ON RIMS AND RIDGES

THE

LOS ALAMOS

AREA SINCE

1880

✳ ✳ ✳ ✳ ✳ ✳ ✳ ✳ ✳ ✳ ✳ ✳ ✳ ✳ ✳

On Rims & Ridges

HAL K.

ROTHMAN

UNIVERSITY OF

NEBRASKA PRESS

LINCOLN & LONDON

Copyright © 1992 by the University
of Nebraska Press
All rights reserved
Manufactured in the United States of America

The paper in this book meets the minimum
requirements of American National Standard for
Information Sciences – Permanence of Paper for
Printed Library Materials, ANSI Z39.48–1984.

Rothman, Hal, 1958–

On rims and ridges: the Los Alamos area since
1880 / Hal K. Rothman.

p. cm. – (The Twentieth-century American
West)

Includes bibliographical references and index.

ISBN 0-8032-3901-7 (alk. paper)

1. Los Alamos Region (N.M.) – History.

I. Title. II. Series.

F804.L6R68 1992 91-24418

978.9'58 – dc20 CIP

For Lauralee and Talia

CONTENTS

* * * * * * * * * * * * * *

List of Illustrations	ix
Acknowledgments	xi
Introduction	1
One. Before the Anglo	5
Two. Industrial Values and Marginal Land	20
Three. The Coming of the Archaeologists	39
Four. A National Park for Archaeological Study	56
Five. Competing Interests in Limited Space	84
Six. Broad Horizons for a New State	106
Seven. Interlocking Empires	125
Eight. Bureaus in Lockstep	151
Nine. Transformed by the Government	176
Ten. Barbed Wire and Watchtowers	207
Eleven. A Typical American Community	233
Twelve. Emerging from the Cocoon	258
Thirteen. Gridlock!	287
Epilogue	315
Notes	317
Bibliographic Essay	359
Index	365

ILLUSTRATIONS

✳ ✳ ✳ ✳ ✳ ✳ ✳ ✳ ✳ ✳ ✳ ✳ ✳ ✳

PLATES

Following page 178

1. A bridge built by Harry S. Buckman across the Rio Grande
2. Archaeological ruins on the Pajarito Plateau
3. Santiago Naranjo on the foot trail into Frijoles Canyon
4. The Tyuonyi Excavation, 1910
5. Plateau homesteads, 1920s
6. Horse-drawn wagons on the Pajarito Plateau
7. Harold H. Brook, Judge A. J. Abbott, and Ida Abbott
8. Harold H. Brook's farmstead
9. Harvesting beans
10. Edgar L. Hewett, 1921
11. Ashley Pond's dude ranch in Pajarito Canyon
12. *Partidarios* standing watch over sheep near the Valle Grande, 1935
13. Archaeologists' tents in Frijoles Canyon
14. Members of the El Rito de Los Frijoles field school, 1910
15. U.S. Forest Service cabin in Frijoles Canyon

16.   Adobe cabins at the Frijoles Canyon Lodge

17.   The road into Frijoles Canyon

18.   The portal linking Frank Pinkley's development and the
       ruins farther west

19.   Frank Pinkley's development in Frijoles Canyon

20.   Calisthenics at the Ranch School

21.   Los Alamos after the war

22.   Watchtower and gate at the Los Alamos installation

23.   Aerial view of Los Alamos, 1969

MAPS

The Los Alamos region, xvi

Bandelier National Monument, 1915, 121

Bandelier National Monument, 1934, 194

Frijoles Canyon developed area, 195

A C K N O W L E D G M E N T S

Any book is a long and complicated endeavor that requires the emotional, moral, and financial support of many people and institutions. This one is no different, except perhaps that the list is longer than usual.

Two people did more to help me with this study than probably even they possibly imagine. Melody Webb encouraged me to see the broad outlines of this project from the day I first walked into her office in 1985. She pushed me toward better scholarship and writing, broader thinking, and a professional approach to the topic. Bill deBuys offered me the benefit of his vast knowledge of natural history and the history of New Mexico. Over an abysmally bad meal in the basement of a church in Hutchinson, Kansas, he helped me lay out the process of change that became this book. He also answered strange questions, fielded late-night phone calls, and generally provided perspective and insight. Bill, Ann, and their family opened their home to me during my frequent trips to New Mexico, and their gracious hospitality and good company made traveling a joy.

Many others, too numerous to name, all contributed to this book. Dorothy Hoard of Los Alamos provided the perspective of someone who had participated in many of the events in this book and had studied many others. Her insights and refinements have given me even broader perspective. My colleagues Bill Unrau and Bill Richardson each took time from their busy schedules to read the manuscript and offer comments. Rory Gauthier offered me the benefit of his vast knowledge of the history of archaeology. David J. Weber and the participants in his 1986 NEH summer seminar on the Hispanic Southwest taught me much I needed to know. Dieter Berninger, Adrian Bustamante, Manuel Gonzales, Al Hurtado, Federico Sánchez, David Sandovál, and the rest of the group offered encouragement, insight, and comaraderie when I most needed it. This book is significantly better for the efforts of all these people.

At various archives and collections, numerous people offered me their assistance. Richard Crawford and Bill Creech helped me negotiate the National Archives. They showed me sources I might have otherwise overlooked, convinced me that if I tagged the correct document and paid the fee, a copy would arrive at my house, and generally made my stay in the Washington, D.C., area easier. Theresa A. Strottman worked at the New Mexico History Library when I began this project; by the final research trip nearly five years later, she was with the Los Alamos Historical Society. There she, Hedy Dunn, and previously, Linda Aldrich provided new sources, corrected errors, and made me feel at home and welcome. At Bandelier National Monument, Virginia Robicheau, my partner in oral histories, helped me wade through myriad sources. Craig Allen also provided help, as did former Superintendent John Hunter, former Chief Ranger Kevin McKibbin, John Lissoway, and many others. Laura Holt at the library of the Laboratory of Anthropology in Santa Fe kept the place open just a little late one night so I could finish my research. Bill Tydeman opened special collections at the Zimmerman Library at the University of New Mexico on a Saturday to accommodate my hectic travel schedule. Martin Kohout took an inconclusive and incomplete clue and found the precise papers for me in the National Archives.

This book could not have been completed without the financial support of some very important people. When I first got out of school and had no job, my parents, Rozann and Neal Rothman, had faith enough in my work to help defray the costs of my existence. They have since been known as the PGF—Parental Grant Foundation. Without their support, emotional and financial, I would now probably be driving a cab. When I arrived at Wichita State University, my chairman, John E. Dreifort, had enough confidence in a newcomer to help me get two summer research grants. That kind of support is invaluable at the beginning of a career. It resulted in grants from the Fairmount College of Liberal Arts and the Office of Research Administration at Wichita State University in successive summers, which gave me valuable time for this book. For the immense trust revealed by a willingness to back up their faith with their check-books, I am grateful to all these people.

I wrote this book in five different places—Los Alamos, Santa Fe, Dallas, Spokane, and Wichita. Like me, the book lacked a home for the longest of times. Only when I met my wife, Lauralee, did I find one. The project began to come together at the same time. Her love, support, patience, and inquisitiveness made me persevere. This book is for her and our daughter Talia. Without them, it would never have been finished.

"Back then, we lived on rims

and ridges up there."

—Homer Pickens

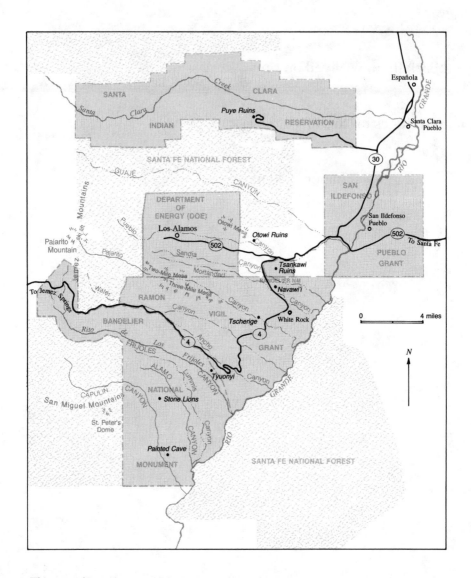

This map of Los Alamos and the Pajarito Plateau area shows the important features of the region in the post–Second World War era.

INTRODUCTION

L ate on a typical summer afternoon in northern New Mexico, the sun drops behind the Jemez Mountains and bathes the area to the east, the Pajarito Plateau, in an array of glorious golds, reds, and browns. As the evening skies darken, the light creates an eerie glow amid the broken mesas and canyons of the region. From atop Tsankawi Mesa, vaguely in the shadow of the mountains to the west and overlooking the Rio Grande valley to the east, the view is of a complete world. To the north, Española, Abiquiu, and the San Juan and Taos mountains form a rim to the bowl of the valleys of northern New Mexico. To the east, across the Rio Grande, the Sangre de Cristo Mountains rise, imposing their power on the entire area. To the southeast and south, a glint from the glass of Santa Fe and its environs appears, and in the distance is the hazy image of the very tip of Sandia Peak, what the Tewa Indians call Turtle Mountain, and the Sandia Range outside of Albuquerque.

Facing the Jemez Mountains, the heart of the Pajarito Plateau unfolds. It is a land of immense contrast. Its muted colors and seeming solitude entrance people who have grown up in noisy cities. Well-worn foot trails and mounds of prehistoric blocks remind modern people that they are not the first to admire its beauty. But the spires of the installations of the modern town of Los Alamos offset the darkening sky. The red and white of painted water towers contrasts with the darker tones of natural vegetation. Power cables strung along the canyons and atop the mesas create horizon lines of their own. The glow of electric lights reaches Santa Fe. The

1

two main roads to the town of Los Alamos are visible, and the occasional whine of an automobile engine intrudes upon this serene world.

The Pajarito Plateau emits an illusion of submission to the whims of modern humanity. Paved and dirt roads traverse the plateau. The most important of these, New Mexico Highway 4, loops the area, passing through Los Alamos, White Rock, and Bandelier National Monument, but a drive on its pavement permits merely a cursory look at the mysteries of the region. It is a road designed by modern people specifically for their needs: easy access and rapid movement. Like an interstate, it reveals only a small piece of the world through which it passes. The towns it connects seem presumptuous in their self-importance, American suburbs deposited randomly in a foreign environment without regard to points of interaction.

The Pajarito Plateau is much more than its modern state indicates. Layers of human and natural history and culture intertwine to reveal a complicated mosaic of human desire and its impact on the physical environment. Its story is of a narrow area of marginal land, for centuries sought only for seasonal use, opened to modern civilization by technology. The passage of this place from remote backwater to twentieth-century icon, a place peripheral in its importance and ironically selected to become significant as a result, was indeed fraught with the peril that accompanies the replacement of one culture by another, however peaceful that transition.

Bringing the Pajarito Plateau into the mainstream of American society meant significant changes in the way people utilized the land, the way they perceived it and its importance, and in the character of the land itself. Before 1879, when the railroad, the consummate symbol of industrial America of the nineteenth century, crossed the upper Rio Grande valley, the Pajarito Plateau was open and unrestricted. There were no rules or laws governing use of the land and its resources, and a loose sense of communal ownership existed. One hundred years later, not a square inch of land in the region remained unclaimed; two or more entities argued over any specific piece. Signs forbidding passage and use abounded, and because of the inherent limits of usable space, the market value of the region seemed locked into a perpetual cycle of ever increasing monetary value. This transformation, from an open world to a world of barriers, from backwater to subsidized protectorate, is the subject of this book.

This process was traumatic for most of the people who initiated the

change as well as for those it affected. The Pajarito Plateau was and is inherently marginal for modern commercial economic use; its sandy soils
are thin, its rainfall intermittent, and its timber suspect. Individuals rep-
resenting industrial America sought to culturally and economically colonize this region, but though they succeeded in controlling the land, its
marginal character repeatedly thwarted their dreams of economic riches.
Yet the region contained more than economic potential, and its archaeological ruins offered the answer to the aspirations of others while simultaneously serving as a backdrop for the development of an institutional
society. That society, with its rules and regulations, spawned federal entities that superseded prior conflicts between individuals. Soon the institutional structure of the U.S. government was at war with itself on the
plateau, a conflict that dominated two decades. It was resolved only with
the initiation of Project Y, the arm of the Manhattan Project that developed the atomic bomb. The Los Alamos National Laboratory, the institution directly descended from Project Y, became the driving force in the
subjugation of the plateau as well as the source of economic sustenance
for the majority of people on the plateau. After 1945, the expansion of this
entity drove the growth of the region.

In this respect, the experience of the Pajarito Plateau serves as a microcosm of the social, cultural, and economic experience of the American
West in the twentieth century. Its status as a backwater, remote to the concerns of the great engines of economic progress, was typical of the West.
The transformation of the area from preindustrial world to peripheral participant in the modern one mirrors the experience of thousands of western communities. In 1880, the region was a frontier periphery of an indus-
trializing society. The insufficiency of its resources transformed it into a
colony administered by the federal government. No form of commercial
economy native to the area succeeded in casting off the reliance of the
plateau on the markets and systems of delivery of the rest of the nation.
As a result, federal presence served as the economic backbone of the region. With the Second World War, the plateau was selected as the location
of a permanent federal presence, bringing it toward the mainstream in a
subsidized and ironically peripheral fashion. The result was a culture
both dependent and independent, sustained by money from elsewhere
yet rooted to the place.

In this, the people of the Pajarito Plateau are different only in degree
from people in much of the rest of the West. Pajaritans are completely and

visibly dependent on federal allocations, a fact that most of them openly acknowledge. Others in the West delude themselves. But this situation has not benefited everyone. The application of industrial values to the preindustrial and nonwhite people on the plateau created a dependency among them, one repeated in a seemingly infinite number of places throughout the West. The social, cultural, economic, and political consequences for Hispanos and Native Americans were devastating.

As a microcosm of the experience of the American West, the Pajarito Plateau provides an excellent case study. Harnessed for federal purposes, with a micro-city sustained by federal funding as its economic heart, the plateau offers a glimpse of the future of the West. Many of the problems faced today throughout the West were addressed before 1960 on the Pajarito Plateau. If the region serves as a barometer of the future of the West, the years to come will be significantly more difficult than those that have passed. The major issue on the plateau in the late 1980s was pressure for space. A sort of environmental gridlock had been reached, creating a situation in which no entity in the region could improve its status without a commensurate loss by another party. In the West, culturally full of the promise of infinite space with resources to match and poorly grappling with a reality far different, this is a harbinger of a chilling future.

BEFORE

THE ANGLO

1

Environmental change in northern New Mexico was part of a larger process that began the instant Christopher Columbus landed in the New World. Old World plants, animals, humans, and microbes rapidly overwhelmed the parts of the New World that bore the greatest ecological resemblance to the Old. Throughout the Americas, fast-spreading European flora and fauna replaced native species, in some cases threatening the survival of native peoples as well as their biotas. In these "Neo-Europes," places like the pampas of Argentina, the Australian grasslands, and the agricultural cornucopia of North America, the portmanteau biota of Europeans—everything from their domesticated and soon-to-become feral animals to their breath-borne and venereal diseases—facilitated wholesale environmental and cultural change.[1]

What had existed before the arrival of Europeans was inexorably altered. For approximately ten thousand years after the Bering Strait land bridge receded and Alaska and Asia were again on opposite sides of a body of water, the Americas were separated from the rest of the planet. A regime different from that of Eurasia developed, accentuated by the isolation of this hemisphere from the commercial, military, and social interaction that took place elsewhere on the globe. As a result, native peoples in the Americas developed traditions, practices, cultures, and mores all their own.

The area that became the American Southwest underwent a cultural evolution determined by its natural resources and the technologies of the people who lived there. Between roughly 9500 and 6000 B.C., Paleo-Indians known today as the Clovis people roamed the Southwest in search of herds of grazing mammoths and other large animals attracted by the then moist and lush grasslands of the region. By 8500 B.C., changes in environmental conditions had doomed all of these animals except the bison, and gradually the hunters gravitated east, toward areas more suited to their skills. They were replaced by foragers, who had to make do with a great deal less. Water became the commodity crucial to their existence, and life focused on riparian environments. Two distinct patterns of life— the Cochise tradition, centered in present southeastern Arizona, and the Oshara, in the northern parts of the region—developed. The most indicative characteristic of each was an extraordinary degree of adaptability. Protoprehistoric people struggled to survive, and they shaped their culture to make the most of the environment in which they lived.[2]

Their ability to adapt to their environment led to a major development in prehistoric life: the gradual rise in the importance of agriculture. Cultivation of corn and squash spread slowly north from central Mexico until sometime after 500 B.C., and the two crops became the basis of a new, more settled way of life. As people learned to depend on agriculture, communities were formed, replacing the looser groupings of foraging peoples. More sophisticated social organization followed. In the next one thousand years, the transformation to an agricultural life, complete with surplus, leisure, and new technologies, occurred in most of the Southwest. By A.D. 500, the various peoples of the region had become the forerunners of the Anasazi, Hohokam, and Mogollon groups, whose ruins dot the landscape of the Southwest.[3]

The Pajarito Plateau of northern New Mexico was part of this matrix of cultural development. Although evidence of inhabitation before A.D. 900 is scant, in the subsequent three hundred years, aboveground pueblos became common, spreading as far north as modern-day Taos. After about A.D. 1100, and increasing with astonishing speed after A.D. 1200, the population of the region grew. An influx of emigrants from the Chaco Canyon region arrived in what is now central New Mexico, bringing the accoutrements of their civilization. The contrast between this world and the one that immediately preceded it was dramatic.

The new arrivals contributed to the emergence of what archaeologists have determined was the penultimate stage of cultural development in the region. As population increased, architecture and material culture became more sophisticated and trade emerged as an important form of exchange not only of materials such as obsidian and turquoise but also of ideas, technologies, goods such as ceramics, and people. Surpluses allowed the development of new and better crafts, further facilitating trade and the exchange of knowledge that accompanied it. The size of individual pueblos grew during this phase, suggesting more substantive community organization, and life improved for the people of the Pajarito Plateau.

But this period of achievement was not without pitfalls. The people were dependent on the physical environment, which—in an arid, mountainous region, cold and snowy in the winter—was not always forgiving. Their growth in numbers precipitated greater use of already scarce resources. Drought forced the abandonment and reoccupation of some pueblos while others were simply left behind. Population was also affected. Periods of actual decline in numbers occurred beginning before A.D. 1300, usually tied to a change for the worse in the physical environment. Trade ties to the Hohokam and the Casas Grandes peoples southwest of the Pajaritans also dissolved as those cultures collapsed. They were replaced by new trade partners on the plains, presumably the descendants of the earlier hunters and gatherers who had gone east.

The change in partners altered the nature of exchange. When trading with similar culture groups, the Anasazi of the Pajarito Plateau had sought ritual items, but plains trade focused on subsistence and utilitarian goods. The exchange of ideas lessened as pueblo people were confronted with different cultures with which they did not share cosmology, a resource base, or technologies. The people of the plains lacked the ability to maintain the cultural facets of trade, but they did have food and materials that added to the life of the pueblos.

But even trade could not protect the pueblos from gradual decline as their resource base became more limited, their surplus was used up as a result of climatic changes, and the activities that enriched their lives were put aside as survival became an all-encompassing task. Extended droughts such as the one that lasted from roughly A.D. 1245 to 1295, as

well as a general decline in temperature resulting from a small planetwide
Ice Age that peaked during the sixteenth century, caused the people who
inhabited the pueblos of the plateau to migrate to lower elevations. By
A.D. 1600, they had abandoned the larger pueblos, and despite occasional
attempts at resettlement, by 1800 the lowland pueblos of San Ildefonso
and Santa Clara to the northeast, Pojoaque to the east, and Cochiti to the
south had become the centers of Native American life in the region.[4]

Elsewhere in the world, changes in attitude, spurred by commercial desires, technology, and the ethnocentric cosmology of European Chris-
tianity, caused a linking of the worlds long cast apart by natural forces.
The arrival of Columbus began a process of environmental and cultural
transformation greater than any other before or since. The encounter, as it
has come to be called, ignited the greatest transformation of biology, demography, and culture known to human history.

Europeans set out from their continent with a variety of motives,
among which commerce, rivalry with other European powers, the desire
to spread their faith, and scientific curiosity ranked high. The ethnocen-
trism of Europeans impeded their ability to understand native cultures,
but in many cases, a conspiracy of technology, demography, and co-opta-
tion made comprehension unnecessary. Although some Europeans pondered the differences, most proceeded under the assumptions of six-
teenth- and seventeenth-century Christian cosmology. Self-righteous,
armed and willing to exercise their military power, and biologically hardened to diseases they carried with them, the Europeans who left home for
places afar found many parts of the world that were ripe for economic,
cultural, and environmental transformation. Yet colonialization was more
than raw conquest. It included cultural amalgamation, exchange of ideas
and technologies, and changes in the physical environment.[5]

In the New World climates most like Europe, transformation became a
relatively simple process; elsewhere, along the equator, and in the
swamps of South Carolina, the tropical rain forests of Central America, or
the deserts and mountains of New Mexico, European peoples, plants,
and animals found conditions much less suited to their health and wel-
fare. In these marginal places, the removal of native ground cover did not
precipitate replacement of indigenous flora by opportunistic imports. Instead a combination of self-aggrandizing native plants and imports reshaped the landscape. Europeans found themselves susceptible to disease, although rarely of North American origin. In eighteenth-century

South Carolina, malaria decimated whites while their slaves, possessing a hereditary West African resistance carried in the same gene responsible for sickle-cell anemia, thrived.[6] The constant moisture and humidity of lowland equatorial regions also proved an enemy of Europeans, as did the harsh desert climate of the Southwest.

The process of transforming these comparatively inhospitable lands into thriving Neo-European colonies rested on economic desirability. Such places usually became important to Europeans and their descendants when the land offered the potential to produce commodities in demand in the European world and when the technology existed to bring them to market. Without these preconditions, places where climate and vegetation differed greatly from those of Europe did not attract large numbers of Europeans.

The collision of cultures in what became New Mexico offers an example. Arid, desertlike, rugged, and unforgiving, this land, along with its indigenous people and its flora and fauna, seemed to resist the intrusion of European portmanteau biota and culture. As varied and diverse as any other area on the continent, New Mexico was and is characterized by a scarcity of resources important to the sustenance of people from humid climates. In this it differed from Neo-European parts of the New World, places where the plants, animals, and people of the Old World systematically overwhelmed every aspect of life that had preceded them.

Although the Spaniards who came to New Mexico recognized the similarities between what they found and the Old World homeland from which they came, New Mexico held relatively little appeal for them. In New Mexico, European flora generally fared well when planted near water. But Spaniards and Pueblo Indians had to carefully nurture fruit trees, melons, wheat, and chilies not near rivers. These plants did not proliferate as did European ones in other parts of the Americas. Compared with places like Peru, where such European imports as turnips, mustard, mint, chamomile, endive, and spinach grew wildly, defying attempts to keep them out of cultivated fields, or like Australia, which became a major producer of livestock within fifty years of the settling of Botany Bay in 1788, New Mexico experienced a less dramatic kind of environmental change.

Two circumstances, both cultural, influenced this process. Unlike the English, the Spanish did not colonize in large numbers. Instead they established a system of economic dominance based on the natives' support of Spanish institutions. In addition, there were places much easier and much more productive to colonize than the far reaches of a sparse frontier. New Mexico did not offer the Spanish the kind of bounty that they desired and to which they had become accustomed elsewhere in the Americas.

The Pueblo Rebellion of 1680 highlighted the difference between places like New Mexico and those that accommodated pastoral and agrarian Europeans. Three generations after contact in Europe-like parts of the New World, native populations and social organization were usually destroyed. In contrast, despite eighty-two years of epidemic disease, droughts, and harsh Spanish rule, the Pueblo Indians of New Mexico were sufficiently powerful to drive the Spanish south of the Rio Grande and even to vent their frustration against European institutions by symbolic gestures such as building a kiva—a Pueblo religious ceremonial chamber—within the church compound at Pecos. Unlike many other indigenous peoples and their cultures after contact with Europeans, the Pueblo Indians and their cultures were strong and vibrant, their people healthy, and their disdain for the Spanish evident.[7]

After the Spanish reconquest in 1693, the peripheral location and status of New Mexico and its decidedly un-European climate attenuated the brunt of the encounter with the Spanish. Although European influence in New Mexico became significant, European animals did not reproduce there in the prolific fashion that characterized the pampas, Australia, or the eastern United States. Old World plants withered in the dry heat, and European peoples did not replace indigenous ones. Instead, they intermarried, creating a mestizo population and a hybrid culture that retained elements of its primary components.

Economic and political factors also played a role in the slower transformation of New Mexico. By the nineteenth century, few Spaniards and Mexicans had ventured so far north, and New Mexico remained an isolated outpost. Even the expanding Republic to the northeast did not pose a significant threat until after 1835. Before that time, Americans in search of land were more likely to head to the hospitable environs of central Texas. The few who arrived in New Mexico found the most fertile land already taken. As late as 1840, the number of foreign residents of New Mexico remained minuscule.[8]

The combination of these factors meant that remote places like the Pajarito Plateau, less than thirty miles from the center of Spanish New Mexico, experienced a less comprehensive impact from the European port-manteau biota than did the fertile river valleys elsewhere in New Mexico. Until the late nineteenth century, northern New Mexico offered Neo-Europeans little but the potential for subsistence. The primary value of the Pajarito Plateau was as a buffer between settlements and the *indios barbaros*: the Utes, Navajos, Apaches, and Comanches who threatened New Mexico. Only when the Denver and Rio Grande Railroad built a narrow-gage railway that crossed the Rio Grande valley in the late nineteenth century did the descendants of Europeans—in this case, Americans—begin to assess the economic potential of the region.

The Pajarito Plateau is located in the heart of the upper Rio Grande valley. West of the river and nestled at the base of the Jemez Mountains, the plateau offers a view of the natural past. More than one million years ago, two massive eruptions spewed ash from a volcanic cone, located where the open plain of the Valles Caldera, or the Valle Grande, on the Baca location No. 1, is today. These ash flows cooled to leave the soft tuff rock that characterizes the plateau. Subsequent erosion carved deep canyons into the plateau, leaving the dissected topography of elongated mesas and steep-walled canyons found today. Throughout time, a variety of ecological communities developed on the Pajarito Plateau. At the time of European contact, piñon-juniper and ponderosa pine probably dominated the majority of mesa tops in the region. Fauna found the region appealing, and a large range of animals, including bear, elk, deer, and other species, inhabited the region.[9]

In 1880, three distinct areas, defined as much by human beings as by topography, composed the Pajarito Plateau. The southern third of the plateau, stretching from the Cañada de Cochiti Grant to the north rim of Frijoles Canyon, caught the imagination of early travelers. One observer wrote that this area included "the most stupendous canyons, the wildest scenery," and afforded "the grandest panoramas to be seen in New Mexico."[10] The region was rugged, and its angular trails made travel on horseback difficult. Except in Frijoles Canyon, the primary point of interest for visitors to Bandelier National Monument, the canyon bottoms were too narrow for agriculture, and the sharp rise of the canyon walls precluded traditional settlement. The sparsely vegetated, tablelike mesas offered little cover. The sandy soils of the region limited agricultural potential. Only El Rito de los Frijoles, in Frijoles Canyon, provided perennial water. The ruggedness of this portion of the plateau kept it largely uninhabited.

Human-drawn divisions created the middle area, the Ramón Vigil Grant. This eighteenth-century Spanish land grant extended from the north rim of Frijoles Canyon to the seasonal creek in Guajes Canyon near the present-day town of Los Alamos. Although nineteenth- and twentieth-century accounts reported seeps and a perennial stream in the westernmost segment of Pajarito Canyon, which bisected the grant, and another perennial stream in the aptly named *Abrevadero* (watering hole), or Water Canyon, there were few other constant sources of water. But the Vigil Grant encouraged human inhabitation. It was neither as rugged nor as inaccessible as the southern third of the plateau. The topography of this grant did not impede settlers. Its mesas did not tower over surrounding canyon bottoms, and the canyons themselves were much wider than those south of Frijoles Canyon.

Prehistoric Native Americans found the middle portion of the plateau very hospitable. The number of ruins on the Vigil Grant exceeded those south of Frijoles Canyon. The tract contained Tschirege, the largest prehistoric pueblo on the plateau; Navawi'i, the pueblo of the game traps; and many other smaller ruins. Within a short distance of the arbitrary northern boundary—drawn in 1877 by General Land Office surveyors as they recast the northern line of the grant—stood thousands of additional prehistoric dwellings.[11]

By 1870, the Vigil Grant had a long history that separated it from the unreserved land surrounding it. Land grants to *vecinos* (a term that in colonial New Mexico meant citizen and taxpayer) served two purposes under Spanish rule. They allowed people to be rewarded for military service without any real cost to the crown, and they peopled the remote peripheries of the empire. The Vigil Grant fit this pattern. In 1742, Viceroy don Gaspar Domingo de Mendoza granted the tract to a former soldier named Pedro Sánchez. When he requested the tract, Sánchez contended that he had difficulty supporting his wife, twelve children, three orphan nephews, and servants. The document may have been a forgery, but during the eighteenth century, no one challenged Sánchez's claim to the marginal tract of land on the periphery of the far northern frontier of New Spain. His grant served the needs of the state. Providing a frontier buffer against marauding Native Americans, the grant was a target that would be attacked before the communities of the valleys to the east.

The land remained in the Sánchez family until 1851, when an heir, Antonio Sánchez, sold the rights of eight of the eleven heirs to the grant to José Ramón Vigil for a yoke of oxen, thirty-six ewes, one ram, and twenty dollars in cash. Vigil claimed his purchase under American law, and his name was attached to the tract. He and his family lived on the plateau, building a home just east of the point where Los Alamos and Pueblo canyons met.[12] Ironically, Vigil's homestead was outside the boundaries of the property he owned, but during his lifetime it never mattered. As in many cases in northern New Mexico, the boundaries of the grant were drawn loosely.

The remaining section of the plateau, beginning at the northern border of the Vigil Grant and extending to the thirty-sixth degree longitude line that bisected Española, differed from the other two segments. Between Frijoles Canyon and Puye Mesa, the vertical, rugged mesas of the southern area gave way to softer, more rolling contours. The land sloped more gently toward the Rio Grande, and close to the Pueblo of Santa Clara, the ascent toward the mountains was more gradual than further to the south. The canyons opened into meadows, and although there was no more water north of the grant than anywhere else, wider canyons, seasonal creeks, and the lower elevation of the valley floors created more abundant, equally fragile grass cover.

Few permanent Hispano settlers replaced the Indians of prehistory, and until the 1880s, the Pajarito Plateau remained open to whoever sought it. Even during the nineteenth century, when Hispanos greatly expanded the boundaries of their settlement in the Southwest, few permanently settled the Pajarito Plateau and the Jemez Mountains. Instead they progressed along the Rio Puerco to the west and up the valley of the Rio Grande to the east. *Indios barbaros* made the Jemez Mountains dangerous for lone cattle- or sheepherders. The lack of perennial streams on the Pajarito Plateau and its frequently inhospitable winters largely confined inhabitation to the summer. In accordance with Spanish policy throughout New Mexico, Hispanos had clustered around the pueblos in the valleys— San Ildefonso, Santa Clara, and Pojoaque—across the Rio Grande and slightly to the north of the abandoned remains of the bustling communities of prehistory. The plateau retained spiritual importance for Native Americans, but it faded from the central position it had held before A.D. 1500.[13]

Between 1500 and 1880, Hispano and Indian life-styles in the Pojoaque and Española valleys surrounding the Pajarito Plateau changed little. After the Spanish reconquest, Hispano communities that grew around the

Pueblos practiced a subsistence regime that took advantage of the fertility of the alluvial soils and the water available for irrigation around the Rio Grande. Primarily valuable for summer pasture, the plateau remained sparsely settled, a place to take animals when the temperature in the valleys rose. Crops, orchards, and stock dominated the economic lives of these *pobladores*, and they became an integral part of the region.

Throughout the nineteenth century, Anglo merchants, mountain men, and settlers filtered into New Mexico. Their trade goods attracted local interest, and the large number of animals they brought began to destroy ground cover around major trading centers like Santa Fe. But only their trade goods made an impact in the Española and Pojoaque valleys. The people there had little to offer merchants, and their land was remote, away from the patterns of commerce dictated largely by the Santa Fe Trail. In comparison with the swelling of Santa Fe with Anglos, the Pojoaque-Española region remained generally devoid of Anglo encroachment. Before 1880, life continued at a preindustrial pace.[14]

But by themselves, the surrounding valleys did not contain the resources to provide economic sustenance for their inhabitants. Throughout the nineteenth century, the timber and grasses of the plateau broadened the economic possibilities of the people who lived at lower elevations. During the summer, when most of the water in the valleys dried up and crops and orchards covered every irrigable acre, residents took their animals up to the higher elevations of the plateau. They sought grass for their small herds, and the frequent afternoon rains in the Jemez Mountains assured a more constant supply of surface water. Many residents cleared patches of land and raised crops. With seventy-five square miles of open land, there was plenty of grass and timber for anyone who needed it. In comparison with the valleys, where people squeezed along the Rio Grande and its acequias—irrigation ditches—the plateau offered abundant land.

Geographic constraints often determined patterns of use for the variety of cultures in the region. The pueblos of San Ildefonso and Santa Clara were closest to the northern third of the plateau, and they controlled most of the bottomland that bordered the Rio Grande, largely north of the current location of the Otowi bridge. Native Americans utilized this more gently sloped area, north and west of Puye Mesa. Hispanos from places like La Cienega, Thornton (Santo Domingo), and the area around Bland made the difficult ascent from the south to use the rugged southern portion, whereas their counterparts from the vicinity of San Ildefonso appear to have gone to the central portion of the plateau with greater regularity, for it contained the Vigil Grant. More easily accessible than the southern portion, the grant became the center of Hispano grazing on the plateau.

Like many other land grants, the Vigil Grant functioned as common property. Although it was originally a private land grant, the way in which the *pobladores* used the grant turned it into an informal community grant. Many of the people in the Pojoaque and Española valleys were blood relatives of the owners of the grant; many more were related by marriage. As elsewhere in the Rio Arriba region, a visible sense of interdependence dominated interaction between people in the valley and those on the plateau. Despite frequent arguments among members of the extended group that used the grant, an informal social compact dictated that unused land belonged to any member of the extended community who needed it. Kinship by blood or marriage strengthened cultural ties. This arrangement had important social and economic consequences for the Hispanos who lived around San Ildefonso. It ensured that the narrow world they inhabited provided for all.[15]

People invariably modify their physical environment, and the *pobladores* of northern New Mexico were no exception. The stock that Hispanos brought to the plateau and the mountains above initiated minor patterns of change in the ecology of the grasslands. The Pino family from La Cienega, southwest of Santa Fe, regularly brought sheep to their camp in Frijoles Canyon in the last decades of the nineteenth century. They planted beans and other crops for their own use, trading only the occasional surplus they produced. They allowed stock to graze freely during the days, and at night they quartered the sheep in prehistoric caves. One man, Pacifico C. de Baca, built a cabin on the eastern fringe of Frijoles Canyon late in the nineteenth century. Some accounts suggest that the structure had a basement, implying that C. de Baca also raised crops, most likely beans, and may have spent some winters there. Observers also noted that prehistoric irrigation ditches from Frijoles Creek had been used during the nineteenth century, presumably for agricultural purposes.[16]

Natural and human-induced fire played a greater role in transforming the physical environment than did grazing livestock. Before the 1790s, a substantial fire occurred on the average of every twelve years at elevations below 9,150 feet. Between the 1790s and 1893, the years of the greatest documented use of the region by the *pobladores* before the implementation of fire-suppression techniques, the rate decreased to every five years. Major fires occurred in 1861, 1873, and 1893. Although some of these fires were natural in origin, the vast majority resulted from human actions, either inadvertent or planned. This pattern of fire changed the composition of timber on the plateau, which also contributed to accelerating the transformation of timbered land into high-elevation grassland. The emergence of stands of white fir furthered the process, since fire rapidly consumed this species. As white fir spread, the potential for more severe and wide-ranging fire increased.[17]

The result of this cyclic burning was that after forest land burned, much of it became grassland. This served the interest of those with livestock, for fires continuously renewed the land they used as pasture. Fire replenished the nutrients in the soil and led to a thicker, more stable grass cover. During the period before the widespread suppression of fire, animals sought the better grasslands while other forested areas burned, beginning the process of generating new grasslands. This fluid process of transformation characterized the region before the 1880s.

Whether or not this pattern resulted in an equilibrium that fostered a semiconsistent rotation of pasture and forest, it did ensure that there was enough grass for the small number of animals that herdsmen brought up from the valleys during the first seventy-five years of the nineteenth century. After the pacification of the Navajos by the American military in the 1860s, stock rustling rarely occurred. Herdsmen often released animals in the spring and returned for them later in the year. The residents of the valleys had plentiful land on the plateau. No barriers to the movement of animals existed anywhere in the region. Fire helped rejuvenate the area, annually creating new areas of grassland.[18]

As late as 1877, the Pajarito Plateau appeared visibly abundant. When Stephen E. McElroy and Daniel Sawyer surveyed the Ramón Vigil Grant for the General Land Office of the Department of the Interior in 1877, they found appealing land. The western portion of the grant contained a "fine growth of large Pine timber," and piñon and cedar trees covered the area closer to the Rio Grande. The grazing potential of the region also impressed the surveyors, with "the grass being of good quality and plentiful," and the two men "saw considerable live stock herds of sheep and cattle grazing in different parts of the tract." In the eyes of these men who routinely assessed the economic potential of land, the area was "valuable for its excellent grazing capacity and its large timber supply." Regardless of any predisposition to exaggerate as a means to encourage settlement, Sawyer and McElroy seemed genuinely impressed with the area they surveyed.[19]

Like many other parts of the Southwest, the Pajarito Plateau was an ecological trap. Its thick grama grasses, abundant ponderosa pine trees, and numerous bears, wild turkeys, and other game at higher elevations promised much to the nineteenth-century eye. The land seemed cornucopian, and to a degree, it was. Compared with places like the Argentine pampas, which by 1500 was "broken, worn, and incomplete—like a toy that has been played with too roughly by a thoughtless colossus," the plateau seemed profusely fertile.[20]

Although the surveyors' inspection suggested that the area had significant economic potential, in reality its commercial value had already begun to diminish. Traditional grazing practices offered little respite for the land, and as grasses became more scant, the amount of combustible vegetation declined. This meant that annual fires did not produce as great a quantity of nutrients as they previously had, leading to more sparse vegetation. Hispano and Indian herdsmen followed practices that initiated the replacement of mesic native plant species with more desiccated xeric plants, which provided poor forage, or with nonnative "exotics." On the plateau, the relatively small number of cattle and sheep and the comparatively large land base mitigated the effect of livestock on the vegetation. Although the approximately two hundred animals grazing the area in a typical summer before 1880 did little immediate damage, they laid the basis for long-term change in the composition of plant species in the region.

The impact of grazing was localized around water sources. Herdsman often took their stock up to the plateau to search for fresh grazing even before grasses at lower elevations began to sprout. Sheep in particular sought young plants, decimating many species before seeding. As a consequence, in the most heavily grazed areas, shortgrasses—like blue and side oats grama, false buffalo, needle and thread, and galleta—and forage plants and shrubs rarely reproduced. By midsummer, the animals were foraging off the stems instead of the flowers of plants. In this situation, even fire could not significantly improve pasture. Without vegetation to combust, fires did not release enough nutrients to create a healthy grass cover for the following year.

But the pockets of damage this created had little effect on the plateau as a whole. With an old-growth timber cover, ranging from piñon-juniper at lower elevations to ponderosa pine higher up and interspersed with Douglas fir in the canyons, and with wildfires that regularly kept forest stands open, replenished soil nutrients, and renewed the vigor of ground cover, herders had little trouble finding new pasture after they had exhausted a small area. Yet each new area of pasture was farther from sources of perennial water and, consequently, was more arid and fragile. Animals traveling to water further damaged the plateau. Not only were there isolated areas of damage; there were also trails to sources of water.[21]

The patterns of fire and use posed problems for the future. In situations of more intensive use, the grazing lands of the *pobladores* and Indians fared poorly. In the eighteenth century, there had been a number of Hispano settlements in the Rio Puerco basin, stretching from Cuba on the west side of the Jemez Mountains to the Rio Grande near Albuquerque, but Navajo raids drove the Hispanos back. After American troops forcibly removed the threat of the Navajos, Hispanos began to resettle the basin. Overgrazing so badly eroded fragile alluvial soils that by 1951, more than ten thousand acres of irrigable land near the river had been lost to cultivation. With the ground cover destroyed, rampaging floods and arroyos became common. In other similar areas, the tiny sharp hooves of sheep left trails that opened the way for opportunistic plants and decimated large areas of forage land.[22]

Before the 1880s, the Pajarito Plateau had escaped this mass destruction, but not because of any intrinsic conception of managing land to preserve its productivity. Locations like Frijoles Canyon, which was limited in size, was hospitable, and was close to water, showed signs of overgrazing. Plants from the drier, lower elevations became common, and forage in the canyon proper became more scarce. But use of the area continued. Neither cultural prohibition nor an understanding of the fragile character of the Pajarito Plateau prevented herdsmen from overgrazing this seemingly abundant area. Yet the herdsmen lacked the quantity of stock to make more than a short-term impact on a limited area of even such a marginal place. At a pace imperceptible to the human eye, the Pajarito Plateau became less suited to animal husbandry.

Survival of the plateau and its traditional users depended on a relatively constant state of change. By the 1880s, the patterns of use were age-old; they had become part of the cultural fabric of the region and, more important, caused no visible damage. As long as roughly the same number of animals used roughly the same acreage and as long as natural and human-induced fires altered the composition of a relatively constant percentage of the plateau and the mountains, the rate of environmental change remained stable. More than anything else, this situation required an open world, without restrictions on the movement of herdsmen and their animals, without fences, and without the pressure to produce for a cash-based market economy.

This open quality was the first casualty of the arrival of Anglo commerce. With the coming of the railroad, the conditions that masked incremental change in the environment disappeared—and so did the plateau as it had been for nearly one thousand years. The patterns of use sowed the seeds of an ominous ecological future, of which the Ramón Vigil Grant became the focus.

2

With the coming of the railroad in 1880, the economic, social, and cultural institutions of Anglo-American society that transformed the West became significant in the upper Rio Grande valley of the New Mexico Territory. These forces were part of a dynamic process that altered both the physical environment and the lives of Hispanos and Native Americans in the region. As a result, environmental conditions on the Pajarito Plateau changed irrevocably, as did the lives of the people who lived there.

Industrialization, the rise of the market economy, and the development of the railroad transformed American life. These new systems created vast linkages that had not previously existed and established a dollar worth for western commodities that had minimal prior value because they could not be delivered to market. Industrialization made the acquisition of capital and the means of production the new measures of wealth. In the West, people still sought the preindustrial equivalent, land. Yet the market economy changed the value of that land. No longer did mere ownership connote wealth and freedom. The value of land was predicated on the kind of products it could deliver to the markets of the East. The change in the structure of the economy limited real success to a few fortunate individuals and to the powerful interests that bankrolled western industry. It also put tremendous pressure on westerners to produce marketable raw materials such as cattle, minerals, and crops. The result in much of the West was an economy that was extractive, exploitive, and little short of colonial.

The requirements of the new economy contrasted with a mode of community living established in tradition and theoretically protected by the Treaty of Guadalupe Hidalgo. Preindustrial Hispano life had stressed cooperative individualism, an interdependence among extended families and neighbors. Yet the market economy disrupted long-standing patterns of living without providing adequate replacement. Nor were nonwhites the beneficiaries of the economic and cultural climate of the time. Entrepreneurial capitalism ranked people hierarchically on the basis of their supposed economic and cultural merit, and non-English-speaking nonwhites fared the worst. Displaced economically, relegated to second-class status, and left vulnerable in law despite formal promises of their protection, the people of the plateau found that the narrow economic base that sustained them could not withstand even largely unsuccessful efforts to integrate it into the market economy.

The environmental change wrought by the application of this set of values to fragile land accelerated an ecological process that had begun as soon as the Spanish came to New Mexico. The mountains and deserts of the Southwest were unlike the more humid parts of the North American continent or Europe, and American influence brought more environmental and cultural change in a few years than Spanish practices had produced in nearly three hundred. The technological advantages and the nationwide networks of the nineteenth-century changed long-standing patterns of land use. New practices altered the physical environment of even the most remote areas of northern New Mexico. The cultural systems that had preceded Anglo commerce ceased to function effectively, and American institutions, shaped by the values of an industrial society, filled the economic gap, often to the long-term detriment of people who preceded Anglo-Americans in the region.

In the Pajarito Plateau area, Hispanos bore the brunt of these changes. They lacked the land base, however threatened, of their Native American neighbors. Like indigenous peoples around the globe who faced the effects of European-based industrial culture, the majority of Hispanos found themselves confronted with a complicated matrix that their culture had not taught them how to address. They became players in a game whose rules they did not always know.

The Santa Fe Trail was the geographic and commercial route into New Mexico as well as the primary avenue of cultural interaction; its path was the center of a gradual process of combining cultures. The parts of New Mexico closest to the trail experienced the greatest Anglo cultural influence. The land around the trail became enmeshed in the national market, its trees and grasses coveted by cattlemen and timbermen.

In general, the further the location of a tract of land from the trail, the less impact industrial culture had on it. Marginal land close to the trail, and subsequently the railroad, had greater commercial value to Anglo businessmen; access to the national transportation system exponentially increased the worth of any tract. Land distant from this network lacked the factor crucial in making its economic development and exploitation important: proximity. The difficulty and expense of conveying the resources and products of marginal land to the national market often superseded the value of those products.

The location of the Pajarito Plateau shielded it from speculation. Two railroads, the Atchison, Topeka, and Santa Fe (AT&SF) and the Denver and Rio Grande (D&RG), competed for access routes through the mountains and toward California. The AT&SF followed the best-known route: the Santa Fe Trail. Forced off the trail by the battle over Raton Pass in 1878, the D&RG moved more slowly. As the rails progressed closer to Santa Fe in the late 1870s, the marginal land along the path of the AT&SF became more attractive. Speculators looked greedily at lands along the prospective course of the railroad in northeastern New Mexico. For people concerned with profit, places like the Pajarito Plateau offered too little gain at too great a risk, particularly if there were lands available closer to the trail and the railroad.[1]

As late as the end of the 1870s, the lands of the Ramón Vigil Grant and the rest of the Pajarito Plateau were far from the central corridor of Anglo enterprise in New Mexico. The land grants of the northeastern part of the state were directly in the path of men in search of land for industrial commerce. While the "Santa Fe Ring" and a number of the surveyor generals of New Mexico defrauded residents of other grants, the Vigil Grant went largely unnoticed by the avaricious power structure. As long as entrepreneurs could capture the wide-open cattle country of eastern New Mexico, they had little need for the area north of Santa Fe and west of the Rio Grande. In comparison with the llanos of the northeast, the Vigil Grant terrain was rugged and inhospitable. The people of the Española and the Pojoaque valleys continued to pasture their animals on the grant.[2]

The D&RG, pressing southward, brought Anglo influence to the Pajarito Plateau. In 1879, the D&RG began to build narrow-gage tracks through the Rio Grande valley, changing perceptions of the value of land west of the river. To make peace with the AT&SF in 1880, the D&RG agreed to build no farther south than halfway between Conejos, Colorado, and Santa Fe, and the progress of the railroad slowed. The Pajarito Plateau was in the area in which the D&RG agreed not to build, further limiting its potential in the eyes of investors. But land speculation was one of the leading industries in New Mexico, and some sensed that the railroad would eventually reach Santa Fe. To them, areas like the plateau were sources of potential profit.

The D&RG's narrow-gage railway, the Chili Line, eventually reached from Antonito, Colorado, to Santa Fe, creating new communities and economic opportunities in its wake. In 1880, just to the north of Santa Clara Pueblo, where the line originally ended, a railroad town called Española sprang up, in the words of an early Anglo visitor, "in the midst of hoary old Spanish towns and Indian Pueblos." As late as 1885, the town was "a baby city [a] nondescript collection of canvas tents and board shanties on a flat beside the river," dependent on the whims of railroad barons for any chance of a future.[3] That hope became reality when the railroad reached Santa Fe in 1887.

As it had elsewhere in New Mexico and the West, the railroad provided a link to a world that few of the Hispano and Native American residents of the region had ever experienced. New commodities became available in northern New Mexico, and new markets for the foodstuffs and livestock produced in the region also developed. In turn, the raw assets of the region—its seemingly untrammeled grazing land and old-growth timber—attracted the attention of Anglo investors. In the rush to serve burgeoning eastern markets, speculators eyed every tract of land near a railroad.

Easy access to a network of national railroad lines meant that even a place as remote as the Pajarito Plateau could be harnessed for the needs of people in American cities. Although few assumed that the mountains of the Rio Arriba hid a cornucopia, there was much land that had economic potential. To investors, that spelled profit, the prospect of which increased the value of land along the D&RG line. Speculation in land became rife.

Anglo perceptions of the value of land like the Pajarito Plateau were very different from those of prior inhabitants of the area. Anglos saw what Sawyer and McElroy, the government surveyors in 1877, had seen: commercial grazing and timber potential. The added allure of the proximity of the railroad also figured in the equation, and Anglos offered what seemed exorbitant prices for land along the proposed route. The Rio Grande valley boomed. Men like Frank Bond, who opened a general store in Española in 1883, saw fortunes in the making and began aggressive pursuit.

But these new values signaled change in the region, and Hispanos bore its brunt. Unlike their Native American neighbors, they had great difficulty proving their claim to lands ceded to them by Spanish and Mexican administrations. Although the U.S. government had approved the land holdings of all the pueblos except Zuñi and Laguna before 1860, Hispanos met with comparatively little success when they asked the American government to affirm their claims. Community ownership, which American law did not recognize, posed significant problems, as did the use of land to which no individual held title. American courts did not regard traditional practices of the *pobladores* with the sympathy of the Spanish and Mexican legal systems. Hispano land received few of the protections extended to Native Americans, and much Hispano land was transferred to Anglo ownership under dubious circumstances.[4]

Unlike many other grants in northern New Mexico, the Vigil Grant went through an orderly transition from Hispano to Anglo ownership. In the early 1870s, Ramón Vigil, already more than seventy years old, was prepared to sell his land. Father Thomas Aquinas Hayes, Archbishop Jean Baptiste Lamy's priest-in-residence at Santa Clara Pueblo, offered Vigil four thousand dollars for the grant. Hayes's position at the pueblo made him familiar to the people of the Española and Pojoaque valleys and presumably facilitated his purchase of the grant. Vigil accepted Hayes's offer.[5]

Hayes was the transitional figure in the Anglo acquisition of the Vigil Grant. As an Anglo priest working at Santa Clara Pueblo, he bridged the gap between different worlds. Hayes knew everyone in the valleys, and garbed in a clerical collar, he commanded their respect. If there were disputes, Hayes functioned as an adjudicator. His motive for the purchase could not have been speculation. In 1871, there was little inkling that a railroad would cross the Rio Grande valley. Nor did he impinge on traditional patterns of use. For the first eight years of his ownership, Hayes served merely as custodian of the land.

The coming of the railroad changed the value of land in northern New Mexico. In 1851, when Ramón Vigil acquired his land, it had subsistence value; by 1880, adjacent to the proposed path of the narrow-gage railway, it had considerable cash value. Father Hayes blossomed into a successful land speculator. He realized that the Vigil Grant had become a marketable commodity, and he took steps to insure its value. While in Rome in 1879, he sold the property for sixteen thousand dollars and repurchased it for the same price, presumably to increase the value of the land on paper. In 1884, after the railroad had come to the region, Hayes made his ultimate deal when Winfield R. Smith, a wealthy Milwaukee attorney, and Edward P. Sheldon, a Cleveland industrialist, purchased the tract for one hundred thousand dollars—by the standards of the day, an astronomical cost of more than three dollars per acre.[6]

During the territorial period, similar events occurred throughout New Mexico. Land became desirable to Anglos as it became linked to transportation systems that could carry to market what it produced, and grants that had belonged to Hispanos and Indians gradually fell into Anglo hands. The sale of the Ramón Vigil Grant to Father Hayes was part of a larger pattern, different only in that its transfer inspired little initial animosity. To the east and south of the Sangre de Cristos, at Pecos Pueblo, Hispanos acquired parts of the original pueblo league from Indians as early as the 1820s. Although the Pecos Valley contained a number of thriving Hispano communities by 1880, at least one title to the entire pueblo league bandied about New York City in the hands of speculators. This group, none of whom had ever seen Pecos, offered the title as collateral in a number of different situations. At Las Trampas, farther to the north, Anglo speculators alienated the *ejido*, the common area, of a Spanish land grant by 1902 and turned the timber and grazing lands of El Valle and Las Trampas into a private pasture for their sheep. Gradually, by fraudulent, deceitful, or legitimate means, Anglos acquired a large portion of the best and most accessible Spanish and Mexican land grants.[7]

The new owners and their allies, both Anglo and Hispano, saw land not as a place to make a home but as the basis for a fortune, and land values dominated territorial New Mexico. The owners utilized the railroad and the growing national markets, and many of them, including some Hispanos, became powerful in territorial politics. Smaller landowners and their communities had difficulty combating the potent acquisitive instincts of men like Thomas B. Catron, who at one point owned more than one million acres in northern New Mexico and was part of the loosely connected cabal referred to as the Santa Fe Ring.[8]

On the Pajarito Plateau, Anglo ownership signaled changes in time-honored practices. Like many Spanish and Mexican land grants, the Vigil Grant had informal boundaries. The traditional northern end of the grant was the seasonal creek in Guajes Canyon; its western limit was long considered the peaks of the Jemez Mountains. In 1877 the surveyors Sawyer and McElroy drew an arbitrary line for the northern boundary of the grant and marked the western edge at the base of the mountains. After Hayes returned from Europe in 1881 he protested the survey, but his claim was denied. With their one hundred thousand dollars at stake, Smith and Sheldon decided to challenge the boundary that the General Land Office survey had established. In 1885, the office denied their claim, ruling that Hayes's acceptance of the 1877 survey bound future purchasers of the land as well. Even with Henry Atkinson, the notoriously corrupt former U.S. surveyor general for New Mexico, as their attorney, the new owners did not prevail. Sheldon was so disgusted that he offered his portion for sale, and George Fletcher purchased it for forty-four thousand dollars in 1885.[9]

The practice of formalizing commonly accepted boundaries revealed a major difference between Anglo and Hispano cultures, a difference that put Hispanos at a disadvantage. Because the extended network of families shared the grant and its environs, the determination of exact boundaries rarely was an issue for the *pobladores*. There was little pressure to decide formal lines. Community usage precluded demarcation.

Whereas a blurry boundary seemed typical to Ramón Vigil and his neighbors, Smith, Sheldon, and Fletcher needed to know exactly what they had purchased. The desire to define boundaries suggested a stronger sense of proprietorship, which in turn implied that the new owners would be less tolerant than their predecessors had been of others who sought to use their land.

These men shared the dominant values and cultural assumptions of late-nineteenth-century industrial America—growth, progress, development, and profit. They differed from other residents of the area in their perception of the tract. Like the majority of their generation, these men believed in competitive commerce as a civilizing factor. They also could not afford to let the Vigil Grant lie fallow. They had too much money invested in the land. As absentee landlords, they sought tenants who could make enough money off the land to pay both the taxes and a stipend to its owners.

After 1868, cattle became the most significant industry in the Southwest. Texas cattlemen drove their cattle to the railheads in Kansas, in the process creating a persistent mythology. But as ecological entities, the llanos of West Texas were fragile, and overgrazing spurred by the possibility of fortunes impoverished the range. The land showed the effect of a booming market and repeated intensive use. By the early 1880s, large sections of former grazing land had become useless to cattlemen. When a number of states enacted legislation to protect rangelands, cattlemen searched for new range, which turned out to be either marginal land that was not previously worth grazing or areas so small or so remote as to preclude large-scale ranching. The Pajarito Plateau qualified on all counts. The railroad gave the region access to the national market, an added advantage for cattlemen. As Smith and Fletcher searched for tenants, cattlemen sought tracts of land like the Vigil Grant. It was only a matter of time until the two sides came together.

In the 1880s, Texans found the Pajarito Plateau. In 1883, after much of the rangeland in West Texas had become desert as a result of excessive grazing, the Texas legislature passed ordinances limiting use of the range. A parade of Texans came to New Mexico to find fresh rangeland, and one, W. C. Bishop, leased the plateau. Bishop headed a large operation that handled more than three thousand head of cattle, and soon spotted, dark brown animals offset the red and gold of the landscape of the plateau. Hispanos later recalled never having seen so many animals in their lives.[10]

The Texans established new patterns of use of the Vigil Grant. Pajarito and Water canyons, both of which bisected the grant, had traditionally been the focus of grazing on the plateau. Both these places had perennial water sources, and Hispanos clustered their animals about them. The Texans also understood the value of these two canyons and used the lower part of Pajarito Canyon as their headquarters. Bishop and his *mayor-*

domo, a man named Cliff, lived there, as did their men. They built a bunk-house and put up a number of fences, creating corrals and marking pasture.

The Texans created competition for the limited resources of the plateau. In response to their appearance, many of the Hispanos who used the plateau for pasture changed their patterns. A number, including Crestino Montoya and Martin Luján, took their cattle off the grant. Another, Nepomoceno Valencia, went to work for the Texans, who allowed him to keep his few cattle on the grant. Juan Montes Vigil took his cattle to Mortandad and del Buey canyons, still on the grant but north of Pajarito Canyon, where the Texans centered their enterprise. But his calves wandered back to Pajarito Canyon, where they had been born and raised.[11]

The Texans caused substantive changes in the ecology of the plateau. The economic promise of the region was an illusion created by its high altitude and lack of intensive use for hundreds of years. The Pajarito Plateau received an average of ten to fourteen inches of rain per year, far short of the minimum required for unirrigated agriculture. Its bunchgrasses were rooted in a thin layer of topsoil formed over thousands of years. Once the grasses disappeared, leaving the land defenseless and vulnerable to erosion, they would not soon return. Sporadic grazing taxed resources; a large-scale endeavor altered the physical environment.

The arrival of Bishop and his cattle also affected the communal nature of the use of land on the Pajarito Plateau. The Texans realized that the area around Pajarito Canyon could not provide for subsistence and commercial economies simultaneously. After the first year there, they modified their practices. Instead of concentrating their cattle around the water sources, the Texans let cattle roam the grant and, in a time-honored western tradition, the area beyond its vague boundaries. This squeezed out Hispanos and their animals.[12]

As the competition for land increased, relations between the lessors and their neighbors deteriorated. Hispanos and Indians owned too few animals to fill the plateau. From their point of view, the Texans seemed determined to monopolize every strand of grass on the grant. Animosity already existed elsewhere between Hispanos and Texans. In 1841, Texans attacked New Mexico in an effort to annex it to the Lone Star Republic; in 1843, a leading New Mexico merchant, Don Antonio José Chavez, was murdered by Texas ruffians along the Kansas leg of the Santa Fe Trail.

During the Civil War, Texan raiders under the Confederate flag worsened their dismal reputation in the New Mexico Territory. Under American rule, Spanish-speaking New Mexicans fared badly, and Hispanos feared violence by Texans. Some of the people who took their stock to the plateau withdrew.[13]

Whether or not the Texans intimidated Hispanos, the result was the same. The people who had traditionally used the Pajarito Plateau as an *ejido* were forced out of large stretches of pasture. But competition for land was not new in New Mexico. Pueblo Indians had previously accused their Hispano neighbors of the same practice.

This pressure was a harbinger of trouble. Two groups, embodying different values and practices, perceived the plateau as central to their interests. The area was limited in size and productive potential, and coexistence was impossible. In a frontier world beyond adjudication, in a territory with a tradition of corrupt administration, and with each side sure that its claim was just, the potential for conflict escalated.

Natural conditions deferred a permanent resolution of this situation. The harsh winter of 1886–87, the second in succession, destroyed Bishop's cattle enterprise, and the plateau returned to its historic state. Deep snow blanketed the entire region from October until April, and many of the cattle froze or starved. Although Bishop tried to revive his herd in the spring of 1887, he saw the trap into which he had blundered. In 1888, he packed up what remained of his herd and returned to Texas.

After the cattlemen left, herders from the valleys filled the opening. They too had suffered from the severe winters. Alejandro Montes Vigil had lost eleven of his eighteen cattle in the winter of 1886–87. Yet unlike the Texans, Hispanos did not have a choice about moving on. The plateau and its environs were their world. They brought their animals back to Pajarito Canyon, using both the corrals and the bunkhouse that the Texans had abandoned.[14]

After the departure of the Texans and perhaps in response to their appearance, cabins sprang up outside the Vigil Grant. Most of these belonged to valley residents who used the plateau for grazing. North of Frijoles Canyon at the base of the Jemez Mountains, Severo Gonzáles had a ranch composed of two homestead sections. On nearby Three-Mile Mesa, Pedro Gómez y Gonzáles and his family settled. In 1894, Benigno Quintana patented a homestead in the vicinity, and David Romero, whose family had pastured animals on the plateau for generations, soon followed. In 1896, William Carpenter White settled a parcel adjacent to the Quintanas, who taught Spanish to White's children. Antonio Sanchés settled near a muddy pond fed by rainwater, raising livestock and growing crops. Some of these *ranchitos* were seasonal; others were year-round endeavors. Other small homesteads dotted García Canyon, just south of Puye, where people used the cut blocks from nearby ruins for their homes. At least one settler, Juan Luis García, also owned land in Española. To the isolated residents of the Pojoaque and Española valleys, the short reign of the Texans seemed an aberration.[15]

Yet Bishop and his cattle had a complex, deleterious, and permanent effect on the Vigil Grant. Modern calculations indicate that the carrying capacity of the thirty-two thousand acres of the Vigil Grant would have been about three hundred head of cattle. By stocking the grant with ten times the number that could graze the tract without decreasing the productivity of its range, Bishop likely initiated a chain reaction. The overstocking reduced the vigor of forage plants, inhibited reproduction, allowed opportunistic plants from lower elevations to move in, and probably eliminated more favored species of forage. The effect was compounded near sources of water. Cattle depended on reaching water, and their hooves created extensive trails, leading to soil movement, erosion, and ultimately, the mortality of plant species, particularly the edible wild plants that congregated around water sources. In turn, the buildup of dead vegetable matter diminished, destroying soil and plant reproduction, limiting the fuel for natural fire, and contributing to altering the historic pattern of ecological change.

The cattle also interfered with the natural regeneration of the range. Trampling of grasses and cropping of immature plants limited the amount of fuel for wildfires, and fire suppression, which began in earnest as homesteaders came to the plateau, ended the existing pattern of regeneration on the range. Changes in fire patterns meant that more timber grew on the plateau, and the overgrazed range could no longer carry ground fires and thereby reduce the density of trees. Both of these conditions impaired the regeneration of the vigorous grass understory necessary to sustain grazing. Fewer nutrients were available on the range, and the mulching litter layer that kept the soil moist disappeared. Xeric plants —species that thrive in hotter, drier zones—began to overwhelm plant life native to higher elevations. The result was the general desiccation of the soil and, ultimately, a diminished economic potential for the land.[16]

In such an arid, economically marginal region, the impact of wide-spread overgrazing lasted for generations. Ecological communities in arid areas like the Pajarito Plateau required hundreds of years to recover from severe disturbance, and when significant soil loss was involved, the damage could be permanent. Because the soils were highly erodible, the excessive removal of ground cover by overstocking created a major disturbance—the depleted ground cover and excessive erosion persisted more than one hundred years later. In short, Bishop and his cattle sprang the ecological trap. Mass grazing permanently decreased the quality of range on the Vigil Grant and initiated a process that led to other commercial uses of land not well suited to the demands of industrial society.

The appearance of the Texans was also a precursor of the spread of Anglo material culture to peripheral areas like the Rio Arriba region of New Mexico. The tenets of industrialism and the drive for cash profits entered the world of subsistence economics. Anglo practices of land use signaled the end of traditional life on the plateau and in the surrounding valleys. Even though the Vigil Grant briefly reacquired its traditional, *ejido*-like status, its value to seasonal users decreased. As its soils became more desiccated, opportunistic desert plants and shrubs like snakeweed replaced native grasses at higher elevations, and the plateau became a less dependable source of sustenance.

The demise of Bishop's cattle operation left the owners of the Vigil Grant in a difficult situation. Their vast capital investment compelled them to seek development schemes. As absentee landlords who made their fortunes in other businesses, they did not know the terrain well and would not have recognized the damage that the grazing enterprise caused had they visited New Mexico and looked at the land. At the time, no one understood the relationship between short-term overgrazing and long-term destruction of natural resources. From Smith and Fletcher's point of view, the land still had economic potential. What they needed was a tenant who planned to develop it.

Besides grassland, timber was the other important commercial asset of the Vigil Grant. In 1898, after a few years in which no commercial development took place on the Vigil Grant, the partners leased the timber rights of the grant to Harry S. Buckman, a lumberman from Oregon living about fifty miles north of Española in Tres Piedras, New Mexico. Buckman built a small town that he named after himself at the spot where the Chili Line from Santa Fe reached the east bank of the Rio Grande in White

Rock Canyon and began to wind toward Colorado, about eleven miles south of Española. Buckman initiated full-scale timber cutting on the plateau. Soon there were lumber camps in Water Canyon, about five miles northwest of the ruins at El Rito de los Frijoles. A new kind of commercial culture took root at the base of the Pajarito Plateau.

Buckman made his living by cutting timber on contract from Spanish land grants that fell into Anglo hands. He leased the Vigil Grant after he finished cutting the Petaca Grant, near Tierra Amarilla, about fifty miles to the north along the railroad. As his work there showed, Buckman had little regard for the land or the absentee landlords with whom he made his bargains. He saw dollar signs where trees stood and cut timber indiscriminately. Yet northern New Mexico made his business tenuous. In marginal country, he nearly always scrambled to break even. The Vigil Grant was no exception to this pattern.[17]

A timber contract for the Vigil Grant was no guarantee of a profitable endeavor. The grant contained about two thousand acres of prime timber —in Buckman's words, "a small body"—as well as large sections of more marginal kinds and much scrub timber. Before Buckman leased the right to cut, a number of the mill owners in the area had passed over the opportunity. Buckman paid ten thousand dollars for the privilege of cutting the timber, a price he later recounted as "sure full value." He had to build his own road from his railroad depot in the town of Buckman to the sawmills he established on the mesas. This cost him nearly six thousand dollars, an investment he planned to recoup by acquiring scrip, which he could trade for government land elsewhere, and by purchasing timber from some of the settlers in the region.[18]

In his approach to the timber business, Buckman typified western entrepreneurs. The timber itself was not sufficient for him to make a profit, but his real intention was to trade scrip with the government under the terms of the forest lieu provision in the act of March 1, 1898, thus giving up his holdings in New Mexico for land in the Pacific Northwest covered with tall Douglas firs. This potential to acquire valuable federal land, often with the cooperation of corrupt officials, made dubious deals into profitable ones for many entrepreneurs.[19]

Buckman's situation on the plateau remained precarious. His contract with Smith and Fletcher required a five-thousand-dollar down payment, and the costs of roads, machinery, labor, and shipping all contributed to high overhead. Pressed by the outlay of capital, Buckman sought ways to increase profits. These led him into conflict with the Hispanos who continued to use the plateau.

Rumors about Buckman's business practices abounded, the most damaging of which accurately contended that he violated the terms of his contract. The pact allowed him three years to cut trees that were more than eight inches in diameter at the base. The contract gave him an additional five years to collect and ship all the timber. Under considerable pressure to pay his creditors, Buckman did not always obey the dictates of the contract. His tie gangs roamed the plateau in search of timber, often cutting smaller trees. This practice reduced large sections of immature forest to stump. The absentee landlords had little idea of what Buckman did, but the descendants of the Sánchez family were unhappy with developments on the plateau. In 1900, they filed a suit against Fletcher and Smith, charging that the contract with Buckman was illegal because it ceded timber rights to the entire grant, whereas the defendants owned only eight-elevenths of it. They sought redress from American courts.[20]

Resistance to the expropriation of land grants in northern New Mexico took a variety of forms. Beginning in the 1870s, Hispanos perceived real threats to their way of life and their land. The tension over competition for grazing lands dominated these controversies in the Rio Arriba region. Hispanos' responses included tactical violence and organized guerrilla resistance as well as political activism and involvement.[21]

In 1889–90, one of the most potent outbursts of violent resistance erupted. Throughout northern New Mexico, and particularly in the area around Las Vegas and the bitterly disputed Maxwell Land Grant, a Hispano group called *Las Gorras Blancas*, "the White Caps," combated land-grabbing by cutting the barbed-wire fences that symbolized restrictions on their way of life, by destroying telegraph wires, and by burning the ranches of Anglos and of Hispano "collaborators." Ironically taking the name of Anglo nativist groups that intimidated nonwhite non-Protestant Americans, these "night riders" enjoyed the support of the Hispano community, as well as the tacit approval of elements in the Anglo community that perceived large monopolistic cattle empires as a threat to the growth of the region.[22]

The battle fought by *Las Gorras Blancas* was as much a class struggle as a racial one. Stretching in a wide swath from the northwest corner of New Mexico to an epicenter in the vicinity of Las Vegas, it inspired the creation of above-ground political resistance in the form of a new political party that ultimately became part of the national agrarian movement. El Partido del Pueblo Unido began with tremendous energy and had a number of very early successes in developing a political base for Hispano resistance to Anglo commercialism. Yet it became an amalgamation of the desires of a number of different groups and, like the Populist movement itself, was short-lived. But the emergence of organized political response showed that both legal and extralegal resistance could be effective.[23]

Buckman's endeavor ignited a different kind of Hispano resistance, at least in part the result of the orderly transfer of the Vigil Grant. The change in usage of the grant was in no way part of a pattern of deceit or fraud. Vigil had sold the land to Hayes, who had sold to the Anglo industrialists, and even when the Texans brought their cattle to the region, at least some Hispanos continued to use the tract. By 1900, process of law had governed the Vigil Grant for a long time. Bringing the issue to court seemed to offer a chance at the most satisfactory solution.

The case was a drawn-out affair, typical of litigation over land in New Mexico at the turn of the century. The plaintiffs based their contentions on the terms of the sale to Vigil in 1851. According to their testimony, Antonio Sánchez sold the rights to eight-elevenths of the old Sánchez Grant to Vigil. Three of Sánchez's siblings refused to sell and retained their right to the land. The original bill of sale supported the Sánchez contention. David Romero, who had homesteaded on the plateau, testified that Hayes had acknowledged the claim of the plaintiffs when he allowed the family of José Francisco Durán, direct descendants of Antonio Sánchez's sister Victoria, to graze their stock on the grant without exacting a fee. Hayes also was rumored to have offered to purchase Durán's share.[24] Former Territorial Governor L. Bradford Prince handled the case for the plaintiffs, who wanted a share of the fees that Buckman paid Fletcher and Smith. A prominent Santa Fe attorney, Eugene A. Fiske, defended Fletcher and Smith.

Both Prince and Fiske were players in the circle of leaders who made up the ruling cabal of the New Mexico Territory. This cadre held almost every important post in New Mexico, and its influence outweighed that of the federal appointees sent from Washington to administer the territory. The members competed among themselves, and their allegiances shifted regularly depending on their individual interests in specific situations. Prince and the land baron Thomas B. Catron were charter members of the Santa Fe Ring. Although both were Republicans, Prince and Catron were often at odds. From 1889 to 1893, Prince served as governor of the territory. Fiske served as U.S. district attorney while Prince was governor, earning the sobriquet "Prince's poodle." He also served on the territorial supreme court. In 1895, Catron regarded Fiske as a sworn enemy; less than two years later, during the controversy between Governor Miguel A. Otero and Catron, Prince and Fiske were both allied with Catron. With Prince's dominance of their relationship, an adversarial meeting between Fiske and Prince smacked of collusion.[25]

No matter who pleaded their case, rural Hispanos often had difficulties understanding Anglo law and its procedures. An alien legal system had been imposed on them, and it devalued or ignored the social customs that were an integral part of their way of proving ownership. Land titles in New Mexico were in chaos, offering Anglo and Hispano speculators the opportunity to manipulate the system. Neither the American government nor its legal system offered support to Hispanos. Court papers and other official documents were generally printed in English, which few Spanish-speakers outside of Santa Fe and Las Vegas could read. The values of Hispanic New Mexicans contrasted greatly with those of Anglos. Even the presence of the highly respected Prince as the attorney for the plaintiffs could not offset the structural disadvantage at which the plaintiffs began.[26]

The case was decided in a court where American laws and suppositions reigned. Prince showed that when Antonio Sánchez sold the grant in 1851, he sold only eight-elevenths of it. Three of his siblings expressly did not convey their rights to Vigil. Prince used the testimony of Juan and Alejandro Montes Vigil to show that both Ramón Vigil and Father Hayes had recognized the rights of the descendants of the three Sánchez siblings who had not sold. Although Prince attempted to show that even the Texans respected these rights, testimony proved inconclusive on that critical point. But according to Prince, his clients' unhindered seasonal use of the grant constituted compelling evidence of their claim.[27]

Prince's evidence would have been substantial under Spanish or Mexican law, but in an American court, the defense had ways to circumvent his contentions. Fiske countered with a tactic that often proved successful in territorial courts. He knew that as a result of poverty, disregard, or lack of knowledge or understanding, Hispanic claimants were unlikely to pay land taxes. Fiske centered his questioning along this line. With the testimony of the deputy assessors of Santa Fe County, Alfred Hinojos and

Ambrosio Ortiz, and their counterpart in Bernalillo County, J. J. Sheridan, Fiske showed that between the time Hayes sold the grant in 1884 and 1900, none of Vigil's or Sánchez's descendants paid taxes on the land. In an American court, this was damning evidence of a lack of proprietary interest.[28]

Although Hispanos had a long history of use of the region, they had little that proved any right of ownership to the satisfaction of a culture that insisted on documentary evidence. Fiske's contentions seem to have swayed Judge John R. McFie, who had previously served with Fiske on the supreme court of New Mexico Territory. In 1905, despite a preponderance of circumstantial evidence in their favor, the plaintiffs lost the case when McFie ruled that their evidence was "of a hearsay nature and of uncertain value."[29] American law devalued Hispano experience and testimony. After the ruling, the Pajarito Plateau belonged wholly to the representatives of the industrial age.

In 1903, while the case was pending, Buckman packed up his tents and left the region. He tried to lease the Cebolleta Grant near Santa Fe through Prince, but the deal fell through. No one in northern New Mexico ever heard of him again. Buckman sold the bridge he had built across the Rio Grande to the Bradys, who owned a lumber mill near Las Truchas. The Bradys dismantled the bridge and took it to their mill by wagon. Buckman left only the small town of Buckman, rusting sawmills, thousands of tree stumps, and his name as evidence of his presence.[30]

Buckman's timber enterprise damaged what remained of the native ecosystem on the Vigil Grant. Bishop's cattle had devastated the native grasses. Buckman had consumed a sizable portion of the old-growth timber. The destruction of the grass cover and the spread of low-quality forage plants further affected the livelihood of Hispano ranchers. The natural world was changing before their eyes, and herdsmen had to take their animals farther to find good pasture. Increasingly they competed among themselves for rangeland of declining quality.

Even more significant, Buckman's enterprise introduced new economic options in the region. As the land became poorer, people who depended on it needed to augment their livelihood to maintain their material standards. Buckman's operation had required many workers. The building of the road, the operation of the sawmills in Water Canyon, and the transportation of timber to the railway were all labor-intensive activities. Buckman's paychecks had considerable allure, for they offered the ability to purchase canned goods, implements, and other newly discovered "necessities" that the railroad brought to the region.

The timber enterprise transformed the economy of the region. Many of the people in the region, both homesteaders on the plateau and residents of the valleys, had worked for Buckman. William C. White had driven a wagon team that carried timber from the plateau to the rail depot in the town of Buckman. Many of the Hispano homesteaders had helped build the roads or had worked as "tie choppers." The timber enterprise altered the pastoral mode of living to which they had previously adhered.

All of these factors combined to further a complicated process of incremental economic, social, political, and environmental change.[31] Each stage of the process pushed the people of the area closer toward dependence on outside markets. Native American and Hispano populations found themselves with less of the plateau at their disposal. The Vigil Grant, its productivity demolished by Bishop and to a lesser extent by Buckman, was no longer available. The density of Hispano and Native American stock outside the Vigil Grant increased, and more animals competed for less grazing land. Anglo overgrazing extended the impact of earlier, limited overgrazing by Hispanos and Native Americans. Cattle and sheep trails were no longer centralized around water sources. Larger herds also drove game and predators higher into the Jemez Mountains, and the black bears, wild turkeys, and pumas that had characterized the pre-1880 plateau became more scarce below elevations of eight thousand feet. The advantages of the plateau as a subsistence environment quickly disappeared, and the people who depended on it had to find new sources of sustenance.

The effect of the new uses of land was a gradual process of impoverishment for most of the people who lived in the region. Before the lumber camps and tie gangs, few Hispanos or Native Americans worked for anyone else. Instead, they grew foodstuffs, tended animals, and traded for the items, like coffee, sugar, and matches, that they could not produce themselves.[32] Currency was scarce, and labor was a commodity to be bartered, not sold. Buckman's crews received cash for their labor, and the influx of money enabled the people of the region to buy the attractive goods in the stores by the railroad in Española.

With motives born of desire and necessity, Hispanos and Native Americans began to participate in the cash economy. As their traditional base of existence offered them less, many Hispanos entered the market to trade for foodstuffs and machine-made factory tools. These were expensive and often required credit—the final step in becoming a part of the cash economy. Storekeepers like Frank Bond began to amass fortunes as the people who had subsisted for generations developed new material expectations. An embryonic imitation of the lifestyle of turn-of-the-century America appeared on the Pajarito Plateau.

Economically, this situation created growing divisions in northern New Mexico. The vast majority of people quickly became used to purchasing implements and goods. They sought currency, often through employment. But the jobs available to Hispanos and Native Americans were generally low in status and pay, and the goods and the credit necessary to purchase them were expensive. A cycle that ground Native Americans and Hispanos downward began as these people lost the confidence and assurance granted by their traditional culture and economy, however meager in comparison with the rewards of industrial society. Gradually they became participants in an economic system that valued them for their labor, and although many made incremental gains by material standards, the price of the increasing distance from the traditional values frequently offset those advantages. Material expectations inspired by exposure to industrial technologies changed cultural perceptions.

The first attempts to integrate the plateau into the market economy were largely unsuccessful for Anglos who tried to secure a fortune. The commodities of the plateau were few in number, poor in quality, and generally worthy of only a rapacious and limited effort. Yet even these failed attempts had a significant effect on life in the region. Anglo commercial culture had appeared, its accoutrements beginning to play a role in changing values and perceptions. The land and its relationship with the people who depended on it began to be transformed.

Simultaneously, another group of Anglos discovered the attractiveness of the Pajarito Plateau. Their concerns were cultural, scientific, and aesthetic rather than economic. They too had plans for the plateau and sought ways to achieve their goals. They too needed the land and its resources to implement their programs. Their presence only complicated an already strained situation.

THE COMING

OF THE

ARCHAEOLOGISTS

3

During the 1890s, commercial interests signaled the emergence of a market economy on the Pajarito Plateau, yet this was not the only significant influence of Anglo-American culture to reach the region. The plateau contained much more than natural resources. On the south side of nearly every canyon and on the tops of most mesas lay the abandoned villages of earlier inhabitants of the plateau. Some of the complexes were as large as six hundred rooms, others as small as four. A vast network of footpaths worn into the soft tuff of the region led from pueblo to spring, from mesa top to cave dwelling. It was a mystical world of an abandoned civilization, the likes of which were unequaled in the United States.

As the region opened up, these ruins began to attract the attention of a widening circle of people around the world. Indian culture, extant and prehistoric, came into vogue, and scientists and travelers, the curious and the self-aggrandizing, became interested in the origin, development, and prospects of the natives of the North American continent. The question of the fate of Native Americans had perplexed American society for more than a century, but as Indian populations continued their decline to the point of extinction, reformers thought that a concerted effort to save them was necessary. Indians and their prehistoric ancestors became an important topic of discussion among educated, affluent, and influential Americans.

The ruins of the Pajarito Plateau became enmeshed in the growing interest in native culture. Among those who were interested in the region was Adolph F. A. Bandelier, a lean and craggy forty-year-old who had trained himself as an anthropologist under the tutelage of the founder of modern anthropology, Lewis Henry Morgan. On October 23, 1880, Bandelier and his guide from Cochiti Pueblo, Juan José, reached the south mesa of Frijoles Canyon. Below them, Bandelier could see the remains of an extraordinary civilization. The ruins of the great community house, Tyuonyi, as well as innumerable cave dwellings, cavate lodges, and the remains of many talus houses, greeted him.[1] After a difficult, half-hour climb down the steep sides of the canyon, Bandelier rushed across El Rito de los Frijoles, the creek that divided the canyon, and carrying his ever-present measuring stick, he began to inspect the hollowed-out cave openings of the prehistoric dwellings extending nearly a mile and a half up and down the canyon bottom. He had discovered a place previously unknown to Anglo-America.

A scientist by inclination, Bandelier was also the first tourist to come to Frijoles Canyon. The canyon appealed as much to his emotions as to his intellect. It was "the grandest thing I ever saw," he wrote in his diary that first evening among the box elders.[2] Bandelier had entered a world apart from the modern one, and besides its obvious advantages as a locale for study, he was entranced by the sentience of the place. He recognized that although he was the first, many more would follow him to the previously isolated corners of the Pajarito Plateau.

Bandelier's penchant for travel revealed much of the prehistoric Southwest to a growing audience. For the better part of the next twelve years, he explored ruins and pueblos throughout New Mexico, Arizona, and northern Mexico and used his multilingual skills to research documents from the Spanish era in the Southwest. Based in Santa Fe in a little house on what is now De Vargas street, Bandelier wrote extensively, publishing his "Historical Introduction to Studies among the Sedentary Indians of New Mexico" and "A Visit to the Aboriginal Ruins in the Valley of the Rio Pecos" in the *Papers of the Archeological Institute of America* in 1881. His most famous scholarly work, *Final Report of Investigations among the Indians of the*

Southwestern United States, Carried on Mainly in the Years from 1880 to 1885, followed, as did his only novel, *Die Koshare,* translated into English as *The Delight Makers.* As the protodiscipline of anthropology focused on the description of prehistoric remains, Bandelier became a mythic figure among his peers.[3]

Bandelier was the first Anglo to systematically explore the Southwest, but others soon followed. His work spurred an increasing awareness of the prehistory of the North American continent. Some of this interest focused on the Pajarito Plateau. In 1887, James and Matilda Coxe Stevenson, who represented one faction within John Wesley Powell's Bureau of Ethnology, surveyed the ruins at Puye, almost due west of Santa Clara Pueblo. Gradually American scientists became aware of prehistoric ruins.[4]

After the pronouncement of the closing of the westward frontier in the 1890s, anything associated with the open world that preceded the spread of the American Republic became popular. Railroads promoted the West with lantern slides, illustrations, calendars, and paintings by famous artists such as Thomas Moran. A back-to-nature ethos permeated the settled parts of the country. Indians and their costumes, cowboys, and Wild West shows became integral pieces of the popular culture of the 1890s as Americans longed nostalgically for an image of the vigorous and demanding world that preceded the westward spread of civilization.[5]

Throughout the Southwest, herdsmen, homesteaders, and cowboys capitalized on these sentiments. They found that an eager public would pay sizable sums of money for the pots and bowls that they found or dug up in prehistoric ruins. Purchasers coveted tangible remains of the aboriginal past as valuable pieces of a world now gone. They sought to retain the spirit of that world by possessing artifacts associated with the past. Marketing American prehistory became a cottage industry in the region.

Archaeological ruins near transportation lines were directly in the path of the curious and avaricious, and as denizens of a culture that placed primary importance on possession of land, many southwesterners found nothing wrong with digging up the past and purveying it as a bounty of civilization.[6] Typically the ruins were visited by people who did not respect them. As Anglo settlers fanned out across the river drainages of the Southwest, they found that the land had prior inhabitants. The numerous pots and baskets, not to mention ruins, were a nuisance to farmers and ranchers. Nor was it illegal to sell pots overturned by plows, dug up with a pick and shovel, or found on the surface. Settlement was only the first stage in the assault on prehistory. The arrival of the railroad in a particular locale usually signaled the beginning of more widespread digging.

In northern New Mexico, the railroad that brought Anglo commerce also brought new faces. Anglos were fascinated with accounts of the ruins and followed the directions of their Hispano and Native American neighbors to see these spectacular remains. Yet many of these "explorers" were destructively curious, and the ruins of the Pajarito Plateau suffered along with those elsewhere in the Southwest. In a typical account, "Buckskin Joe," a local character in Española, took Birge Harrison, an eastern writer and artist fascinated with the Southwest, his wife, Eleanor, and a group of other visitors to the ruins at Puye, about eight miles southwest of Santa Clara Pueblo. At the ruins, Buckskin Joe regaled his audience with tall tales and, with a flourish, showed them a human skull. In Harrison's words, "then ensued a general stampede in search of relics." Harrison and his friends found arrowheads, decorated pottery, and other prehistoric tools and implements in perfectly preserved cave dwellings with the original whitewash on the walls. Satiated after a few hours with their prehistoric plunder, the members of the group returned to Española.[7]

The actions of such visitors resulted in the wholesale destruction of prehistoric ruins. These structures and the artifacts they contained fascinated visitors, and like Buckskin Joe and his friends, the tourists wanted to take what they found with them as souvenirs or curiosities. In the West, this was accepted behavior; westerners operated on a "first-come, first-served" basis in almost every aspect of the physical world. Nor was prehistoric pottery remarkable from the point of view of most homesteaders. It was something to shatter with the plows of progress unless a buyer was readily available. Prehistory was one of the few perquisites of life in the Southwest. At the end of the nineteenth century, artifacts were as free for the taking as was rangeland or a homestead in this arid region.

The situation placed the ruins of one-thousand-year-old civilizations in serious jeopardy. Some visitors treated relics with disdain. They wrote their names on painted walls, defaced prehistoric pictographs painstakingly drawn in the char of the cave ceilings, and used masonry and stonework for campfires or shelter. Many fragile and easily accessible ruins were quickly demolished, their walls destroyed or overturned. Most of the visitors kept the artifacts they found – ollas (clay pots), potsherds, woven baskets and nets, and other tools and implements. These quickly scattered with their owners to all parts of the nation and the world, where they were no longer protected by the arid climate of the Southwest. Some pieces crumbled and broke; others disintegrated into dust.[8]

Depredations worried a growing constituency in the scientific world. Beginning with the establishment of the Smithsonian Institution in 1846 and augmented by the founding of the Peabody Museum at Harvard University in 1866, the systematic study of Native Americans, American prehistory, and archaeology became a focus of American scientists. They developed a discourse of their own, founding journals such as the *American Antiquarian* and the *American Anthropologist*. Frederic Ward Putnam became the curator of the Peabody Museum in 1875; his actions made him a major force in the development of American archaeology. A plethora of organizations followed. By the late 1880s, anthropological study had been removed from the realm of the enlightened amateur and had become accepted as both an avocation and a vocation.[9]

Museums became the central cultural institutions in the evolution of the twin disciplines of anthropology and archaeology. The museum best mitigated social change, explained relationships between preindustrial and industrial people, and showed there was order in industrial society despite its seemingly chaotic nature. The museum contributed to the socialization of a public faced with a new and confusing industrial order. It gave validity to life in an industrial society while it inculcated Americans with the values of the industrial age. Order did exist in the new world of machines, albeit in a different fashion, the message of the museum affirmed. Exhibits and fairs showed the might of industrial culture; in contrast, archaeology and anthropology presented the inferiority of aboriginal cultures.[10]

John Wesley Powell's Bureau of Ethnology, which became the Bureau of American Ethnology in 1894, played a leading role in interpreting this cosmology. Powell, the one-armed former Civil War major who had rafted the Colorado River through the Grand Canyon in 1869, became an important force in federal policy as the U.S. government tried to answer questions on the role and fate of Native Americans in a postfrontier, industrial world. Powell posited that ethnological study would provide information to guide federal policy, and his charisma and status assured the founding of the new bureau in 1879. Yet there was a deeper purpose to the bureau. Powell sought a coherent scientific unity that presented a moral universe to replace the empirical chaos dominating American sciences at the time.

In short, Powell sought to place anthropological study within a framework so that it could serve pragmatic social purposes.[11]

Buoyed by the high esteem in which leaders in Washington, D.C., held Powell, the Bureau of Ethnology found a niche in the federal bureaucracy. Science had become the panacea for a changing society, and anthropology played an integral role in establishing continuity between past and present. In a transition period in which organizational and group efforts began to supersede individuals, Powell gave his ethnologists leeway reminiscent of that of surveys of the 1870s. Yet Powell's commitment to the moral education of the public resulted in a "party line," in the words of John Swanton, a prescient bureau ethnologist and linguist. The conclusions of the research of Powell's bureau were foreordained, "predetermined by [the bureau's] prior commitments" to the concept of progress. This paradox permeated the bureau under Powell.[12]

The ethnologist had become the latest claimant to the role of "boonbringer"—the figure who, by experiencing wilderness, returns to civilization with concepts of value to a society out of touch with its roots. The ethnologist emerged to take this role at the time of the first widespread dislocation of traditional agrarian life—the era of industrial culture, replete with urbanization, railroad development, factories, clocks, and the creation of a class system. In the post-Darwinian era, the ethnologist was the successor to the cloth as explainer of human action and creator of a unified worldview. As a scientist, he had the best position to learn the secret of regeneration and prosperity. The prize with which bureau ethnologists returned, a "romantic aboriginal cosmology for a callow, disenchanted people," offered assurance in an age of change.[13]

At the time, anthropological and archaeological study differed in the eastern and the western halves of the nation. The study of the Southwest lagged behind similar endeavors east of the Mississippi River, where enlightened amateurs and protoscientists had studied for more than a generation. While those who studied the Mound Builders engaged in debate over questions of analysis and comparison, in the West, the primary mode of discourse was description. The Southwest possessed a seemingly endless supply of ruins to be "discovered" and subsequently described and was host to a comparable list of government-financed surveys and military expeditions. For scientists interested in the subject, there was abundant material to digest, and ethnologists from Powell's bureau strove to uncover even more. Their comprehensive solution to the problems of the industrial age required understanding a complete world-view.[14]

During the 1880s, the Southwest held particular appeal for bureau ethnologists. Such luminaries as Frank Hamilton Cushing, James and Matilda Coxe Stevenson, Washington Matthews, and Jesse W. Fewkes studied the region. Not surprisingly among a group of people seeking to offer pure knowledge to the public, powerful rivalries developed. The most potent pitted Cushing, Matthews, and John Bourke, the army lieutenant-ethnographer par excellence, against the Stevensons and Fewkes on questions of method, integrity, and preeminence. Perhaps the most insightful of the group, Cushing was erratic at best, and his behavior fueled the conflict. The role of boon-bringer required alienation from mainstream culture, something Cushing easily accomplished. He failed, however, to achieve the reconciliation necessary to present the gift of understanding to debased industrial society. Powell's paradox of individual and institution haunted the bureau as a result, but by the end of the decade, Powell's bureau had created a structure for scientific inquiry in the Southwest.[15]

Federal and public interest in the anthropology and archaeology of the Southwest grew as a result of the work of the bureau and its role in constructing the moral universe at the center of Powell's cosmology. The prehistory of the Southwest also became a focus of the romantic notions of eastern elites. A group of Bostonians including the governor of Massachusetts, Oliver Ames; Mary Hemenway, the sponsor of one of Cushing's southwestern expeditions and a great patron of anthropological study; Oliver Wendell Holmes; Anna Cabot Lodge; R. Charlotte Dana; Francis Parkman; and Edward Everett Hale petitioned to their U.S. senator, George Frisbie Hoar, to reserve a four-story adobe ruin in central Arizona called Casa Grande. Passed by Congress in 1889, the Casa Grande Ruins Reservation was created by President Benjamin Harrison in 1892.[16] Yet Casa Grande was an exception, a single case, and as scientists became convinced that Congress needed to consider some kind of general legislation to protect antiquities, the destruction of southwestern ruins continued. Vandals and souvenir hunters tore through sites from Colorado to the Mexican border, turning over walls in search of artifacts.

These tangible remains were the great prizes of the early history of southwestern archaeology. In an era with a romantic conception of the immediate past, artifacts took on symbolic value. For collectors, they became evidence of an anchored past, an understanding of continuity in human cultures as well as a mythic, romanticized picture of human experience. On a temporal level, this craving led to ruthless competition among museums, individuals, and others for the best collections. The value of the prehistoric past as anything other than fodder to alleviate the woes of industrial society was overlooked. No laws regulated acquisition, and southwesterners looked at collectors as crazy people chasing something useless. But collectors offered cash, often a rare commodity, and throughout the region, people willingly cooperated in the search for artifacts. Museums sponsored expeditions, purchased relics from anyone who offered, and generally sanctioned unrestricted chaos in search of advantage.[17]

Ironically, at the beginning of an era stressing the management of natural resources by trained experts, there were no rules that protected other kinds of treasure in the West. The experts that clamored for regulations in forestry and hydrology competed vigorously for access to prehistoric artifacts and structures to enhance the positions of their institutions. Blind to conflict of interest and resulting depredation, federal and private excavators hurried to enhance their personal reputations. Natural resources required scientific management to ensure fair distribution and continued availability, but nonrenewable cultural resources were pillaged wholesale. Issues of public good had not yet emerged from the chaos of the transition to an industrial society.

Many people dug in ruins in search of profit, but one man came to epitomize the exploitation of American prehistory. Richard Wetherill, an iron-willed rancher from Mancos, Colorado, discovered many ruins in the Mesa Verde region of southwestern Colorado during the 1890s. He excavated first for his own edification, later for commercial ends. In 1892, he and Gustav Nordenskiold of Sweden made a collection of artifacts that returned to Europe with Nordenskiold.[18] Jingoistic Americans pointed to this as purposeless despoliation of the American past for the gratification of European sensibilities, and Wetherill became the focus of the anger of different groups. Unconcerned with the clamor of easterners and unaffected by derogatory remarks, he ignored the complaints and continued to dig. Wetherill's work also attracted positive attention. He, and the artifacts he found, represented the state of Colorado at the Columbian Exposition of 1893 in Chicago. There Wetherill came to the fore.[19]

The Columbian Exposition presented a culmination of the experiences of the European in the New World. Designed to commemorate the four-hundredth anniversary of the arrival of Columbus in the New World, the fair also juxtaposed the "White City," the beacon of progress, with the Midway Plaisance, where ethnology was on display for public consumption, along with popular amusements labeled the "honky-tonk sector" of the fair. Frederic Ward Putnam of the Peabody Museum took charge of the anthropological exhibits, and the National Museum and the Bureau of American Ethnology added separate displays. William Henry Holmes directed the exhibit of the bureau with assistance from Cushing, the ethnologist James Mooney, and others. They presented groups of figures of Native Americans, offering "pictures from life" as a replacement for the pieces of sculpture that had represented aboriginal culture at earlier expositions. For the first time, numerous living Native Americans also were present.

Despite attempts to portray the nature of Native American life, the raucous atmosphere of the Midway, the "Royal Road of Gaiety," overshadowed the seriousness of the venture. The fair introduced the American public to evolutionary ideas in a way that could not help but demean Native American cultures. The Indians who participated were ridiculed and abused; not yet romantic figures of a distant past, they were still a threat to the progress embodied in the White City.[20]

The Columbian Exposition was an important moment for American anthropology and archaeology. Despite the way in which the public interpreted the material presented, anthropologists had gone far toward offering Americans a feel for native cultures. During the 1890s, the two disciplines also began to professionalize in the United States. The first formal training programs started; in 1894, a German-Jewish emigré, Franz Boas, directed the first American Ph.D. in anthropology at Clark University, and in 1899, he went to Columbia University and developed the first comprehensive graduate program. The exposition gave anthropologists an eminence that would otherwise have taken years to acquire. Newly trained professionals saw the Southwest as their crucible. It was uncharted territory from which they could make a reputation and achieve greater peer recognition for their discipline.

Not surprisingly, there was a moral point that could be derived from the study of Native Americans. In essence, it differed little from the message offered by the juxtaposition of the White City and the honky-tonk entertainment of the Midway. The vindication of progress was the objective,

John Wesley Powell would have asserted. Anything else was the moral equivalent of bankruptcy in an era of unbridled public pronouncement of faith in growth.[21] This was a heavy weight for professionalizing disciplines.

As anthropologists and archaeologists developed scientific standing, Wetherill became a threat to their future. The collections he made attracted considerable interest in Chicago, and he emerged as a minor star there. Yet to protoprofessionals with something to prove, Wetherill became anathema. He had both the knowledge and the desire to thwart them. Wetherill knew the location of more southwestern ruins than any other living Anglo, and he neither hesitated to dig nor deferred to the scientists of his time. With motives inspired in part by fear and jealousy, anthropologists and archaeologists were outraged by Wetherill's actions. To protect its growing interests, the scientific community galvanized against him. Scientists redefined their terminology to create a category for Wetherill. After Wetherill excavated Chaco Canyon, another extraordinary prehistoric area, the derogatory label of "pothunter" was attached to his name.

Many of the people at the Bureau of American Ethnology had no more training in archaeology or anthropology than did Wetherill. Powell, Holmes, Cushing, and others were all self-trained, as were the vast majority of people interested in archaeology at that time. What they and other scientists had that Wetherill lacked was official sanction, and this sometimes arbitrary designation came to separate those who labeled and those who were labeled as pothunters.[22]

Largely to prevent Wetherill from excavating where he chose, accredited professionals and their supporters began to raise a cry for legislation to protect southwestern archaeological ruins. Like many of the attempts to support preservation in the nineteenth century, the impetus for such legislation came from the East. With a romantic conception of both Native Americans and the task they undertook, easterners led in the struggle for preservation. Pockets of support in the West existed.

Westerners who supported the idea of preservation came from two distinct categories. Some were people of extraordinary foresight who realized that the future meant the end of perceptions of abundance and the acceptance of a regulated world. These people acquiesced to an imposed structure in the name of the common good. Others used issues like preservation to impress order on a chaotic society. From this point of view, issues like despoliation of prehistoric ruins were part of a larger process of change that replaced the open, allegedly individual West with an institutional society that promised material rewards for cooperation. Self-interest and public spirit combined in many supporters of preservation, and among this group, Edgar L. Hewett headed the charge.

Lean and prematurely balding, the young Hewett had a prominent chin and firm jaw that showed his resolve. His eyes revealed the insecurity of his background. Raised on a farm in western Illinois, Hewett followed an unlikely path to a career in archaeology. His insatiable desire for knowledge drove him to Tarkio College in Missouri, where he became a teacher. He began his career in the Midwest, moving progressively westward until he settled at the Colorado Normal School in Greeley. There Hewett discovered and voraciously read the works of Adolph Bandelier and became infatuated with the prehistoric Southwest.

Living in the West allowed Hewett and his first wife, Cora Whitford Hewett, to explore. They spent their free time satisfying a familial wanderlust. Hewett designed a camp wagon to hold all their necessities, and their two prize horses, Don and Dot, pulled them from Greeley into the mountains every summer. They traveled the West and Southwest from Yellowstone to Chihuahua, inspecting archaeological ruins and feeling the freedom of living in an open world. Among the places they found entrancing was the Pajarito Plateau.[23]

In 1896, Hewett began to apply the knowledge he had acquired from Bandelier's writing. The Hewetts packed their camp wagon and surveyed the ruins of the Pajarito Plateau, Bandelier's El Rito de los Frijoles among them. On hot, dusty summer days, Hewett and his Indian guides, Weyima (Antonio Domingo Pena), Potsonutse (Diegito Roybal), Oyegepi (Santiago Naranjo), and Aguaono (Juan Gonzales), "tramped every mile" of the plateau, its "stillness and mystery . . . undisturbed" by modern life. In Hewett's words, his Indian friends were "part of the scenery," of a piece with the surrounding world, and Hewett tried to emulate their behavior and feelings. He later recalled that "it took [him] quite a while . . . to disturb the soil [he] felt was sacred; longer still to spoil the scene with scientific papers."[24]

Hewett faced the classic paradox of the romantic archaeologist-anthropologist. Like Cushing and others, he sought both to convey the knowledge of the innocent—the healing power of a culture not yet debased by civilization—and to protect that culture from encroachment. Yet these two ends were mutually exclusive, leaving Hewett the surveyor-explorer in possession of an immense secret of great cultural value and Hewett the author as a violator of the trust of his guides. This dilemma was unsolvable; it accounted for Hewett's self-proclaimed initial hesitance to disturb the soil as well as his reluctance to muddy the mystery of prehistory with scientific articles and books.

Hewett's retrospective romanticism typified the nature of archaeological thinking and writing at the end of the nineteenth century. Responding to the unrestricted expansion and growth that characterized the Gilded Age, archaeologists sought a more simple world, unsullied by the aspirations of aggressive industrialism. Hewett believed there was no calling higher than that of archaeologist—the one who established the links between distant past and present, who showed progress as continuity and change over time. With the increasing acceptance of Native Americans as an exciting curiosity instead of a threat to public safety, romantic archaeology took on a significant role in creating an American mythology.

Despite his romantic sensibility, Hewett was a pragmatic person. When he became the president of New Mexico Normal University in Las Vegas, New Mexico, in 1898, his activities on the Pajarito Plateau intensified. With students from the teachers college, Hewett surveyed and mapped many of the ruins in the area. Increasingly, he spent his summers almost exclusively on the plateau. A scholar, albeit one without formal archaeological training at that time, he became a well-known figure in the cultural affairs of the Southwest.[25]

Like many who came in contact with the ruins of "lost" civilizations, Hewett became obsessed with prehistory. Fascinated with the Pajarito Plateau and possessing boundless energy and an unquenchable desire for knowledge, Hewett devoted himself to studying the region. He recognized that he had the opportunity to be the Christopher Columbus of southwestern archaeology, to be the first to discover the ways of the prehistoric inhabitants of the area, and learning to understand prehistory became the singular objective of this driven man. For a time, Hewett's vistas were those of the Pajarito Plateau.

Preserving its archaeological ruins from encroachment and paradoxically for his own study became one of Hewett's primary goals. Following the example of many European and American archaeologists in the nineteenth century, Hewett sought an exclusive domain. The Pajarito Plateau fit his criteria. Despite private ownership of the Vigil Grant and wide-

spread seasonal use of the region, in the view of the American government, the bulk of the area belonged to no one. Hewett could use it as he
pleased with little worry of intrusion by those who might tarnish the mysteries he sought.

Unfortunately, from Hewett's point of view, anyone else who wanted
some of this land could claim it under the terms of the Homestead Act of
1862. The General Land Office (GLO) was responsible for the public domain, but in the 1890s, its myriad obligations prevented it from paying attention to unusual features on its land. The adjudication of homestead
claims largely occupied GLO field officers. Both to protect the ruins and to
ensure his right to explore them, Hewett wanted to elevate the protection
of archaeological ruins to a position of unparalleled importance within the
GLO. But as the situation stood, there was no way to restrict anyone from
digging in the ruins of the Southwest.

Hewett's objectives trod on the values of westerners. He needed a way
to protect archaeological ruins from vandalism, but the idea of federal
control over western land made him and many other westerners suspicious. Raised in the nineteenth-century tradition that made individuals
the masters of their destinies, Hewett also understood that the twentieth
century would require cooperation between self and society, the individual and the government. He cast his lot with the cooperative future and
began to seek ways to remove land with archaeological ruins from the
public domain.

Hewett and other westerners were critical to the success of any move to
preserve antiquities in the West and Southwest. By the 1890s, many westerners resented the intervention of the federal government in western affairs. Although white settlers welcomed the military when Native Americans threatened settlement, sectional conflict loomed when legislation
that restricted the use of resources in the West reached the floor of Congress. As a leading educator in New Mexico Territory, Hewett had much
to offer the scientific community. He represented another kind of West,
the forward-looking side of the region, and his presence went a long way
toward diffusing cries of elitism and opportunism directed at advocates of
preservation. Hewett became a leader in the fledgling movement.[26]

In 1900, Hewett's archaeological credentials were no better than those
of Richard Wetherill. Neither man had any formal training, and both dug
primarily to make collections of artifacts. Yet Hewett saw his objectives as
different from those of the cowboy from Mancos. He sought artifacts for

the knowledge of prehistory, whereas men like Wetherill wanted only the monetary profit from the sale of artifacts. The effect of an excavation by either was the same; only the attribution of motivation differentiated scientists and amateurs.

Wetherill and Hewett epitomized the differences between nineteenth- and twentieth-century values in the West. In the eyes of the trained specialists creating the federal natural resource bureaucracy, Wetherill was merely a cowboy. He represented the open, individualist America of the frontier, whereas Hewett linked himself to the burgeoning federal system of regulation. Used to living in a harsh world determined by the desires of individuals and stubborn to a fault, Wetherill did not understand the federal bureaucracy, nor did he care to. He refused to listen to people who told him what he could and could not do, and when the twentieth century intruded on his life, he simply ignored it. Hewett's background taught him a similar set of premises, but his foresight and experience as an educator made him see the future more clearly than Wetherill. Rather than defy the government, Hewett learned to influence its decisions.

Hewett had to balance the nineteenth-century attitudes of his background and the twentieth-century world with which he cast his fortunes. Raised to believe that individual initiative was the way to success, he recognized that life in postfrontier America required cooperation between ambitious individuals and the commercial and political infrastructure. Hewett knew that to achieve his goal of protecting archaeological sites, he had to learn to work with the burgeoning federal bureaucracy and its members who addressed questions of natural resources.

In 1900, Hewett had no legal right to prevent Wetherill or anyone else from excavating anywhere on the public domain. No laws specifically governed archaeological sites on public land, although some government officials believed that such places were protected by general legislation applying to the public domain. Hewett devoted his immense personal energy to the effort to create a law that preserved valuable pieces of the prehistoric heritage of the North American continent. A power play developed, with Edgar L. Hewett at its center. A twentieth-century professional with scholarly aspirations challenged the "first-come, first-served" mentality of the nineteenth-century West.[27] There were new forces shaping American horizons. After more than two decades of a caveat emptor society, many middle-class Americans had had enough of the excesses of the business community. Beginning with the Sherman Antitrust Act in

1890, Congress began to respond with legislation to counter blatant avarice and exploitation. The closing of the frontier made Americans aware that there were limits to the continent, and efforts to conserve its natural resources gained credence. By 1900, the pieces of a full-scale social revolution, with faith in the science, technology, and progress embodied in the White City of the Columbian Exposition, were in place, waiting only for a charismatic leader for guidance.

But Progressivism, the label given to this set of beliefs, was also a backward-looking movement. It sprang from the middle class, disenfranchised by the aggressive capitalism of the late nineteenth century. Many Progressives sought to restore an earlier order, in which their social class had played a more significant role. Predicated on the assumption that everyone shared the same value system, Progressivism became a hegemonizing force in American society. There were "good" values and laws, and Progressives implemented them with little concern for other social groups. Legislators believed that they passed laws that would better American society, but they often felt that the laws did not apply to themselves and their peers. In a posture that mimicked traditional religion, new laws were corrective measures designed to lead the unknowing to the proper path. The iron hand of self-conscious morality guided Progressive America, and its followers sought to shape the United States in their image.[28]

The Progressive view was also socially skewed. The middle and upper-middle classes dominated the loose confederation of reformers, and their decisions often reflected only that perspective. Predominantly eastern and urban, Progressivism addressed largely urban issues. In the wide-open, sparsely populated West, it fizzled. But many Progressives believed that the entire country subscribed to their values, and they took the compliance of the nation for granted. Progressive legislation often lacked punitive measures, as if its authors believed that passing a law was tantamount to ensuring fealty to it. Progressivism was a product of a time during which the concept of progress had only a faint tarnish applied by the iconoclastic and curmudgeonly. The goals of the movement reflected the increasing influence of science on American society.[29]

Hewett's perspective included many of the assumptions and biases of Progressive America. Although his only real credential was a master's degree in pedagogy, he believed that no one but "professionals" like himself should be allowed to excavate archaeological sites on public land.

Like many others in the late 1890s, he saw rules and laws as a way to make unruly elements comply with his desires. In his mind, however, the rules he advocated did not apply to people like himself. He and his peers had better motives and so were exempt. In this cavalier fashion, Hewett reserved for himself the right to excavate where he chose, regardless of any restriction that might become law. He also realized that he needed solid allies in the federal bureaucracy.

The Department of the Interior was a natural ally for Hewett, for it was in the process of modernizing the West by applying Progressive-era sensibilities to regional issues. Interior administered the public domain and was inundated with homestead claims, disputes, and jurisdictional questions. Yet during the last decade of the nineteenth century, it began a number of campaigns to curtail indiscriminate cutting of timberland in the West. Other programs to protect exploited natural resources followed. With this precedent, Hewett and other advocates of preservation had only to convince the appropriate (GLO) officials that protecting archaeological ruins ought to be added to their already sizable realm of responsibility.[30]

Fortunately for Hewett, federal employees in a number of agencies and departments agreed with this new perspective. During the 1890s, southwestern ruins attracted the attention of the American public as an outgrowth of general interest in the conservation of natural resources. GLO special agents began to inspect many of the ruins in the Southwest. In response to the charges of pothunting leveled at Richard Wetherill, as well as to more ordinary forms of vandalism and defacement, the GLO increased the number of its inspections of archaeological sites during the second half of the decade. Federal officials became aware of the marvelous ruins that still belonged to the government.

In an America without a western frontier, the need to preserve vestiges of the tradition of westward expansion grew in importance. Without legal options that allowed the permanent reservation of valuable historic and natural features, GLO officials revived the policy of "temporary withdrawal," under which specific tracts were reserved until the government decided for what purpose the tract was best suited. Temporary withdrawal prevented homestead entries, mineral claims, and other ruses by which individuals might attempt to claim valuable archaeological, historic, or natural places as their own.

Temporary withdrawal was not a remedy for the problem of protecting archaeological ruins in the Southwest. It was a stopgap measure, necessary because of the lack of federal legislation. A temporary withdrawal was a paper decree. It prevented expropriation of the title to the land on which the ruins stood, ensuring that no one could legally claim a tract containing important features. This kind of proclamation deterred only people who obeyed the law and had little effect on what at the time was a more serious issue: the unauthorized excavation and depredation of archaeological areas. Access even to reserved land was not restricted, and anyone could still go to ruins and dig for relics. Only the unlucky might be caught during the infrequent visits of a GLO special agent.

For Hewett, the situation posed a major problem. Unlike government officials, Hewett regularly saw the declining condition of prehistoric ruins. On his frequent trips to the plateau, the evidence of the activities of people such as Buckskin Joe and his friends confronted Hewett. Ever prescient, he recognized and feared the result of the continuation of unchecked activity of this nature.

But stasis seemed likely to continue indefinitely. In the West, people such as Hewett, who advocated a system of care for ruins, were a distinct minority. Other concerns dominated the horizons of westerners—the most important being the drive to spread "civilization" to even the most remote parts of the region. Despite the growing number of scientists, aficionados, and leaders in the East who appreciated the significance of the story of humanity on the continent, archaeological ruins still had only marginal importance in the West.

A NATIONAL

PARK FOR

ARCHAEOLOGICAL

STUDY

4

✳ ✳ ✳ ✳ ✳ ✳ ✳ ✳ ✳ ✳ ✳ ✳ ✳ ✳ ✳ ✳ ✳

When Hewett, Cushing, Fewkes, and other anthropologists and archaeologists looked at the Pajarito Plateau, they did not see the grasses and timber that supported commercial and subsistence use. To them, the mounds indicating subsurface ruins, the scattered artifacts, and the innumerable cave dwellings represented stores of knowledge and understanding, a salve for the cultural woes of fin de siècle America and a crucible in which to establish their discipline. To Hewett in particular, the plateau was a magnificent laboratory that sheltered the kind of synthetic knowledge to which John Wesley Powell and his bureau aspired.

Hewett hoped to preserve the Pajarito Plateau from depredation. The dichotomy in his romantic point of view—his vision of the archaeologist as the noble leader, conveying and resolving mystery to an eager public, and his desire not to disturb the buried past—made preservation of the ruins his singular goal. If the ruins were protected, Hewett would not have to resolve his dilemma immediately. By 1900, he had become a vociferous opponent of pothunting, complaining to the GLO about Wetherill's activities in Chaco Canyon.[1] Wetherill's cavalier attitude threatened all in which Hewett believed.

Yet preservation left few options. Temporary withdrawals only deferred permanent decisions. Forest reserves, game preserves, and other similar designations did not address issues of archaeological preservation. As late as 1906, no law specifically forbade the expropriation of artifacts and other relics from federal land. Advocates of preservation were left to rely on the presumption that the federal government owned everything its lands contained.[2]

The only way to permanently reserve an area of the public domain was to establish a national park. Occasionally an archaeological area, such as Casa Grande in Arizona, might be the subject of a petition to Congress, but permanent preservation meant entry into the national park category. There were only a few national parks, and none preserved ruins. Most parks were physical parallels to the heritage of a conquering, westward-moving people, who pitted themselves against a rugged environment. That West was still nearby; only in the 1890s had the idea of the closed frontier gained credence. To many, that world still seemed real. Yet simultaneously the West of the pony express rider, the buffalo hunter, and the Indian was passing into the realm of myth, creating a sensibility of its own among the public.

National parks at the turn of the century had a number of features in common. All contained spectacular scenery—the mountaintops of Mount Rainier National Park, established in 1898, showed one type, the glorious Yosemite and Yellowstone parks another. Most were carved from land that seemed to have little commercial economic value at the time of their creation, and most were large areas. They represented the grand features of the continent in a fashion appropriately labeled scenic monumentalism.[3]

Even at the turn of the century, battles over the creation of national parks were often fierce. Local constituencies saw little advantage in the establishment of a park, and the reservation of western land for any purpose played to westerners' cultural paranoia. Outnumbered in Congress, seeking economic prosperity, and suspicious of restrictions, westerners resented federal rules and regulations. National parks could easily be construed as a threat to economic survival and individualism, and often were.

As such, national parks were a poorly suited vehicle through which to preserve prehistory. In general, the Department of the Interior, the federal agency in charge of the parks, discouraged the proclamation of national parks when park bills permitted commercial use of grazing and timber resources within park boundaries. These symbols of grandeur must be pristine, emblematic of the power of the subdued continent. They must seem untrammeled by civilization, revealing an image of the challenges that the people of the nineteenth century had faced.

This image of preservation was ill suited for protecting archaeological ruins in general and the Pajarito Plateau in particular. Unlike the high country of Mount Rainier, archaeological ruins showed that humans had found use for the area. Many ruins were in river basins, the very places that Anglo settlers sought when they came to the arid Southwest. In addition, the Pajarito Plateau had inherent commercial value. Less than a decade before, cattlemen and a timber company had developed its resources, and the influx of homesteaders suggested that the pattern would continue.

Even more important, preserving archaeology was categorically different from preserving scenery. There were more ruins in the Southwest than could possibly be counted. Not all of them could be preserved. Advocates would have to make choices among them. More complicated was the question of the land between desired ruins. National parks were expansive areas, offering grand vistas, natural features, and other spectacular phenomena. At the turn of the century, making a case for a similar mode of preservation of archaeological ruins was difficult. If advocates did not offer an area large enough to resemble the existing parks, they risked being told that their proposal did not include features of national-park caliber. If they suggested an expansive area, such as the Pajarito Plateau, they were certain to infringe on the economic goals of their neighbors.

But a national park for the Pajarito Plateau was the only choice available to Edgar L. Hewett in 1900. In 1899, he began to lobby for protection of the region. In response to Hewett's queries, John F. Lacey, the chairman of the House Public Lands Committee and an outspoken advocate of conservation, requested that the GLO initiate a bill to create a national park on the Pajarito Plateau. Late that year, the GLO commissioner, Binger Hermann, ordered J. D. Mankin, an agency clerk, to New Mexico to inspect the ruins.[4]

Like Bandelier and Hewett before him, Mankin was amazed to find himself in the midst of a lost civilization. The plateau was covered with evidence of human habitation. Atop many of the mesas were abandoned pueblos, and the south face of nearly every cliff contained innumerable cave dwellings. Prehistoric pottery and tools were scattered across the surface. Astonished by the sophistication of the construction, Mankin felt that he had stumbled on a place worthy of the interest of the nation.[5]

His reaction was not uncommon. In the few years since the Columbian Exposition of 1893, the general attitude toward Native Americans had softened. Indians no longer represented a threat to the ideal of progress and instead had become part of American mythology. The Columbian Exposition had shown Indians as relics of savagery contrasted with the achievements of industrial society. Despite the efforts of the Bureau of American Ethnology in 1900, the nomadic Plains Indian still dominated the public image of the Native American. Particularly after the advent of Buffalo Bill's Wild West Show, Sitting Bull and the Dakota Sioux came to represent the scope of pre-European culture in the West. Only a small minority of people recognized that pre-Columbian inhabitants of the continent had lived in permanent communities, and fewer still had seen the extraordinary evidence of those civilizations.

Another current in U.S. policy toward Native Americans found merit in the ruins of these "civilized" Indians. As their way of life changed, Native Americans were threatened by extinction. Federal policies forced them to assimilate, but their ability to survive in an industrial society remained in question.[6] Places like the Pajarito Plateau and Mesa Verde dispelled widespread notions about Native Americans in an era when the Indian was a valued relic of a wild past. The ruins of settled villages were important evidence to counter the feeling that no native culture had merit of its own and was worth preserving, as well as ammunition for those who favored assimilation of Native Americans into the mainstream. If Native Americans could farm and live in communities, this argument offered, they might find a place in the modern world.

Impressed by the ruins, Mankin advocated the establishment of 153,000 acres as the Pajarito National Park, but even this recommendation offered a less-than-perfect solution. Persuasive and determined to assert his convictions, Hewett significantly shaped the report. Mankin deferred to the insistent and more educated Hewett. Although the idea of an archaeological national park was unwieldy, Hewett had no alternative. He believed that its establishment at the Pajarito Plateau would prevent the wanton vandalism afflicting other archaeological sites in the Southwest.[7]

With good reason, Hewett pushed for the immediate establishment of a national park. As the bill was being prepared for introduction in Congress, the romantic scientist's dilemma confronted Hewett. "Irresponsible parties are making preparations to invade the territory in the early spring," Hewett informed Mankin, "with a view to opening the rooms of the Communal Dwellings and exploring the caves for relics."[8] Hewett's greatest fear—that people other than himself, people with motives far more base, would defile the prehistory of the Pajarito Plateau and that he would not be able to stop them—had become reality.

Hewett's conception of a national park stressed protection of the ruins in the region. National park status offered two major advantages: permanent legal authority and military administration. The embryonic tourism that had begun at places like Yellowstone and Mount Rainier did not enter into Hewett's thinking. His goal was simple: protection of the ruins from depredation at the hands of the callous, the avaricious, or the curious.[9]

This objective differed from those that underlay the establishment of the earlier national parks. The Pajarito Plateau had little in common with the existing parks, and its scenery did not compare. No precedent for a national park of primarily cultural or scientific value existed. The history of economic use of the land surrounding the ruins meant that vocal constituencies would oppose any proposed park.

Under any circumstances, establishing a national park at the turn of the century was not easy. Congress had to pass a bill creating each park, and in 1900, the chances of most proposals were remote. National parks were a recent idea. The first national park, Yellowstone, dated from 1872, and during the 1890s, Yosemite, General Grant (now included in King's Canyon), Sequoia, and Mount Rainier national parks followed. All included spectacular scenery and rarely impinged on commercial interests.

Despite Hewett's repeated pleas, there was little change in the situation. Congress did not act on the bill, and Hewett continued to urge GLO Commissioner Binger Hermann to promote the establishment of the park. The increasing number of people who came to the primary ruins in the region, Frijoles Canyon, Tschirege, Navawi'i, and Puye, worried Hewett. With his romantic sensibility, he tried to respect the past, but interlopers began to destroy his domain, forcing him to a decision regarding his own relationship to the ruins. Vandalism increased in the summer of 1900, Hewett contended, and the damage to valuable sites was incalculable.[10] The choice of whether to respect the past or to dig and convey its secrets to the American public—was being taken from him.

GLO officials also were ready to act. The idea that the government should assert itself in social issues was gaining momentum, and in the West in 1900, the disposition of the public domain was the primary concern. Late in the year, the GLO transmitted Mankin's report and a draft of its bill to Lacey. On December 21, 1900, the congressman proposed it on the floor of the House as H.R. 13071. Lacey's committee received the measure and on January 23, 1901, reported favorably on it.[11]

But the proposal ran up against the economic needs of westerners. Forest reserves were being established throughout the West; on George Washington's Birthday in 1897, President Grover Cleveland reserved more than twenty-one million acres of the West in new forest reserves. "King George had never attempted so high-handed an invasion of the rights of Americans," thundered a memorial to Congress from the Seattle Chamber of Commerce. Nevertheless, the reserve proclamations, and westerners' resentment of them, remained.[12]

New Mexicans felt particularly threatened by the prospect of the reservation of more land. In 1900, New Mexico was a territory. Its governor was appointed in Washington, D.C., it had no U.S. senators, and its one congressional delegate had little influence. From the point of view of the territory, decisions that shaped its future were made by people unaware of its concerns. The national park proposal confirmed this feeling. The park had little to offer people whose livelihood depended on grazing and timber.

That westerners were unhappy about reservation of land was not news, and Lacey attempted to assuage people in New Mexico Territory. The House Public Lands Committee limited the bill it received. One new provision allowed the secretary of the interior to permit grazing within the park. Most people in northern New Mexico made at least part of their living in ranching, and many were concerned that the park would restrict their livelihood. Without concessions to livestock owners, no park proposal stood a chance of local approval.

Such concessions were an uncomfortable reality for park advocates during the early years of the twentieth century. At the time, national parks had neither a management bureau nor a specific constituency, and the reason for their existence was not yet clearly defined. Local interests usually outweighed national ones, particularly in questions of the use of land in the West. While more and more leaders expressed a desire for federal regulation of western land and its resources, the machinery to implement such decisions was inadequate. Nor had the idea of conservation achieved consensus. Despite the opposition of the Department of the Interior, new park legislation frequently required concessions to meet the needs of local communities.

Another change seemed more innocuous, but in reality became the source of many years of strife. On the grounds that an English-speaking public would mispronounce the name "Pajarito," the committee proposed that the name of the new park be "Cliff Cities."[13] Ever concerned with details, Hewett objected. He found the new name inaccurate and strenuously opposed so titling any national park. "Cliff Cities" could describe numerous areas in the Southwest, he asserted, but "Pajarito" preserved a traditional name for the region. The choice of an appropriate name became an important side issue in the process of establishing a national park on the Pajarito Plateau.

The first step to park status was the creation of a temporary withdrawal. On July 31, 1900, Commissioner Hermann of the GLO ordered the temporary withdrawal of the tract that Mankin and Hewett previously suggested. Ranging from the Puye ruins in the north to the Cañada de Cochiti Grant in the south, Hermann's withdrawal included more than 238,000 acres, most of the area Hewett had surveyed, as well as nearly all the known pueblo ruins. The withdrawal secured the land while proponents worked for the passage of a park bill in Congress.

Despite Hermann's withdrawal, the first serious attempt to create a national park on the Pajarito Plateau went no further than the proposal stage. The confluence of economic interests and the dubious value ascribed to preservation of any sort halted the idea.

Grazing interests protested the size of the withdrawal. Preservation was the province of an elite few, and some wondered if archaeology was a valid reason for the withdrawal of large areas of uninhabited land. Congressmen rightly saw that the park proposal before them was different from the existing national parks. It seemed to defy the conception of national parks as scenic areas. The House of Representatives did not act on the bill, which expired along with the Fifty-sixth Congress.

While Hewett and his friends wrestled with Congress, homesteaders continued to move onto the plateau. By 1900, new homesteads joined the ones already standing at the base of the Jemez Mountains. David Romero and his family settled on the plateau before 1900, as did Pedro Gómez y Gonzáles, who lived on Three-Mile Mesa. In the same time frame,

William Moses, Donaciano Gomes, and Miguel Sánchez also began homesteads. Buckman's foreman, a Cherokee Indian named James Loomis, stayed and, in 1902, settled on the border of the Vigil Grant. His homestead was later known as the Anchor Ranch. The Pino family of La Cienega, south of Santa Fe, used Frijoles Canyon as a base for their sheep-herding activities. Some of the family members lived in caves, and at one point, they built a small cabin east of the Tyuonyi ruins.[14] Early in the twentieth century, more than twenty cabins dotted the area north of the Vigil Grant at the base of the Jemez range.

The lives of homesteaders differed little from those of the seasonal users who preceded them. Many of the Hispanos were part of the net-work of extended families who had traditionally used the plateau. They sought the best grazing and timber lands, farming some of their acreage. Many followed the traditional patterns, roaming in search of pasture and using land that they did not own, either on the Vigil Grant or elsewhere. They too discovered archaeological ruins, although most were more inter-ested in the grazing capabilities of the land than in the artifacts it held. Some used prehistoric caves as nighttime corrals for their sheep. Others used surface ruins for shelter.

Anglo homesteaders faced a different set of problems. Unlike their His-pano neighbors, they were not part of an intricate social structure, and alone, they lacked a strong sense of community. The Pajarito Plateau was home, but for Anglos, "home" did not mean generations of tradition, as it did for Hispanos and Indians. This difference, that home had connota-tions of economic success as well as of place, contributed to an important distinction between Anglo and Hispano activities in the region. In 1900, Anglo families on the plateau already planted crops for market. Hispano families still practiced a regimen that more resembled subsistence.

The influence of Anglo culture was pervasive. Goods in the stores in Es-pañola and the pay that Hispanos and Indians received from a growing range of employers gradually changed the nature of farming and ranch-ing on the plateau. More and more people augmented their income by working for Anglo commercial interests. Homesteaders also began to see their land differently, producing crops for sale as well as for family use. This brought them closer to the market system and dependence on Anglo institutions.

The presence of the homesteaders and their increased desire to use land for market purposes pointed out the most critical problem that

Hewett and the preservationists faced. The land they wanted for their archaeological national park included vast tracts of timber and grazing land to which the homesteaders needed access. The ruins merited preservation, but in New Mexico Territory in 1900, protection could not come at the expense of the commercial use of natural resources. Although the homesteaders themselves had little influence, large landowners, of whom Frank Bond of Española had become one, felt threatened by the idea of preservation. The homesteaders were vocal. A number of letters appeared in the *Santa Fe New Mexican,* eliciting the sympathy of other influential people in the territory.[15] As long as efforts to protect prehistory focused on vast tracts of land containing natural resources with commercial potential, opposition from all levels of New Mexican society remained a strong possibility.

The swirl of interests complicated Hewett's position. As long as he lacked scientific credentials, his position in the archaeological discipline was tenuous. The Pajarito Plateau was his professional ace in the hole. With its ruins, he could forge a considerable reputation. Although Hewett took a sympathetic view of Hispanos and Indians, he shared the patronizing attitudes of his time. He did not want to deny homesteaders the right to pasture animals and cut timber, but from his point of view, preserving ruins was a great moral good. The ruins were top priority to an aspiring scientist and cultural leader who saw archaeology as the most noble of human callings and the apogee of human experience. Hewett knew that if the status quo persisted, his future as an archaeologist might be destroyed before he had the chance to uncover it. The situation required a new remedy.

Three basic areas containing ruins interested Hewett, and in 1900–1901, the federal government owned two of them. In 1875, after the dismissal of a land grant claim in district court, Frijoles Canyon and the entire area between the southern boundary of the Vigil Grant and the Cañada de Cochiti Grant to the south had been returned to the public domain. The second area, the ruins at Puye, were also on public land, and the temporary withdrawal of 1900 included both areas. When compared with the third tract, the Ramón Vigil Grant, the other two were relatively safe.[16]

But Hewett believed that the Vigil Grant was by far the most important to the park proposal. It had much more than the economic value that Bishop and Buckman tried to develop. The largest prehistoric pueblo on the plateau, Tscherige, overlooked Pajarito Canyon, the headquarters of the old cattle operation. Navawi'i, the pueblo of the game traps, lay northeast of there.

Hewett coveted the grant for his archaeological national park. In his interpretation of the prehistoric world, the grant included two of the best examples of the highest stage of pueblo culture.

The presence of the commercial interests also drove home the need for swift action. Buckman entertained visitors at his lumber camps and sawmills, and while his men built the road and cut trees, his guests lived a life of simple but exquisite pleasure as the guests of the backwoods gentleman. The visitors had free reign in a world choked with the ruins of a prehistoric civilization. The curious, intrigued by the freedom with which they could explore, found a world of astonishing beauty, mystery, and meaning. Harry Field, a guest of Buckman's in 1900, discovered "rich flowers of many hues all around, trees of bright green foliage on every side, birds of tropical plumage flitting from bough to bough; and on either side the massive stone walls of the canon rising up to the rugged edge of the mesa far above." The canyons swallowed Field, and the sights and sounds left him in awe.[17]

The prehistoric features of the region impressed Field as much as its natural attributes. The hollowed-out cave dwellings made an impression on people whose usual homes were constructed of wood, brick, or stone, and the number of dwellings astounded visitors. The caves were of a "beehive shape inside," Field wrote many years later, "and you can see the black openings all along the side of the canon, and also one above another . . . cunning steps leading from one cave to another are cut out of solid rock." Life in the canyons showed evidence of a sophistication that far exceeded the level then expected of the aboriginal inhabitants of the continent.

Putting distance between oneself and modern society had become desirable in a culture that seemed to have lost track of its past, and visitors to the Pajarito Plateau had an opportunity unparalleled in the United States. "The scene was delightful," Field continued. "As I thought of the bricks and mortar which meet one's gaze in a civilized community, I absolutely envied this primitive race of men; the glories and beauty of their surroundings." The pristine isolation of the area was compelling even in 1900. A visitor felt like the only person in the world.

Imaginative visitors like Harry Field had great respect for the ruins and sometimes wistfully envisioned this long lost world. "As I stood there that fine sunny day, among the homes of a dead nation; I fancied myself back in the past," Field mused. "The dry creek bed was full of clear water; I saw the cave dwellers back in life again, sitting at the entrance to their caves; I saw the little ones playing amongst the stones of the creek and leaning over the bank looking into the clear water below." In the romantic tradition, Field was content to imagine the past and did not disturb it. Although he saw with a romantic's glow, he sought to appreciate the simplicity of the prehistoric world on its own terms.

Had they met, Hewett would have sensed in Harry Field a kindred spirit. Others were not so respectful, and Buckman's guests became a constant worry for Hewett. His fears were driven home during the summer of 1901, when the Reverend G. S. Madden of the booming mining town of Bland, New Mexico, showed his friend George Townsend Cole around the plateau. The youngest son of California Senator Cornelius Cole, G. T. Cole was a lecturer who had sketched, photographed, and made maps of ruins and pueblos throughout the four-corners region. He also painted watercolors, a skill for which he later received regional acclaim. Guests of Buckman's, the two men had free reign on the Vigil Grant, and as Hewett seethed, they collected a number of surface artifacts. They took away what they could carry and stored the rest under the railroad station in Buckman.

The trip enraged Hewett, and when he found out about the artifacts in Buckman, he used his influence to stop Cole and Madden. Hewett enlisted Mankin, the GLO clerk, who contacted a GLO special agent, S. S. Mathers. Mathers headed to the plateau to assess the damage and found evidence of excavation, which he reported to his superiors.[18]

The GLO agents did what Hewett wanted, but the situation backfired. Hewett was adamant about preventing unauthorized work, and at his insistence, Mathers and Mankin treated the incident as if it were a violation of federal law. Mathers seized the artifacts that Cole and Madden left at Buckman Crossing and filed a complaint against the two men. The U.S. attorney in Albuquerque, William B. Childers, informed Mathers that Cole and Madden had not broken the law. Soon after, the Department of the Interior censured Mathers for overstepping the bounds of his power and ordered him to return the artifacts to Cole and Madden.[19] The GLO men were confused. They had acceded to the demands of an important cultural leader of New Mexico and, as a result, now faced the ire of their superiors.

When confronted with the charges, Cole and Madden quickly defended their position. Madden telephoned Mathers and told him that
Cole had a permit from the secretary of the interior that allowed him to
visit, sketch, and photograph ruins throughout the Southwest. Cole confirmed this in a letter to the commissioner of the GLO and further insisted
that he and Madden had not excavated public property. The small
amount of excavating that Cole acknowledged was within boundaries
that Harry Buckman had showed them. Buckman told the two men that
they were working on the Ramón Vigil Grant.[20]

During his conversation with Mathers, Madden leveled serious coun-
tercharges at Hewett, and Mathers developed a new perspective on the
situation. Madden claimed that Hewett's activities were the most detrimental impact on the ruins. It was not the last time that Hewett would be
charged with having a double standard that validated his actions but that
prohibited those of others. The events troubled Mathers, who decided,
"The pot [was] calling the kettle black . . . I think they are both guilty of
the same thing." Hewett's dictatorial methods angered Madden, and after being censured by his superiors, Mathers had no idea whom to believe. The situation became a standoff. Madden and Cole kept the artifacts
they had taken. Hewett remained worried.[21]

Again Hewett faced the dilemma of the romantic anthropologist, the
boon-bringer and purveyor of secret knowledge. He had not yet begun to
"disturb the soil," in his retrospective phrase; he held the secrets of prehistory close. Two men happened along, collecting artifacts and theoriz-
ing about prehistory without the base of knowledge that Hewett believed
he had. Hewett could not stop them, either from digging in ruins or
spreading what he labeled inaccurate information. By holding the secrets
he knew too close, Hewett risked giving up his domain to people he
termed charlatans. He reacted to people such as Cole and Madden as if
they were defilers of a sacred place. Hewett fancied that his work was different—that he empathized with Indian culture—and the cooperation he
received from nearby Pueblo Indians confirmed his sense. He wanted to
protect the plateau, but he had to reveal its secrets if the world was to appreciate it. Nor did he have an effective way to stop people with purposes
similar to his own.

The dispute with Cole and Madden was an important battle for Hewett.
He learned that he did not yet have the influence he desired. Cole and
Madden had as many friends as he and, worse, as much right to the ruins

of the Pajarito Plateau. The episode also affected Hewett's power base: his friends at the bottom of the GLO hierarchy had tried to protect his interests and got only trouble for their efforts. Hewett's reputation was challenged, and he discovered intolerable limits on himself. It was one thing to label an ordinary cowboy like Richard Wetherill a pothunter; it was another to accuse a minister and his friend, the son of an influential western senator, of the same thing.

Incidents like the one with Cole and Madden forced Hewett to consider excavation. He could see that the two men shared an impulse that had become common. By 1901, stories of random excavating abounded in western newspapers, confirming the worst of Hewett's fears.[22] If he did not begin to dig, to sully the spirit of the past with pick and shovel, the influx of people to the region would narrow his choices and destroy whatever archaeological treasures lay beneath the ground. In response to the threat of depredation, Hewett designated responsible archaeology—his work —as the crucial mission. He planned to salvage the history stored in the mounds of the Pajarito Plateau, history that he believed less-principled depredators would sell on the commercial market. To Hewett, the process of excavating southwestern prehistory became a race between competitors with different motives.

The incident with Cole and Madden also drove home the necessity for immediate legislation. The two men were only one example of a trend in the Southwest. From Grand Gulch to the Gila River, southwestern ruins were at the mercy of whoever happened along. The danger to structures increased in direct proportion to proximity to railroads and trails, and most of the ruins were close to a water source or travel artery. If no law restricted the behavior of people like Cole and Madden, Hewett firmly believed that one should.

The incident served as a catalyst for Hewett to support the creation of legislation for the general protection of American antiquities, and it led him to broaden his contacts with the federal government. Hewett learned that the decisions affecting archaeological ruins in New Mexico came from Washington, D.C. He needed a closer relationship with the center of power. In 1900, Hewett had traveled to Washington and introduced himself to the scientific community. He met the aging John Wesley Powell and his assistant, William Henry Holmes. But Powell was old and ill by 1900, and the Bureau of American Ethnology had declined with him throughout the 1890s. Powell's immense presence protected the bureau as long as he was well. When he took ill, a battle for succession began, leaving government ethnology in disarray. Astute in political matters, Hewett recognized that the impending turmoil precluded action on his concern. He also intuited that Holmes would play an important role in any change at the bureau, and a relationship developed between the two men.[23]

Yet Hewett had encountered only the scientific side of the administration of ruins. His interests differed from those of the bureau, where the dominant philosophy stressed material collections and their presentation. Hewett wanted to preserve ruins, and the people who made those decisions were located elsewhere, in the General Land Office of the Department of the Interior.

In 1902, Hewett boarded a train at Lamy, New Mexico, and returned to the capital in search of support for his plan. There he sought out the people who could help him solve the issues he faced. The question of Powell's successor was the lead issue at the bureau. Powell himself favored W J McGee, but Samuel P. Langley, the reclusive and lonely secretary of the Smithsonian, wanted William H. Holmes. A battle that would culminate in an investigation the following year had already begun. Issues of science were not preeminent at the bureau in 1902. Hewett instead went to the old U.S. Patent Office building, a two-block-long monstrosity between F and G streets and Seventh and Ninth streets northwest that housed the Department of the Interior. Friendly with GLO field officers in the West, he now cultivated their superiors. After meeting the commissioner and his assistants, he reintroduced himself to the people at the heart of Washington science as well as to the members of the House Public Lands Committee. Hewett's move to become an influential player began in earnest.[24]

Yet Hewett remained powerless to stop the growing disarray among the advocates of preservation. On January 9, 1902, Lacey had reintroduced to the Fifty-seventh Congress the same proposal he had made in 1900. The bill had not changed, and opposition in New Mexico Territory had not decreased. The daily newspaper in Santa Fe, the *New Mexican*, expressed its fear that the new bill, H.R. 8323, was just another way for the federal government to seize control of large tracts of land in New Mexico. The paper supported the principle of a national park filled with archaeological ruins, but its editor, Max Frost, a longtime participant in the affairs of the seemingly defunct but still powerful cabal labeled the Santa Fe Ring, feared that further withdrawals would damage local commerce.[25]

Frost's editorial asked the territorial delegate, Bernard S. Rodey, to oppose the bill. The residents of New Mexico did not see giving up their land to serve an ostensibly national purpose as a beneficial move.

The response of the *New Mexican* showed the issues that caused resistance to the establishment of national parks. Local interests did not perceive any economic advantage in the new park, and someone like Frost, an advocate of accessible land, accurately reflected the view of most residents of the territory. National parks offered little except symbolic value. Tourism in the American West had little impact on the economy of the region. There were few automobiles, the railroad industry was just beginning to promote travel in the Southwest, and the national park idea had yet to develop. Few thought of the new parks as profitable endeavors, and area merchants and businessmen did not see any direct benefit from the proposal. In 1902, New Mexicans perceived land and its produce as their only marketable commodity. The permanent withdrawal of two hundred thousand acres would severely restrict the development of ranching and farming. It was too large a gamble for those who already had an investment in stock and equipment, as well as for those who serviced the livestock industry. "Not an acre more than necessary should be included in the area reserved," thundered an editorial in the *New Mexican*. The area was "being plastered up with forest and other reservations" that included "at least three times the area necessary to serve" their intended purpose. From this perspective, the park proposal was just another way for the federal government to hamper the right of an individual to make a living.[26]

New Mexicans were responding to Theodore Roosevelt and his conservation-oriented land policies. Roosevelt was the charismatic leader that Progressive reformers had sought. His administration aggressively developed programs that western constituencies consistently opposed. Westerners resented the power of the federal government over what they felt was their land, and Washington had a long history of what people in the West considered meddling. The president had unchecked power to permanently reserve any tract of forest in the public domain for conservation purposes, and the GLO could use the temporary withdrawal. By 1900, more than twenty million acres of western timberland had been reserved by executive fiat, and from a regional perspective, that was enough. Land withdrawals inevitably met strong resistance in the region, and many believed that Washington bureaucrats too often made the decisions that determined westerners' economic future.[27] To some, Lacey's Pajarito Plateau proposition seemed another example of government officials whimsically taking away someone else's ability to earn a living. The battle over the park embodied the same kind of conflict between public good and individual rights as did the story of Richard Wetherill.

Western pressure reminded advocates that they needed to pursue a conciliatory path. Already the author of a number of conservation bills, Lacey was in the process of designing another one. The new measure, authored by Hewett and eventually titled "An Act for the Preservation of American Antiquities," provided for the reservation of limited archaeological and scenic areas at the discretion of the president. Lacey recognized the importance of support in the West not only for the Pajarito Plateau national park proposal but also for his attempt to preserve antiquities. He knew that westerners had to be satisfied before any of his measures could pass Congress.

These factors, and Hewett's persistent coaxing, persuaded Lacey to revise the park bill. A pragmatic accommodation, the new measure, H.R. 7269, stood a better chance of passage than its predecessors. To appease local stockmen, Lacey reduced the size of the proposed park from the original 153,620 acres to fifty-five sections, about 35,000 acres. Although the new bill did not allow grazing or other forms of commercial use within the park, the substantial reduction of the area of the park satisfied stockmen. When Lacey reintroduced the bill in Congress in 1903, it seemed that the park might soon become reality.

But the pacification of commercial interests did not take preservation advocates into account. After 1900, anthropologists and archaeologists recognized the significance of preventing vandalism in southwestern ruins, and they wanted a voice in the resolution of conflicts like those concerning the Pajarito Plateau. The two disciplines consolidated their status during the 1890s and developed and applied new power after 1900. Spurred by Teddy Roosevelt's boisterous swaggering and the xenophobic nationalism that followed the Spanish-American War, scientists realized that American antiquities had considerable cultural value. Reverend Henry Mason Baum, the founder of the Records of the Past Society and the editor of its journal, headed an extensive campaign to establish a favorable intellectual climate for legislation promoting archaeological preservation.[28]

From the perspective of the scientists, protecting archaeological remains was of paramount importance. The archaeologists valued research in protected prehistoric sites above any economic consideration. With an elitist view typical of their era, scientists regarded the concerns of local residents as immaterial in comparison with their own lofty cause. The scientists by no means represented the only view favoring the establishment of an archaeological national park, but they often did not agree with others advocating different means to the same end.

Lacey's compromise bill received a lukewarm reception. The reduction of acreage hurt support in the scientific community. The park would be too small for the kind of research that Hewett planned, and earlier supporters of the idea became less enthusiastic. Baum offered his opinion on the park proposal; during the summer of 1902 he had visited the Pajarito region. Although Baum lacked formal training, he saw himself as the preeminent living Americanist. The Chaco Canyon region impressed Baum, and he thought it warranted park status. But on his return to Washington, Baum belittled the qualifications of the plateau in the *Records of the Past* journal.[29] The readers of the journal included many influential archaeologists, and Baum's remarks were a damning blow that soon haunted the park effort.

Baum's stance against the Pajarito park was the start of an extended period during which any semblance of unity among advocates disappeared. This fragmentation created rifts not only among supporters of the park proposal but in the entire preservation alliance. Baum's stance angered Hewett, and he came to despise Baum. The antipathy continued as the two men became heads of rival factions. Hewett's influence among archaeologists and anthropologists gradually increased, whereas Baum's declined after 1904. Although Hewett became the pivotal figure in both the Pajarito Plateau national park and the Antiquities Act controversies, the conflict delayed the passage of legislation to preserve American antiquities for nearly five years.[30]

The attempt to establish a national park on the plateau encountered other difficulties. As Lacey's bill passed through the various levels of the Department of the Interior, new opposition arose in the Southwest. In January 1903, Clinton J. Crandall, the superintendent of the Santa Fe Indian School and the agent for area pueblos, sought to extend the boundaries of the Santa Clara Reservation, near Española. He discovered that his proposed extension was already reserved under the temporary withdrawal of July 1900. Dismayed, Crandall told his superiors that the ruins would be safer in Indian hands than as a national park. Baum's contentions offered ample evidence that the park idea was flawed. The Indian claim antedated the park proposal, he insisted, and it should take precedence.[31]

Crandall's opposition created new tensions. What had been an issue between disparate groups outside the federal government now included two different bureaus in the Department of the Interior. The Bureau of Indian Affairs and the GLO were relative equals. The two had different missions and constituencies, and when they sought jurisdiction over the same tract, the situation typically prompted an inspection of the area. Departmental officials selected GLO Special Agent S. J. Holsinger.

Holsinger was the field representative of the Department of the Interior for archaeological inspections in the Southwest. Before the Pajarito proposal, he visited Chaco Canyon to report on Richard Wetherill's unauthorized excavations. In late 1902, he broke up a ring of pothunters in Arizona and inspected the Montezuma Castle and other archaeological locations as well as proposed national park areas like the Petrified Forest. No one else in the federal government knew the Southwest better, and when the Department of the Interior needed an important inspection, it nearly always called on Holsinger.[32]

Open land only twenty years before, by 1903 the Pajarito Plateau had become a mosaic of conflicting interests. The situation embodied a new concept, foreign to Americans not two decades before. The small amount of land in the region and the myriad ways to use it created a world of limits. The mere forty square miles of the plateau could not fulfill the desires of all sides. Advocates of archaeological preservation lined up in favor of an expansive national park. Local stockmen needed the same land for their stock and expressed the traditional western fear of centralized authority. Native Americans objected to Anglos encroaching on their religious shrines. Timber interests wanted to influence the disposition of forested sections. Stockmen, area homesteaders, the Santa Fe community, and area Hispanos and Pueblo Indians would all have to be satisfied before the issues on the plateau could be resolved.

Compromise, another concept foreign to the world of individualism, was an integral part of any solution. As the ones trying to alter patterns of use in the region, park advocates sensed that to achieve their ends, they would have to make concessions. Unlike other park proposals, the Pajarito park had obvious economic potential. Stockmen ran territorial New

Mexico, and park advocates recognized that they had to allow grazing in the proposed park to secure the support of this important constituency. Reluctantly, they agreed that a park with grazing was better than no park at all.

Ironically, this concession revealed the difference between Hewett's conception of a national park and the standards being set up in other situations. Because his park actually was a ruse to preserve the ruins for archaeological study, Hewett did not learn the expectations of the cadre of national park supporters. Instead he simply enlisted their support, only to find that their objectives and those of the scientific community diverged.

Hewett did not object to grazing within the park. To him, this was inconsequential, irrelevant to the study of prehistory. His park was not reserved for its pristine scenery but for its subsurface treasures. Other park advocates felt differently. Holsinger's mission seemed the best way to sort out the issues. Hewett supported it in the hope that despite entrenched opposition, a national park that included all the important ruins could still be achieved on the plateau.

Holsinger arbitrated many similar cases, but few had the complexities of the Pajarito park situation. The confluence of interests there created a situation in which the gains by any group necessarily dictated losses on the part of every other. Each group had its idea of the value of the plateau, but all the plans applied to the same space. There was little room for compromise. If any interest group gave ground, it could not achieve its ends. Similarly, if one of the groups succeeded, all the others were thwarted. In 1904, the modern concept of a world of limits had become reality on the Pajarito Plateau.

Holsinger's visit was the social event of the season on the Pajarito Plateau. Each group presented its position to Holsinger; Crandall, Hewett, and others all pushed for his support. Sorting out the situation required patience and wisdom. A conscientious public servant, Holsinger tried to fairly evaluate all the contentions. His trip revealed that preservation advocates had been shortsighted. The park would affect life in many ways that the legislation did not address. Yet Holsinger concurred most closely with park advocates as he assessed the positions of people previously ignored.

Holsinger was asked to assess a number of questions with broad-based impact, all of which had to be resolved for the park to succeed. Some he addressed with his characteristic insight. Others exposed his own pre-conceptions. The expansion of Santa Clara Pueblo to include Puye was a critical issue. Holsinger took a patronizing view of the Santa Clara Indians, disagreeing with Crandall's assertion of their need for land. But encroachment by Hispanos had long been a primary complaint of the Indians. In 1904, Pueblo Indian land received little protection from the federal government, a result of a U.S. Supreme Court decision in *United States* v. *Joseph* in 1876 that had in essence placed the pueblos outside of federal Indian law. Some pueblos, such as Pojoaque and adjacent Jacona, had been overwhelmed by their neighbors and had all but disappeared. By 1913, the federal government estimated that twelve thousand non-Indians lived within the boundaries of the various Pueblo Indian grants. Although Holsinger did not believe that the pueblo needed more pasture land, he did support adding some land near the Rio Grande to alleviate the pressure from encroachment. His solution was far too simple for an issue that had become the focus of a legal battle and congressional action.[33]

The use of the timber of the plateau was another issue that advocates barely addressed. Local use predominated, with homesteaders and residents of the valleys cutting timber for their needs. Some commercial companies had begun to consider the heavily forested higher-elevation land in the Jemez Mountains and south and west of Frijoles Canyon. The timber constituency would not oppose the current park bill, since Lacey's revised proposal did not include the disputed areas.

Conscious of the growing threat to ruins and influenced by his experience with Richard Wetherill, Holsinger concluded that the best solution was to establish on the Pajarito Plateau a national park that included all the major ruins in the area except those in the forested areas and to allow stockmen to graze animals within the park's boundaries. He incorrectly claimed that provisions for the development of the park already existed.[34] With vandalism in the ruins remaining endemic, Holsinger's plan received strong local support, headed by Hewett. Reserved status was necessary.

There appeared to be no further objection to the establishment of the national park. The House Public Lands subcommittee considered Holsinger's report and revised the bill to allow the secretary of the interior to permit grazing within park boundaries. The committee also decreased the size of the new park once again, creating a forty-section tract that included the Otowi, Tsankawi, and Puye ruins, all north of the Ramón

Vigil Grant. The El Rito de los Frijoles ruins that had so entranced Adolph Bandelier were outside the proposed boundaries. Separated from the proposed park by the Vigil Grant, Frijoles Canyon was surrounded by impressive stands of timber with commercial value.

Given the lack of government influence over private landholders and the limited significance of national parks in 1904, there was no way to include Frijoles Canyon as a contiguous section. This did not disturb park advocates. The temporary withdrawal of 1900 contained the canyon, and few provisions for the administration of national parks existed in 1904. It would be as safe outside the park as within its boundaries.

The compromise bill satisfied government interests. The Bureau of Forestry in the Department of Agriculture approved the new plan, as did the acting commissioner of Indian affairs, A. C. Tonner, and the new GLO commissioner, W. A. Richards. Park proponents in the government believed that they had legislated all possible opposition out of the bill, and passage appeared imminent.

But political considerations impeded progress toward the establishment of the park. Despite the general concurrence among federal agencies, many New Mexicans were still uncomfortable with the ramifications of a national park. From their perspective, federal agencies governed too much of New Mexico. The power-hungry cabal that ran the territory fed on this sentiment, and a national park within the state remained a controversial measure. When the newest version of the park bill was introduced in a House of Representatives Public Lands Committee hearing on January 11, 1905, it was paired with a bill to establish the Mesa Verde (Verde) National Park. Both bills were closely tied to the movement to preserve American antiquities, which the Lodge-Rodenberg Bill personified in 1904 and 1905.

The Lodge-Rodenberg Bill, backed by the Reverend Henry Mason Baum of the Records of the Past Society, represented federal attempts to preserve southwestern antiquities. At the end of the prior congressional session in 1904, Assistant Secretary Richard Rathbun of the Smithsonian Institution had gone to the floor of Congress and blocked its passage. The bill angered westerners, for it gave the secretary of the interior unlimited discretion over unreserved public lands. It also accentuated the Hewett-Baum rivalry. The heavy-handed Baum alienated GLO officials, who turned to Hewett to create an antiquities bill that westerners could accept. With Lodge-Rodenberg on the floor of Congress, western resolve to oppose national park bills strengthened, and it seemed that politics would prevent the preservation of American antiquities.[35]

For many westerners, creating any new national park was synonymous with extending the discretionary power of the president. None of the proposals for the protection of American antiquities curbed executive power. Westerners feared the consequences of unchecked initiative and often opposed even the most meritorious legislation, whether directed toward establishing a park or not. The Pajarito Plateau proposal was further hampered because some in Congress believed that approving an archaeological national park was tantamount to tacit approval of a measure like the Lodge-Rodenberg bill. With guaranteed opposition to any measure that restricted the use of western land, passage of legislation that allowed preservation became even more difficult.[36]

The battle lines were clearly drawn, and the Pajarito Plateau national park proposal became a pawn in the process of compromise. Attempts to create the park pitted eastern scientists against local and regional interests determined to devour their piece of the American natural resource pie. In the end, the Pajarito Plateau national park proposal became a conflict in the larger battle between the individualist philosophy of nineteenth-century America, embodied in men like Richard Wetherill, and the ordered, bureaucratic, twentieth-century world that would soon replace it.

The most prominent representatives of the new century were the professionals in the newly sanctioned scientific disciplines of anthropology and archaeology. By 1905, the scientific community had made a serious commitment to the concept of preserving American antiquities. Bandelier's sojourns had opened the way, and Victor and Cosmos Mindeleff, Jesse Walter Fewkes, Walter Hough, William Henry Holmes, Hewett, and numerous others began explorations that sought to record knowledge as well as collect artifacts. The ideals of the science of man, as anthropology was frequently called, had been reconstituted when Holmes succeeded Powell at the Bureau of American Ethnology. The new leadership gave more active support to preservation, for the future of American anthropology was linked to its ability to protect the prehistoric remains of aboriginal culture.

As bills to preserve archaeological ruins surfaced in Congress, the scientific community made sure that legislators heard its point of view. At the Pajarito and Mesa Verde committee hearing, such luminaries as Francis W. Kelsey, the eminent classicist from the University of Michigan and secretary of the Archeological Institute of America, lined up to show support for both the bills. Henry Mason Baum, whose view of the region had changed after another visit to the area in 1904, also addressed the committee. The plateau was an integral piece of the southwestern crucible for homegrown sciences, and the support of the eastern professional community was unequivocal.

Edgar Hewett was less comfortable with the proposal, as was New Mexico Territorial Delegate Bernard S. Rodey. But even though Hewett expressed some reservations, he generally favored the plan. Rodey felt otherwise. A dynamic Albuquerque lawyer with a driving personality and ties to railroad interests, Rodey resisted the intrusion of the federal government into state land matters. Rodey enjoyed the distinction of being closely allied with Thomas Catron, one of the primary land-grabbers and later a U.S. senator from New Mexico, while managing a solid working relationship with Catron's enemy Miguel A. Otero, who was governor of the territory from 1897 to 1906. This meant Rodey spoke for both factions in the New Mexico power structure.[37]

With such diverse support, Rodey was determined to make a bold stand against federal intervention in the affairs of the territory. He extended his opposition to unrestricted executive reservation of the public domain to the park proposal. When Hewett remarked that too much forest land in New Mexico was already withdrawn, Rodey concurred loudly. If all the ruins were lined up, Rodey said, an area ranging from Española to the Colorado border might be reserved. He had no doubt that such a measure adversely affected the interests of his friends.

Rodey's opposition had little to do with the park itself. He was more concerned with a principle—restricting executive power. While Teddy Roosevelt stalked the White House, such efforts were futile, and Rodey's regional perspective made him the butt of jokes. To the laughter of the committee, Congressman Eben W. Martin of South Dakota asked Rodey, "How would the size of the State of New York suit you as a limitation [on possible reservations for the preservation of antiquities]?" Rodey testily replied, "Well, we have been reserving New Mexico for about sixty-eight years." He added that the secretary of the interior, Ethan Allen Hitchcock "might get in reservations of that size. [He] is pretty radical [and] is liable to do almost anything."[38]

Sounding the concerns of his constituency, Rodey damaged the case for the Pajarito park. His alliance with the dominant forces in the territory led him to take an extreme position, and he offered typical western resistance to federal plans. Voters in New Mexico Territory did not favor granting the federal bureaucracy additional power. Rodey was New Mexico's one elected representative in Washington, D.C., and his opposition muted support.

Simultaneously passing other bills to preserve antiquities also proved difficult for preservation advocates. Lacey's Public Lands Committee reported favorably on the Pajarito proposal, and it went to the floor of the House of Representatives. The bill remained there throughout 1905, along with a number of measures for the preservation of American antiquities and the bill to establish Mesa Verde National Park in Colorado. Given a variety of options, the politicians, it seemed, could not choose.

But the specter of Richard Wetherill continued to shape interest in American antiquities. The self-trained archaeologist from Mancos, Colorado, was anathema to the professionalizing discipline. Accredited scientists discounted Wetherill's discovery of the prepueblo inhabitants of the Southwest, later labeled the Basketmakers, and Baum regularly defamed him in print. Edgar L. Hewett also complained to the Department of the Interior about Wetherill's digging. Sites that Wetherill worked, such as Mesa Verde and Chaco Canyon, became priorities in the federal scheme of preservation. The consensus among government officials and scientists was that Wetherill had to be stopped. The best way to restrict him was to reserve the locations that he dug.[39] If he excavated after the federal government extended protection to an area, he could be prosecuted.

As it became apparent that only one of the two archaeological park bills was going to pass Congress, Lacey made a choice dictated by the near-hysteria over Wetherill's excavations. The establishment of an archaeological park had to convey a message to potential depredators of a cultural heritage. Since Wetherill excavated at Mesa Verde, the reservation there was a more potent statement, and Lacey threw his support behind the Mesa Verde proposal to show would-be pothunters that their behavior would not be tolerated. Facing political reality, he left the Pajarito Plateau proposal behind.

Conditions on the Pajarito Plateau also changed, determining the fate of the first serious effort to establish a national park on the plateau. When the commissioners of the GLO and the Bureau of Indian Affairs met to discuss Holsinger's report, they agreed on additions to the holdings of the Santa Clara Pueblo. In July 1905, Theodore Roosevelt added forty-seven square miles, including the Puye ruins, to the reservation, a great deal more than the commissioners had recommended. Early in 1905, the United States Forest Service was established and located in the Department of Agriculture. The existing forest reserves were transferred to its realm, resulting in the bifurcated administration of the lands sought for the national park. Later that year, the establishment of the Jemez Forest Reserve also hurt the chance for a national park. Frijoles Canyon and the rest of the area south of the Vigil Grant was included in the new reservation.[40]

In Hewett's view, these changes greatly diminished the potential of the Pajarito park. The area's ruins had been parceled out piecemeal, and the new proposal contained little of archaeological value. The park proposed in the bill before Congress contained none of the three most important groups of ruins: Puye, Frijoles Canyon, and the Ramón Vigil Grant. After the enlargement of Santa Clara Pueblo, only the ruins of Otowi and Tsankawi were still included. The Department of the Interior could not depend on acquiring the privately owned Ramón Vigil Grant, which included the ruins of Tschirege and Navawi'i. Under such circumstances, the effort to establish such a limited area hardly seemed worthwhile, and Hewett concurred with Lacey's decision. He openly moaned that the proposition was dead.[41] Although William H. Andrews, Rodey's replacement as the New Mexico delegate, introduced another measure to establish a Pajarito national park on March 28, 1906, the bill made little headway.

But the issue of a law to protect American archaeological ruins made greater progress. Late in 1905, Hewett drafted his "Act for the Preservation of American Antiquities." It allowed the president to proclaim as a national monument any section of unreserved federal land with significant historical, scientific, or cultural interest. No longer was national park the only category of permanent reservation. The monument category was more flexible, allowing for the inclusion of all kinds of features. The preservation constituency united behind the bill, which passed both houses. In early June 1906, Roosevelt signed it into law. Mesa Verde National Park followed later in the same month. There was no sign of a Pajarito Plateau national park.

Nineteen-hundred-and-six was the year of archaeology in Congress. The heady climate inspired great confidence—American scientists truly thought that the public heard their message. The passage of the Antiquities Act and the Mesa Verde park bill within three weeks of each other offered strong support for that supposition, showing a greater public interest in establishing archaeological national parks than ever before.

Ironically, in 1906, the Pajarito Plateau park proposal lacked a significant archaeological component. The most important sites on the plateau were within the new Jemez Forest Reserve, on the Santa Clara Reservation, and on private land. Compromises had deprived the park bill of its primary features. The prehistory of the plateau was beyond the reach of advocates at the best moment for the creation of an archaeological national park. As a result, the Pajarito Plateau missed a unique moment in the history of American preservation.

As a leader among archaeologists in the Southwest in the early 1900s, Hewett should have been able to orchestrate the establishment of the park. His influence over the GLO and the Department of the Interior was at its zenith between 1904 and 1906, and at the same time, he became a power in the Archaeological Institute of America. He served as GLO Commissioner W. A. Richards's advisor on archaeology and preservation. While turmoil raged at the Bureau of American Ethnology, Richards turned to Hewett to draw up a survey identifying four distinct river basins brimming with archaeological remains. Hewett also published articles in the *American Anthropologist*, authored a bureau report, wrote the Antiquities Act, received the approval of the Archaeological Institute of America and the American Anthropological Association for the act, testified frequently in front of Congress on archaeological questions, and remained a close friend of John F. Lacey's.[42] After Baum was ousted in the aftermath of the Lodge-Rodenberg debacle, Hewett was even appointed a contributing editor of *Records of the Past*. In 1906, Hewett was as close as anyone could be to the sources of power over questions of preservation and land.

After Lacey's death in 1917, Hewett contended that the congressman had abandoned the Pajarito project in favor of the Mesa Verde bill, but his charges do not bear close scrutiny.[43] Hewett was capricious, and it seems a stronger probability that after he inspected Mesa Verde for the Department of the Interior in March 1906, he himself gave up on the abrogated Pajarito project. From Hewett's point of view, without either Puye or Frijoles Canyon and with minimal likelihood of acquiring the Ramón Vigil Grant, there was little point in accepting an inferior national park for archaeological study at that time. With the widespread popularity that archaeology enjoyed, Hewett's confidence seemed appropriate. Better opportunities would certainly arise.

But in this assumption, Hewett was wrong. The mosaic of interests that made up the Pajarito Plateau in 1906 became only more complicated. As new people came to the region, competition for the limited resources of the area increased. The primary battle participants were in place. Hewett and others would play variations on the same theme for the following thirty years.

At the turn of the century, the Pajarito Plateau became enmeshed in controversies typical of the era. Different groups of people, with different value systems, sought to utilize the plateau to achieve their goals. The same kinds of battles occurred throughout the West. What made the plateau peculiar was that its limited amount of space showed the conflicts in high relief. As the tenor of the time emphasized limits to abundance, programs from elsewhere began to be applied on the plateau. The result was a conflict between the value system of people who sought to make a living from western land and those who sought to regulate its use and administer it for noncommercial purposes.

The nature of issues under debate on the plateau also changed. Competing interests were no longer exclusively economic. The values of scientists looking to make an issue of the significance of prehistory to a changing society were juxtaposed with the economic interests of commercial groups and indigenous residents and settlers. All looked at the plateau through different prisms. At least temporarily, their incommensurable goals seemed compatible, and a resolution to the issues they addressed seemed a distinct likelihood.

But the demise of the proposal of 1906 meant the end of the idea of a national park for archaeological study on the Pajarito Plateau. The nature of the constituency that supported preservation changed, and scientists increasingly represented a minority view. Future attempts to create a national park in the region focused on the value of the ruins from a commercial perspective. Archaeological justifications of future proposals took second place to economic ones as national parks became an important way to attract tourists to the American West.

From the aborted park proposal of 1906, Edgar L. Hewett emerged as a leading figure in American anthropology and archaeology. The early battles between competing interests taught him important lessons. His pres-

tige and power grew, and he consolidated his position as the primary archaeologist of New Mexico. After 1906, Hewett extended his influence in
the scientific world, the federal bureaucracy, and New Mexico Territory.
He became the one who determined the success or failure of efforts to ar-
range the disposition of land on the Pajarito Plateau.

5

✳ ✳ ✳ ✳ ✳ ✳ ✳ ✳ ✳ ✳ ✳ ✳ ✳ ✳ ✳ ✳ ✳

The early years of the new century were a vibrant time in the Southwest. As railroads traversed the region, the American public saw it in a new light. Thanks largely to the efforts of the Atchison, Topeka, and Santa Fe Railroad, the Southwest ceased to be a lonely, godforsaken desert, the home of Apache Indians and Gila monsters, and became the last land of opportunity south of Alaska. The AT&SF promoted the romance of the Southwest, and Americans looking to "see America first," in the phrase coined by the noted writer and southwestern luminary Charles Lummis, flocked to visit. Miners, farmers, and ranchers came in search of good land, and midwestern tuberculars lined up at spas and sanitariums throughout the arid region.[1]

Government agencies began to regulate the previously open Southwest. Homestead laws applied to federal land in the region, and as Anglos came to the Southwest, their law overruled the common practices of the Hispanic and Indian past. In the three years following the passage of the Antiquities Act of 1906, the GLO proclaimed seven archaeological areas as national monuments.[2] Advocates of preservation saw their plans bear fruit, Anglo commercial interests determined the future of tracts with long histories of traditional use, and the twin ideals of technology and progress began to reshape the Southwest.

But even though the values of American society affected the nature of life in the region, southwesterners did not readily acquiesce to the tenets of an industrial world. The area was still an economic frontier, its Native Americans only recently subdued by the American military. Distances between communities were vast, and communication sometimes was ineffective. The economy of the region remained colonial; the Southwest still traded raw materials for finished products. Good land remained scarce, and competing interests embodying different value systems fought bitterly to dominate the best tracts.

On the Pajarito Plateau, disparate groups consolidated their positions and became more entrenched. Under the terms of the Forest Homestead Act of June 11, 1906, the government opened arable areas within national forests, as forest reserves had been retitled in 1905, to settlement.[3] On the plateau, this made more land available, and the number of homesteaders in the region increased. With the support of the new U.S. Forest Service (USFS), some settlers augmented subsistence with commercial endeavors. National park advocates still held high hopes for the region, archaeologists like Hewett valued its cultural resources, and the temporary withdrawal of 1900 remained in force. The problems remained. Anthropologists and archaeologists worried about the destruction of their crucible, and Hispano and Indian residents of the area watched the continued narrowing of their world. Except for the largely disenfranchised Hispanos, whom the Anglo world ignored, each group held its position. But the plateau could not contain the dreams of everyone who sought its varied treasures.

The confluence of interests and the limited amount of space in the region made the national park proposal the focus of local animosity. A large restricted area threatened the livelihood of homesteaders, indicated limits of the jurisdiction of the Forest Service, which would cede administration to the Department of the Interior, and raised the ire of those who opposed federal control of the West. Posturing became rife and argument intense as each group tried to impress its views on the others.

There were two distinct positions after 1906. The contingent of scientists and preservationists sought to preserve the area. Homesteaders and their ally, the USFS, valued the economic potential of the area above its intangible cultural attributes. The relatively small size of the plateau intensified the conflict. Both factions wanted to use the same tracts of land in different fashions. Initially, the perspectives seemed compatible, but in reality, they became mutually exclusive.

Hewett emerged as the pivotal figure in the future of the Pajarito Plateau. His career blossomed as he became a powerful member of the scientific community. After Territorial Governor Miguel Otero ousted him from the presidency of the New Mexico Normal School during a political controversy in 1903, Hewett developed his professional credentials. He saw that he needed an advanced degree and, in the middle of his life, changed directions to facilitate his climb to prominence. Hewett made himself an accredited archaeologist. He began work on a Ph.D. in archaeology under the auspices of the University of Geneva, completing this degree in 1908. His role as peacemaker in the aftermath of the Lodge-Rodenberg debacle also won him many friends, and he spent most of 1905 in Washington, D.C., as a fellow at the Smithsonian Institution.[4] In the capital, Hewett became a fixture in preservation circles.

Hewett also initiated the process that rescued Santa Fe from its doldrums. After 1880, the importance of Santa Fe decreased. The main line of the AT&SF bypassed the town, stopping instead in Lamy, some twenty miles away. Even the completion of the Chili Line in 1886 had little impact on the ominous trend. Without a direct link to the markets of the rest of the nation, Santa Fe had little to offer. Its population dropped from 6,635 in 1880 to 5,603 in 1900 and 5,072 in 1910. Santa Fe seemed on the way to the oblivion of towns outside the realm of new technologies.

Hewett built cultural institutions that breathed new life into the city. His work brought two important constituencies to Santa Fe: writers and artists who came for the ambience and visitors who came to see a glimpse of what the railroads presented as a quaint and romantic past. The first of the institutions was the School of American Archaeology, a new branch of the Archaeological Institute of America, founded in 1907. Hewett's lobbying located the school in Santa Fe, and he became its first director. He retained this position until his death in 1946.[5] The school was the first piece of Hewett's cultural empire. It and a subsequent development, the Museum of New Mexico, which Jesse L. Nusbaum and Kenneth Chapman helped develop, created a climate that made Santa Fe hospitable to people of artistic temperament.[6] By 1910, Hewett had few peers in southwestern archaeology, and no one was more critical to the cultural future of Santa Fe.

By developing Santa Fe as a cultural center, Hewett unwittingly bifurcated support for his park proposal. Writers and artists came to Santa Fe to rest their souls, and by viewing the past through ethnocentric prisms, no matter how sympathetic, they commercialized northern New Mexico more widely and rapidly than even the AT&SF. As a result, the local business community learned the commercial value of archaeology, hurting the chances of the establishment of a national park for archaeological study.

In 1910, archaeology still rode a wave of popularity in the United States. Articles about southwestern ruins permeated the popular press. Professionals such as Frederic Ward Putnam, who directed the Peabody Museum at Harvard University from 1875 to 1909, and self-trained experts like William Henry Holmes, John Wesley Powell's successor at the Bureau of American Ethnology, helped promote prehistory. For many Americans, the archaeology of the Southwest became a fair rival for the history of Europe and the Middle East. But of the early leaders in the field, only Hewett and Byron Cummings, then of the University of Utah, lived in the West. As a result, the majority of excavations before 1910 involved eastern professionals and westerners with knowledge of the location of ruins. Two heirs to a soap fortune, Fred and Talbot Hyde, financed Richard Wetherill's excavation at Chaco Canyon. Wetherill ran the enterprise, but George W. Pepper, who had studied under Putnam at Harvard, intermittently supervised the dig. This kind of alliance typified archaeological excavation early in the century.[7]

Hewett was a pivotal addition to the scientific community. His credentials made him a much more acceptable key to the crucible of American archaeology than cowboys like Wetherill. Hewett made himself invaluable by offering undergraduates from eastern schools a chance to do southwestern fieldwork during the summers. Alfred V. Kidder and Sylvanus Morley, who would both become prominent archaeologists, apprenticed with Hewett in 1907, and others such as Earl H. Morris and Neil Judd followed. Jesse Nusbaum, a tall gangly youth whose head seemed too big for his body and who owned the first motorcycle in Santa Fe, also apprenticed with Hewett.[8] A summer with Hewett became a rite of passage for aspiring American archaeologists.

But as a science, archaeology was undeveloped. There were so many undisturbed ruins in the Southwest that the earliest fieldwork consisted mostly of surveying and describing sites. Archaeological technique was in its infancy, and in the half generation since the outcry against Richard Wetherill, little had changed. Professional excavators still concentrated on tangible prizes that would look nice in a museum case. Collecting pieces of prehistory was the philosophy of excavation. Discovering a site was as important as excavating it, and scientists rushed from the discovery of one ruin to another.

Often, the results of a professional excavation and of an amateur pot-hunting foray were perilously similar. Excavators frequently left large, exposed holes in the ground where they dug. On occasion, they neglected rudimentary stabilization of walls and structures, and the work of accredited professionals was indistinguishable from that of unauthorized vandals. The major difference between the types of excavating was that the collections made by professionals ended up in the hands of learned societies and museums instead of private individuals.[9]

In 1910, archaeology remained a descriptive discipline with roots in American romanticism. It had vast popular appeal, and its forms permeated American cultural life. The Columbian Exposition of 1893 had first presented the public with the scope of Indian cultures in North America, and the great expositions of the first decade of the twentieth century, including the Louisiana Purchase Centennial Exposition in St. Louis in 1904, featured buildings of exhibits devoted to cliff dwellings and dwellers. Enlarged photos of Chaco Canyon decorated the grillroom in the new Hotel Astor in Times Square, where fashionable New Yorkers went to dine and drink. Because of the attention, and the lack of scientific technique and data, archaeologists painted a picture of the past that was largely based in American preconceptions about prehistoric life.[10]

The pueblo dweller replaced the nomadic Plains Indian as the dominant image of the aboriginal West. In an era searching for moral justification of the principle of Indian assimilation, the sedentary Pueblo peoples offered Anglo-Americans hope for the remaining Native Americans. Indians who lived in towns and who farmed could be loosely construed as precursors of western civilization; in the deterministic view of the time, they were more highly advanced than their northern peers.

Among purveyors of this kind of description, Hewett rose to the fore. He made inferences about prehistoric life by drawing analogies to modern pueblos, but like most others in his discipline, he had difficulty substantiating conclusions. Archaeology had not yet developed a standardized analytical format. Romantic description remained paramount, and Hewett's stylish writing and considerable sensitivity and foresight distinguished him from his peers.

Yet the rush of activity dampened one aspect of Hewett's romanticism. He could no longer let the history in storage in the mounds of the Pajarito Plateau lie undisturbed. Incidents like the one with Cole and Madden, as well as the growing number of students who came to the Southwest, finally took the decision out of his hands. As trained archaeologists crowded the Southwest, Hewett tightened his hold on the Pajarito Plateau ruins. He began to excavate as early as 1903, abandoning his ideal of a world undisturbed in the face of consistent encroachment.

Hewett approached excavation with energy, enthusiasm, and visions of empire. By 1910, he held excavating permits from the Forest Service for the Frijoles region and from the Department of the Interior for Puye and other ruins within the proposed withdrawal. He also had permits for other archaeological sites throughout the Southwest.[11] Although each permit required his presence during work at the site, his prestige in the region was so great that the GLO and the Forest Service allowed him vast leeway. Hewett did not have to abide by the terms of the Antiquities Act he had authored. In 1907, he excavated Puye and from 1908 to 1912, the ruins of Tyuonyi, the great community house in Frijoles Canyon.[12] Hewett published his findings through the School of American Archaeology and became a fixture on the cultural landscape of New Mexico. Few challenged him, and he came to see the plateau as his personal project in prehistory.

As he carved out his territory, Hewett followed a time-honored tradition in his chosen field. Completing a dig was a long and involved process that required a number of years, and like migratory birds, archaeologists returned to their favorite locales each summer. Archaeologists dating as far back as Heinrich Schliemann, the talented amateur who rediscovered Troy in the 1870s, viewed their excavations as personal property, and many guarded their sites jealously. American archaeologists east of the Mississippi River did the same.[13] What made Hewett different was that he staked his claim on a large area that included a multitude of ruins rather than on a specific site. He could not possibly excavate every site of importance on the Pajarito Plateau, but he could prevent others from digging there.

Hewett was not alone on the Pajarito Plateau. The paucity of perennial streams in the region meant that the area remained in seasonal use long after there were permanent settlements in nearby valleys and even in the higher and less hospitable Sangre de Cristo Mountains, east of the Rio Grande valley. Homesteaders, commercial interests, and the traditional communities in the surrounding valleys all had economic claims on the region, but few took the time to establish permanent tenancy. The traditional pattern of seasonal use continued, oblivious to the encroachment of a scientific world. Business interests sought the stands of timber on the Vigil Grant and to the south, and after Buckman left, the plateau contained a number of local sawmills. Although Hewett controlled the archaeology of the plateau, he did not dominate those who saw its value in dollars and cents.

Homesteading received a boost after the establishment of the Forest Service in 1905. The USFS aided local commerce whenever possible while teaching the tenets of Progressive-era utilitarian conservation. Its policies helped farmers, ranchers, and timber and grazing enterprises. A system of permits allowed access to federal rangeland, and rangers sought to convey the principles of scientific management to the people of the Southwest.

Yet this agency had problems with the very people it hoped to help. Conservation often had preachy overtones, sometimes seeming as if its message came from the pure to the infidel. In addition, some national forest land in northern New Mexico had once been part of Spanish and Mexican land grants, and almost 80 percent of USFS lessees were Hispano. Late in the nineteenth century, land barons like Thomas B. Catron had acquired this land under dubious and sometimes fraudulent circumstances and had later exchanged it with the government. As a result, Hispanos sometimes had to pay to graze animals on land that their ancestors owned. A clash of values also impeded the relationship; natives of the region clung to their traditions while forest rangers limited grazing on lands that Hispanos had formerly used whenever they chose. An uneasy tension resulted—Hispanos derogatorily labeled the Forest Service "La Floresta," and rangers pondered the recalcitrance of the people they tried to help.[14]

The Jemez National Forest, of which the plateau was part, stretched far into western New Mexico. The headquarters for the forest was in Cuba, a rough town in which rangers were thoroughly resented and in which two were thrashed in 1908. Because of tension between the agency and a local political leader there, the USFS focused its attention on the Cuba–Rio Puerco region.

Nevertheless, USFS policies helped develop the Pajarito Plateau. The incentive of seemingly good land available for the price of improvement continued to attract new settlers. The northern mountains offered a better opportunity than anywhere else in New Mexico. More people chose the area at the eastern base of the Jemez Mountains, in the shadow of the Otero family's Baca Location no. 1, for their homes. Many families had already settled there, and despite the high elevation, the land held promise for ranching and farming. By 1910, there were thirty-five homestead claims on the eastern slope of the mountains.[15]

Homestead life on the Pajarito Plateau was not easy, and it accentuated the differences between the deep-rooted Hispanic culture and that of the relatively transient Anglos who came to the region. Life was lonely, and the winters at higher elevations were long and harsh. Hispanos who homesteaded the plateau were in the midst of an extended social and familial network. Their lives and culture were rooted to that place. Many Hispano families had lived in surrounding valleys for more than two hundred years, and when they left their homesteads in the mountains, they moved to the valleys and spent the winter with the family of a brother or sister or resided with parents. The social structure encouraged the presence of more than the immediate family under a single roof.

Anglos who settled the region had little cultural sustenance. Most moved to the region in search of opportunity, many after failing elsewhere. Their families were far away, and so were their roots. They sought a definition of success shaped by industrial culture as much as by land, and they did not see the area in spiritual terms. In their view, the plateau was a potentially profitable commodity. But the growing season was short, and the rigors of winter lasted long. There were few Anglos in Española and Pojoaque, and few Anglo settlers had permanent ties to New Mexico. Their isolation exacted a toll. Many became heavy drinkers. Others became storytellers and "lie-swappers." They had little other respite from cabin fever.

Few could make a living exclusively from their land, fragmenting Anglo culture even more. Extended families in the Hispanic pattern were rare, and the frenetic search for a living made family life an infrequent luxury. The men often went elsewhere to work, leaving their families for as much as six months at a time. Culturally locked into the cash economy, young Anglos found the idea of a subsistence existence unpalatable.

Many shared the experiences of George White, a son of William C.

White. As a young man, George White bounced around northern New Mexico and southern Colorado like a Ping-Pong ball. In 1905, he scraped out a living breaking maverick cattle and horses in the Jemez Mountains, then took a job in the mine at Bland. After a near tragedy when the mine collapsed on top of him, he and his father went to Mancos, Colorado. The two men worked there briefly, but the younger White soon returned to the plateau to drive a team for a lumber company. He lived in a cabin in the Española Valley with his wife. When she died of complications resulting from childbirth in October 1907, he returned to the family homestead in the Jemez Mountains. He stayed for a year, raising crops and presumably letting psychological wounds heal. In 1909, White went to work for the New Mexico Lumber Company near Tierra Amarilla and soon after started work for the Forest Service building a telephone line in the Carson National Forest. He returned to the plateau when the USFS began to construct another telephone line from Pojoaque to the Jemez Mountains.[16]

Although the family homestead was home to people like George White, it was really only a place to which to return. Home was wherever the paycheck was. The cash-dominated Anglo economy fostered transience, impeding White and his neighbors as they tried to develop cohesive social underpinnings that would bind them to the place. Often having histories of failure elsewhere, most did not see their relationship to the plateau as permanent. The paychecks from elsewhere that sustained their way of life also accentuated their restless tendencies.

In northern New Mexico, Hispano culture was more stable, its communities stronger and more cohesive. When young people left home to work for the sawmills or railroads, they had more than personal aspiration in their hearts. They pioneered the cash economy, venturing into an increasingly foreign world to bring back necessities for their families. But they left a cohesive social unit behind them, the roots of a regional community. Their absence was to benefit the family, and their relatives filled the void they left. Their sweethearts stayed behind, as did many of their friends, who preferred the rigorous life in the village to one filled with what they saw as the corrupted values of English-speakers. Hispano tradition taught that the respect of a person's neighbors was more important than material possessions, and the young people who upheld tradition knew that they also fulfilled an important social role, one lacking in the world of Anglo homesteaders. The community continued, with its feasts and celebrations, sometimes isolating those who left.

It was an unarticulated division of labor. After the ascent of the cash economy, Hispanos needed cash to pay the taxes on their land. When goods like metal plows and kitchen ranges became available, currency became even more important, and young men and women were sent to earn the dollars that purchased modern necessities and comforts. Those who stayed behind maintained traditional culture while those who left carried the key to a presumed economic prosperity.[17]

The plateau was on the periphery of the Hispano world, and the rules of the villages did not always apply. Homesteaders differed from the people of the valleys. They formalized their time-honored practices in land patents, reaching a level of accommodation with the Anglo world that their cousins in nearby villages did not. They abandoned common patterns of living, instead building homes that did not abut those of relatives with adjacent property. In an integrated world of economically and culturally marginal Anglos and Hispanos, homesteaders adapted to life on the periphery.

More widespread availability of goods and use of credit dramatically changed economic life in the Pajarito Plateau area. Cash-crop farming became prevalent, and new patterns of land use emerged. Before 1880, Hispano agriculturalists raised crops primarily for their own consumption. If a surplus existed, they traded for necessities. By the early twentieth century, their emphasis had changed. As the experience of Victor and Luisa Romero and their six children showed, cash crops assumed prominence in agricultural activities.

The Romeros were typical of homesteaders on the Pajarito Plateau. Victor's father, David, had begun to homestead the plateau early in the century, and the younger couple followed his lead. In 1913, they staked a claim to an adjacent parcel. Each spring, in their horse-drawn wagon laden with supplies, they left San Ildefonso for the plateau. Of their fifteen acres, thirteen were tillable, and these the Romeros filled with beans and corn. Until the end of the First World War, beans were the primary cash-crop commodity. The Romeros harvested 1,200 pounds of beans in 1913; 300 pounds of beans and 4 *fanegas* (roughly 2 1/2 English bushels) of corn in 1914; and 2,100 pounds of beans and 1,800 pounds of corn in 1915.

Cash-crop farming did not cause homesteaders to abandon subsistence ways entirely, but these activities became less important. The Romeros planted peach, apricot, and cherry trees, watermelons, and a variety of vegetables, including squashes, for their own use. They also harvested native wild plants like *quelites* (a wild spinach), *verdolaga* (purslane), *osha* (wild celery), and *amole* (yucca), the last used to make soap. Ernest and Ernestina (Montoya) Romero, who both grew up on the plateau, fondly recalled the abundant wild strawberries growing on the canyon walls. Nevertheless, the amount of tillable land planted in marketable crops revealed the importance of the cash economy.

Despite the native abundance, the lot of homesteaders resembled that of sharecroppers in the South. They too took seed and implements on credit, paying interest to merchants in the valleys. As long as their yield and the market prices remained high, their situation was stable. But the land became less productive as a result of constant use. Bean and other crop prices plummeted in the aftermath of World War I, and the economic viability of homesteading measurably decreased. The people who lived on the Pajarito Plateau remained poor, but their situation worsened. They had experienced what Anglo material culture had to offer, changing their expectations and enticing them further into the Anglo market. They also owed interest and principal for commodities that they had taken in the better years. The result was a sociocultural and economic magnet that pulled them closer to the mainstream.

In part, this resulted from the marginal status of the plateau. Although it was adjacent to the most heavily populated areas of the north, it was a frontier of the regional community. Despite the beginnings of a distinct community sense, accentuated by marriages such as that of Bences González, the son of Severo González, and Ernestina Romero, the daughter of Victor and Luisa Romero and granddaughter of two plateau pioneers, its homesteaders identified the nearby valleys as their home. Families such as the Romeros returned to San Ildefonso in the winter, and Antonio Sanchés and many others were buried there.

The interdependent village social structure of the Sangre de Cristo Mountains, typified by the acequia (irrigation ditch), was not a powerful force on the plateau. The region was an economic frontier for Hispanos, much as were the mines and beet fields of Colorado. Instead, as its population grew, the loose-knit community centered around institutions such as the school, which Bences González developed after discerning in 1921 that there were 130 parents on the plateau. The small log shack in the back of González's home began to replace the social rituals and attendant customs of the villages as the primary avenue of socialization.[18]

Cash-crop farming was ecologically dangerous in a marginal area like the plateau. Modern agricultural science was in its infancy, and few people understood the need for techniques such as crop rotation. Like people everywhere else, homesteaders on the plateau planted the same crops in the same places year after year. Within a decade, productivity usually declined, damaging the land, further impoverishing its people, and increasing their dependence on the cash economy.

Anglos and Hispanos all lived lives of deprivation in northern New Mexico, but the realities of the region shaped Hispano experience. The rigors of life, the years of little, were part of their heritage, and in lean times, their social system offered support. Many were not aware of changes beyond their narrow existence and thus did not miss what they did not know. Anglo migrants came to the region to find opportunity and were often disappointed by the illusion of fertility. They craved property, for in their culture, land measured wealth. On the plateau, plenty of land was available. Even though the opportunity it offered was often illusory, the land Anglos claimed was their own, and they guarded it zealously.

As others settled on the plateau, Anglo culture began to establish more than a foothold in the area. Among the new settlers was the attorney for the northern pueblos, Judge A. J. Abbott. The Judge's son, Albert J. Abbott, a USFS ranger, had visited Frijoles Canyon in 1906 and discovered the remains of a number of homesteads, including the adobe house of the Pacifico C. de Baca family. He told his father about the area's charm, and in June 1907, the Judge and his wife, Ida Patton Abbott, followed the "right track over the *right* mesa" to the canyon. Their four-day sojourn left the Abbotts as impressed as Bandelier and Hewett with the "beauty, grandeur and solemnity of the surroundings." They found "a spot for an ideal rustic home" on El Rito de los Frijoles and resolved to return the following spring.[19]

Mimicking the age-old pattern of use, the Abbotts saw Frijoles Canyon as a fine place to spend the summers. But the Judge did not plan to run stock in the classic sense, preferring instead to keep animals for the use of his family. The Abbotts built a home across El Rito de los Frijoles from Tyuonyi and, under the terms of the act of June 11, 1906, filed a claim on much of the canyon area. The judge even planted crops so that his spread complied with the Homestead Act of 1862. Albert Abbott had previously told his superiors in the USFS that Frijoles Canyon would make a fine headquarters for Forest Service activities in the Jemez area, and the agency built a ranger station just beyond Abbott's "Ranch of the Ten Elders." Although the Abbotts remained in the canyon, their land claim could not be perfected.

When Hewett excavated Tyuonyi in the summers of 1908 and 1909, he and the Abbotts became good friends. Sharing similar educational, political, and cultural backgrounds, they found each other's company a pleasant surprise. The relationship also benefited both parties. The Abbotts depended on Hewett for supplies and contact with the outside world during their time in the canyon, and they enjoyed being associated with a man of his prestige and energy. In return, Hewett used Abbott as his eyes and ears during his absences from Frijoles Canyon. Hewett also used the plateau to promote his archaeological activities, and the Abbotts hosted many visitors sent by Hewett. Abbott was a respected jurist, well-known in the Pueblo and Hispano communities of the nearby valleys, and Hewett's standing with natives of the region improved because of his relationship with the Abbotts.

Next to Abbott, the most important person on the plateau was Harold H. Brook. A slight but outspoken man with deep-set, hollow eyes, Brook was determined to succeed as an agriculturalist. He graduated from the Illinois College of Agriculture in Jacksonville and shortly afterward contracted tuberculosis. Like many turn-of-the-century Anglo migrants, Brook left the Midwest for the drier southwestern climate. But Brook differed from many of the other new settlers. When he arrived in New Mexico in 1907, he brought with him an innovative, entrepreneurial spirit, faith in the scientific technology of the Progressives, and technical expertise far beyond that of his neighbors on the Pajarito Plateau.

Brook became a pivotal figure, for he was the first to believe that the region held the potential for more than subsistence. The availability of land attracted him, and he believed that the techniques he had learned in college would make him a success. In 1907, Brook purchased a quarter section with a little pond, paying twenty-five dollars in back taxes that the Sanchés family could not pay after Antonio Sanchés was killed by a falling boulder. Here Brook founded the Los Alamos Ranch, where the Fuller Lodge stands in the present-day town of Los Alamos, spent five thousand dollars on modern machinery, and took up cash-crop farming to patent homesteads claimed by him, his mother, Martha Brook, and his partner, William M. "Mack" Hopper.[20]

By Brook's account, homestead life on the plateau was not easy. Brook was on his own, for his workers were undependable, the weather was unpredictable at best, and the resources of the plateau were limited. With his training, Brook could forge an existence, but only with great difficulty. Capital equipment made his situation better than that of his neighbors. They faced the same conditions he did but lacked the benefit of up-to-date technology.[21]

Homesteaders soon found themselves in the center of a dispute between federal agencies. The creation of the USFS, its acquisition of the forest reserves, and the temporary withdrawal of 1900 confused boundaries on the Pajarito Plateau. Because the national forests were under the jurisdiction of the Department of the Interior in 1900, the GLO had made the original temporary withdrawal. After the transfer of the land to another federal agency, GLO officials nevertheless considered the order valid. To the USFS, the temporary withdrawal of 1900 was just another piece of paper in a vast pile. In the chaos that followed the transfer of more than twenty million acres of forest land to the USFS, no one thought to see if any kind of claim on the plateau existed before the establishment of the Jemez Forest Reserve. After passage of the act of June 11, 1906, the Forest Service allowed settlers to file for ownership of land that the GLO had withdrawn from entry in 1900. But the GLO had final approval of the title to any tract of public land, and officials decided that the temporary withdrawal precluded permanent claims within its boundaries.

Although a bureaucratic lapse on the part of both agencies accounted for the confusion, the situation had much more grave meaning to westerners. Their paramount fear—that the property of an individual could be taken at the whim of the federal government—resurfaced. People far from the locus of power found another in an endless sequence of reasons to resent federal intrusion into their lives.

Harold H. Brook, the first to discover the error, became the advocate for the rights of homesteaders. In 1909, Brook found that his claim was within the boundaries of the temporary withdrawal of 1900. USFS officials told him he could not perfect title to his land, but Brook had every intention of defending his investment. He angrily wrote Hewett, well-known as the primary backer of the park, and blamed the confusion on the Forest Service, which had allowed him to apply, and the GLO, which had granted him conditional title. Brook felt that he had been treated unfairly and wanted Hewett to exclude from the park proposal the farmland at the base of the Jemez Mountains.[22]

The developing antagonism brought back arguments that had damaged the case for the park in 1904 and 1906 in a new and more potent form. There were more homesteaders and additional jurisdictional conflicts in the region. Hewett recognized that the situation did not further his goals. He also understood Brook's point of view. The 153,620-acre temporary withdrawal of 1900 threatened to choke off settlement all over the plateau. Brook's complaints had merit, and the politically experienced Hewett searched for a solution.

With the passage of the Antiquities Act in 1906, Hewett could preserve ruins without having the land between various ruins fit standards designed for dramatically different situations. He recognized that excluding the homesteads would silence much of the opposition to the preservation proposal. He had written the Antiquities Act based on his experience on the plateau, and with the complications that the homestead situation caused, a national monument seemed a more conciliatory solution than a national park.

The Antiquities Act had given the federal bureaucracy new alternatives. By 1909, the new category, the national monuments, had proved well suited to the preservation of archaeological areas. There were no expectations about national monuments. Under the terms of the act, the GLO could formalize temporary withdrawals without congressional approval. Most monuments created before 1909 were areas withdrawn before the passage of the act. Monuments were often small areas, and more important from the local point of view, the Department of the Interior generally permitted grazing within monument boundaries. The category was an eclectic hodgepodge; national monuments existed for no other reason than that they were special in some way.[23]

Yet since 1900, the Department of the Interior had sought a large park on the plateau, and changing its perspective took time. The long history of bills left an imprint, and Hewett had been a staunch supporter of the park idea. Yet he worked to change the point of view of the GLO. In November 1909, Hewett suggested that the department undertake another survey of the region, with the objective of establishing a national monument. If a smaller area was reserved in a national monument, the temporary withdrawal could be invalidated, and Brook could perfect his claim. Settlers could continue to make their living in the region, and the ruins could be preserved as well. It was precisely for cases like this that Hewett and Lacey had created the Antiquities Act. A monument seemed an optimal solution.

After Hewett began to press for a resolution, government agencies again started to sort out land questions on the Pajarito Plateau. The Forest Service requested the opening of the entire 153,620-acre withdrawal to settlement. The Department of the Interior was reluctant to surrender its claim and proposed that the USFS permit homesteading only in the withdrawn areas that fell within the Jemez National Forest. In the view of the department, the USFS had no right to determine the future of the area outside the forest reservation. The GLO wanted to keep that section withdrawn pending final disposition. Secretary of the Interior Richard A. Ballinger asked the Forest Service to determine the exact location of important ruins within the national forest. Ballinger also directed GLO Commissioner Fred Dennett to order another study of all the ruins outside the national forest. For this purpose, Dennett ordered U.S. Examiner of Surveys William B. Douglass to the plateau.[24]

Douglass was an important figure in the evolution of federal preservation in the United States. Responsible for land surveys in the Southwest, he was an ardent supporter of federal attempts at ruins preservation, yet like many of his contemporaries, he disparaged the motives and actions of others while doing as he pleased. Douglass was one of the first whites to see the natural bridges and rainbow bridge in Utah, and he selected the ruins that became Navajo National Monument after being informed that they were threatened by unauthorized excavation. He was a firm believer in orderly excavation of archaeological sites. He crammed his GLO reports full of archaeological descriptions and his own suppositions, watching with a jaundiced eye as archaeologists rushed to the Southwest to make their reputations. He also engaged in excavations of his own, often without the very permits he chastised others for not possessing.

In 1909, Douglass took a position that later affected the future of the Pajarito Plateau ruins. He challenged Hewett and Byron Cummings and their excavation in the newly established Navajo National Monument. Hewett was never present during the course of the excavation, and Cummings planned to train students at the site, a common practice among archaeologists. Douglass, regarding the entire episode as a breach of professional ethics, complained to the secretary of the interior that Hewett did not abide by his own regulations. Douglass was not impressed with Hewett's reputation and, in essence, called Hewett, the man who had developed the label "pothunter," an officially sanctioned pothunter. Sensitive to the vagaries of a public reputation, Hewett never forgave Douglass. The consequences of their arguments affected the development of the Pajarito Plateau for the next fifteen years.[25]

By 1910, Hewett had become an important figure in Santa Fe. With the help of Alice C. Fletcher and Francis W. Kelsey of the Archaeological Institute of America, he established the reputation of the School of American Archaeology. More maneuvering led to the creation of the Museum of New Mexico in 1909, and Hewett assumed the directorship of both organizations. He promoted archaeology like a carnival barker, and the graceful tone of his work aroused the interest of many. Hewett became the most important scholar of prehistory in New Mexico, and he wielded his influence like a war club.[26]

Hewett's dislike for Douglass was so strong that he used the entire force of his position to thwart Douglass's work, and the reservation of the ruins on the Pajarito Plateau was impaled on their mutual distaste. When Hewett found out that his plea for a monument brought Douglass to survey the portion of the plateau outside the Jemez National Forest, he regarded Douglass's presence as a threat to his authority.

Douglass's presence greatly complicated Hewett's situation. Hewett was a man of vast ego and even larger ambition. Douglass was a nemesis with the power to wound; Hewett had learned as much at Navajo. Hewett wanted to reserve the ruins that were not protected—the ones that he and his crews were not yet excavating. Frijoles Canyon and Puye were already secure: the Abbotts, whom Hewett trusted, lived in the canyon, and Hewett's crews were at Puye. But Douglass presented the same kind of threat that he had the year before. Hewett was notoriously lax about who excavated under his permits. He was present intermittently, which had caused Douglass to complain about the Navajo excavation.

Hewett correctly assumed that another effort to reserve Puye was afoot. Puye was not Hewett's goal for a reservation on the plateau. Douglass would try to stop the excavation there, Hewett knew, and he immediately began to use his influence to thwart his rival. In Washington, D.C., in the spring of 1910, he angrily told GLO Chief Clerk Frank Bond that he objected to the idea of a Puye national monument.[27] Back in New Mexico, he generated opposition to Douglass's survey.

Hewett knew that the cantankerous Clinton J. Crandall at the Santa Fe Indian School would object to any attempts to take Puye from the Indians. Both men were aware of the rampant thievery of land in New Mexico. In 1911, the law protected neither Native Americans nor Hispanics from the legalized alienation of their land. Speculators thrived, and to honest government officials and the few others with a sense of justice, the situation was an oozing sore that besmirched the idea of democracy. Crandall had made significant inroads in protecting the pueblos. The addition of the tract including Puye to the Santa Clara Pueblo in 1905 was largely the result of his effort. The prospect of the government trying to reclaim what it had only recently granted the Santa Clara Indians appalled him. Crandall complained to his superior, Commissioner of Indian Affairs Robert G. Valentine, reiterating the objections he raised in 1903. Even a national monument would hurt Santa Clara Pueblo.[28]

But Douglass was carrying out the orders of the secretary of the interior, and Hewett found himself obstructing the aims of his old friends in that department. He had to be very careful. Departmental officials took a dim view of interference in their plans, even by their friends. Consequently, Crandall became the public representative for Hewett's perspective. Neither the Indians nor Hewett stood to gain anything if Puye became a national park or monument. Hewett convinced Crandall that the monument would cost the Santa Claras grazing and timber land. There was still no bureau to manage the national parks, Crandall pointed out, and at its best, national monument status was a dubious distinction. "Mr. Hewett would regret very much to see any change made in the present management of these cliffs," Crandall indiscreetly informed his superiors.[29]

Again, incommensurable concerns had to be compared. The monument that Douglass advocated curtailed the rights of Native Americans. Much more than the preservation of tracts of ruins was at stake. A higher ideal, that Native Americans should be accorded enough land to survive, was an integral part of the thinking of reformers such as Crandall. From this perspective, the Pueblo Indians were particularly attractive. Living in towns and practicing agriculture, they embodied the hope that Indians could assimilate in a participatory fashion and could be useful, if limited, members of industrial society.

Yet among Native Americans at this time, the Pueblo Indians were the lone beneficiaries of federal policy. The Dawes Act of 1887 had been designed to facilitate assimilation, but it had failed to make inroads. Instead it allowed legal expropriation of Native American lands. In part as a result, the idea of assimilation for Native Americans no longer included the goals of homogeneity and citizenship. By the first decade of the new century, political leaders began to envision a lower level of social participation for Indians and other nonwhite people. This change served the needs of a hierarchical, plural industrial society in which race played an important role in determining access to power and stature.

Land extensions such as the one at Puye were anomalous in the first decade of the twentieth century. Despite the unique situation of the Pueblo Indians, current trends ran counter to Native American rights. Indian agents systematically carved up allotments, assuring dependency and poverty for Native Americans. In the case of the Pueblo Indians, a substantial land base helped maintain the traditional life-style. Yet they too were vulnerable to encroachment, for pueblo land was not protected in the manner of reservation land granted by the U.S. government. As a result, Hispano and Anglo settlers moved onto most pueblos. In cases such as Pojoaque Pueblo, intermarriage and the steady appropriation of the best lands led to the decline of the pueblo as a functioning entity. Support for the pueblos gained strength after 1900, but protection became genuine only in 1913, when the U.S. Supreme Court forbade further alienation of pueblo land in *United States* v. *Sandoval*. By 1911, the trend to protect the pueblos had begun. The Puye monument proposal found few supporters.[30]

Hewett's motives were not wholly altruistic. He also wanted to protect his interests and, conceivably, to enhance his reputation by solving what had become a time-consuming problem for the GLO. His animosity toward Douglass, his fear of the GLO official's power, and his self-interest played an important role in Hewett's support of the idea of a national monument and in his opposition to the establishment of a national monument at Puye.

Although Douglass never called for taking Indian timber or grazing land, Hewett's influence far outweighed the facts, and his tactics swayed Crandall. Despite his vested interest, Hewett was well-known as a friend of Native Americans in the area. If Hewett believed that a national monument was not a worthy enough prize for the transfer of land away from the pueblo, then Crandall was sure that Douglass's proposal would not benefit his constituents.

Hewett's efforts diminished the chances of the establishment of a national monument at Puye. As Hewett expected, on July 27, 1910, Douglass filed a report that recommended the establishment of a national monument including the Puye ruins. But Hewett had cultivated the Bureau of Indian Affairs, and in part as a result of his efforts, Assistant Commissioner for Indian Affairs F. H. Abbott asked the GLO to eliminate Puye and the other ruins on the Santa Clara Reservation from the national monument proposal. GLO Commissioner Fred Dennett asked the secretary of the Smithsonian Institution, W. D. Walcott, to decide whether there ought to be a national monument at Puye.[31]

Hewett's influence also reached Smithsonian Institution circles, and he battled the idea of a monument at Puye there. He and the Bureau of Indian Affairs put together an intense lobbying effort. On October 26, 1910, Walcott used the exact words that Hewett had spoken to Crandall the previous summer to inform the GLO that he thought a national monument was unnecessary. Without Frijoles Canyon on Forest Service land and with Puye on the Santa Clara Reservation, little reason to pursue the idea remained. The other important ruins were on the privately owned Ramón Vigil Grant, and a national monument proclamation could not include them. Two days later, Dennett informed Walcott that he was dropping the proposal.[32] Hewett had thwarted Douglass, and the Puye national monument idea was as dead as the earlier park proposals.

Two important consequences emerged from the fray. Residents of the region found no reason to trust federal agencies. A monument could have allowed the settlers to perfect their claims, but when Douglass surveyed Puye instead of the ruins of the Jemez Mountains, Hewett was compelled to oppose the establishment of a monument. This subtlety escaped most of the people in the region; when they found that the situation was not resolved, homesteaders felt betrayed. Only in 1914 did the GLO perfect Brook's title. Nor did the GLO understand Hewett's vehement objections to an idea that he seemed to have supported in the recent past. Those who did not observe the situation closely were baffled.

The efforts to reserve ruins on the plateau had become fragmented. No longer did a broad proposal that encompassed all the important ruins exist. Instead, the effort had broken up into attempts to separately reserve each area. Under different kinds of administration, Puye and Frijoles Canyon were separated by the Ramón Vigil Grant, which was also covered with ruins that Hewett coveted. The idea of a national park had been abandoned and, with it, comprehensive preservation for the ruins of the plateau.

Other developments limited the chance that the Vigil Grant could be included in any monument or park. Brook had interests besides his farm. He, Robert G. (Archie) McDougal, who homesteaded the section south of

Brook's, and B. S. Phillips, the owner of a small sawmill near Española, formed the Ramon Land and Lumber Company to purchase the Vigil Grant. Brook and his partners paid twenty thousand dollars as a down payment on the fifty-thousand-dollar selling price of the property in 1910 and invested in milling equipment. Brook and his partners surmised that Buckman had left more than two thousand acres of old-growth timber on the grant, which gave the new company a considerable margin with which to work.

Like Bishop and Buckman before them, Brook and his partners saw the timber of the plateau in terms of profit. They hoped to capitalize on the needs of the Atchison, Topeka, and Santa Fe Railroad. To compete with the Panama Canal, the AT&SF planned to increase its efficiency by building an additional set of tracks through the Southwest. Brook and his co-directors realized that despite competition from A. B. McGaffey and the Santa Barbara Tie and Pole Company in the Sangre de Cristo Mountains, the Vigil Grant offered a chance to profit.

But the U.S. government challenged the Ramon Land and Lumber Company. After its initial payment, the company had begun to cut timber on the northern side of the grant. Government officials, claiming that the timber the company cut came from the adjacent national forest, filed a lawsuit against Brook and his partners. In the course of the action, the company went bankrupt, and the United States Bank and Trust Company (USB&T) of Santa Fe took over responsibility for the grant. Napoleon B. Laughlin, a founder of the bank, hired Hiram B. Cartwright, a land speculator from Santa Fe, to supervise the grant, and the two men battled the government in court. Thanks to the efforts of a Washington, D.C., attorney, Patrick Loughran, the USB&T won the case in 1913, but the victory came too late for the Ramon Land and Lumber Company. It dissolved under the strain of the debt it had acquired in the attempt to purchase the Vigil Grant.[33]

Even though the USB&T offered the tract to the highest bidder, the government was loath to acquire land for park or monument purposes. There were too many places of significance in the public domain to spend money to reacquire land. For the time being, little could be done. Tschirege and Navawi'i remained on private land, the Forest Service continued to administer El Rito de los Frijoles, and the Santa Clara Indians guarded Puye.

Ironically, by the time the Ramon Land and Lumber Company disintegrated, Hewett had achieved many of his goals without the help of legislation. Douglass, an explicit threat to Hewett's domain, had used his position with the GLO to put Hewett on the defensive. By preventing Douglass's effort to place his excavation under federal jurisdiction, Hewett could continue his work at Puye indefinitely. Hewett's friends, like A. J. Abbott in Frijoles Canyon, watched the ruins and prevented depredation whenever possible. With close ties to both the Forest and Indian services, Hewett excavated anywhere on the public land of the plateau that he chose. By 1910, he had created the situation that he had sought when he first presented the idea of a national park in 1900. The status quo suited Edgar L. Hewett very well, and he protected it zealously.

Yet as a result of the confusion, the different interests became even more polarized than before. All consolidated their positions, and entrenched, they too fervently guarded what they had. Although Hewett had been successful in stopping an unpalatable solution in the short run, in the long run, the confusion that began between 1906 and 1910 left solutions on the Pajarito Plateau to people with narrower visions and baser objectives.

6

✳ ✳ ✳ ✳ ✳ ✳ ✳ ✳ ✳ ✳ ✳ ✳ ✳ ✳ ✳ ✳ ✳ ✳

Statehood was an important step for New Mexico and its people. After more than sixty-one years of territorial status, a kind
of limbo that both caused and resulted from the unique qualities of the state, New Mexicans became part of the Union. The
sense of membership that statehood conveyed followed decades of attempts to prove that this bilingual anomaly did in
fact belong with the other forty-six states. New Mexicans re-
joiced, if for no other reason than that they could now run their
own affairs.[1]

Despite the cultural differences of the newest state, the
forces of Anglo commerce and industry were well entrenched,
and leaders now sought the perquisites that territorial status
had denied New Mexicans. Down on the list, below total self-
determination and representation in the U.S. Senate, were issues such as a national park that would display the special features of the New Mexico landscape and its unique record of the
human past.

This pork-barrel objective rated high for both of the territo-
ries admitted to the Union in 1912. Arizona and New Mexico
each wanted a national park as a symbolic representation of
their new status. Congressman Carl Hayden led the charge in

Arizona. He sought to convince the GLO that an area between Tempe and Phoenix ought to be designated as a park. Instead, in 1914, that tract became Papago Saguaro National Monument. In New Mexico, Thomas Catron, who had made a successful transition from land-grabber to U.S. senator, also worked toward a national park. Department of the Interior Inspector Herbert W. Gleason inspected the Pajarito Plateau in 1913 and urged Catron to become involved. Catron already had a similar idea. He planned a bill for the following congressional session.[2]

As in previous cases, the new effort began without even a cursory inspection of the corpses left from prior battles. In the aftermath of the Puye debacle, Hewett consolidated his gains on the plateau. His excavations continued, and he continued to train aspiring archaeologists in the ruins. Neil Judd, who later performed important work at Chaco Canyon, spent the summer of 1910 in Frijoles Canyon. Alfred V. Kidder, who began his study of southwestern archaeology with a set of vague instructions from Hewett in 1907, worked at the Frijolito ruin on the south rim of Frijoles Canyon from 1909 to 1914.

Yet there was a more irresponsible dimension to Hewett's training. The School of American Archaeology ran a summer school that in two to three weeks taught the basics of archaeological technique to a collection of students, hobbyists, aficionados, and affluent thrill-seekers. Hewett added to his already extensive support and, in the years following 1910, developed a genuine archaeological empire on the plateau. The government agencies that renewed his excavation permits every year did not challenge him, and most of the other people in the region were not interested in the ruins. An eerie peace settled on the plateau.

Hewett benefited the most from the quiet. He tightened his hold on the region. In 1912, he asked the Forest Service to replace its Frijoles Canyon ranger with A. J. Abbott. Abbott's connection to the Bureau of Indian Affairs made him an important figure to the northern pueblos. He was known for his fairness, and his relations with Native Americans in the area were excellent. Abbott had also become increasingly dependent on Hewett's resources, and the insistent archaeologist had a measure of control over the judge. Hewett knew his interests were safe in Abbott's hands. But the foresters did not comply; despite his son's position in the USFS, Abbott had none of the qualifications necessary for appointment as a ranger. In 1916, the USFS did make Abbott custodian of the ruins, leaving the administration of the national forest to uniformed personnel.

Hewett's power also was manifested in other areas. His opposition to Douglass in the Puye dispute had confused advocates of preservation. Hewett had been their leader, and his opposition to a preservation project forced many to reevaluate their stance. Preservation had become very complicated, quieting park advocates for nearly half a decade.

But statehood and Catron's new power in Washington, D.C., helped gather momentum for a new attempt to establish a national park on the Pajarito Plateau. On February 14, 1914, Catron entered S. 4537, "A Bill to Establish the National Park of the Cliff Cities." Because this measure poorly described the boundaries of the park, Catron soon replaced it with a revised measure, S. 5176. Elsewhere in the capital, the U.S. representative from New Mexico, Harvey B. Fergusson, followed Catron's lead. He authored a companion measure, introduced in the House of Representatives on March 18, 1914.[3]

William B. Douglass headed local support for the new bills. After his inspection of Puye in 1911, Douglass settled in Santa Fe. He joined the local chamber of commerce, the forum for civic-minded leaders of the community. Economic problems persisted even though Santa Fe had begun to become a haven for artists and writers. Railroad promotional efforts had attracted increasing numbers of tourists to the region, and enthusiastic local leaders sought ways to entice more. The cultural base that Hewett helped develop offered one way to increase the importance of the city. Aware of the growing value of tourist travel in the Southwest, the chamber of commerce contemplated a number of development schemes.

The most promising was the bill Catron proffered, a national park that consolidated ruins from the Santa Clara Reservation, the Jemez National Forest, and the public domain. Yet the chamber of commerce had a very different reason for its national park. Unlike Hewett, the chamber wanted a symbol of the unique features of the state with which to continue to develop Santa Fe as a destination for the expanding horde of American travelers.

The West was becoming a vacationland for Americans. Tamed at least symbolically by the institutions of a powerful industrial culture, the West was an icon of the affirmation of progress. As Americans traveled unmolested in this formerly dangerous land, they proved to themselves that their way was right, their destiny was divinely inspired, their values were true and correct, and their actions in the nineteenth century had been necessary.

The expositions that had become a hallmark of American life confirmed this intuition. From Philadelphia in 1876, fairs of cultural validation progressed westward. The first one located west of the Mississippi River opened in Omaha in 1898. St. Louis followed in 1904 with an exhibition to commemorate the centennial of the Louisiana Purchase, and in 1907 and 1908, fairs in Portland and Seattle made the concept of exposition as transcontinental as the Republic itself.[4]

California also made its mark. In 1915, San Francisco celebrated the Panama-Pacific International Exposition while San Diego held its own regionally oriented fair, the Panama-California Exposition. Both of these commemorated the opening of the Panama Canal the previous year. The two cities had been in competition for a world's fair. The smaller San Diego lost but succeeded in working a compromise supporting its more narrowly focused effort. The result was a fair in San Diego that presented the anthropology of the Southwest and Latin America as a means to demonstrate the progress of the human race.[5]

Edgar L. Hewett played a major role in the design of the fair in San Diego. In 1911, during the planning stages, he accepted the post of director of exhibits. It was an ideal situation for Hewett, one that encouraged him to broaden his power base. The San Diegans had money—always in short supply in Santa Fe—and the ability to attract an audience. There Hewett could place some of his protégés, develop support for his interlocking institutions, and again take the lead in transmitting anthropology and prehistory to the American public.[6]

For Santa Feans, the fair in San Diego and Hewett's prominence in it created an opportunity. To reach the fair, anyone traveling from the East had to cross the Southwest, most likely by rail. The railroads had actively promoted travel in the region, which in turn contributed heavily to its growth. The business community in Santa Fe wanted to capitalize on the increase in travel that the fair would create. The organizational arm of local commerce, the Santa Fe Chamber of Commerce, recognized the potential in Catron's bill and actively supported it. Chamber members hoped to use the new national park to attract tourists headed to and from the exposition.[7]

By 1914, Santa Fe had become a culture in flux. The boom in archaeology had increased the importance of the community, and Hewett's status attracted national attention. The location of the School of American Archaeology in a southwestern backwater was a major coup d'état. Hewett, the promotion department of the AT&SF, and Fred Harvey, who managed the hotels that the AT&SF established and who later branched out into his own tourist business, together cultivated the traveling public. Writers and artists continued to arrive in search of an illusory simplicity and purity that they could not find elsewhere. Santa Fe became Mecca for some; its age-old, timeless character appealed to residents of burgeoning American cities, people in search of the essence of life.[8]

Hewett and his peers valued many of the same characteristics, and they fought to keep Santa Fe an anachronism in the modern age. Hewett had an empire in northern New Mexico, and he did not relish being challenged. As it was, the town fit Hewett's temperament and sensibility, and he wanted it populated by people who were sensitive to its blend of cultures. Progress was important, but retaining the character of this unique place held equal significance.

There were only a handful of prominent Anglos in Santa Fe, and they functioned in a tight-knit social world. The chamber of commerce meetings were their forum, and here the owners of the biggest businesses in town made their plans. Their idea of growth and development and Hewett's view sometimes were at odds, but besides the chamber, no other social venue existed. The organization included bitter rivals such as Hewett and Douglass, but personal battles had little place during meetings of the chamber. These people perceived each other as members of the same social class, and polite decorum was the rule during discussions in this gentlemen's forum. No one, not even Hewett, could risk the ostracization of his peers when there were so few local substitutes for interaction.

Hewett had many more responsibilities than the average member of the chamber. Besides the School of American Archaeology and the Museum of New Mexico, he raised money for archaeological expeditions to Central and South America, trained young archaeologists, and supervised digs all over the Southwest. The San Diego exposition gave him another realm of interest, one he readily could mesh with the goals of his friends in Santa Fe.

Hewett and members of the chamber of commerce often found themselves on opposite sides of important issues. Some of these conflicts involved specific issues, but frequently personal distaste overwhelmed genuine disagreement. In particular, Hewett and the president of the organization, Harry Dorman, became fierce rivals. In September 1913, Hewett destroyed a chamber of commerce scheme to advertise Santa Fe as the oldest city in the United States. He solicited the opinions of Adolph Bandelier, Frederick Webb Hodge of the Bureau of American Ethnology, and Charles F. Lummis, who all agreed that Saint Augustine, Florida, was entitled to the distinction of oldest city. Before Hewett's campaign, the chamber of commerce had ordered 12,500 envelopes with the disputed logo printed on them. After Hewett pointed out the discrepancy, the chamber could not use the envelopes. An angry Dorman charged that had Hewett expressed his opposition publicly at the outset, the chamber of commerce would not have ordered the envelopes and would have been spared the cost. Hewett had undermined the chamber at a moment when the organization could ill afford the expense. The chamber was not always a solvent entity. It rented space from Hewett in the Museum of New Mexico, the old Palace of the Governors, but the account was often in arrears. Shortly after the logo incident, Hewett asked the chamber to pay up or leave. Dorman was livid.[9]

Hewett's behavior in this situation was indicative of his confrontational style. He had to win and could be very divisive in the process. Picayune in his adherence to detail and likely to hold others to a higher standard than he required of himself, he was difficult to please. Nor did he battle in a forward fashion. He rarely aired objections in public, instead fomenting opposition in half secrecy. After he marshaled the facts, he went public, often destroying unsuspecting foes and certainly winning their animosity and sometimes hatred. In a small community like Santa Fe, however beholden to the institutions he had established, this approach won him few friends.

Among Hewett's other adversaries was Bronson L. Cutting, the owner of the *Santa Fe New Mexican* and later U.S. senator from New Mexico. After graduating from Harvard, Cutting moved to New Mexico for his health. He bought the *New Mexican* and developed a power base that included former Governor Miguel Otero, the man who ousted Hewett from the presidency of the New Mexico Normal School in 1903. Hewett had a run-in with Cutting in 1910, when he told the newcomer that a man with whom his sister was keeping company was a notorious local womanizer. Cutting gruffly told the older man to mind his own business, and the two developed mutually unfriendly feelings. The logo debacle confirmed Cutting's suspicions of Hewett.

It also gave Cutting an economic reason to dislike Hewett, and this led to accelerated hostilities. The chamber of commerce was an important entity in Santa Fe, and its members were Cutting's advertisers. For reasons of his own, Cutting allowed Dorman to use his newspaper to attack Hewett. Dorman called for Hewett's ouster from both the School of American Archaeology and the Museum of New Mexico and accused Hewett of repeated "intruding and meddling" in an effort to dominate the chamber of commerce. Although Cutting offered Hewett space to respond to the allegations against him, Hewett ignored the opportunity. Predisposed to even the score, he preferred to wait until he could unleash his full fury.[10]

The attack on Hewett was not the end of Dorman and Cutting's assault. On October 27, 1913, the *New Mexican* printed unfavorable opinions of Hewett's character and research in a bold-lined box on the front page. Three of Hewett's leading professional detractors—Franz Boas, one of the most highly regarded American anthropologists, who had resigned from the managing board of the School of American Archaeology in disgust with Hewett two years before; Alfred M. Tozzer of Harvard University, who had worked in Mexico at the same time as Hewett; and George A. Dorsey of the University of Chicago—criticized Hewett's professional standing and his dominance of the Santa Fe cultural scene.[11] The material fueled a drive to oust Hewett.

To some degree, the opposition of Hewett's peers was inspired by professional rivalry; it also resulted from a generally held perception that Hewett debased the profession. Hewett had become very successful in an extremely short time. In a four-year period, he went from the fringe of American archaeology to the position of director of the only institution in the American Southwest sponsored by the Archaeological Institute of America. He also promoted incessantly, in a fashion that many of the more scholarly of his peers regarded as inappropriate. Hewett's efforts made him both powerful and famous, and others certainly resented his advancement. Hewett was never a meticulous scholar, and at this time he rarely published. Those who did not like him characterized him as a charlatan with a smooth delivery and a boisterous swagger.[12]

Seething, Hewett bided his time and prepared for an opportunity to fight back. He took some measure of revenge at the annual meeting of the Archaeological Institute of America in Montreal in February 1914. Dorman had repeated his complaints to Hewett's peers, hoping for a response similar to the one published in the *New Mexican*. But among archaeologists, Hewett had as many supporters as detractors, and Dorman found himself in an untenable position. The eminent classicist Francis W.

Kelsey, a long-time ally whom Hewett characterized as a "rapid fire-gun," humiliated Dorman.[13] Vindicated, Hewett chuckled to himself all the way back to Santa Fe. But he saved the full fury of his retribution for the attempt to establish a national park.

Hewett perceived that the chamber of commerce wanted to intrude on his empire. He believed that Douglass, Dorman, and Cutting were involved in a conspiracy to strip him of his hard-earned position, and although they failed in Montreal, they stood a better chance of impeding Hewett's desires in New Mexico. Cutting had begun to develop the political influence that would lead to a U.S. senate seat two decades later. He was also tremendously wealthy, offering another avenue to build support in the always cash-poor region. Hewett feared Douglass, and Dorman became the object of his contempt. This triumvirate presented a challenge from which Hewett believed he had to protect himself.

Besides the animosity, Hewett and the chamber had different conceptions of the national park. Hewett stressed archaeological research, but the proposal put forward in 1914 was designed to facilitate tourism. As the incident with Cole and Madden in 1901 established, visitors to the plateau were threats to the integrity of Hewett's work. A park for commercial purposes also could curtail his excavations. The chamber of commerce appointed Douglass head of its national park committee, and Hewett decided that the primary goal of the project was to divest him of his empire. He began to clandestinely oppose a national park on the Pajarito Plateau.

The embarrassment in Montreal showed Dorman that Hewett's professional power base was much too strong for local adversaries, but it hardly showed the range of Hewett's influence. Chamber of commerce members did not know that Hewett's ties to the federal bureaucracy were even stronger than his links to the scientific community. Hewett also knew politics in the Santa Fe area and could easily create opposition where none had previously existed. Much to the eventual consternation of Dorman, Douglass, and their supporters in the chamber of commerce, Hewett held the upper hand.

Park supporters nevertheless remained optimistic. Douglass tried to facilitate the passage of Catron's bill. He rewrote it to appease Native Americans, the Bureau of Indian Affairs, and livestock interests. Douglass also tried to pacify growing USFS resistance with a provision that made the Forest Service responsible for the administration of grazing leases within the new park. The Santa Fe community publicly favored the bill, and chances of passage seemed better than they had since 1905.

Then opposition arose in a new quarter. The commissioner of the GLO, Clay Tallman, told Undersecretary of the Interior A. A. Jones, a New Mexican, that the lands in the proposal were too scattered for inclusion in a national park. The chamber of commerce wanted a national park only because Congress would appropriate money for it. Money was not available for monuments. Tallman believed that with grazing allowed, a national park would be indistinguishable from a forest reserve.[14]

Tallman's statement reflected the status of national parks and monuments in 1914. Despite the symbolic connotations of the titles, few of the parks and none of the monuments were carefully managed. No federal bureau was exclusively responsible for national parks and monuments, appropriations for the upkeep and maintenance of the parks were erratic, and there were no departmental employees charged with full-time responsibility for any specific park area. In a number of the western parks, the military provided the existing administration. In 1914, national-park status offered no more protection than did a national-forest designation.[15]

An archaeological national park would have been an anomaly in 1914. Despite the creation of Mesa Verde in 1906, natural areas stood a better chance of becoming national parks. Hewett had authored the Antiquities Act to protect archaeological areas, in the process creating a new category of nomenclature. In the era of the creation of Glacier and Rocky Mountain national parks, the cultural message of the national parks paid little attention to prehistory but instead emphasized the splendor and grandeur of the continent. When Tallman contested the proposal, he expressed the genuine concerns of federal officials.

The Santa Fe Chamber of Commerce responded to Tallman's assertions quickly and vehemently. In a scathing letter, G. H. Van Stone, its secretary, asserted that the lands requested were contiguous, and he assailed Tallman's credibility. Van Stone also objected to Tallman's claim that the area was protected by Indian police and the Forest Service. Both agencies had other priorities. Managing archaeological ruins was a responsibility for which USFS and Bureau of Indian Affairs employees were not trained. Worse, there was no way to restrain collectors. Any institution could request a permit and take away artifacts.[16]

Emotional and hyperbolic, Van Stone made the case for the establishment of a national park. Despite his emphasis on protection, the true aim of the chamber was to attract new visitors to the region. Van Stone was carried away by his enthusiasm. Hewett had already dug Puye and Tyuonyi and had surveyed many other sites. Archaeological science had little place in any park proposed by the chamber of commerce.

The conflict between scientists and commercial interests became public. Since Douglass had arrived in Santa Fe the two groups had been working toward a different end through similar means. The park label was important to the chamber because it connoted national significance. Gradually Americans were becoming aware of national parks, and a park in northern New Mexico could become a good drawing card for travelers, as well as an asset for the forty-seventh state. Veiled in that commercial attraction was the archaeologists' goal, adequate protection for the ruins.

But from Hewett's point of view, the new arrangement was not an advantage. For his purposes, the ruins were already protected. The creation of a national park would bring at least some callous and malicious visitors. He correctly assumed that as long as Douglass and his friends were in the vicinity, preventing depredations might also interfere with his work. In 1914, Hewett controlled the disposition of the archaeology of the Pajarito Plateau. The national park represented a new kind of authority, more potent than those he previously overcame. With Douglass and the chamber of commerce behind the proposal, he could not help but see his previous objective as a threat.

Hewett was of two minds on this particular proposal. The opposition of the GLO diminished the chances of passage, so in a characteristically Machiavellian maneuver, he announced that he favored the park bill.[17] He was not yet ready to challenge the objectives of the hierarchy in Santa Fe, and in essence, the boundaries of the proposal differed little from those that Hewett supported in 1904. Open opposition would harm the alliances he had spent nearly two decades building, and lukewarm support for the bill suited his ends. It was the purpose of the park and its supporters, not its boundaries, that made Hewett wary.

Hewett also wanted some of the credit if the park became reality. If the obstacles were surmounted, an all-encompassing archaeological national park would further the ends of the School of American Archaeology and certainly offer its director greater prestige. A national park would afford better protection for the ruins than they previously received, and if the School of American Archaeology could continue its excavations in at least some of the sites, the new park would be an important triumph. Hewett had originally recommended Mesa Verde as a national park, and if his name was associated with the establishment of the second archaeological national park, he would once again show the range of his influence. He might also catapult beyond the reach of his rivals, possibly even to the pinnacle of his discipline.

By 1914, Hewett had made his mark in the Southwest and sought new areas to conquer. His professional focus shifted away from the Pajarito Plateau. In 1911, he and Sylvanus Morley, one of the first Harvard students who had come for a summer with Hewett, excavated Quirigua in Mexico, and Hewett made plans to go to the Middle East. But he remained the primary builder of cultural institutions in New Mexico, and the plateau continued to be significant to him. It was the place that inspired the quest for understanding that dominated his life. The School of American Archaeology also had its summer school program on the Pajarito Plateau. It offered a convenient training ground for others interested in doing fieldwork and served to broaden Hewett's connections with the professional community and the public.[18]

With Hewett's public support, the project seemed even more likely to succeed. The chamber continued to barrage the Department of the Interior with testimonials to the advantages the park would provide for the Pueblo Indians, as well as the benefits ethnologists and tourists would derive from a resident Indian population within the park. Chamber members regularly informed A. A. Jones of the broad local and national support for the bill, and on April 21, 1914, the chamber passed a resolution requesting rapid proclamation of the park.[19]

Yet there were other forces with which to contend. Congress acted in a typically deliberate fashion, and changing conditions disrupted the delicate stasis. In the spring of 1914, new owners purchased the Ramón Vigil Grant. These affluent easterners altered the balance of power on the plateau. On April 9, 1914, a consortium of prominent industrialists—Roy Chapin, the president of the Hudson Motor Company in Detroit; Henry B. Joy, the president of the Packard Motor Car Company; David L. Gray; and Paul R. Gray—purchased the Ramón Vigil Grant. Ashley Pond, a local dreamer who was also the boyhood friend of the four men, acted as their agent in the transaction and received a one-fifth share of the property.

Pond barely averted a swindle. To settle expenses and realize a profit, the United States Bank and Trust needed fifty-six thousand dollars for the grant. One of the officers of the bank, Frederic "Fritz" Muller, offered Pond the grant for eighty thousand dollars. Pond agreed, and Muller stood to profit twenty-four thousand dollars for merely transferring the land. Santa Fe was abuzz with rumors of the sale, and Pond discovered he was about to be cheated. He circumvented Muller and purchased the grant from the bank for its asking price of fifty-six thousand dollars.[20]

The new owners followed in the pattern of many other wealthy Anglos in the Southwest, fancying themselves masters of a baronial estate. They planned a resort, of which each had a different vision. One wanted a little cabin to live the simple life, and others favored a cross between a cowboy bunkhouse and a modern hotel. With this issue unresolved, Ashley Pond and his family moved to the grant in 1914. They lived in Pajarito Canyon in the old lumber company headquarters, which Pond renovated. Later that year, he opened the Pajarito Club as sort of an embryonic resort. But the four easterners rarely visited, and Pond was unable to run the place by himself. For a time, Harold H. Brook, who was still reeling from the demise of the Ramon Land and Lumber Company, managed the estate while Pond planned his dreams.[21]

The men from Detroit were businessmen, and after they realized that they would have little opportunity to enjoy their land, they decided to make a profit from it. Pond was not equal to the task of management, and his partners never trusted his judgment, particularly when they had to foot the bill. Pond initiated costly improvements that the partners thought were unnecessary. When he tried to buy cattle, which he claimed to need to prevent wild grass from growing rampant over the grant, the four men ignored his telegrams. Pond continued to advocate new expenditures, and the partners soon agreed that their childhood friend's business sense was minimal. Chaos resulted. Although Pond lived at the grant and owned 20 percent of it, he lacked the capital for development. His partners had the resources, but they would not entrust the future of their investment to Pond's whims. As its owners vacillated, the land lay unused.[22]

The Vigil Grant drove a wedge into the heart of the national park proposal. After the easterners purchased the grant, the Department of the Interior again faced a noncontiguous park, this time divided by the recreational estate of the wealthy group. Advocates began a chain of accusations and counteraccusations. Hewett was unhappy: the Vigil Grant included prime archaeological ruins. The Santa Fe Chamber of Commerce believed that wavering by the government caused the loss of the Vigil Grant, and Department of the Interior officials again questioned the validity of the park proposal. As the bickering escalated, other powerful opponents asserted themselves.

The Department of Agriculture strongly opposed the park bill. Secretary of Agriculture D. F. Houston objected that the bill lacked provisions to differentiate the park from a national forest. Because Douglass's campaign to please everyone left the Forest Service in charge of grazing within park boundaries, the administration of the new park was divided between the Departments of the Interior and of Agriculture. This disturbed Houston, who did not object to a national park if the bill included clauses encouraging development but who would not approve a national park that was essentially a national forest under the administration of the Department of the Interior.[23]

When Douglass learned of Houston's objections, he tried to negotiate a compromise. He met with Don P. Johnston, the Forest Service supervisor in the Jemez District, to work out the problems. Senator Catron was also in Santa Fe, and he, Johnston, Douglass, and the national park committee of the Santa Fe Chamber worked out an agreement. Representative Fergusson reintroduced the changed bill on May 14, 1914, as H. R. 16546. With all the interested parties satisfied, the chamber resumed its campaign to sway the New Mexico delegation in Washington, D.C. In letters to Fergusson and Catron, Douglass gushed over the popularity of the measure.[24] The chamber saw its own position enhanced by advocacy and urged immediate passage of the bill.

Although Douglass thoroughly countered local objections, the odds against the establishment of a park remained strong. All the players in the national arena were not yet in agreement. Despite Johnston's cooperation with Douglass and the chamber, Secretary Houston was not convinced of the need for restrictive protection of the Pajarito Plateau. In early June, he expressed his sympathy for the idea to New Mexico Governor William McDonald but also asserted that he did not yet see the need for specific park legislation. The tireless Douglass immediately worked to alter the bill to meet Houston's objections, but in his capacity as a federal surveyor, the Department of the Interior sent him to western New Mexico before he could completely satisfy Houston.[25] Before he returned, new problems erupted.

Officials at the Interior Department had never been convinced that the proposal had merit. The bill had been drawn up without the help of the GLO, and its boundaries included much land already claimed or reserved. When GLO Commissioner Clay Tallman reported to the Senate Public Lands Committee on S. 5176 that July, he expressed additional reservations about the project. A 94,275-acre area in the southern and western part of the proposal did not contain suitable surface ruins, and he recommended its exclusion. This paralleled the request Harold Brook had made in 1909. The park proposal also contained the entire Santa Clara Reservation, requiring an opinion from the Bureau of Indian Affairs. Such a measure assured fair representation of each entity within the department. But Tallman's perspective changed after the summer of 1914. He became a lukewarm advocate, arguing that the park was a good idea because it gave "a uniform jurisdiction" to the ruins on the plateau.[26]

Even with Tallman's grudging concurrence, S. 5176 was far from assured of passage. The bill remained a focal point of controversy at the Department of the Interior. Many within the department thought the bill was too great a compromise. It contained provisions that permitted development of natural resources within park boundaries if economic value was discerned. This vague description set a dangerous precedent and presented future problems. In addition, the Forest Service retained its right to grant grazing permits within the area, another unusual procedure. At the discretion of the secretary of the interior, the Forest Service could also manage areas of the park as if they were part of a national forest. Secretary of Agriculture D. F. Houston consistently objected to this clause, reiterating that if the area was to be a national park, it ought to be reserved as such.

Douglass's effort to appease the Department of Agriculture backfired. By trying to please everyone, he succeeded in raising additional questions, and the half-park, half–national forest area met the needs of no one. The lack of consistency in the proposal fragmented supporters of the park. They agreed only that the principle of a reserved area was a good idea; implementation and administration were far from resolved. Each change Douglass made pacified one group but alienated others.

Ultimately, neither the Department of Agriculture nor the Department of the Interior supported the park proposal with any enthusiasm. It seemed that all Douglass's bill would do was complicate the administration of the region. In October 1914, Assistant Secretary of the Interior Bo Sweeney recommended that a Senate committee reject the bill.

The Department of the Interior lacked an intradepartmental mechanism to properly manage the park. Sweeney asserted that the department wanted to wait until a bureau of national parks was established before pushing the project any further. Then, "competent persons connected therewith" could determine the feasibility of a national park on the Pajarito Plateau. Beginning in 1912, a move for a bureau of parks had begun in earnest, and late in 1914, the founding of a new agency seemed likely. Waiting provided an excellent alternative. Sweeney sent a copy of the letter containing the unfavorable recommendation to Scott Ferris, the chairman of the House Public Lands Committee, along with his request that the House committee table the bill.[27]

Without the support of the Department of the Interior, this attempt to establish a Pajarito Plateau national park was finished. The bills on the floor of Congress did not meet the existing standards of the Department of the Interior. Threatened by the aggressiveness of Douglass and the Santa Fe Chamber of Commerce, and aware of the slew of inferior national parks created during the first decade of the twentieth century, Interior Department officials agreed that the park should not be established. Their decision stalled congressional efforts.

The Department of Agriculture also remained unsympathetic to the entire park idea, and the failure of existing proposals gave Houston an opportunity to develop other plans. He ordered an inspection of the area to find a compromise that preserved ruins and allowed the development of economic potential. A national monument fit the bill. Because Frijoles Canyon was included within the boundaries of the Jemez National Forest, a monument established there would be the responsibility of the USFS. Houston and the Forest Service could protect their domain from the Department of the Interior, preserve the ruins, and help homesteaders and timber and livestock interests.

In July 1915, Will C. Barnes, the chief of grazing for the agency, and Arthur Ringland, the USFS regional forester for Arizona and New Mexico, made the inspection that Houston requested. They visited the region on horseback and discussed the merits of national-park status with Judge Abbott in Frijoles Canyon. Abbott had seen the Catron bill but did not approve of its boundaries. Echoing Hewett's perspective, he thought that the area proposed was far too large. Including Frijoles Canyon, the Stone Lions, and the Painted Cave in a protectorate was sufficient. Around a campfire in the canyon, the men agreed that a national monument was

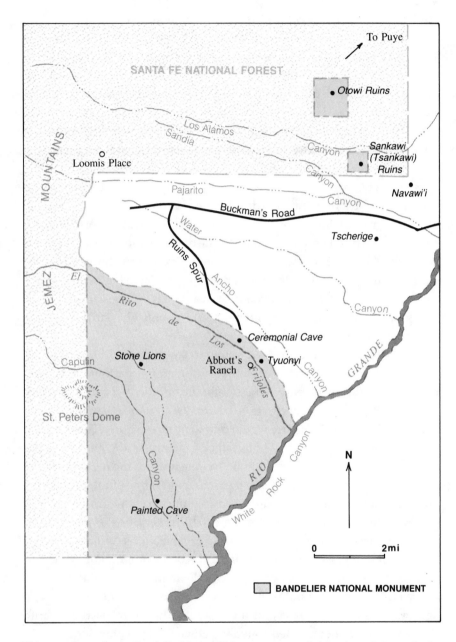

This map, drawn from a Bandelier National Monument map of 1915, shows how poorly the monument protected the prehistoric features recommended in earlier park proposals. Of the four major ruins of the plateau, Puye, Tscherige, Navawi'i, and Frijoles Canyon, only the latter was included in the reserved area.

the ideal solution. Abbott and Barnes then suggested that the area be named for the recently deceased Adolph F. A. Bandelier.[28] After Stephen T. Mather, the assistant secretary of the interior in charge of national parks and soon-to-be first director of the National Park Service, told Secretary of the Interior Franklin K. Lane that the monument idea predated existing park bills and posed no problem if a national park bill later passed Congress, the proposal was expedited. On February 11, 1916, President Woodrow Wilson proclaimed the 22,400-acre Bandelier National Monument.

The monument itself seemed a timely compromise that resolved the issues of the plateau, but in reality it fell far short. The establishment did leave natural resources open to development and protected some archaeological ruins, solving the primary problem of the decade before. But new conditions inspired new views of the value of the region. In particular, the chamber of commerce and Hewett offered different purposes for reserving the ruins yet advocated the same designation. This rivalry superseded the homesteader-preservationist rivalry that the legislation seemed designed to address. The monument solved only the surface issues. Deeper questions remained.

Federal officials also expressed opinions, and their importance in the region had increased. What separated the national park effort in 1914 from that of 1906 was more than a difference in the objectives of advocates. In 1914, federal agencies exerted greater influence than they previously had, and their influence would only continue to grow. The USFS had replaced homesteaders and the livestock industry as the loudest opponents of the park. Forest Service policy set the tone for the region, and the foresters found themselves speaking for a broad range of interests in the area. This new development suggested a significant change in the balance of power on the plateau. Before the establishment of the monument, change occurred because individuals and organizations contacted federal agencies and requested action. The initiation of the monument by the Forest Service indicated a more direct role in the management of the region, as well as the codification of the views of one constituency in a federal agency. These steps meant that increasingly, the future of the Pajarito Plateau would be determined by federal officials, albeit ones sympathetic to the needs of westerners. Federal control of land for the good of people in the region grew in proportion to the increased visibility of the federal agencies that managed land.

This level of management typified the era. In the first two decades of the 1900s, regulation of individual activities by federal agencies seemed the best way to restore the order submerged in the advent of industrialization. In the West, the effort was more pronounced as westerners felt the imposition of values that responded to and were designed for the more populous parts of the nation. Yet despite frequent western recalcitrance, the forces of an institutionalized and regulatory society began to affect western life.

The creation of the monument was a victory for the utilitarian conservationism embodied in Forest Service policy. It suggested that success in the future would come through influence on government agencies. USFS officials and many local residents regarded the park as the prime threat to the commercial development of the region. The USFS alternative stopped the park, melding individual and bureaucratic interests. This fusion of interests suggested an alliance, but in reality, foresters and the people they hoped to help had different perspectives. When faced with a situation that threatened them both, the two groups united. As a result, the monument seemed an appropriate compromise. It protected ruins but did not lock up large areas of the Pajarito Plateau. The vast majority of the region remained open to commercial development. The monument allowed the Forest Service to protect its domain while also offering some ruins special designation. It solved Houston's and Hewett's problems but did little for the chamber of commerce.

No federal bureau yet represented the interests of the preservation advocates. Hewett's park proposal for protection of ruins was dead, but without federal support, so was the park for tourists. The disparate groups that favored preservation and the federal agencies instrumental to its success had not yet developed rapport. Preservation was also a concept that required greater explanation than did conservation. As a result, preservation advocates lagged behind utilitarian conservationists after the USFS took the lead in orchestrating compromise.

In 1916, the commercial value of forest land clearly outweighed the cultural value of ruins on the Pajarito Plateau. A mosaic of interests competed in the region. Only a small minority of Americans were interested in archaeology, and although the prospect of a "lost civilization" on this continent had its attractions, Americans in general did not yet value the heritage of non-Western cultures. National parks had not yet developed into prominent attractions, and their economic value to a region was limited. Their value was largely symbolic. They were places that represented the Anglo-American quest to subdue the continent and that revealed the environment in which mountain men and traders, road makers and civilization builders, horse thieves and land speculators had struggled.

To locals, that quest was real. Area residents were from far the social reforms of the early twentieth century, and only a few appreciated the notion of conservation. The timber and pastureland of the Pajarito Plateau held their future, and to reserve it denied area residents their chance to achieve dreams of prosperity. A national park might be important to a resident of New York City, but to a family dependent on plateau grazing land for its subsistence, a park was a dangerous extravagance.

The establishment of the national monument did not end land disputes on the Pajarito Plateau. It complicated the mosaic, for it gave each interest group, from homesteaders to preservationists, a taste of success. All the participants gained experience and stature as a result of the first battles, and they again tried to put their beliefs into practice.

But the era of individual triumph ended. After 1916, the key to success on the plateau was working relationships with institutions. With the founding of the National Park Service in August 1916, preservation advocates found a federal agency to match the USFS. Two federal agencies with distinctly different points of view spoke for interests in the region. They grappled with a fervor that equaled that of their predecessors. Disputes over the comparative value of the Pajarito Plateau were only beginning to get complicated.

INTERLOCKING

EMPIRES

7

The creation of Bandelier National Monument was an attempt to solve the complex problems of the Pajarito Plateau in a simple fashion. It was a twentieth-century remedy, conceived and promulgated by people with faith in the values of an institutional society. But many in the Southwest did not share this belief. Isolated in an as yet undeveloped sector of the nation, they saw themselves as pioneers in the fashion of their nineteenth-century predecessors. Southwesterners often resented even the government agencies that sympathized with their plight. They had legitimate reasons for their fears. By 1916, the burgeoning federal bureaucracy controlled the fate of public land, and the protests of homesteaders had little direct impact on policy.

The compromise that Ringland, Barnes, and Abbott fashioned was little more than an agreement to disagree on future disposition of the region. But the actors in the drama changed, with federal agencies replacing individuals. No longer would the opinion of people such as Harold Brook be an important part of the dialogue over issues of land use. Instead, the values of federal agencies and competition for administrative control became the dominant motif of conflict in the region.

This struggle typified the West early in the century. Throughout the region, federal officials and agencies sought to promote their sense of the way things should be. At times, their perspectives coincided with those of the people of the region. More often, orchestrating the growth of the West involved establishing federal land protectorates that in effect regulated local economies. Although this hardly affected large landowners, it fostered a pattern of dependence and resentment among the less affluent. It also made average homesteaders far less important than they had been before.

The national monument escalated tension on the plateau. It contributed to the polarization of the federal agencies with the greatest stake in region, the Forest Service and the Park Service. The two had different ideas of the meaning of a national monument. To the Forest Service, which saw itself as the representative of homesteaders and economic interests, a national monument was, in the words of the forester Frank A. Waugh, "frankly a makeshift."[1] The Park Service, which advocated preservation of the area for its cultural value, saw an opportunity for acquiring land and implementing their ideas.

Federal agencies competing for control of the region complicated Edgar L. Hewett's position. Part nineteenth-century individualist and equal portion twentieth-century empire-builder, Hewett found that his personal loyalties, professional objectives, and social conscience were at odds. He needed to find the juncture of his contradictory positions. In a world of absolute values, he had few choices. The emergence of a federal agency concerned with preservation made his situation even more difficult. The Park Service was his logical ally, for he and its representatives believed that the concept of preservation had merit. But the foresters were part of the power base Hewett had developed. He also had to contend with the aspirations of local boosters. Hewett was drawn to both sides in the battle over the plateau.

The establishment of the monument did little to quell the desire of park advocates. William B. Douglass and his friends at the chamber of commerce continued to seek their park, despite their earlier pummeling at the hands of the Department of the Interior. They saw the establishment of the monument as a prelude to eventual park status for the region. After the Barnes-Ringland expedition in the summer of 1915, Douglass, himself hard of hearing, publicly lambasted the Interior Department for its "deaf ear," and the chamber appointed another committee to work for passage of the bill.[2] Douglass founded the New Mexico National Parks Association to further the park effort. There he could speak as a private citizen, and his superiors in the department could not stifle him. Senator Catron soon enlisted in the cause, and in December 1915, while the documents for the monument were being drawn up, he introduced another measure, S. 2542, to establish a national park on the Pajarito Plateau.

Although Secretary of Agriculture D. F. Houston's initiation of the national monument antedated the bill, Catron believed that the public supported his project. He was powerful and, he told himself, popular. Passage of the bill would increase the prestige of the new state. Catron planned to replace the existing monument with a new and larger national park, a scheme that also appealed to Stephen T. Mather, the energetic promoter who became the first director of the National Park Service.

The two men formed a formidable alliance. Mather wielded considerable influence. He had made a fortune in borax and had social and political ties to every important member of Congress. The powerful Catron's support gave the new bill instant national and regional support. The Santa Fe Chamber of Commerce was also thrilled. Without even seeing the new measure, the excited Douglass publicly supported it in a December 1915 letter to the editor of the *New Mexican*.[3]

The new bill again centralized decision making in Washington, and homesteaders and ranchers objected because it ignored their situation. S. 2542 allowed the secretary of the interior to prohibit grazing at his discretion. The Forest Service had begun to regulate range in the West and Southwest, much to the consternation of western ranchers. Hispanos in northern New Mexico were particularly affected. Some of the range that the foresters administered had once been the common areas—*ejidos*—of Spanish land grants. As a result, Hispanos had to come to "La Floresta" to request permits to graze their animals on land that had once been theirs. The prospect that a federal official could whimsically further restrict their grazing did not win the support of homesteaders, ranchers, or leaders of the livestock industries. Some feared that the bill was a ruse that would set a precedent for greater abrogation of grazing rights.[4]

The outcry came from sources that had traditionally opposed the park. Homesteaders and ranchers led the charge. Harold Brook expressed the prevailing point of view in a letter to the *New Mexican*. "The settlers [of the region] contend," Brook wrote, "that the difference between the benefits gained by the judicious handling of the ruins, as they are, and the benefits gained by a park, would not justify the unfair unreasonable ruination of a great many homesteaders."[5] More important than Brook, Frank Bond opposed any bill that could forbid grazing on the plateau.

In the words of a man who once worked for him, Bond was a "tough old buzzard" who built an empire of his own in northern New Mexico. He had come from Canada to join his brother, George, who owned a wool-processing plant at Trinidad, Colorado. Frank Bond ran out of money in Pueblo, Colorado, and took a job painting its courthouse to earn his fare. The brothers later sold their plant in Trinidad and in 1883 started a mercantile business in Española, where they brokered lambs and wool. Their mercantile store carried the most up-to-date farm implements and goods, and Bond shrewdly traded with Anglo, Indian, and Hispano alike.[6]

Shaped by the harsh western environment, Bond was resilient and could often be merciless. After acquiring the common area of the Las Trampas Grant, he disregarded the Hispanos whose families had settled the grant in the 1740s and who retained only their personal plots after his purchase, referring to them as "squatters." Observers of the New Mexico scene rated his altruistic sentiments as nonexistent.[7] Raising sheep also became part of Bond's empire, and before 1900, he financed other people's sheepherding under his version of a Spanish system called *partido*.

Partido à la Bond was typical of the ruthless system that prevailed at the turn of the twentieth century. The system had its beginnings in Spanish practice, but like the environment of the region, it was harnessed to suit entrepreneurs and speculators. *Partido* had been a joint venture in which owner and herder shared profit and loss, a way for a father to help a son get started. Although the system had harsh features in the Spanish era, under Bond it amounted to little more than sharecropping. A herder leased a fixed number of ewes, usually for a three- to five-year period, and paid annual rent, typically three hundred pounds of wool and twenty to twenty-five lambs per one hundred ewes, each of the lambs weighing no less than fifty-five pounds. Although in theory small herdsmen stood to profit, in reality they were impoverished. The system nurtured Bond's empire.

Bond's shrewd business practices gave him considerable leverage over sheepherders in northern New Mexico. By 1900, Frank Bond monopolized grazing land in the region. Each land purchase he made controlled an area ten times as large. *Partidarios* had little choice. They took his sheep along with their own, and Bond assigned all cost and risk to the *parti-*

darios. Their stock served as collateral. Bond collected a fee for each animal on his range, including the ones he leased. *Partidarios* also had to outfit themselves from his store, where he charged inflated prices and a flat 10 percent interest rate for cash loans. Typically expenses mounted, and *partidarios* were fortunate to be able to keep their own sheep at the end of a contract.

When Bond leased national forest land for *partidarios* to run sheep, he made sure the USFS recorded the transaction in his name. After three years of use, forest grazing rights became permanent, and placing the lease in his name allowed him even greater control over the herdsmen who watched his ever growing flock. Soon Bond controlled the best federal range, as well as leases for private land and more than one hundred thousand acres leased from the AT&SF railroad. As Hispanos' access to Indian land was increasingly limited, small stock owners had to become *partidarios* to find grazing land. By the 1930s, only three of Bond's *partidarios* were not deeply in debt. With fewer options for Hispanos, heads of households replaced younger, single men as herders. This change reflected a narrowing range of economic possibilities for Hispanos.

Bond profited in numerous ways from his *partidarios*. He and his companies made money from the lambs that were partial payments for the lease, the rental of rangeland, the sale of rams to herders, the commodities sold in the store at exorbitant prices, the high interest rate charged on debt, the lambs and wool received as payment for debt, and the middleman's fees levied for brokering lambs and wool. Many of the *partidarios* could not pay their debts, creating an immense tax deduction for Bond. His land and sheep were assessed at less than half their value. Controlling the range by ownership and lease and its users by their debts, Bond created an ironclad sphere of economic influence.

Bond worked to preserve this structure. Few *partidarios* fared well, and those who did faced obstacles to prosperity. One found no winter range or lambing grounds for rent. He sold his flock to Bond, who promptly leased it back under less favorable conditions. When another leased only one-fourth of his flock, Bond limited the grazing land available to the man. Such practices perpetuated the system, and Bond became the most influential man in the Española Valley.[8]

As it had earlier elsewhere in New Mexico, commercial sheep grazing changed the environment for the worse. It compounded the earlier effects of cattle grazing and timber cutting and damaged the fragile landscape of the Pajarito Plateau. Sheep climbed steep slopes that more clumsy cattle could not negotiate, and their sharp hooves left tiny, zigzagged trails along the sides of mesas. They sought different plants than did cattle, finding the bunchgrasses of the canyons relatively unpalatable compared with the shortgrasses of the mountains. Like cattle, sheep favored new forage. "Once they get a taste of new grass sprouts," Harold Brook lamented, "they won't eat anything else, [even the] tons of good hay all around." Ponderosa pine, juniper, and piñon overlapped at about seven thousand feet in the plateau area. Although climate and exposure dictated which would regenerate in a disturbed area, the result was an altered environment. At higher elevations, the problem was highlighted. As smaller numbers of cattle began to replace sheep in the 1920s, large numbers of conifers moved onto the south-facing grasslands of the Jemez Mountains.[9]

Perhaps the biggest change that Bond made in the economy of the region resulted from the creation of a system of credit. When Bond allowed *partidarios* to take what they needed against their expected yield, he encouraged the kind of instant gratification that urban industrial Americans had begun to expect. Yet in an agriculture- and livestock-based economy where cash and other sources of credit remained scarce, *partidarios* found themselves with fewer options than did their counterparts in cities. Villagers who had been landowners became debtors. Ironically, an early victim was Alejandro Montes (Vigil), Ramón Vigil's descendant who testified in *Sanchez* v. *Fletcher*. In 1901, Bond sent his attorney to collect a debt that Montes could not pay. The network of institutions that supported the credit system in American cities did not exist on the Pajarito Plateau. In bad times, all that stood between *partidarios* and disaster was the dubious social conscience and generosity of Frank Bond.[10]

Bond's empire grew. In 1908, Bond & Nohl, Bond's store in Española, grossed $41,358.01; a decade later net sales reached $495,369.52. Bond increased his control in the region as well. In 1917, he leased the one-hundred-thousand-acre Baca location No. 1, the Valle Grande, from the Otero family, and in April 1918, he purchased the Ramón Vigil Grant from Chapin and the other Detroit businessmen. One year later, he solidified his hold when he purchased the Baca location.[11]

Both Bond and Hewett now had empires on the Pajarito Plateau, but little strife developed between these two strong personalities. Sheep did not interest Hewett; Bond was scarcely aware of archaeological ruins. The two men saw the value of the land from different perspectives. The twin empires could coexist in the same place because what interested one did not disturb the other. The monument—the status quo after 1916—served both Hewett and Bond very well.

The idea of a national park intruded on this unlikely peace. Hewett's park and Bond's empire could coexist, but the plans of the chamber of commerce posed a threat to both. Their park seemed designed to encircle Bond's holdings, possibly limiting use of the land that Bond needed for his sheep. Since Bond ruled much of the region and was a man who did not like to be opposed, park advocates found themselves in a difficult situation. Bond handled adversaries with celerity, eliminating rival merchants and other competitors with harsh tactics. Those who owed him money knew how wrathful he could be. If such a powerful force believed that the establishment of a national park would have an adverse impact on his business, park supporters faced an uphill battle with residents of the area.

Bond had countered the trend toward federal management of the plateau. With his holdings and an array of leases for federal grazing land, he—not "La Floresta"—held the key to the economic future of the people of the region. His holdings nearly rivaled those of the foresters, and he had the ability to offer credit. Despised, envied, and feared, Frank Bond held sway over a larger portion of life on the plateau than did the USFS.

Bond and the Forest Service both opposed the park idea, but their perspectives were diametrically opposed. Bond did not want more restrictive federal management of grazing land. The Forest Service wanted to continue its programs on the same land, educating the public and managing the resources in its care. Although foresters also feared restrictive management, the loss of their holdings was an even greater threat to the agency. With two powerful entities committed to stopping the park, advocates found themselves with much work to do.

From its inception, the park effort bred surprising alliances, and the latest variation was no exception. After nearly a decade of rivalry, Hewett and Douglass found themselves ostensibly on the same side of an issue. Despite their immense personal dislike for one another, they agreed on one thing: as more people settled the region, the opportunity to protect the ruins of the Pajarito Plateau was slipping away. A national park in the region became a project of singular importance.

But Hewett found Catron's measure unsatisfactory and attacked it in the annual report of the School of American Archaeology for 1915. Although no one in New Mexico responded to Hewett's charges, the potential for conflict between unlikely allies became more evident.

The level of animosity between Hewett and the chamber of commerce seemed to preclude even superficial agreement. In Santa Fe, chamber meetings were the only forum for debate among civic and social leaders. Nevertheless, the lines between the factions blurred considerably as the interests of both sides were threatened. Each side needed the other—neither had much success achieving its objectives alone—and a joining of the proposals seemed to be the best avenue to success. In February 1916, Hewett met with the national park committee of the chamber, still hostile territory, to resolve differences and agree on strategy for moving forward.

Despite their long-standing rivalry, Hewett and Douglass agreed on a number of issues. Neither was satisfied with the way in which the new bill protected Indian rights. They also agreed that the bill must permit grazing in order to mollify Frank Bond and the homesteaders. Local opposition could be fatal. These obvious flaws had to be rectified if the bill was to stand a chance of passage.[12]

The shaky coalition dissolved in minutes. The xenophobia of the turn of the century had not died. Since Catron's bill named the park "Pajarito," chamber members raised an old objection. To their ears, "Pajarito" was no easier to pronounce in 1916 than it had been in 1900. Their goal was to attract the American public. For this purpose, "Cliff Cities" was a better choice of name. Hewett objected as vehemently as he had in 1901, but he held his tongue. There were other issues he thought more important.

Hewett's quiescence and lack of open objection to the various proposals deceived his adversaries. They took his silence to mean compliance when in fact, Hewett remained quiet while laying an elaborate trap for his rivals. He had a score to settle with Dorman, and the circumstances favored him. Of all the chamber of commerce members, only Douglass had experience with the federal bureaucracy. In contrast, Hewett wielded his power like a club. Unbeknown to Douglass and the chamber, Hewett was in the process of leading the park effort astray.

As always, Hewett's issue was the advancement of science, and this gave him a concrete reason to object to the new measure. Parts of the Catron bill seemed specifically designed to stop his fieldwork. To receive his wholehearted support, the new park had to allow the continuation of archaeological research. Catron's bill also prohibited the removal of original and duplicate artifacts from the state, an eventuality that Hewett feared. In building the collection of the Museum of New Mexico, Hewett often exchanged New Mexico artifacts for others. In some cases, he gave artifacts to museums and individuals in an effort to gain support or curry favor. He also sanctioned expeditions, from all over the country, that made collections on the Pajarito Plateau. He had no legal right to do so, but when he began these practices, no one objected. They became an integral part of his empire, and Hewett's cultural cottage industry rewarded him with the gratitude of the museum profession. He could not support a bill that affected the disposition of artifacts.

As a result, Hewett, Douglass, and the chamber agreed that the existing park bill was untenable, and they reached a temporary compromise. They proposed instead a division of the region into four national monuments. Along with the existing Bandelier monument, they requested a Pajarito national monument, north of the Ramón Vigil Grant and including the northern bank of the Guaje River and its ruins. Puye and Shu'finne were to become Santa Clara National Monument while the ruins in the Jemez Mountains were to be included in Jemez National Monument.

Douglass's habit of appeasing dominant influences seemed to have paid off. The collection of national monuments would preserve most of the important ruins on public land while leaving the USFS in charge of enough forested land to implement its mandate. Few in the federal bureaucracy could object to an approach as direct and inexpensive as this one. Grazing interests also stood to benefit from this solution. Frank Bond could continue to run his sheep, and he could lease federal land for stock. Franklin K. Lane, Woodrow Wilson's secretary of the interior, had only to approve, and Hewett's connections in Washington could shepherd the bills to the president's desk. A satisfactory arrangement looked plausible.

Despite the change in tactics, the goal of proponents remained the same. The four monuments were a way station to eventual park status.[13] Yet the coalition lacked the solidity of the opposition. Even though Hewett and Douglass could agree on the principle of a national park, further compromise was necessary if the project was to have a chance to succeed. They also had to be prepared for a backlash from the sheep industry if their effort appeared insensitive to its interests.

The fragile coalition did not last long, and Hewett used the situation to punish his former rivals. Though Hewett knew that Douglass had asked Catron to withdraw the bill so that he could refine it, in April 1916, Hewett republished his earlier attack on S. 2542 in *El Palacio,* the journal of the Museum of New Mexico. This time, everyone in the state who was concerned with cultural questions read the piece, and the battle between Hewett and Douglass resumed with new vigor.

According to Hewett, the bill was poorly conceived and unnecessary. S. 2542 had too many compromises. It had little support in New Mexico, he contended, and passage would unduly restrict archaeologists. The catalyst for an increase in tourism was railroad advertising, not the park designation, Hewett insisted, and no one in the state would gain from the establishment of a national park.[14]

To some extent, Hewett's final point was valid. The promotional efforts of the railroads in 1916 did determine the destinations of travelers more than did the national-park designation. But the argument was a straw man—the timing of Hewett's attack was designed to thwart both Douglass and any national park for commercial ends. Although Hewett contended that he did not make his remarks "in the spirit of opposition," such a public pronouncement from a man of his stature took the issue from the elite of Santa Fe and assured the demise of S. 2542.

After reading Hewett's account of the shortcomings of the new measure, Douglass felt betrayed. He charged that Hewett misled the public. Douglass believed that despite opposition to S. 2542, the idea of a national park on the Pajarito Plateau was popular. He showed that he could count on support from Bond as long as a proposal allowed grazing within park boundaries. The governor of New Mexico and federal officials also supported the project. The park would make a sizable economic contribution to the region, for its many visitors would be fed and lodged in northern New Mexico.

Douglass also attacked Hewett's motive for opposing the bill. Douglass still regarded Hewett as a glorified pothunter, an activity that the bill would stop. Excavators would have to leave the relics they discovered in New Mexico, preventing the kind of wanton excavation that Hewett supported. One such instance occurred at the Otowi ruins in the summer of 1915, where Lucy Wilson, an educator with no prior archaeological field experience, dug in the ruins and collected artifacts for the Philadelphia Commercial Museum. Her crew badly damaged the site. The new bill would end that kind of excavation, Douglass argued, for no one would be able to take artifacts to museums on the coasts. Such a direct attack fired an already tense situation.

Douglass stressed the willingness of park advocates to compromise. He reminded his readers that the New Mexico National Parks Association, of which he was the driving force, had requested the withdrawal of the Catron bill. The proponents knew, Douglass reiterated, that a bill restricting grazing on the plateau would not work. In an effort to salvage support for the project, he announced that he was designing another measure that would satisfy everyone once and for all.

Douglass attacked Hewett personally, renewing the feud that had so recently appeared to be winding down. He charged that Hewett had written the disparaging article only because the Santa Fe Chamber of Commerce rejected Hewett's suggestion to call the park "Pajarito" instead of "Cliff Cities."[15] Douglass contended that Hewett wanted the public to confuse the Catron bill with the concept of a park, thereby protecting people like Lucy Wilson, people who Douglass believed were destroying the remains of prehistoric civilizations throughout the Southwest.

It was as if the two men were back in the Navajo National Monument controversy of 1909, arguing about who should be allowed to excavate the ruins. In the decade since their first confrontation, neither had wavered at all. Hewett still saw southwestern archaeology as his personal domain, and Douglass still insisted that the ruins belonged to the government and that everyone, including Hewett, should excavate only by permission. The two were equally to blame for the impasse; each was adamant that he was correct, and both refused to consider contrasting points of view. Each believed his perspective provided the best solution. But in New Mexico, Hewett held the upper hand.

No stranger to controversy, Hewett once again used his influence to thwart the wishes of his neighbors. His article destroyed the "gentlemen's forum" that had been the center of the dialogue, polarized the different factions, and prevented discussion of the park issue. Hewett's opponents speculated that to preserve his position, he had insidiously worked against the park all along. Hewett insisted that no park was better than a bad one. At the moment when the concept of a national park on the Pajarito Plateau needed all its advocates, they were squabbling with each other rather than furthering their common goal.

Hewett's arguments had surface merit, but closer inspection revealed his idiosyncrasies. By Hewett's definition, his contention that no serious depredations had occurred on the plateau in the preceding decade was true. But he and Douglass defined *depredation* quite differently. Vandalism, to Hewett, was an excavation that he did not sanction. Through the system of permits and the watchful eyes of people like Judge A. J. Abbott, he prohibited such unsanctioned digging. Despite Hewett's often self-serving motives, there were no restrictions on his activity.

Douglass had more rigorous, albeit equally self-serving, standards. Southwestern ruins belonged to the American people, Douglass believed, and he wanted professionals to do the work in such sites. He took a dim view of excavations by untrained people like Lucy Wilson, insisting that only accredited archaeologists should be allowed to dig on federal land. But Douglass was not without the guilt of tainted excavation. He mimicked Hewett's habit of holding others to rules to which he would not adhere. In his role as a surveyor for the GLO, he performed a number of excavations, including one on Chacoma Peak in the Jemez Mountains, a sacred place to Tewa Indians, and another at Ojo Caliente, to the north and well out of Hewett's domain. Hewett later labeled the Chacoma Peak excavation pure vandalism. As the GLO agent S. S. Mathers had noted in 1901, the pot was calling the kettle black.[16]

The question became one of influence, and Hewett's word far outweighed Douglass's. Hewett had spent nearly two decades building a power base in Washington and New Mexico, and if he said that depredations did not occur, then many in the Washington bureaucracy believed him. Hewett was so powerful that despite Douglass's protestations, Lucy Wilson's Otowi excavation continued for two additional summers. Only those who disliked Hewett gave credence to Douglass's shrill complaints.

It was possible to excavate on the Pajarito Plateau only with Hewett's permission, and he sanctioned the work of whomever he chose. He held simultaneous excavation permits for nearly every important ruin in the region. Yet some of those Hewett allowed to excavate were amateurs, no different from men like Cole and Madden, the two who had encroached on Hewett's empire in 1901. Despite Hewett's support, and the fact that *El Palacio* published these excavators' findings, they were real pothunters, the onerous label attached to Richard Wetherill two decades before.

In 1916, Hewett opposed a national park in order to preserve his control of the area. The establishment of Bandelier National Monument had allowed the continuation of his reign. Hewett had vast influence on Forest Service policy-makers, and the protection of archaeological ruins was an ancillary issue to the USFS. The status quo served Hewett's purpose better than any proposed change. The park proposition could have ended

Hewett's rule, for the Department of the Interior would exercise greater control over excavations within the new park. Hewett's power would be threatened, and his ability to oversee excavation curtailed. Hewett could not allow this situation. If he could not grant people like Lucy Wilson permission to excavate, he would lose a major means of building national support among his peers.

The less astute Douglass did not understand the implications of Hewett's behavior, and his attempts to unmask Hewett were largely unsuccessful. Douglass was not privy to the extent of Hewett's maneuvering. He believed that Hewett acted spitefully out of sheer egomania. Douglass recognized that Hewett's article was a ploy to confuse the public in the hope of turning locals against the idea of a park in the vicinity, but he never understood why Hewett created this and other obstacles. Hewett's motives were simple: he supported the idea of a park as long as he had input into its rules and regulations and its creation would not cost him his special position. When Hewett believed a park proposal would strip him of his hard-earned advantage in the competitive world of archaeology, he fought it with the intensity and verve he brought to any conflict.

In spite of the extended controversy and the confusing perspectives placed before them, New Mexicans generally continued to support the concept of a ruins national park. The New Mexico Federation of Women's Clubs offered its support in 1917, and the membership of the New Mexico National Parks Association continued to grow. Although an adverse report from the Department of the Interior killed the disputed S. 2542 at the end of the sixty-fourth Congress, Douglass made inroads in broadening support. But advocates had much to do before they could consolidate their position.

Park advocates believed that modern amenities in the Pajarito region would further their cause. The Pajarito Plateau was still a long way from civilization, and a trip to Frijoles Canyon remained a strenuous undertaking. Travelers took the old Denver and Rio Grande narrow-gage Chili Line railway from Santa Fe to the Buckman crossing in White Rock Canyon on the Rio Grande. Traversing the river was not an easy task. The bridge across the river regularly washed away in flooding caused by snowmelt from the mountains, and by 1916, the existing structure was in danger of collapse. From Buckman, travelers had two options, horse or foot, to cover the last fifteen miles to Frijoles Canyon. Beyond Buckman, water was scarce, and the first four or five miles were straight uphill over the dusty trails cut by Buckman's laborers in 1900. Travelers went across the mesa tops, past the abandoned sawmills of Buckman's enterprise and the Ramon Land and Lumber Company in Water Canyon to the Frijoles Canyon trailhead. During summer or early fall, the most feasible times to visit, the entire trip could be quite uncomfortable.

After 1910, various companies offered tour trips out of Santa Fe. E. J. Ward and a man named Comers, who ran the Rocky Mountain Camp Company, organized some of the earliest. The company began with pack trips and, in the summer of 1914, offered its first auto tours. Frijoles Canyon was the usual destination; at the time, it took more than three hours to drive the twenty-seven miles. Ward owned two touring cars, an Oberlin 85 and 86, the former a four-cylinder, four-seat conveyance, the latter a six-cylinder, seven-passenger model. The company also had a Willy's Overland, a Kripp, and a Chevrolet as well. The tours left Santa Fe before eight A.M. and climbed the Buckman Hill, which was usually in "terrible condition," as one veteran of the trip recalled. The car then wound through Pajarito and Ancho canyons and made its way up to the rim of Frijoles Canyon shortly after eleven. Negotiating the steep foot trail into the canyon took another half hour, and the visitors usually arrived in the canyon at lunchtime. The Judge and Ida Abbott provided a sumptuous noon meal, with fresh fruits and vegetables from the garden they kept, for seventy-five cents to one dollar per plate. The "wonderful feast" was the "high spot" of the traveling day, Ward recalled many years later. After the meal, the guests looked around the canyon, climbed back up the steep side of the canyon or rode out on a burro, got back in the touring car, and returned to Santa Fe.[17]

Not everyone came by automobile, and many of these visitors planned longer stays in the canyon. By traversing the plateau on foot or in a wagon, these people saw more than did the automotive day-travelers. To foot travelers in particular, Frijoles Canyon was an oasis in comparison with the rest of the plateau. Grace Spradling Ireland, who with her husband made the two-day journey from Buckman on foot in September 1917, found Frijoles "a welcome sight for there were 2 or 3 patches of corn & gardens & a small house. But best of all a lovely little stream of water."[18] The canyon was an outpost of relative comfort and familiarity in a world devoid of the accoutrements of civilization.

The experience of people like the Irelands, who made an effort to reach Frijoles Canyon on its own terms, differed from that of visitors who came in automobiles. Because of the difficulty, those who made it up the hills, over the mesas, and down the final steep embankment to Frijoles Canyon had the luxury of being in a world apart from modern life. Frijoles Canyon became a base during their stay, and some of these people made day or overnight trips to nearby sites like the Shrine of the Stone Lions in the Bandelier backcountry. Some, like the Irelands, had their "sleeping apartments up in the caves" and their "kitchen and dining room down by the stream."[19] It was an idyllic existence, far away from the rigors of modern life.

Although visitors like the Irelands loved the brief interlude of solitude in their lives, the archaeologists who worked in the canyon tired of the loneliness and lack of communication with the outside world. Neil Judd, who trained with Hewett and later became an important archaeologist in his own right, remembered the disappointment of a Harvard man who came to the canyon the day after the Jack Johnson–Jim Jeffries heavyweight boxing title fight on July 4, 1910. Having heard that there were Harvard men in the canyon, the visitor gave the Harvard "nine" from the top of the trail into the canyon. Instead of the desired response, all he heard were irritated voices asking who had won the prizefight.[20] Hot, tired, and overworked by the ever-demanding Hewett, the youthful trainees missed the outside world.

Those who came to stay on the plateau left the noises, sounds, and smells of city life behind. They had few preconceptions about the region, since no guidebooks existed to tell them what they could not miss. Arriving by foot or on burro compelled close contact with the physical sentience of the plateau. There were few modern roads, and most of these were merely trails. As visitors moved along the network of thousand-year-old foot trails that crisscrossed the region, they chould choose from the many natural amenities of the plateau. The only fences they had to cross were the borders of their imagination. Their feet raised the dust of the ages as they hiked and rode through the mesas and canyons.

Although most of the visitors were not archaeologists, they could still get a feeling for aboriginal life on the plateau. No one told them not to climb into caves or collect pottery sherds, and many took souvenirs with them. The Irelands found a stone hatchet and a smoothing stone, and "had great sport trying to find enough pieces to make a whole pot."[21] It was an experience that no hotel or resort could equal. While they traveled, visitors gave up the comforts to which they were accustomed and lived a life closer to that of the prehistoric inhabitants of the plateau than to that of their counterparts in New York City. The effort required to reach Frijoles Canyon enhanced the experience for all but the most jaded of visitors.

Although Frijoles Canyon was the most frequent destination, visitors experienced more than the attractions of the canyon. In 1910, Judd reported that black bears roamed all over the region, and mountain lions were also seen. The Irelands, who camped in caves on the way to and from Buckman, heard coyotes howling while they slept and hunted rabbits for their breakfast. Like many, they did not know what to expect when they embarked from the town of Buckman. When they returned, they had acquired a heightened appreciation and healthy fear of the natural world to accompany the feeling that they had seen something truly special. "I was really sorry to leave that state," Grace Ireland wrote as her train made its way over the Raton Pass and into Colorado, "for there had sprung up within me a great liking for it."[22]

As its charm became known, the Pajarito Plateau attracted visitors and settlers alike. Among them was Dick Boyd, E. J. Ward's cousin, who like many other Anglo settlers, arrived in northern New Mexico as a result of problems with tuberculosis. Originally from Indiana, he came to New Mexico from Oregon, after doctors there told him that he would not live another week in its moist climate and probably would not last a month in the Southwest. A year later, he brought eighty-seven registered Morgan mares from Oregon and summered them in the Valle Grande on a lease from Frank Bond. His family, which previously lived in Raton, New Mexico, as well as in Indiana, Oregon, and northern California, soon followed him.[23] After Boyd's parents, John and Martha, bought out the aging Judge Abbott's lease in 1919, Boyd joined Ward's business.

The increase in visitors brought on by touring-car operations accentuated the need to protect the ruins. Visitors meant no harm, but they did collect pieces of pottery during their stay. The number of pleasure-seekers steadily increased, and although the actions of any one of them were of little consequence, as their numbers multiplied so did their impact.

Tourists were both a blessing and a problem for advocates of the park, and increased travel led to more lobbying. Each tourist was a potential supporter of the idea of a park. Each had a congressman and two senators, and most people who came to Frijoles left believing that the ruins ought to be preserved somehow. But greater numbers of tourists each year would have a deleterious effect on unsupervised ruins, and the implications of the compound effect of two decades of visitation were staggering. Douglass and his friends renewed their quest with new urgency. The moment to establish a park seemed to be passing.

The sixty-fifth session of Congress saw the introduction of three new bills proposing a national park. On March 1, 1917, Catron introduced S. 8326, and Congressman William Walton introduced House Bill 3216 shortly afterward, on April 16. New Mexico Senator A. A. Jones, the former undersecretary of the interior, introduced his measure, S. 2291, on May 11. Advocates thought that again they had a solid chance of passage.

The fledgling National Park Service was inundated by propositions for a national park in north-central New Mexico. The phone lines between Capitol Hill and the Park Service offices were constantly engaged as the discussions increased in intensity. The New Mexico State Legislature overwhelmingly supported the national park idea, and Governor W. E. Lindsey drafted a memorial that urged the creation of a national park. In early 1918, with the memorial in hand, Douglass took a leave of absence from the GLO and went to Washington to promote the project.[24]

Douglass faithfully did the legwork as more problems arose with government agencies. On February 26, 1918, Douglass gave the memorial to Secretary of the Interior Franklin K. Lane. He also sent the memorial and copies of S. 2291 to the U.S. forester and the commissioner of Indian affairs. Finally, on March 8, 1918, Douglass met with Horace M. Albright, the assistant to Director Stephen T. Mather of the National Park Service, to discuss the project. Albright was eager to go ahead with the project, but because Puye was part of the proposal, the Park Service had to consult the Bureau of Indian Affairs.

The Park Service was a new entity, and despite its aggressive and innovative leadership, it had little power as an agency. In the late 1910s, it had a two-pronged mission: to promote the existing national parks, and to seek land—usually from other federal agencies like the Forest Service and Bureau of Indian Affairs—for new parks. In tune with the burgeoning consumer ethic that fully emerged as World War I ended, the Park Service had the tools to market the national parks to the American public. But it lacked the organizational structure and influence to achieve that goal.

Indian Affairs officials saw no reason to help this upstart bureau that sought their land, but the ever zealous Albright tried to outmaneuver them. Indian Affairs sought to evaluate the impact of the proposal on the

Santa Clara Indians. Albright was informally told that the superintendent of the Santa Fe Indian School, Frederick C. Snyder, opposed the project. Albright orally requested that the Bureau of Indian Affairs hold its opposition until Albright could investigate further. The bureau acquiesced until early 1919, when the Park Service again asked for approval. The commissioner of Indian affairs explained the delay and informed the Park Service that his office opposed the inclusion of the pueblo in the park.[25]

Despite the opposition, Albright wanted to proceed with the project. The Park Service could circumvent the Bureau of Indian Affairs. Albright made this case in a telegram to Mather: "Regardless of Indian Office believe we should favor Cliff Cities project to extent of delaying final report to Congress pending investigation."[26] But Albright made little progress, and the Department of the Interior rejected the various bills.

New national park bills bloomed during the spring of 1919, and the Park Service began to prepare for its first serious acquisition attempt in the Pajarito region. Senator Jones offered S. 666, "Creating the National Park of the Cliff Cities," on May 23, 1919, and he revived a bill approximating Catron's ill-fated S. 2542 on July 1. Mather decided an inspection was necessary and selected Herbert W. Gleason, who had reported on the region in 1913. Gleason assessed a number of proposed parks in the Southwest during that summer.

Traveling by train, Gleason reached the region in early June to begin his inspection. He visited Bandelier National Monument and the detached sections, Otowi and Tsankawi, as well as Navawi'i, Tschirege, and the other ruins. He also met with Douglass at his camp near Ojo Caliente where the surveyor was excavating a large mound, with the southwestern author Mary Austin in Española, and with Santiago Naranjo, Hewett's old guide who had become the governor of Santa Clara Pueblo. All offered their opinions on the idea of a park, and surrounded by a variety of viewpoints, Gleason added his perspective.

Gleason worried that the ruins might be further damaged by amateur excavators and called himself a "violent advocate" of the park proposal. Protection of the plateau was imperative. What he saw of the work of earlier expeditions greatly influenced him. Gleason was "righteously indignant" when he discovered the way the Wilson expedition had left the site. He was particularly appalled that Wilson had been "heaping up rubbish in the effort to secure pottery relics." When Gleason discussed the matter with Douglass at his excavation camp near Ojo Caliente, Douglass reminded him that the excavators were only educators. No archaeologist himself, Douglass convinced Gleason. Presumably unaware that Douglass lacked credentials, Gleason later insisted that only trained archaeologists be allowed to excavate on government land.[27]

Despite the obvious need for protection of the ruins, Gleason recognized opposition to the project. Even though tension between the Forest Service and the Park Service was escalating, he believed that the livestock industry posed a more significant obstacle than the foresters. Frank Bond vehemently opposed any bill that did not specifically permit grazing within park boundaries. Gleason realized that a compromise with stockmen would further the chances of the park.

Hewett's position puzzled Gleason, and he accepted the explanations then current among Douglass and his clique. Between 1916 and 1919, Douglass had learned much about Hewett's motivation, and his later assessments were closer to the truth. Douglass convinced Gleason that Hewett was inordinately self-serving, and Gleason reported that Hewett's "opposition (concealed) is based on the fact that he will be shorn of his present authority and prestige if the park is created."[28] Gleason knew only what he was told of Hewett's position, and his evaluation did not do justice to the complexities of Hewett's strategy.

Hewett feared any administration that would curtail his privileges. He had been wary of the Park Service since 1916, when Mather had informed Hewett that he could not petition for a three-year excavation permit for Puye. Until Mather had become assistant secretary of the interior, Hewett's requests had been approved without question.[29] Hewett often evinced symptoms of paranoia, and he feared conspiracies. Douglass's relationship to the Department of the Interior did little to quiet his fears. Hewett believed he could not trust the Park Service.

Gleason's activities confirmed Hewett's suspicion that the Park Service meant to stop his work. Santiago Naranjo, the governor of the Santa Clara Pueblo and an old friend of Hewett's, worried that the creation of a park would permit excavators to dig in the burial sites of the pueblo. He complained of indiscriminate digging on the Santa Clara Reservation and wanted "to be able to say to these would-be diggers just where they may dig."[30] Aware of Secretary of the Interior Franklin K. Lane's prior support of Indian rights, Gleason promised the governor that he and his successors would have the authority to prevent digging. Reports of Gleason's promise perturbed Hewett. Despite Hewett's long friendship with

Naranjo, the agreement seemed aimed at curtailing his privileges. If the Park Service became responsible for the ruins on Santa Clara lands, Hewett's summer schools at Puye would be curbed, if not terminated.

For a proposal to succeed, proponents still needed to resolve the grazing issue. Douglass contended that a "no grazing" stance by the Department of the Interior meant no park. He told Gleason to retain a clause permitting grazing in any bill. Mary Austin told Gleason that she believed in "intelligent grazing." Gleason thought that grazing was an overrated issue, for the area was generally a winter pasture for cattle. Sheep pasture was even less of an obstacle. Bond owned most of the sheep in the region, and he grazed them on the Ramón Vigil Grant and the Baca location. Hewett's old friend, Will C. Barnes, chief of grazing for the Forest Service, noted that most of the federal rangeland was inadequate for sheep.[31]

In Gleason's estimation, the threat of conflict over livestock was miniscule. He told Douglass to muster the park supporters and "frame a bill which would incorporate their ideas and then thrash out with Mr. Albright the question of grazing." Douglass took Gleason's advice and implored Albright to allow grazing within the new park. Douglass repeated his contention that without the support of stockmen, the project was doomed.[32]

At its inception, the Park Service had a defensive posture. Mather and Albright developed a conception of the way they wanted to shape the system, but they lacked funds, staff, and organization. As a result, the standards for national parks were not yet formalized, and even though grazing was anathema, particularly in areas with extraordinary natural features, the Park Service would compromise in specific cases. Albright informed Douglass that the latest revision of the bill contained a clause allowing grazing and that he did not see it as a problem.

Douglass was elated by Albright's concurrence, for with the grazing issue resolved, only one source of opposition remained. Hewett continued to oppose Douglass's park projects, publicly focusing on the "Cliff Cities" name. He preferred his own choice, the "Pajarito National Park," believing that the use of Spanish and Indian names ought to be continued. On occasion, he even suggested renaming Bandelier National Monument.

Hewett began to play the two federal bureaus against each other. He still feared Park Service restrictions on his research, and the foresters also worried about encroachment by the Park Service. Mather and Albright had already developed a policy of aggressive pursuit of the transfer of land from the USFS. Hewett joined the Forest Service in what Douglass described as "its effort to defeat this legislation."[33]

Since the creation of the Jemez Forest Reserve in 1905, Hewett had been the primary archaeological client of the USFS. He had great influence among its personnel. Forest Service officials like Barnes were Hewett's personal friends, and the district foresters and the supervisor of the Santa Fe National Forest, Don P. Johnston, greatly respected Hewett. He served as their unofficial advisor on archaeological issues, and by the early 1920s, his word on such matters carried great weight among foresters in the Southwest.

Again protecting his interests, Hewett played an instrumental role in creating the conflict between the Forest Service and the Park Service, a conflict that would dominate the Pajarito Plateau throughout the 1920s. Almost from the day the Park Service was created, a rivalry existed between the two agencies. They had overlapping missions and constituencies and often coveted the same parcels of land for their programs. During the late 1910s, Hewett's constant positioning fueled the existing conflicts, and his prestige gave him the influence to keep the two sides wary of each other. Both sides respected his knowledge and experience, and he manipulated them to his own advantage.[34]

Hewett had always been prescient if not clairvoyant about the forces shaping the future. He realized that institutions and federal agencies were rapidly becoming more important than individuals in the battle for control of the Pajarito Plateau. Even an area as peripheral as this one had come under the influence of industrial America. Hewett's future depended on his ability to get along with whichever side triumphed. He already had important influence over the foresters. Sensing the future power of the Park Service, Hewett learned much about it. When he opposed the park in 1919, he did it through the Forest Service, ensuring that he was not visibly blamed for most problems and that the ones in which he was involved did not cause irreparable damage.

Gleason was far less astute. A minor character in the drama, he was not always aware of the problems that had existed before his arrival in New Mexico. His assessments were too often based on superficial analysis and on the opinion of the last person with whom he spoke. After his discussion with Naranjo, he presumed that the Santa Clara Indians had no objection to the inclusion of their reservation in the national park. In fact, this issue split the pueblo badly. His focus on the stockmen as the primary source of opposition was also off the mark.

He did correctly assess the issue in question. Commercial use of natural resources on the plateau had become the center of the dispute, but the most important adversaries were not the government and local stockmen. Instead, the Park Service and the Forest Service began a divisive battle over the incommensurable values of the plateau. The Park Service emphasized archaeological preservation and inspirational scenery, and the Forest Service focused on commercial timber use and grazing policies.

Gleason inadvertently fed the rivalry, and he received a lesson in bureaucratic tact from Mather for his efforts. On one occasion, Gleason declared that the creation of a large national park in the region was imminent, and when Gleason's comments filtered back to Washington, U.S. Forester Henry Graves was "very much disturbed." Gleason also made Mather's plans public, something that the director preferred to avoid. "It is best to be careful and not commit yourself on propositions like this," Mather cautioned his old friend.[35]

But the damage was done, and Gleason's remarks came back to haunt the Park Service. When Gleason, Douglass, and Mather met in Mather's office in October 1919, the Forest Service hierarchy had begun to object strenuously, arguing that the commercial value of natural resources in the region outweighed any value of preserved ruins. In 1919, the Forest Service remained the more powerful of the two, and the Park Service changed its plans.

Mather looked for ways to establish the national park without starting a war with the Forest Service. At the meeting with Gleason and Douglass, he asked if a park could be created without including any national forest land. It would be possible, Douglass replied, but the new park would lose its most important features. Frijoles Canyon was within the national forest, and Frank Bond owned the Ramón Vigil Grant. The Park Service had no money to buy the grant, and Douglass discounted Bond's altruistic sentiments. This meant that the Frijoles Canyon ruins, Navawi'i, and Tschirege were sure to be left out of the proposal. The group agreed that it would be best to get a national park, no matter what the limitations, and worry about extending it later. Douglass drew up a map and bill for Congress.[36]

Such a rapid ad hoc move created an entirely new set of problems. Expedience instead of any notion of preservation dictated the terms of the latest proposal. Douglass chose the new boundaries by determining which agency had jurisdiction of the lands in question, not by assessing the cultural value of any portion of the plateau. The proposal itself seemed incomplete. Someone had a claim on nearly everything on the plateau. Between national forest land, private grants, and Indian reservations, there was little left from which to create a national park.

The very purpose of the proposed park was at issue, and the Park Service left itself open to questions about its motives. Before the meeting in Mather's office, the ruins of the area provided the reason for creating a park. The latest proposal, drawn up by the leading advocate of the park, at the request of the director of the Park Service, did not include Bandelier National Monument, Otowi, Tsankawi, or Tschirege. Douglass's draft clearly outlined an inferior national park, of the same caliber as Sully's Hill in North Dakota or Platt in Oklahoma. If the new proposal went any further than Mather's desk, it would seem that the Park Service wanted a national park exclusively for the sake of having one. The Department of the Interior owned the reputation of being the most corrupt entity in Washington, D.C., and Mather could not offer its detractors any fresh tidbits.

Douglass's proposal was unsatisfactory, and it led Gleason to suggest a different solution to the problem. In Gleason's assessment, the new proposal was not worthy of national-park status, a sentiment that Mather and others shared. Gleason suggested a tactic that the Park Service would come to favor: ask for a great deal more than can possibly be acquired, and settle for more than was initially thought possible.[37]

From Gleason's perspective, Puye was the primary prehistoric attraction in the region. It was easily accessible, unlike the more spectacular Frijoles Canyon, which could be reached only by descending a steep trail. Gleason argued that any national park established in the region must include the Puye ruins. Once the park was established, adding the existing national monument and the land between the two sites would be a logical step.

During the late 1910s, the Park Service had begun to develop standards for the national park category. Douglass's truncated proposal was clearly inferior to the Grand Canyon, Lafayette (Acadia), and Zion national parks, the latest additions to the system. Encompassing only 60,800 acres of the 195,000 that Douglass had proposed in 1914, the proposed park contained few of the prehistoric features of the region. Some in the agency thought it barely worth the effort to research the status of the lands involved.[38]

During Mather's tenure as director, the Park Service frequently took a pragmatic approach to acquisition issues; in this case, prescient opposition stopped the creation of an inferior park, for which the agency would later have had to apologize. The proposal resulted from more than a decade of special-interest conflict and was not the kind of national park envisioned by Mather. Success in his "park game" remained complicated.

The elevation of New Mexico Senator Albert B. Fall to the office of secretary of the interior in 1921 did not simplify the situation. An advocate of anything that increased his personal estate, Fall had earlier proposed an "All-Year Round" national park, to be created from a disconnected horseshoe of land surrounding his ranch in southeastern New Mexico. Although Fall's project had neither the scenic nor the archaeological importance of the Pajarito proposals, Mather could only tactfully resist his superior's alternative. After the various bills died at the end of the congressional session in 1919, the little time Mather had to devote to a New Mexico national park was spent quietly thwarting Fall.[39]

In the meantime, Hewett worked clandestinely to damage the chances of future park projects. His manipulations were so successful that New Mexico Senator A. A. Jones would become disgusted with the entire idea. First, in 1919, Hewett assisted Jones in drawing up the "Pajarita National Park" bill, which Jones proposed on July 1, 1919. Although Hewett called his offering "a radical revision" which would be "acceptable to everyone," the new measure repeated the folly of S. 2542, the controversial Catron bill of 1915–16.[40] Jones's introduction of the proposal revived all of the livestock industry opposition. Jones felt duped, and his interest in the project waned considerably.

The enthusiasm of New Mexicans for a national park on the Pajarito Plateau also started to ebb. There were simply too many different kinds of interests; satisfying ranchers, archaeologists, and federal officials from three different bureaus in two departments seemed impossible. Some in Santa Fe called Jones's bill an attempt to "muddy the waters" and stymie any future attempts to establish a park.[41] By 1920, there were no bills in Congress to establish a park. Even Douglass was out of ideas, and at the end of 1921, the project looked hopeless.

Between the establishment of Bandelier National Monument and the early 1920s, Hewett's opposition killed every attempt to create a Pajarito

Plateau national park. Although the number of visitors to the region grew, substantiating the very kind of use the Park Service promoted, the new agency did not have the influence to capitalize on the situation. Unsure of its position in the federal bureaucracy, it often acted tentatively. Yet Hewett feared this new agency and particularly its director. He thought that the Park Service planned to restrain his excavations. He applied the full force of his prestige, as well as the knowledge and contacts he gained in nearly twenty years of Washington experience, to stop the project, and the change in his position confused the New Mexico public.

Hewett used insidious methods. He attacked obviously flawed bills when he already knew that proponents of the park had disavowed them, and he proposed measures that stood to rankle important constituencies. He confused the public by putting the full weight of his power and prestige against certain bills while supporting bills that he knew other influential New Mexicans would oppose. His tactics were designed to convince the public that the concept of a national park on the Pajarito was flawed. He created a climate of mistrust in Santa Fe, manipulating senators, congressmen, and government officials. Edgar L. Hewett remained master of the ruins on the Pajarito Plateau.

But an irreversible process of institutionalization had also advanced in spite of Hewett's efforts. Hewett recognized that his ability to control his empire was diminishing. When the Park Service proposed a national park, Hewett relied on the Forest Service and the Bureau of Indian Affairs to oppose it. Soon the different agencies encompassed the points of view that homesteaders and preservationists had earlier advocated. By 1920, the battles for the plateau were no longer fought between ranchers and archaeologists. Mirroring the evolution of the American system, government agencies took over the roles that individual citizens and local and state organizations previously played.

The ever astute Hewett recognized the implications of an institutional society. When twentieth-century civilization, with its roads, telephones, and motorcars, began to encroach on the loneliness of the Pajarito Plateau, he could no longer hold on to his empire single-handedly. The world, and even New Mexico, became figuratively smaller places, more crowded with people. The influence of even the most flamboyant individuals, such as Hewett, decreased ever so slightly.

Hewett had successfully made the transition from nineteenth- to twentieth-century man nearly two decades before. Although he remained an outspoken individualist, he learned to work closely with bureaucratic networks to achieve his goals. Hewett became a back-room politician, and he influenced policy through a vast network of contacts. Instead of doing as he pleased without paying attention to rules, regulations, and laws, he shaped the nature of the bureaucratic system that affected him.

By the early 1920s, Hewett recognized the need for a new ally, and the Park Service seemed the most likely candidate. During the 1920s, the relationship between Hewett and agency officials flourished. Hewett left his old friends at the Forest Service behind and replaced them with more dynamic Park Service people. The result was an alliance that led to the most aggressive effort to establish a national park on the Pajarito Plateau. Ironically, the Park Service–Forest Service rivalry that Hewett fueled from 1910 to 1920 would come back to haunt him as the Forest Service vigorously resisted the next round of land-acquisition attempts.

8

✳ ✳ ✳ ✳ ✳ ✳ ✳ ✳ ✳ ✳ ✳ ✳ ✳ ✳ ✳ ✳

By 1921, Edgar L. Hewett's horizons had outgrown the Pajarito Plateau. The national park for archaeological purposes ceased to be his major concern. In the 1910s, he added the director-ship of the Museum of Man in San Diego to his respon-sibilities, oversaw the creation of the Santa Fe Art Museum, began the Santa Fe Indian Market, and also became chairman of the annual Santa Fe Fiesta celebration. He advanced to the role of administrator, performing less fieldwork but shaping the direction of numerous organizations. Hewett's area of in-terest in archaeology became the Middle East, and although he made occasional forays to the location of his earlier work, the Southwest held few mysteries for him. The region served as the basis for his reputation and the center of his power. He still arranged excavations for students and friends, but such work was no longer crucial to him.[1]

Yet Hewett's position atop the archaeological profession was precarious. Always controversial, he made enemies when he successfully captured the School of American Archaeology for Santa Fe, and his incessant campaigning gave his detractors more ammunition. His work became increasingly suspect. He had been a pioneer in the development of American archaeology, but by the early 1920s, the discipline had begun to pass by him. Hewett clung to its traditional descriptive style, augmented with an interdisciplinary approach that encompassed fields such as ethnobotany and art history. To reflect his broadened perspective, in 1917, he changed the name of the School of American Archaeology to the School of American Research. His discipline, however, followed different lines of inquiry.

The new breed of archaeologists did much more than describe, and some in the Southwest developed reputations that surpassed Hewett's. New techniques led to more sophisticated analysis of archaeological sites, and a burgeoning quantitative science replaced the romantic view of Hewett's era. In the late 1910s, Nels C. Nelson, who had studied with Alfred Kroeber at the University of California, made advances by applying the nineteenth-century archaeologist Max Uhle's technique of stratigraphy to the ruins of the Galisteo basin in northern New Mexico. Soon archaeologists began to consider a chronology of cultural sequences in the American Southwest. Throughout the 1920s, Alfred V. Kidder, one of the first three Harvard undergraduates who had come West to gain field experience with Hewett and had studied under A. M. Tozzer—one of Hewett's adversaries—at Harvard, applied stratigraphic technique to the abandoned pueblo at Pecos, New Mexico. It was the largest undertaking attempted in North America, and from it, Kidder made an array of analytical generalizations that revolutionized the field.[2] Hewett's sentient descriptive writing was replaced by a scientific style: impersonal, cold, and professing objectivity. As the new breed of archaeologists ascended, Hewett became an anachronism, albeit an extremely powerful one.

The changes in American archaeology perplexed Hewett. He was fifty-six years old in 1921, and his appearance reflected his power. Bald, his body filled out to fashionably rotund proportions, his face replete with bulldog-like jowls, Hewett retained his piercing gaze. His associates took to calling him "El Toro," the bull, but only behind his back, and bull-like he was. In his mind, he created southwestern archaeology. Pottery sequences of the kind that Nelson and Kidder worked out did not interest him, and the attention the two men received bothered him. The younger men stole his thunder, and as Hewett got older, he liked challenges even less. His reputation and position were at stake.

The Pajarito Plateau held a special place in Hewett's heart, and he could see it changing rapidly. The population of the plateau increased, as did competition for its limited space. The number of visitors to the region

grew, placing the ruins in greater danger than ever before. The benign neglect of the USFS no longer sufficed to protect the area. With the decline of
the ruins of the region a distinct possibility and with more frequent challenges to his preeminence, Hewett needed the support of a government
agency that valued preservation. The National Park Service (NPS) provided the solution.

Since its founding in 1916, Steve Mather's Park Service had become as
dynamic an agency as existed in the federal bureaucracy. Mather was a
congenial man, a promoter of Hewett's caliber. The Park Service flourished under his tutelage, and Hewett respected its success. Mather had a
vision of a comprehensive park system, and his work brought tourists to
the Southwest in droves.[3] Rail passengers led the way, closely followed
by travelers arriving by automobile.

As Hewett became more involved in the promotion of the Southwest
instead of the excavation of its ruins, his and Mather's objectives inter-
twined. As an administrator of a number of museums, Hewett needed
visitors. He also needed sources of funding for his many operations. Professional rivals could derail his plans if he had to rely on the organizations
they controlled. As a result, Hewett strove for public awareness of the importance of prehistory as he modified the original concept of boon-
bringer into one more applicable in the twentieth century. Despite his fear
of restrictions by the Park Service, Hewett came to appreciate the breadth
of Mather's plans.

Hewett and the Park Service gradually began to work together. During
1921 and 1922, Hewett and Assistant Director Arno B. Cammerer developed a cooperative agreement for the excavation and maintenance of
Gran Quivira (Salinas) National Monument, southeast of Albuquerque.
The NPS had no resources for such a remote monument, and it gave
Hewett a free hand. The relationship worked to the advantage of both
parties, and Hewett recognized that the NPS offered better possibilities for
cooperative efforts than did the USFS. Its programs also protected ruins
from depredation. Hewett liked the Park Service people, particularly the
self-trained superintendent of southwestern national monuments Frank
"Boss" Pinkley, and found them interested in his work and supportive of
his goals.

Small and wiry, with the tenacity of a terrier, Pinkley was a straightfor-
ward perfectionist who managed the fourteen Park Service national monuments scattered about the Southwest. From his base at the Casa Grande,

halfway between Phoenix and Tucson, Pinkley assumed responsibility for natural, archaeological, and historical parks within a fifteen-hundred-mile radius. Among the group were archaeological ruins, a Mormon fort, a Spanish mission, and the limestone caverns of Carlsbad. Almost single-handedly, he arranged for their protection and care. Pinkley inspected all his monuments and performed stabilization work in many of the ruins. At a time when the NPS could not finance work in the monuments, Pinkley secured funding from the state of Arizona for the restoration of Tumacacori Mission. Given very little, Pinkley accomplished a great deal.[4]

Pinkley's conception of the national monuments differed from that of the mainstream in the Park Service. During the 1920s, the Park Service was engaged in a battle for survival with the Forest Service. To build national support, Mather focused attention on the national parks. He believed that places like the Grand Canyon and Yellowstone commanded wider public support than did the archaeological sites of the Southwest. With the national parks as his flagship sites, it was to Mather's advantage to have the most spectacular areas in the park category.[5]

Under Mather, the monument category became a storehouse of potential national parks. Establishing a national monument did not require the congressional approval needed for a new national park. Places originally proclaimed as national monuments were often reassigned to the park category. National-park status meant a built-in national constituency and, generally, funding from Washington. Unlike others in the agency, Pinkley took the nomenclatural distinction between the two categories seriously. He opposed the transfer of monuments to the park category and advocated the division of park areas in accordance with the language of the Antiquities Act of 1906.[6]

Pinkley helped develop the tie between Hewett and the NPS. Before the inception of the Park Service, Pinkley trained himself in the ethnology and archaeology of the Southwest. He knew the first generation of southwestern archaeologists and helped some of them in their work. His respect for Hewett laid the basis for cooperation. Pinkley handled the administration of Gran Quivira promptly and efficiently, eliminating one potential headache for the perennially overextended director of the School of American Research. More important, Pinkley always deferred to Hewett in archaeological matters. Hewett came to respect Pinkley, seeing in the superintendent something of himself.[7] The success of the Gran

Quivira excavation made Hewett comfortable with the NPS, leading to further joint endeavors.

There was little animosity toward Hewett within the Park Service. Douglass had made Hewett into a villain in his correspondence with Department of the Interior and Park Service officials, but their interest in Douglass's personal feelings soon evaporated. The Park Service was a new agency, and out of necessity, its leaders cultivated anyone who could help build a constituency. Although Hewett's opposition to earlier park efforts was public knowledge, his power attracted the agency. He would be an important addition to Mather's ever growing list of friends. The NPS was willing to forgive anything Hewett had previously done if it could count on his future support. Soon Hewett and Arno B. Cammerer's correspondence extended beyond the excavation at Gran Quivira.

The Pajarito Plateau continued to interest Hewett and the Park Service. The frequent defeats of the park proposal in the 1910s had dampened the enthusiasm of the Park Service, and by the early 1920s, Mather had given up on the project. Cammerer got it moving again. He involved Hewett, telling him that the federal bureaucracy was out of ideas.[8] The situation fit Hewett's interests and skills. By the middle of the summer, he had worked up his own proposal, which he transmitted to Robert Sterling Yard, an old friend of Mather's and the founder and executive secretary of the National Parks Association.

Hewett proposed a national park on a scale not seen for more than a decade. The park would include the entire range of natural features and archaeological ruins previously suggested: the one-hundred-thousand-acre Baca location—the Valle Grande, which the Española merchant Frank Bond had purchased in 1919; the plateau ruins, including Frijoles Canyon, Otowi, and Tsankawi; and the Santa Clara Reservation, including the Puye ruins. His proposal, Hewett wrote in hyperbolic fashion, "was the greatest thing possible in the way of a national park project that is left in America. The southwest should not be handed a 'lame duck' among National Parks. What I have indicated is of National size."[9]

Ironically, Hewett now advocated a proposal similar to ones he had earlier opposed. In part the change of heart resulted from his belief that the Park Service protected ruins better than anyone else. In addition, his role as initiator of this idea and savior of the Pajarito Plateau park, if it succeeded, offered him the kind of position he coveted. He could create a national park that would serve his needs and develop ties with another federal agency.

During the 1920s, the Park Service established itself as an agency. Mather's land-acquisition program was very successful in southern Utah, where in 1919, he arranged for the establishment of Zion National Park, followed in 1923 by a Forest Service national monument in Bryce Canyon as a prelude to a national park. The Park Service had taken the Grand Canyon away from the Forest Service and had even established a national park, Lafayette (Acadia), on the coast of Maine. Having already built Santa Fe into a haven for travelers, Hewett recognized that the Park Service was the federal agency of New Mexico's cultural future. He did not want archaeology omitted from what was becoming the preeminent category of American tourist attractions.

Hewett recognized that the task he outlined was immense. The main obstacle was the acquisition of private land, including the Baca location, the Ramón Vigil Grant, sections of the Canyon de San Diego Grant, and the parcel of the Santa Clara Reservation that contained Puye. "You indicated, when we talked this over in Washington, that you would like a big job for the Association to tackle," Hewett challenged Yard. "Well, here it is."[10]

Hewett's maneuvering of the National Parks Association was typical of the way in which he worked with government agencies. He defined the boundaries of the project, suggested a method of attack, began to muster other support, and left the responsibility to others. Without extending himself, he put Yard in his debt and was again close to the sources of power in questions of land use.

Nor was Hewett's power base overrated. With his support, the park project had a much better chance of passage than without it. If he could orchestrate the Pajarito national park after countless other attempts had failed, the Park Service would owe Hewett. He would make new friends in Washington and develop unbreakable ties to a federal agency on the rise. The Park Service would need him as much as the General Land Office had two decades before.

The success of the park proposal would also help Hewett regain a leadership role in southwestern archaeology. Nelson and Kidder had begun to make important inroads, and with the development of dendrochronology, archaeologists more and more fashioned themselves as scientists involved in a self-contained dialogue. A Pajarito Plateau national park would revive the romantic archaeology that Hewett favored.

Hewett's actions during the park controversy in 1919 had defined the battle lines between the Park Service and the Forest Service; ironically, if Hewett had joined the initiative then, most likely a national park on the Pajarito Plateau would have come to fruition. But he had helped the Forest Service establish the grounds to oppose the project, and by 1923, the foresters had consolidated their position. The seemingly insatiable Park Service appetite for Forest Service land scared the foresters, and the Park Service's success at acquisition and with the public was even more frightening. Even Hewett's vast influence could not sway Forest Service officials. They firmly opposed any project that took commercially valuable national forest land and reserved it within a "single-use" national park.[11]

A new kind of confrontation began. Previously, the move to bring the ruins under federal administration had involved efforts to displace individuals in order to include the ruins and the timber of the region. By the 1920s, federal agencies battled each other, not individuals. Homesteaders and herders found themselves outside of the decisions that would determine their future. This was a conflict of abstract concepts, utilitarian conservation juxtaposed with preservation. The debaters viewed regional resources in a national framework and worked within a bureaucratic hierarchy to derive equitable solutions. The needs of the people who derived their living from the resources of the Pajarito Plateau became a secondary concern to the reality of bureaucratic debate.

Resistance to the idea of preservation did not prevent the reawakening of propark sentiment. Hewett exerted powerful influence on the press in New Mexico, and as he predicted, newspapers in the state endorsed the new proposal. The leading supporter was Adela Holmquist of the *Albuquerque Herald*, whose July 15, 1923, article served as a catalyst for the reintroduction of a park bill. She and other park advocates lobbied New Mexico Congressman John Morrow, who in April 1924 went to Cammerer for background information on the bill Morrow intended to introduce.

Aware of the series of debacles that dated to the turn of the century, NPS officials proceeded reluctantly. Before 1923, the Park Service invested tremendous time and effort in park proposals on the Pajarito Plateau. With little to show for the efforts and notable success elsewhere, agency officials placed the Pajarito region near the bottom of their list of priorities. Even with Hewett's support, the time for the project seemed to have passed.

The impetus for a major effort by the Park Service had to come from outside the agency, and Bob Yard was willing to further the initiative. He enlisted the assistance of Willis T. Lee of the National Geographic Society. Lee, who had just finished work at the new Carlsbad Cave National Monument, the focus of another drive for transfer to national-park status, was asked to inspect the Pajarito Plateau. Yard understood the politics of the Department of the Interior and the needs of the Park Service. "A lot of good could be done without in the least forcing Mr. Mather's hand," he explained to John Oliver La Gorce, the vice-president of the society.[12]

The interest of the National Geographic Society convinced Mather, and the park progressed from an objective outlined on paper to one pursued by agency personnel. Although La Gorce specifically forbade the involvement of the society in the politics of the issue, Lee went on a fact-finding tour. He concluded that the Hewett proposal merited support. While New Mexico Congressman John Morrow readied a national park bill for submission, on March 5, 1925, Mather went to the Coordinating Committee on National Parks and Forests, a committee formed to address the increasingly vicious conflict between the two agencies, to ask for the enlargement of a number of park areas. His presentation included a proposal for another Cliff Cities National Park.[13]

The members of the committee played important roles in American conservation. Pennsylvania Republican Henry W. Temple, a staunch conservationist and supporter of the Park Service, chaired the committee. Charles Sheldon, of the Boone and Crockett Club, a well-known conservation organization founded in 1887 by George Bird Grinnell and Theodore Roosevelt, Major William A. Welch, of Palisades Interstate Park Commission, Mather, and U.S. Forester William Greeley rounded out the committee. All the members had myriad obligations, and they often sent representatives in their stead. Some of their replacements did more to complicate issues than to resolve them.[14]

The Forest Service again found itself the subject of a land-acquisition proposal. Mather sought the transfer of 195,000 acres from the usFs for the park. Beleaguered, the foresters fashioned their response. On July 10, 1925, the Forest Service informed Mather that it believed the transfer was unwarranted. usFs officials were willing to concede Bandelier National Monument, "provided its size" called for "separate administration." According to the Forest Service report, the natural features were "admittedly distinctive, but not of such grandeur or impressiveness" to belong in a national park.[15]

The usFs focused on the economic value of the land in the region, in the process usurping the right of the Park Service to determine the attributes of a national park. Foresters asserted that the "sole grounds" behind the park proposal were the inclusion of the various ruins on the plateau. According to the Forest Service, these were of greater interest to the scientific community than they were to tourists. This approach obscured the real objection of the Forest Service: the transfer would damage USFS efforts to develop the economy of the region.[16]

By the 1920s, the Forest Service had emerged as a clearly bifurcated agency with one primary mission: timber management. Equal parts frontier individualist and scientific conservationist since its inception, the agency reflected the values of the era in which it was founded. The wise use of resources was its focus, and programs to manage resources took precedence over other activities. Decentralized administration facilitated the combination of individual initiative and regulatory proscription that characterized the agency.

With the ascent of Frank Pooler to regional forester in 1920, the Southwestern Region embarked on a twenty-five-year period of stabilized leadership. Pooler, one of the last to rise through the ranks of the USFS without graduate training in forestry, earned a reputation as a good administrator as he brought more comprehensive management to the region. In addition, under his direction, many programs long designed but not implemented finally took shape. On the Santa Fe National Forest, permits for grazing were reduced to the carrying capacities determined by reconnaissance surveys by 1930. The transfer of large sections of land would threaten such programs.

Yet on the Pajarito Plateau, the USFS was at a disadvantage. The small community of homesteaders and seasonal users was not as substantive a constituency as elsewhere. The Jemez section of the forest lagged behind the Pecos section, and much of the attention in the western part went to more populated areas such as the Cuba vicinity. In addition, the Forest Service lost a number of its rangers to the Los Alamos Ranch School, which Ashley Pond had begun in 1917. The school offered less isolation, fewer nights in tents, a shorter work year, and better pay. Although USFS programs could have helped meet local needs, the Forest Service focused on areas other than the plateau.[17]

Mather and the Park Service did not deny that the ruins were the primary reason they wanted a national park on the plateau. Mather and his second-in-command, Horace Albright, worked to broaden the bound-

aries of the park category, and the Pajarito Plateau presented an opportunity. Mesa Verde, which had already acquired park status, offered ample precedent for another archaeological national park. From Mather's
perspective, the plateau ruins were as important as those at Mesa Verde.

Bound by the mission of their agency, Mather and his staff also resented
the attempt of the Forest Service to define standards for national parks. If
the Park Service could not broaden the definition of "park-caliber" areas,
the park system would remain small. There were few Yellowstones and
Yosemites, a reality that Mather and Albright clearly understood. The future of the system depended on the outcome of battles like the one developing in northern New Mexico.

In an effort to counter the popular success of the parks, the Forest Service took a dim view of the development of Park Service areas. By the
1920s, cooperation among railroads, hotels, and the Park Service had become the basis of a booming industry. The Fred Harvey Company ran numerous hotels near park areas, rail service to the Grand Canyon was a
great success, and nearly every major park offered services for visitors.
Forestry officials focused on this commercialism as a means to stop the
Park Service. They opposed putting an NPS-style resort hotel in Frijoles
Canyon, appealing to more noble sentiments. The Forest Service, with
the "requirements of the seriously-minded interested visitor in mind,"
hoped to protect the area from commercialization. Only a burro trail
reached Frijoles Canyon, and USFS officials correctly assumed that the
Park Service would advocate the construction of a road to the canyon
floor. Foresters clearly stated that they opposed an automobile road into
the canyon.[18] In their view, accommodations would mar the pristine
beauty of Frijoles Canyon. Hotels and roads made many of the national
parks havens for comfort-seekers, and the Park Service seemed more concerned with catering to its visitors than with protecting the attributes that
brought them. This policy left a gap that the foresters hoped to fill.

Ironically, the agency advocating strict preservation was the same one
that repeatedly argued that commercial use had higher value than preservation. Meanwhile the Park Service, charged with preservation, gained a
broad constituency by accommodating visitors. In an effort to blunt attacks, the USFS argued for less-comprehensive amenities. Although the
Forest Service harbored a small cadre of recreation supporters and a similar group of wilderness advocates headed by Aldo Leopold, such positions were outside the mainstream. The focus of the USFS in 1925 re-

mained timber and grazing. But claiming undeveloped preservation as an objective was the only way the foresters could hope to thwart the Park Service. By conceding that the primary value of the region was its archaeological ruins, the USFS offered substantial evidence that the attributes of at least the monument area superseded any commercially viable natural-resource development.

By 1925, the conflict between the Park Service and the Forest Service had become a long-term quarrel rooted in overlapping missions and constituencies. The Coordinating Committee, charged with sorting out this multifaceted rivalry, held hearings and made an inspection tour of many of the proposed areas. The junket highlighted the nature of the controversy and the growing advantage held by the Park Service in some areas.

One such area was the Grand Teton Mountains. Although the Forest Service willingly ceded the region east of Yellowstone National Park to the Park Service, it opposed efforts to include the Tetons in the park. As a result, Senator Robert N. Stanfield of Oregon, the Senate Public Lands Committee chairman and an opponent of the Park Service, held a hearing in Yellowstone. The hearing gave Arizona U.S. Senator Ralph Henry Cameron, a perennial nemesis of the Park Service, a forum. During the meeting, the committee counsel, George K. Bowden, sought to discredit Horace Albright, Mather's alter ego and the superintendent of Yellowstone. Albright deftly turned the charges around, and L. C. Speers, a reporter from the *New York Times*, wrote an account that favored Albright. Four years later, Grand Teton National Park was established.[19]

In other instances, the committee hearings were equally tense. The level of conflict on the Pajarito Plateau had escalated. USFS supporters sought to strengthen their position by arousing local support before the arrival of the committee. A former Forest Service employee, A. J. Connell, who ran the Los Alamos Ranch School, "started a campaign of defamation" against Mather and the park. Connell was an important person in the region, and his threat to close the school if a national park was created indicated the depth of antipark feelings. Insistent, he convinced some area landholders that the Park Service would seize their land, that no one would be allowed to collect even dead-timber firewood, and that the Park Service would ban private cars from the park and force visitors to pay exorbitant fees to ride the "shrieking yellow busses of the transportation monopolies."[20]

Other than Frank Bond, Connell was the most powerful opponent of the park. The Los Alamos Ranch School was the outgrowth of Ashley Pond's dream of a school for boys. Before taking over Pond's failing concern, Connell had been the district ranger for the USFS at Panchuela in the Santa Fe National Forest, and he was loyal to his former agency. The proposal also presented a threat to his operation. The park would surround the eight-hundred-acre property and might impinge on the one road to the school.[21]

In Santa Fe on September 9, the maneuvering for and against the park escalated into public battle. When the Coordinating Committee came to town, neither Mather nor Greeley was present. Greeley sent Assistant Forester Leon F. Kneipp, one of his closest associates, while Jesse L. Nusbaum, at that time the superintendent of Mesa Verde National Park, represented the Park Service. Hewett chaired the hearing, and Park Service officials were certain they would receive support. Hewett traced the history of previous efforts to create a park in the region and, in an ironic case of rewriting the past by outliving his rivals, pointed out the shortcomings of each. Representative Henry Temple stated that he wanted a reading of local sentiment on the issue. As Temple finished, Forest Service representatives took their cue, and efforts to stymie the establishment of a national park in north-central New Mexico began in earnest.

"The Forest Service had all the objectors to the plan lined up for the meeting," Nusbaum recounted, and they sought to convince Temple that the region was not appropriate for a national park. Nusbaum found himself outnumbered as the situation became increasingly partisan. Hewett, the most important advocate of a national park in north-central New Mexico, chaired the meeting but, in no small part because of a rivalry between him and Nusbaum over what would later become the Laboratory of Anthropology, did not come to Nusbaum's defense. Hewett knew how unimportant one meeting was in the larger scenario, and as always, he preferred to fight behind the scenes rather than in front of an audience. Caught unprepared, the park advocates were leaderless and comparatively unorganized. The meeting was a rousing success for the Forest Service and a disaster for the NPS.[22]

The Forest Service and the Park Service had a complicated relationship, and often valid objections to individual proposals were lost to the childish bickering that characterized interagency relations. The USFS had to defend itself from what it saw as wanton aggressiveness by the NPS, and forestry officials regarded the transfer of land as outright submission. USFS policy began to change during the 1920s as the NPS became a major threat. In part as a response to the successes of the Park Service, the Forest Service began to develop recreational programs of its own.[23] Yet the network that Mather built far outdistanced the comparatively haphazard efforts of the foresters.

The Forest Service opposed creation of the national park because its policy placed economic development above the preservation of ruins. Foresters saw range management and timber cutting as the best uses of the region. Even though the Park Service had a history of making compromises that furthered the procurement of land, by the mid-1920s, its successes made accommodation seem like defeat to the USFS. The polarization of the two agencies precluded a middle position.

The Forest Service had a sizable stake in the region. Homesteaders, stockmen, and timber interests, not tourists from afar, composed its constituency. After two decades of management, the forestry programs that had long-term potential to conserve resources were under way. Systematic lowering of the number of permits meant that the range was in better condition, and Pooler's practice of promoting competition among timber companies helped build the base for a solid economy. To the foresters, professional management of natural resources outweighed preservation of large areas of the plateau. If the archaeological ruins could be administered in conjunction with the use of forest land, then perhaps a compromise could be found. A large national park that restricted the use of natural resources in the Santa Fe National Forest was out of the question.

Settlers supported the stance of the USFS. The population of the region had increased throughout the 1910s and 1920s. Many residents depended on the Forest Service for at least part of their livelihood, and most had little appreciation of the commercial value of the ruins. The aboriginal past was simply part of their lives. Every time they hunted or fished, settlers traveled on prehistoric paths, and when they collected their stock at the end of the summer, they often came across ruins. The sites that were so important to Hewett and the archaeologists were merely landmarks in the lives of homesteaders.

Because their experience with the archaeological past was commonplace, settlers did not see the ruins as culturally valuable. Most were too busy trying to scrape up a living in a world without indoor plumbing or electricity. When settlers came to Frijoles Canyon, it was for a special occasion, like the birth of a baby. The ranger station in the canyon provided contact with the outside world: the telephone there hooked into the Forest Service network, and the government representative afforded a measure of security.[24]

By 1925, the tourist industry in the region had begun to flourish. The Boyd ranch attracted visitors to the canyon, and as automobiles became a common means of transportation, travel time to Frijoles Canyon decreased greatly. Visitors did not stay as long, instead returning to their vehicles and continuing on to other attractions. Some looked over the canyon rim at the steep trail to the bottom, gasped, and drove away. More visitors came every year, and although their experiences were different from those of Harry Field in 1900 or Grace Spradling Ireland in 1917, most still appreciated the special qualities of Frijoles Canyon.

The late 1920s was a critical time in the development of the plateau, for as it became accessible, area residents discovered new options. The Forest Service established its programs as the economic base of the region, but growing numbers of tourists offered opportunities for profit that foresters had not considered. Nusbaum knew that plateau residents realized they could make money from visitors, and he saw a way to cut into local support for the USFS. He was certain his performance in Santa Fe had hurt the chances of success for the park.

Although Nusbaum felt embarrassed, the damage to the park cause was minimal. Temple and Morrow remained strong proponents, even though Morrow was surprised at the strength of the resistance of the USFS.[25] Despite the public battering Nusbaum took, it appeared that the national park long sought for the northern half of New Mexico would become reality. Forest Service representatives knew that Temple's support of the proposal put them at a disadvantage. He was the nonpartisan person on the committee, the only member without a vested interest in the outcome. His opinion outweighed all others.

The rivalry between the two agencies often translated into petty behavior by its representatives, and the trip to the plateau was no exception. Kneipp and Nusbaum each sought to make his case to Temple without the interference of the other. Trapped by what he felt was partisan behavior by Kneipp and the other foresters, Nusbaum complained about the behavior of his counterparts. Their machinations, he asserted, deprived Temple of the opportunity to genuinely experience the ruins of the plateau.[26]

Finally, the group ended up in Temple's quarters to pursue an equitable

resolution. The two sides made their arguments, already stale from re-
dundance. Kneipp gave a long, impassioned speech that denigrated the
importance of the ruins, trumpeted the efficiency of the USFS over the
NPS, and questioned the need to sacrifice forest land to allow a national
park large enough to fit the arbitrary standards that Mather and Albright
had established in earlier cases. Nusbaum forcefully repeated the Park
Service position that the large area was necessary to protect the ruins and
the unique physical features of the area. The time to deal with the question had finally arrived. Like nineteenth-century gunfighters, the men
drew their maps and placed them on the table. The process of compromise began.

The two agencies had very different ideas of what constituted an acceptable size for the proposed national park. The Park Service envisioned
a large area, including the existing monument, the Otowi ruins, the Puye
ruins on the Santa Clara Indian Reservation, the Valles Caldera, and the
land connecting the various features. "The boundaries I laid," Nusbaum
informed Mather, "made the Forestry people gasp."[27]

The counteroffer of the USFS was unacceptable to the Park Service. After much consultation, the foresters were willing to cede only the existing
monument, the Otowi ruins, and a corridor connecting the two, a position that reflected the thinking of Barnes and Ringland a decade before.
Nusbaum immediately rejected the proposal. It did not fit NPS officials'
image of the size and stature of a national park. Kneipp made another offer that included an area east of the Los Alamos school that abutted
Otowi, Tsankawi, and Puye and portions of the national forest between
the Santa Clara Reservation and the Vigil Grant, bordering the detached
Tsankawi section of Bandelier. This compromise offered archaeological
control of the plateau to the Park Service, but it created a disjointed park
that was not contiguous. Nusbaum was at his worst in this kind of situation. He vacillated, turning down the offer in no small part in fear of making the wrong decision. Tired after a long day and a longer evening, Temple suggested that a delay might be a good idea.[28]

Unhappy at what it regarded as an acquisitive, one-dimensional land
policy, the Forest Service refused to capitulate. Even under pressure from
Temple and Morrow, agency officials would not acquiesce. With rudimentary elements of a recreational policy beginning to surface within
their agency, Forest Service officials were not prepared to relinquish forest
land to allow the NPS to develop its programs for visitors. The foresters

were willing to cede archaeological administration, but not at the expense of either the development of natural resources in the area or their own embryonic recreational programs.

The Park Service challenged Forest Service management, claiming that forestry personnel were not prepared to administer such an important part of the natural and cultural past of the North American continent. Park Service officials cited the multitude of USFS interests in the region that detracted from its ability to protect the ruins. A decentralized agency, the Forest Service had a vast domain. It was too much to expect rangers to add archaeology and tourism to their long list of obligations. By combining the archaeological importance of the region with the developing conception of national parks within the agency, advocates made the Bandelier area appear to have the combination of values that equaled national-park status.

The tenor of the nation during the 1920s favored the Park Service. A world of marketed leisure had become part of the ethos of the time, and with vacations and automobiles in which to travel, Americans visited the national parks in search of recreation and symbolic sustenance. The return to normalcy meant a degree of self-indulgence for a larger portion of the population than ever before. With its flamboyant leadership and market-building approach, the NPS reflected the sentiments of the time. The Forest Service and its Progressive-era doctrine did not.[29]

The increasingly widespread support for the Park Service grew out of the perception that the USFS sought to do the work of both agencies. New Mexico Congressman John Morrow noted that USFS resistance created the impression that the Forest Service "endeavor[ed] to set up little national parks of [its] own." In 1928, a USFS administrative declaration that made Bandelier part of one of its wilderness preserves reemphasized that perspective.[30] Since the Park Service had convinced Congress and the public that tourism was its business, such resistance made the Forest Service seem to be interlopers.

What the agencies were really debating was how much additional land would be transferred to the NPS. The USFS had offered Nusbaum the primary archaeological features on national forest land; it was only a matter of time until the Park Service acquired Frijoles Canyon and the rest of the existing monument. Forest Service arguments were typically utilitarian, emphasizing the quantitative economic value of the disputed land. A much less tangible value could be assigned to a national park. Each agency felt it should have priority.

Nusbaum may have made a tactical error when he turned down archaeological control of the plateau, but if he did, the mistake was the result of NPS policy. Mather and Albright had crafted the national parks; by 1925, "parks" were large scenic areas. The archaeology of the plateau offered an important piece of the cultural past, but that alone was not sufficient to include the region in the primary category in the park system. This created a difficult situation for park officials. Although they claimed that they wanted the ruins of the plateau, they really wanted a great deal more. As a result, their requests and explanations seemed incongruous, and NPS plans proceeded slowly.

But slowly the Park Service gained an advantage. The cultural construct of the time favored the style of the NPS, and Mather and Albright had become experts at working with Congress. Morrow was a longtime supporter of the various Pajarito Plateau proposals, and state government officials also showed renewed interest. Hewett provided the state with a comprehensive report on the situation, indicating that he still supported the idea of a large park containing all the important features of the region.[31] Hewett firmed up the alliance with the NPS by adopting the mainstream perspective of the agency. This point of view seemed likely to prevail.

The Coordinating Committee sought a resolution, but for more than a year and a half, there was little progress. Neither agency offered the kind of concessions that could create a compromise. The committee's appropriation to fund inspection tours expired on July 1, 1927, and aware of the deadline, Ringland became impatient. Early that year, he decided to send a Park Service official to study the area one final time.[32]

Frank Pinkley was the only legitimate choice for this task. The Southwest was his domain, and no one else in the NPS had his level of experience with archaeological sites. He built the southwestern monuments with little more than the moral support of his superiors. In addition, he stood to benefit from the acquisition of Bandelier, which would be added to his southwestern national monuments group. At the end of April 1927, Pinkley arrived in Frijoles Canyon to make his inspection.

In his isolation, Pinkley developed a perspective that differed from that of the administrative mainstream in the agency. He was naive about the political realities facing the NPS. In the 1920s, he frequently voiced opinions that made his superiors uneasy, and he drifted far from the prevailing views, but the central administration of the NPS trusted his judgment. Albright in particular expected that Pinkley would echo the departmental line on the proposed park. Pinkley would visit and report that a large park, containing more than archaeological ruins, was essential. Anything less than a park that took in everything of interest on the plateau, from Puye to Otowi to the Valles Caldera, fell short of established standards. A national park on the Pajarito must be archaeologically significant, scenically spectacular, and able to compare with the existing members of the category.

These rigid requirements made it impossible for the NPS to compromise about land acquisition if it wanted national-park status for the Pajarito Plateau. If agency officials omitted the scenic mountainous areas, they could be accused of offering a proposition inferior to Mesa Verde. Yet without the archaeological features, they had no basis for a national park. The scenery in the area was noticeably inferior to the likes of the Grand Canyon, Yellowstone, and Yosemite, and the agency could end up with a national park that recalled disasters like Platt and Sully's Hill. Mather and Albright had prevented such embarrassments since the founding of the agency. There was no room for compromise. The Pajarito Plateau became an all-or-nothing proposition.

Despite Pinkley's frequent public outbursts on behalf of the national monuments, his report shocked the agency. "Boiled down," he wrote after his trip, "my report on the [proposed park] is that the scenery is not of park status and ruins do not make a national park, not in any number, kind or quantity; they make a monument." He reiterated his long-standing contention that the ruins were inferior to those at Chaco Canyon and Mesa Verde and presciently noted that the park seemed designed more for archaeologists than for visitors. A visit there would be "a distinct anticlimax" after a trip to Mesa Verde. Since the Frijoles ruins were already protected, Pinkley thought it best that administration transfer to the Park Service. But he heretically asserted, "I would rather see them left as a monument under [the Forest] Service than be transferred to ours as a Park."[33]

Pinkley could not condone the park effort. His monuments group could not afford the damage that a national park with archaeological features was certain to cause. The "park idea" was inflexible. It left no room for compromise, and in Pinkley's biased opinion, the area simply did not live up to established scenic standards. National monuments and national parks had to be distinct if Pinkley's system was to survive. The conversion attempt represented an effort to minimize the legal and conceptual differences between the two categories.

Pinkley found himself at odds with his superiors on a critical policy issue. His report damaged the entire park effort and created a rift in the ranks. If Pinkley's report became public, it would end any chance of convincing the still intransigent Forest Service people that this was not just another acquisitive move by the NPS. The Park Service could not make a move until it had a response to Pinkley's position. Another study was the logical alternative. Horace Albright, the leading proponent of the project, thought that Pinkley saw the proposal from the narrow view of an archaeologist instead of from the "broader standpoint of a national park executive."[34] In a blatantly partisan move, Albright tried to replace Pinkley with someone he could count on. He suggested Nusbaum, of whose support he was assured, as a more qualified evaluator of the situation. But exhausted by the earlier fray and perhaps afraid of the consequences of another blunder for his career, Nusbaum declined.

As a result, the Park Service shifted the Pajarito Plateau national park proposal into the background. Pinkley's report remained confidential. Even friends of the agency were kept in the dark. On January 17, 1928, Hewett wrote the Park Service to find out if the project was still under consideration. More than six months after Pinkley's report, the most important friend of the proposal in the region did not even know the results of Pinkley's visit.[35]

The question hung in a Park Service–imposed limbo until late 1930, when Albright commissioned another study. In 1929, on Mather's death, he had become the director of the agency, and agency priorities again shifted. The Park Service became even more aggressive, and land acquisition at the expense of the Forest Service was a coveted goal. The Pajarito Plateau rose to the top of Albright's list of priorities, and his national park executives were enlisted. In October 1930, Roger Toll, the superintendent of Rocky Mountain National Park and the primary inspector of national park proposals in the West, M. R. Tillotson, the superintendent of Grand Canyon National Park, and Nusbaum went to inspect the region one more time.

Surprisingly, the three agreed with Pinkley. In their view, the region lacked scenery of the caliber of national parks. "The choice," their report read, "seems to be between having a large and important national monument and a rather small and unimportant national park." Although Cammerer thought that the agency should "aim high and then if necessary come down to what is possible," the report persuaded Albright to put aside the park plans. He accepted the monument because he was "quite convinced" that the NPS "had better not try to get a national park in this section," adding ominously, "at least not now."[36]

An influential Park Service supporter who did not participate in agency politics offered an impartial opinion that confirmed the decision. On February 10, 1931, Dr. Clark Wissler of the American Museum of Natural History and a member of the Committee on the Study of Educational Problems in the National Parks, suggested that the Park Service should focus on the archaeological resources of the region instead of its scenery. In his view, the scenery was not up to national park standards. This innocent admission closed the long-standing discussion, for to have a park significant by agency standards required not only archaeological but also scenic value. Late in 1931, Roger Toll took the lead in ending the controversy when he proposed that the agency accept an offer by the USFS to transfer the monument.[37]

The Forest Service's willingness to offer the monument was no surprise. The USFS was in transition. Its initial generation of charismatic and dynamic leaders had been replaced by their underlings, the people who had executed the orders of the first generation—Pinchot, Graves, and Greeley. Major Robert Y. Stuart, who succeeded Greeley in 1928, typified the problems of succession. A weak leader who had only implemented policy until he became chief forester, he had little experience making executive-level decisions when he assumed the top post. He responded ineffectively in numerous situations. In addition, Stuart had a nervous breakdown in 1932, and his mental state was not good between then and his mysterious fall to his death in 1933. By 1925, the USFS had conceded that Bandelier National Monument ought to be administered by the NPS. All Stuart wanted was assurance that access roads through certain areas would remain open to local residents. He hoped that the transfer would satiate his adversaries and remove the pressure on national forest lands. On February 25, 1932, the controversy was finally resolved. The Park Service took the monument.[38]

The transfer of the monument was a more balanced solution to the problems of the Pajarito Plateau than most of the earlier proposals. It adjusted the existing boundaries of the region to fit preconceptions of the cultural and economic value of the area. By the early 1930s, the NPS had begun informative interpretation programs for archaeology.[39] Both sides could accept NPS administration of the already preserved archaeological features of the plateau, particularly if it meant that the USFS gave up only twenty-six thousand acres rather than two hundred thousand. The Los Alamos Ranch School and the homesteaders in the Jemez barely noticed the change of administration in Frijoles Canyon, and the constituency of the USFS remained intact. The Park Service acquired control of the ruins that had been designated as significant on federal land that did not belong to Native Americans. But the question of the disposition of other archaeological areas in the region remained.

Quickly the Park Service changed its approach. As the NPS took over Frijoles Canyon, agency officials once again turned to the Puye ruins. The most obvious way to make the plateau more important in the overall scheme of the park system was to include the Puye ruins in a new national monument. If the agency created a new national monument at Puye in spite of the adverse economic situation in the nation, Albright would have a logical reason to continue to press for a national park encompassing Puye, the detached Otowi Section, and the main portion of the monument. In the context of depression America, consolidation by expansion became an efficient maneuver.

Although Pinkley's report undermined the park proposal, it also raised the question of the administration of Puye. Pinkley believed that Puye should also be administered by the NPS, and on this point, he and Albright agreed. After Toll, Nusbaum, and Tillotson recommended that the NPS accept the offer of the national monument transfer, Albright set his sites on Puye.

As Mather's assistant during the late 1920s, Albright had lobbied for a Puye national monument. He saw the monument as a prelude to an L-shaped national park containing the ruins between Puye and Bandelier.[40] The "monument-first, then-the-park" approach was not new; it had been a cornerstone of NPS strategy since the inception of the agency. William B. Douglass and the Santa Fe Chamber of Commerce had advocated a similar idea in 1916. As director, Albright determined agency policy, and if he had his eye on Puye, the NPS would make an effort to acquire it. By early 1931, a side issue to the transfer of the monument developed. At Albright's instigation, the agency pursued Puye.

The Santa Clara Indians were firmly entrenched at Puye, and to avoid acrimony within the Department of the Interior, the Park Service needed a legitimate reason to propose the transfer. Administration of the ruins became the issue. Conditions at Puye had deteriorated, as a result of both excavation and mismanagement. Professional advisors on loan to the Bureau of Indian Affairs believed that if there was a way to allow the pueblo to retain the money from entrance fees, the Park Service should assume responsibility for the ruins.[41]

An expert who attested that Puye needed NPS-style professional care was precisely the kind of ammunition the agency needed. Arthur E. Demaray, an associate director of the agency, the liaison officer to the Congressional Appropriations Committee, and an early advocate of the proposal, was put in charge of the attempts to create Puye National Monument. He arranged for a group from the appropriations committee to make a trip to the Santa Fe area. Although not favorably impressed with the idea of a national park, the congressmen were convinced that the NPS should administer Puye. Bowing to the reality of the situation, Demaray became an advocate of the Puye national monument idea.[42]

Demaray's position influenced the vision of agency responsibilities in the northern New Mexico area. Although he did not discount the value of a national park in the Pajarito region, Demaray was a pragmatist. He believed that the Park Service ought to acquire Puye for the value of those ruins, not as leverage to create a national park. If a national park was the eventual result, it would benefit the NPS. If not, at least the safety of the Puye ruins would be guaranteed.

The acquisition effort began. Before the Bandelier transfer, Jesse Nusbaum began to explore the possibility of acquiring Puye. While working on the project in 1930, Nusbaum approached Bureau of Indian Affairs Commissioner Charles J. Rhoads and found him favorable to the idea. In January 1932, after Demaray refocused agency policy, the Park Service pushed for resolution. With the tentative commitment of the Indian Bureau, the position looked strong. The proposal recommended joint administration. The NPS would manage the ruins, but the pueblo would continue to receive revenue collected there and would hold veto power over excavations.

To the surprise of Nusbaum and the Park Service, Indian resistance to government interference in their lives dashed all hopes of acquiring Puye. On February 11, 1932, the Santa Clara Pueblo unanimously voted against turning Puye over to the National Park Service. As a result, Rhoads withdrew the support of the Indian Bureau, and Park Service attempts to add Puye to the park system ended. The solidarity of the pueblo surprised Nusbaum. For more than a decade, the pueblo had been divided into a number of factions. In the face of acquisition attempts, the pueblo united. There was more to the story than the vote itself revealed. Puzzled but undaunted, Nusbaum retrenched.

At a dinner party in Santa Fe in March 1932, Nusbaum found out what had happened to his hopes for Puye. Ed Lowrie, a Washington, D.C., newspaperman studying the problem of law and order in the pueblos for the Brookings Institute, was also a guest. Lowrie and Nusbaum had become friends during Lowrie's stay in New Mexico, and the newspaperman had often made use of Nusbaum's knowledge and contacts. Lowrie saw the factionalization of the Santa Claras as the greatest obstacle to the future development of the pueblo. He decided that the best way to unite them was to find a common adversary for the pueblo to oppose. Unfortunately for Nusbaum, the first opportunity that arose involved Puye.

In 1932, Nusbaum directed the Laboratory of Anthropology in Santa Fe and had not revealed his involvement with Park Service efforts to acquire Puye. At the dinner party, Lowrie boasted that his efforts had stopped the NPS. Nusbaum took Lowrie aside and explained his interest in the project. Lowrie, who was quite beholden to Nusbaum, was stunned. "It was a terrible blow," Nusbaum reported, "and I thought [Lowrie] would pass out completely." Lowrie apologized profusely and professed his loyalty to Nusbaum. But the damage was done, and Nusbaum put the project aside. After the uproar died down, he hoped new attempts to acquire Puye would begin.[43]

But NPS enthusiasm for Puye waned as the reorganization of the federal bureaucracy in 1933 became imminent. The Park Service acquired the remaining Forest Service and War Department national monuments as well as a broad array of other areas, and these efforts monopolized agency attention. The Park Service also faced new management problems. After Albright's resignation to enter private business in August 1933, a new and noticeably less aggressive director, Arno B. Cammerer, took charge. He was in a position similar to that of Robert Y. Stuart at the USFS. The Park

Service had to cope with changes in procedure and policy. With new responsibilities and an important role in implementing federal emergency-relief programs, it shifted away from acquiring land on the plateau.

The failure to acquire Puye signaled the end of Park Service dreams of an archaeological national park on the Pajarito Plateau. All the proposals between 1900 and 1930 were predicated on the fact that only a few people would be affected by the establishment of a park. Most of the land recommended for inclusion in the park belonged to federal agencies. Before 1930, interagency cooperation could have established a park on the plateau. By the 1930s, private citizens owned sizable portions of the land between the major ruins. Park proposals affected the livelihood of more than a few remote settlers. Private landowners became a powerful force that had to be addressed.

The nature of federal administration contributed to the deepening quagmire. Unlike Frank Bond and Edgar L. Hewett, the empires of the Park and Forest services overlapped. Federal bureaus implemented comprehensive plans; Hewett and Bond made more limited use of the plateau. As a result, the two federal agencies were in conflict, but Hewett and Bond, embodying equally different points of view, could coexist. Ostensibly, the question of whether archaeological, recreational, scenic, or natural values should take precedence on the Pajarito Plateau forced the issue. But in reality, the agencies grappled because the plateau facilitated their programs and because orchestrating the situation to their advantage offered both of them important benefits. Resolution solved problems of the moment but set no precedents.

In the broader context of NPS-USFS relations, the Pajarito Plateau situation was anomalous. Frank Pinkley was far from the mainstream, his perspective divergent. Statute, not the evaluation of incommensurable values of land, dictated his position. He had a place within the Park Service to protect, and an expansive national park with the combination of important archaeological ruins and mediocre scenery was as unacceptable to him as it was to the Forest Service. His position and personality helped settle the Bandelier question to his advantage, but in the 1930s he paid a high price for his success.

Yet the battle itself contributed to the development of new barriers on the Pajarito Plateau. The NPS and the USFS fought over what each regarded as its territory, and by defining the region as such, they took large areas of the plateau another step away from the open world of the 1880s.

No matter which of the two agencies controlled a larger portion of the plateau, the rules that they made would determine the use of land under federal jurisdiction. Although the agencies did not build fences to mark the boundary of their domains, they created the psychic equivalent.

The battle over the Pajarito Plateau in the 1920s brought federal agencies to preeminence in the region. Previously the institutions of industrial society had made their impact. As elsewhere early in the new century, the denizens of an ordered, regulated society followed to clean up the mess created by unbridled capitalism and to restore a sense of balance to the affairs of the region. That such institutionalization occurred so late on the plateau was testimony to its marginal status.

By the 1930s, the transfer of power in the region to federal agencies was complete. Previously an economic colony, the plateau became a federal protectorate. This transformation accelerated with the depression and the advent of the New Deal. Frank Pinkley had what he wanted on the Pajarito Plateau, and he quickly began to implement his plans for the Bandelier National Monument. Other federal agencies also contributed. With the help of the federal emergency-relief programs during the 1930s, the Pajarito Plateau flourished in a newly dependent fashion.

9

A stirring speech, the pundits acclaimed Franklin D. Roosevelt's inaugural address in March 1933, and indeed the country responded to the words of the dandy-turned-leader elected the previous November. The problems of the depression were immense, but at least in his words, the new president seemed to understand the gravity of the task he faced. Roosevelt's actions during his first one hundred days in office spoke even louder. In this brief period, he began myriad federally funded programs on a scale never before seen in the United States, revived the flagging confidence of millions of Americans, and permanently altered the role of the federal government in American society.[1]

In the West, the New Deal was a godsend. It offered what had been lacking both before and after the stock market crash: a backbone for tenuous local economies and many opportunities for employment. The array of legislation, the initiation of public works programs, and the generally optimistic climate encouraged westerners. Federal programs built an entire infrastructure for the West, down to the roadside shelters a young Lyndon B. Johnson developed as National Youth Administration director for Texas. Federal agencies received money and labor for countless programs and whole ranges of necessary work that had never before been funded. For individuals, the New Deal offered work with a steady paycheck. For many, it was the difference between survival at home and hobo-like vagrancy.

In a remote periphery like the Pajarito Plateau, the New Deal had vast ramifications. Long ignored and generally undermanaged even by the federal agencies with a stake in the region, the plateau stood to benefit from the new programs. But there was a price to pay. The people who ran New Deal agencies and programs had unparalleled power in the devastated peripheries of the nation. Their expenditures sustained economic life throughout the West, particularly in marginal areas such as the Pajarito Plateau. New Deal funding made the plateau and its people even more dependent on the federal government.

The New Deal offered the Park Service unprecedented opportunities. On the plateau, access to money for development favored the NPS, for the USFS spent the 1920s declaring its fidelity to "pure"—undeveloped and therefore inexpensive—recreation. The Park Service had already selected visitor accommodation as its direction, and New Deal programs allowed it to stress service without spending money allocated to the agency. Emergency Conservation Work funds and Civilian Conservation Corps (CCC) labor performed development work in park areas.

But the opportunities that gave the Park Service hope for the Pajarito Plateau also engendered competition with other federal agencies. The emphasis on capital development catapulted agencies like the Bureau of Reclamation, with its newfound emphasis on the construction of dams, to positions of importance in the federal resource bureaucracy. New agencies and bureaus such as the Soil Conservation Service and the Grazing Service were created to address the specific problems of the 1930s in the West and Southwest: destruction of land, drought, and concomitant economic collapse. Closely matched to the government perception of the needs of time and place, these agencies entered the resource management arena. No matter how great the advancement of the Park Service and the Forest Service in the 1930s, these agencies surpassed them and achieved greater importance in the larger scheme of federal programs.

Yet there were dramatic differences between the vision of conservation of the older bureaus and that of agencies such as the Soil Conservation Service. While the NPS and USFS continued their long-standing practices in the area, the depression-era agencies promoted new ideas. Most clear in the programs of the Soil Conservation Service was a desire to use modern science to solve problems, in the process creating a more stable economy without the traditional cycles of boom and bust. The Soil Conservation Service offered technology as the panacea that would remedy not only a lack of knowledge but also the declining condition of the land. Rather than teach conservation practices, its people proposed to reverse the negative effects of historical practice. As a result, farmers, ranchers, and others could continue as they always had, albeit in a more profitable fashion. In many areas, including the plateau, this was an easier claim to make than to uphold.

There was also a decidedly liberal bias to the New Deal. The needs of Native Americans and Hispanos were addressed in a more comprehensive fashion than ever before. Federal investigators sought to understand the economic problems and social context of life in northern New Mexico before implementing programs in the region. This emphasis was new, and its goals contradictory. Scientific education was supposed to be the means to sustain a preindustrial way of life.

These attitudes created a new kind of dependence on the Pajarito Plateau. There the federal government came to the rescue, as it did elsewhere in the United States, but Franklin D. Roosevelt's goal of priming the pump never occurred. Instead, New Deal money and programs reinforced the tendency of local people to see their predicament as the result of circumstances beyond their control and to look to the federal government for sustenance. On the plateau, federal programs simply transferred the economic and cultural dependence of local people from the institutions of American society to the agencies and bureaus devised by its elected officials.

The economic situation of homesteaders and seasonal users of the plateau continued to decline throughout the 1920s. Between 1905 and 1920, the amount of rainfall in northern New Mexico was far above average. Although this was good for crops, the increase in moisture and its often rapid appearance and equally sudden disappearance contributed to a visible increase in gullying. Overused for decades and inherently fragile and vulnerable, plateau land declined precipitously in productivity. Topsoil, in short supply for more than a generation, washed away even more quickly. With remaining soils already taxed by prior use, a greater concentration of homestead activity, lower value for produce sold on the market, more land in cultivation and grazing, and greater expectations of the peo-

1. This is a later version of a bridge built by Harry S. Buckman across the Rio Grande in White Rock Canyon. These bridges, which washed away almost annually, linked the railroad and the plateau, giving market value to the plateau's resources and initiating a cash-crop homestead economy. Photo courtesy of Los Alamos Historical Museum, photo archive HS 478.

2. Turn-of-the-century visitors had free run of the archaeological ruins on the Pajarito Plateau. Photo courtesy of Los Alamos Historical Museum, photo archive HS 3522.

3. Santiago Naranjo—Hewett's guide "Oyegepi" and governor of Santa Clara Pueblo—climbs the foot trail into Frijoles Canyon in 1908. Photo by Jesse L. Nusbaum, courtesy of Museum of New Mexico #48896.

4. *The Tyuonyi excavation in 1910. Excavators such as Edgar L. Hewett were able to uncover the world to which A. F. Bandelier had awakened the American public. Photo courtesy of the National Park Service, Bandelier National Monument.*

5. *This photograph of a number of plateau homesteads shows a typical level of homestead technology as well as a large personal garden. By the 1920s, these homesteaders had become involved in the market economy. Photo courtesy of Los Alamos Historical Museum, photo archive HS 742.*

6. Successful years on the Pajarito Plateau required cooperation among the extended homestead community. With similar levels of technology and strong cultural ties, residents could rely on each other. Photo courtesy of Los Alamos Historical Museum, photo archive HS 623.

7. The few people of the plateau knew each other well. Here Harold H. Brook, the leading agriculturalist of the region (far left), and Judge A. J. and Ida Abbott pose with visitors on the rim of Frijoles Canyon. The Judge, in the back seat, has the long beard; Mrs. Abbott, in the front left seat, wears the large hat. Photo courtesy of Los Alamos Historical Museum, photo archive.

8. *Harold H. Brook's farmstead shows the financial investment of an aspiring agricultural entrepreneur. Brook was far more technologically advanced and affluent than nearly all of his neighbors. Photo courtesy of Los Alamos Historical Museum, photo archive* HS 437a.

9. *Harold H. Brook was the most successful farmer in the region. By bringing in capital from elsewhere, he could afford to hire his neighbors. There was always a pool of labor available. Here they harvest his beans. Yet even Brook's comparatively vast investment could not protect him from the marginality of his land. Photo courtesy of Los Alamos Historical Museum, photo archive* HS 2845a.

10. Edgar L. Hewett in 1912—approaching his zenith. Photo by Jesse L. Nusbaum, courtesy of Museum of New Mexico #7339.

11. *The Pajarito Lodge, Ashley Pond's dude ranch in Pajarito Canyon. Pond renovated this building, which had been the headquarters of a nineteenth-century ranching enterprise. Photo courtesy of Los Alamos Historical Museum, photo archive* HS *2848.*

12. *Partidarios watch Frank Bond's sheep near the Valle Grande in 1935. Photo by T. Harmon Parkhurst, courtesy of Museum of New Mexico #5454.*

13. *These tents were home to the archaeologists who excavated Frijoles Canyon. Photo courtesy of the National Park Service, Bandelier National Monument.*

14. *The El Rito de Los Frijoles field school in the summer of 1910. Front row from left to right: Sylvanus G. Morley, Kenneth Chapman, Percy Adams, Jesse L. Nusbaum, unidentified, Junius Henderson. Back row: W. W. Robbins, Donald Beauregard, John P. Harrington, Frederick Webb Hodge, Edgar L. Hewett, Neil Judd, Maude Woy, Barbara F. Moracco (Aitkin). Photo courtesy of Museum of New Mexico #81918.*

15. *This lone cabin served the needs of the U.S. Forest Service in Frijoles Canyon. Photo courtesy of the National Park Service, Bandelier National Monument.*

16. *The adobe cabins at the original Frijoles Canyon Lodge were the first visitor accommodations in the canyon. The way in which they fit into their surroundings inspired rumors that Frank Lloyd Wright had designed them. Photo courtesy of the National Park Service, Bandelier National Monument.*

17. *The road into Frijoles Canyon was the critical stage in developing services for visitors on the Pajarito Plateau. Photo courtesy of the National Park Service, Bandelier National Monument.*

18. *This portal provided the only automotive link between Frank Pinkley's development and the ruins farther west in the canyon. A temporary compromise, it was closed before the termination of the* CCC *camp at Bandelier. Photo courtesy of the National Park Service, Bandelier National Monument.*

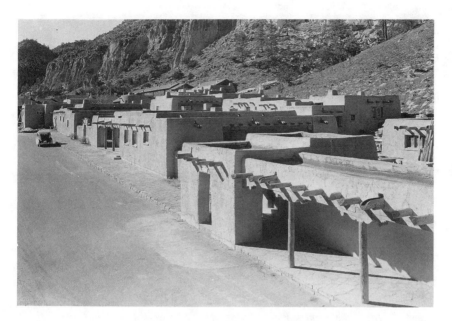

19. *Frank Pinkley's development in Frijoles Canyon nears completion. The complex changed the way visitors approached the area and made the Park Service the most important presence in the canyon. Photo courtesy of the National Park Service, Bandelier National Monument.*

20. *The Big House, as the central building at the Ranch School was called, was the heart of school life. These uniformed students participating in calisthenics attest to the discipline stressed at the school. Photo courtesy of Los Alamos Historical Museum, photo archive R 4169.*

21. *Los Alamos grew dramatically after the war, yet it retained a distinctive military look despite the spectacular scenery. Photo courtesy of Los Alamos Historical Museum, photo archive* EL 1653.

22. *The watchtower and gate at the Los Alamos installation. Everyone who came through the gate needed a pass until 1957, when the facility was opened. Photo courtesy of Los Alamos Historical Museum, photo archive* EL 5958a.

23. An aerial view of Los Alamos in 1969. The community had become a white-collar version of a company town. Photo courtesy of Los Alamos Historical Museum, photo archive RL *5574.*

ple of the region, much of the land in use on the plateau simply wore out. A sustained drought throughout the 1920s and a brutal winter in 1931–32 compounded the problems. By the early 1930s, more than 80 percent of landowners in the Middle Rio Grande Conservancy District were delinquent in tax or mortgage payments. The depression and the dry years of the early 1930s did not cause the problems faced by the people of the plateau, or indeed of the entire southern plains and the Southwest. They simply highlighted the predicament caused by the integration of the plateau into the market economy three decades before.[2]

Yet the standard of living for the average homesteader remained relatively constant. Only in comparison with development elsewhere in the nation had homesteaders fallen further behind in the 1920s. Like other isolated groups in similar places—the Hill Country of Texas, for example—the people of the Pajarito Plateau lived largely in a time vacuum. Minimal contact with the outside world and intermittent exposure to services such as electricity and running water made them anachronistic, as if they were living before the turn of the century.

The conditions under which they lived insulated the plateau homesteaders from the harshest effects of the depression. Most retained an inordinate level of self-sufficiency, and though they remained poor, they depended less on outside institutions for their daily sustenance than did unemployed workers in cities or in the nearby valleys. Most owned their land outright and had for a generation. The Pajarito Plateau was not the heartland of Illinois or Iowa, but it offered a varied subsistence diet from wild plants and homesteaders' personal gardens. Raising their own food set plateau homesteaders apart not only from city dwellers but also from other Hispanos, Indians, and Anglos in the region who had lost their ties to subsistence and were dependent on paychecks. Nor did a return to such an existence significantly damage the self-esteem of homesteaders. For people not far from subsistence, the return to it was less painful and demeaning than for those with closer relationships to the machined miracles of industrial society. During the 1930s, plateau homesteaders did not thrive, but they did survive.

Despite perceptions to the contrary by the Anglo community, in the nearby valleys the depression made life painful. Reliance on the market economy had relegated most natives of the region to livelihoods short of prosperity. Work in beet fields or in mines had become an integral part of life for people in the more highly developed social units in the valleys.

When the depression began, many tried truck farming—direct marketing of their produce—as a way to maintain a livelihood. As their market evaporated, families verged on starvation. Particularly in towns such as Española, people had grown far enough away from subsistence living to be wholly reliant on outside forces. As many as 60 percent of Hispanos in the north needed help from the government. When the institutions of American society collapsed, the very survival of culturally peripheral people in a remote corner of an industrial society was in jeopardy.

New Deal relief programs came close to providing a solution. Although such efforts could not counteract the loss of economic control that Hispanos felt, the Civilian Conservation Corps spearheaded programs that helped. To a degree, federal programs supplanted predepression jobs as the source of cash outside the villages. Vast federal holdings in the region and the previously low levels of funding meant that plenty of work existed when money could be found. The jobs were as physically hard as the Hispanos' previous occupations. The depression supplied the labor, which federal programs provided the dollars to put to work. Hispanos now worked for the government rather than the private sector.

There was no shortage of men for the ccc camps on the plateau. Most of the people in the region were unemployed. Many had been "repatriated"—kicked out of Colorado as a result of their ethnicity—limiting the mobility that had characterized Hispano economic life since the pioneering of the cash economy. In some camps, fathers and sons worked together, but generally ccc programs were reserved for the young. Most workers came from the vicinity of the plateau, and the camps ranged from about 50 to 70 percent Hispano. Only about one of five enrollees was from outside New Mexico, usually from the Texas and Oklahoma panhandles. The workers received one dollar a day—thirty dollars a month—of which they were given five. The remainder was sent home to their families, answering the prayers of the destitute towns of northern New Mexico.

The Española and Pojoaque areas were not exempt from the national trend. There, as elsewhere, businesses disappeared, jobs became scarce, and subsistence existence returned with a vengeance. The influx of ccc-supported dollars initiated the process of restoring the economy. Residents had money to spend, and stores could increase inventories. Slowly, ever so slowly, economic life began anew, supported by federal dollars.[3]

Although rural western communities perhaps provided the best example of the principle of "priming the pump," federal employment also created a long-term problem. Again, workers became dependent on federal institutions, limiting the viability of Hispano systems of self-support. Between 1933 and 1945, many New Mexicans were employed exclusively by the federal government. A sixteen-year-old in 1933 who worked for the New Deal and entered the military during the Second World War could be nearly thirty before the first opportunity to leave government employ arose. The lack of options slowed the development of the infrastructure necessary to wean northern New Mexico from federal money.

But CCC labor solved severe problems for federal agencies in the region. Most found themselves in a difficult position as the 1930s opened. Particularly after the onset of the depression in the winter of 1929–30, the Forest Service lacked sufficient resources to manage all the national forests. Individual forests were still hampered by limited appropriations for fire fighting, trail building, and other management activities, and the timber bust of the late 1920s curtailed an important source of revenue and support for the USFS. Under Forester William Greeley, the Forest Service had courted the timber industry—despite the wrath of Gifford Pinchot, who saw this emphasis as an offense bordering on treason. The agency focused on areas in which the largest companies operated.[4] The western section of the Santa Fe National Forest—the Pajarito Plateau—was not one of these.

The seven-year battle for Bandelier National Monument restructured the division of power in the region. The Park Service had established its presence and, before the end of 1932, had begun its characteristic incremental approach to further acquisition when it sought to add Puye to its holdings. With Bandelier under its administration, the NPS was poised to take advantage of the New Deal programs administered by Secretary of the Interior Harold L. Ickes. The New Deal seemed likely to accelerate the tension between the two leading federal agencies in the region.

Instead, the New Deal and its resources did more to quell the conflict on the plateau than to heighten it. The Park and Forest services, both of which had previously used the figurative equivalent of sticks and stones for armaments in their struggle, found themselves in possession of a much more substantive set of resources. But the new endeavors, the large labor pool, and the sheer amount of money available distracted them from their rivalry. Both pursued intraagency objectives: the deployment of the largess that the New Deal granted and the creation of a system to administer it. The Park Service nearly doubled in size as the result of Executive Order 6166, which transferred everything in the federal system that resembled a park area to the NPS. This meant additional burdens on an already understaffed agency. There were more than one hundred CCC and Emergency Conservation Work camps and side camps in the park system, and more than seven hundred in the national forests. These new responsibilities meant that despite increasing levels of animosity between the Department of the Interior and the Department of Agriculture, the two agencies had little time to fight—except in notable cases such as the Olympic National Park controversy.[5]

The vast funding spurred improvements on federal land, improvements that during the 1920s could not have been considered. For park areas in the West and Southwest, the 1930s became the pivotal decade for development. With New Deal money, areas outside of prior development could finally be integrated into the mosaic of parks that the Park Service promoted. Archaeological areas, long left out of the mainstream, especially benefited.

For the Forest Service, New Deal programs such as those on the plateau were a mixed blessing. In the midst of a crisis in leadership in 1933, the USFS faced significant problems. Because of the vast acreage under its administration, most CCC camps were located in national forests. A decentralized agency with limited personnel, the Forest Service had little experience with large-scale programs of development. Although the national forests had many needs, the emphasis of the agency on timber production continued to preclude other kinds of use. As a result, when the USFS received the CCC, it had few activities suitable for the large number of enrollees available. New programs were necessary.[6]

In the West, better control of fires became the primary goal. Before the New Deal, fire fighting was a haphazard affair. As the agency developed into a bureaucracy in the 1910s and 1920s, its leaders devised an internal system to govern its response to wildfire. Fire policy for the agency was based on the twin ideals of efficiency and science. Yet reality often fell short of planning. Crews were not always reliable. The Forest Service never had enough people to fight major fires on its own, and local help was often limited and undependable. Worse was the assistance available in most emergencies. The pool of unskilled labor in the area became the major source of temporary fire fighters. These Emergency Fire Fighters were marginally useful at best, but they were all that was available under the circumstances. Despite USFS emphasis on utilitarian conservation and the widespread belief that aggressive action against fires cut economic losses, no cadre of trained professionals existed. The USFS lacked sufficient resources.

The CCC solved that problem: enrollees in the camps were trained to fight fires while the programs provided the necessary structural support. The USFS formed special fire-fighting groups from CCC camps, called "Hot Shots." Enrollees took pride in this distinction. Besides actually fighting fires, the CCC enrollees developed the roads, trails, fuel breaks, and other mechanisms that became the basis of the USFS system. Fire management allowed the Forest Service to deploy CCC labor throughout the national forests, not only constructing facilities but also staffing them. It expanded the type and quantity of land the USFS could protect, including that with only marginal economic value. The CCC mandated projects that had previously ranked at the bottom of priority lists. There was no reason not to undertake such programs.

One inherent issue haunted USFS fire policy. The Forest Service was in an ideal situation, but it was temporary. The USFS could create expensive, labor-intensive programs without regard to cost, but when the last of the CCC camps closed in 1942, the Forest Service lacked the money and work force to continue at the level of the 1930s. That model was imprinted in its cultural outlook. As a result, the agency set for itself unrealistic expectations that governed policy for a long time after.[7]

On the Pajarito Plateau, access to resources distracted the USFS from its competition with the NPS. Close, labor-intensive management was the primary need in the Santa Fe National Forest. Since the fusion of the Pecos and Jemez forests into the Santa Fe in 1915, the western portion had never received enough money for adequate administration. Less inhabited and less important, it received less attention. Even in the federal system, the Pajarito Plateau remained the periphery of a periphery.

The New Deal remedied this with a dramatic flair. During the first enrollment period, four camps were established in the Santa Fe National Forest. Each had about two hundred men between the ages of eighteen and twenty-five, and there was no shortage of work for them to do. CCC camps in the region developed fire trails, cleared brush, cut fuel breaks, thinned timber, and planted trees. Although a few picnic grounds and camping areas were included, this sideline did not compare with the efforts of the NPS. As a tool to maintain the national forest, the CCC program on the Pajarito Plateau served its purpose; as a means to keep the USFS in competition with the Park Service for the growing constituency of American travelers, it failed miserably.

The Park Service saw the New Deal as the means to comprehensive development distributed evenly throughout the system. New Deal programs gave the NPS a way to realize extensive "wish lists," using money that it ordinarily did not have. Almost every park area for which the Park Service had commercial aspirations received a share of the federal windfall. Nomenclatural distinctions between park areas became much less significant as the agency acquired national monuments, historic sites, and battlefields in the reorganization of 1933. The vast amount of money that the Park Service had at its disposal meant great changes in development in the park system.

The money from New Deal programs allowed the development of archaeological areas at a much faster rate. Horace M. Albright, who planned to leave the Park Service for private industry shortly after the new administration took office, had the ear of Secretary of the Interior Harold L. Ickes from March until his departure in August 1933. Ickes controlled the disposition of federal relief money, and Albright convinced the secretary that the park system was a high priority.[8] Left out of the development of the system for so long, archaeological areas became prime candidates for attention.

The expenditure of federal money on archaeological areas changed the nature of visitation. Throughout the 1910s and 1920s, the Park Service had pursued a policy of accommodating visitors. New Deal money allowed the development of facilities for the convenience of travelers, which meant that in many cases, visitors no longer had to walk on trails, short or long, to reach archaeological ruins. This changed the visitor's experience, making it less rigorous and more a part of the sedentary twentieth century.

The archaeological monuments where development proceeded most rapidly were those that fit into Frank Pinkley's scheme of development. The Pajarito Plateau and Bandelier National Monument topped his list of plans for the Southwest. Bandelier filled a long-standing gap in Pinkley's plans. Near Santa Fe, it could serve as an entry point for the rest of the southwestern monument group, most of which were far more distant from the railroad and the centers of tourist travel.[9]

After the establishment of the monument in 1915, the Forest Service had administered archaeological resources at Bandelier in a nonchalant fashion. Lacking resources for noncommercial endeavors, as well as the sense that such development was important, the Forest Service did little at Bandelier. This attitude was the catalyst for the efforts of the 1920s. In 1932, when the Park Service assumed control of the monument, the only way to reach the ruins in Frijoles Canyon, the main attraction at the monument, was by a three-quarter-mile winding trail from the top of the mesa. The path intimidated many, preventing the sedentary, the infirm, and the aged from visiting the canyon. Only horses, burros, or feet could traverse the narrow, steep banks.

The situation at Bandelier reflected the policy of the Forest Service. Throughout the 1920s, foresters had scoffed at what they saw as the commercialization of the Park Service. They presented their rivals as accommodationists who would allow the pristine beauty of places like Frijoles Canyon to be destroyed by hordes of visitors for mere commercial purposes. Locked into an exclusionary mindset that was a backside of the legacy of Progressivism, the foresters held their ground. In the official view of the Forest Service, places like Frijoles Canyon were only for those people willing to make the effort to reach them.[10]

But the acquisition of the monument by the Park Service brought about visible changes. Pinkley lined up with those who favored accommodating visitors, and under his management, Bandelier developed in ways directly opposite those of the Forest Service. The monument could serve the needs of the park system, and not incidentally, Pinkley and his southwestern national monument group. Pinkley based his development on two specific features: a road to the canyon bottom, and facilities to receive, guide, and educate the visitors who arrived there.

The Park Service inherited little in the way of a physical plant from the Forest Service at Bandelier. A small, dilapidated ranger cabin, with a telephone line that hooked into the USFS network, comprised the extent of improvements in the area. Forest Service trails were simply cut through the brush, without the gradation, explanatory markers, or directional signs that had become characteristic of the areas the Park Service featured. Many of the cave dwellings in Frijoles Canyon were still filled with decomposing sheep manure from the era when herders penned animals there. To make Bandelier into the entry point that Frank Pinkley envisioned would require extensive development.

From the perspective of the Park Service, the region had tremendous potential. The plateau had become a popular vacation spot before the agency acquired Bandelier, and even as Pinkley laid the basis for the NPS presence, tourism was becoming an important industry in the area. The Rocky Mountain Camp Company and Koshare Tours paved the way with tours during the late 1910s and the early 1920s. The Fred Harvey Company's Indian Detours opened for business in 1926 and quickly became the most popular way to visit the plateau. With headquarters in the La Fonda Hotel off the plaza in Santa Fe and headed by an Englishman named R. Hunter Clarkson, the Indian Detours surpassed the tours of smaller companies.

Harvey's tours accelerated the institutionalization of tourism in the Santa Fe region. The Fred Harvey Company ran an operation aimed at Americans with money to spend, and it offered the very best in accommodations and service. The Harvey Company promoted the Indian Detours in railroad and popular magazines and at its many other hotels and restaurants throughout the Southwest. Travel agents were an even more effective source of business. Erna Fergusson, the noted southwestern writer, trained attractive young women, "the daughters of senators," the advertisements attested, as guides. The women dressed in southwestern clothing and jewelry and were given a Packard or Cadillac touring car— "Road Pullmans"—with a driver to show visitors special places in northern New Mexico. For about one hundred dollars a day, an Indian Detour car could be hired to go anywhere in the Southwest with a reasonable trail. It was an enticing offer, and among those who accepted it were Eleanor Roosevelt, John D. Rockefeller, Jr., and Albert Einstein.[11]

The Indian Detours became even more popular after Hunter Clarkson bought the division from the Harvey Company in 1931. For Clarkson, the business was more than a sideline. He promoted the company throughout the nation, establishing a branch office in Los Angeles replete with a former guide, Henrietta Gloff, who wore "hand hammered conchos and a silver squash blossom necklace," as field representative. Newspapers and magazines published frequent articles about the Indian Detours as national interest focused on the Santa Fe area. The Indian Detours geared up for larger numbers of visitors in each succeeding year.[12]

The surge in visitation and promotion by a major tourist agency changed the way in which visitors saw the ruins of the Pajarito Plateau. An Indian Detours guide met new arrivals at the train station in Lamy and took them to La Fonda Hotel in Santa Fe. From there, guests had many options. There were day trips to Chimayo, the site of the Sanctuario de Guadalupe, nearby pueblos such as San Ildefonso, and the old frontier town of Taos, as well as trips to Bandelier and the Puye ruins. Visitors were in the constant company of guides and saw only predesignated places selected from a list offered by the company. On the preplanned tours, each was a short stop, limited by the timetable established by the company. The managers of the Indian Detours also directed the activities of visitors. The guides' knowledge was limited, their perspective shaped not only by the way in which the company sought to promote the region but by their personal experiences as well. Most were not native south-westerners but were the children of affluence seeking to broaden their experiences. Although they loved the Southwest, they too were outsiders, learning of the region as they showed it to visitors.

The tours were informative, the service was excellent, and the nights at La Fonda were lovely, but in the process, visitors lost something important. "Roughing It in Style" was different from merely roughing it. Motor travel to predesignated sites established and maintained a distance between visitors and life on the plateau. Travelers rarely experienced the rigors of the region; most did not climb mesas or descend along any steep paths unless they made the trip down to Frijoles Canyon. They admired the Jemez Mountains from auto trails, experiencing its splendor from the security of their vehicle. The guides showed visitors specific ruins, imparted well-inculcated information, and whisked them off to another point. Each evening, they returned to La Fonda, where they dined and slept in comfort. The plateau became just another stop in a series of vacation spots, marked by the tire tracks and wider automobile trails of the twentieth century.

Even the most sensitive visitors in the 1920s and 1930s had difficulty experiencing the closeness that people like Harry Field had felt to the place and its prior inhabitants. Visitors could no longer sense the proximity of aboriginal life. Even though Indian Detour passengers often heard the howling of coyotes as they returned in the evening gloom, they were never threatened by the presence of wildlife. Their dinner came cooked on their plate at the hotel; the rabbits, squirrels, and turkeys of the plateau were safe from their need. Visitors did not spend nights in caves or smell piñon and juniper in the morning. They awoke off the Plaza in Santa Fe each day, in the bustle of the little city at the base of the mountains. The water they drank came from basin taps, not mountain streams.

The visitors' experiences did not challenge them or their way of life. Their trip to the plateau served as a counterpoint to modern life, reminding them less of the life of the past than of the distance between themselves and the worlds that came before. They did not give up modern amenities on their visits, and consequently their writings lacked the sense of romance and adventure characteristic of early travelers. The strictures on visitors came from the modern world, and perhaps this explains the number of visitors from this era who stared down from the Tyuonyi overlook and left without trying the trail to the bottom. Their trips to the canyon rim were not difficult, and they were not prepared to make even minor sacrifices to reach the prehistoric past. They passed through the past, seeing it through an automobile windshield. They were not compelled to tune their senses to its rigors.

This perceptual change resulted in the diminishment of the past. The measure of control exerted by the guide services made the experience a commodity shaped as much by the needs of the company and the cost of the trip as by the desire of the visitor. As the number of visitors and the profit from tourism increased, someone was bound to try to dominate the tourist service market. That it was the Fred Harvey Company, with its high standards of quality and unparalleled resources, was fortunate for visitors. The cheap tent camps and tawdry attractions that cropped up near many national parks did not surround the Pajarito Plateau. The care and quality of the Indian Detours ensured that visitors got as far from modern life as they were prepared to go. But the visitors purchased a marketed commodity, and their sensibilities, as interpreted by the company, dictated the terms of the experience more than did the reality of prehistoric or modern life on the plateau.

Yet the establishment of a formal system of visitation did more to protect archaeological relics than had all the previous efforts to create a national park. Under Indian Detour programs, visitors were supervised during their stay. The company determined what they visited, and travelers no longer had the freedom of their predecessors. Guides were able to impede the wanton collection of surface artifacts, and the haphazard digging that characterized early visitation was all but eliminated. Visitors acquired only a passing familiarity with the region, and without the close contact established by early visitors, most were content simply to observe. Their impact on the prehistoric treasures of the region was as limited as their experience.

Frank Pinkley's educational programs in the Southwest were more substantive than those of the Harvey Company, and he was eager to establish the position of the Park Service at Bandelier. The lack of clearly defined USFS policy left a gap that Pinkley could fill with his programs. He pioneered educational work in the national monuments during the 1920s and had definite ideas about the way to develop archaeological areas. He insisted on guided tours through ruins. His staff not only could teach visitors more but also could minimize vandalism and depredation. Pinkley also wanted visitors to know about the Park Service and its policies and to appreciate the efforts of its personnel. The core of Pinkley's preservation philosophy, this became the foundation of NPS policy in the Southwest. Implementing it at Bandelier was never in question.[13]

The growth in interest offered Frank Pinkley an unparalleled opportunity. Santa Fe had become a focal point for American tourists, and through the Indian Detours, people were visiting the plateau and its attractions in growing numbers. If he could elevate the charm of Frijoles Canyon into an educational and aesthetic experience, he might also be able to entice the public to visit more remote monuments like Montezuma Castle, Pipe Spring, and Hovenweep. A well-run Bandelier was an invaluable asset to Pinkley's group of southwestern monuments.

The existing facilities in Frijoles Canyon posed an obstacle to Pinkley's plans. The focus of life in the canyon was the Frijoles Canyon Lodge, located across the creek from Tyuonyi, the community house ruin. In 1925, the Forest Service granted the newlyweds George and Evelyn Frey a ninety-nine-year lease for concessions. Evelyn Frey was the daughter of George H. Cecil, a former USFS official with a sawmill in the Jemez Mountains. The Freys took over the lodge and offered services on the canyon floor.[14]

Frijoles Canyon had developed into a small-scale resort before the arrival of the Freys, and despite the ambivalence of the Forest Service, it became popular. In 1923, the homesteader John Boyd sold his interest there to John Davenport, the brother of his wife, Martha, and to the Reeds, his sister and brother-in-law. They ran the operation until the Freys arrived in 1925. The young couple moved into Judge Abbott's old house, just across Frijoles Creek from Tyuonyi, and established the Frijoles Canyon Lodge. The Freys accommodated those who wanted more than a casual acquaintance with the canyon. They offered home-cooked meals, with fruits and vegetables grown in the canyon, as well as provided cabins and other amenities.[15] Visitors no longer had to brave the inhospitable conditions of an archaeological dig. They could enjoy comfortable surroundings and good food and still have the solitude and mystery of the canyon when they wanted it.

Many who visited Frijoles Canyon were struck by the way the buildings there blended with the environment. The simplicity of the architecture and the use of indigenous materials contributed to this impression. Judge Abbott had built his house out of blocks from the prehistoric ruin of Tyuonyi, and the Freys added cabins made of the towering pines and cottonwoods that dominated the canyon floor. The guest cabins were so attractive and fit in so well that rumors that Frank Lloyd Wright had designed them abounded. Access was exclusively by the steep trail; the only automobile in the canyon was a truck that George Frey took apart, sent to the bottom in pieces by pulley, and put back together. Modern life barely intruded on Frijoles Canyon. Beyond the amenities necessary to snare visitors, there was little evidence of the twentieth century to detract from the place itself.

By the late 1920s, inconsistent Forest Service policy toward archaeological areas had become a great liability. Despite the clearly articulated anti-development stance of the USFS, the Freys and the Indian Detours helped bring nearly four thousand people to Frijoles Canyon each year. The Forest Service lacked firm policy for archaeological areas, and no coherent way to preserve prehistory emerged in the face of this onslaught. Foresters understood that the ruins were important, but they lacked the knowledge and inclination to administer the canyon for visitors. Benign neglect characterized their policy, which carried over to every aspect of archaeological management in Frijoles Canyon. Evelyn Frey later recalled that she gave many tours through Tyuonyi and the Ceremonial Cave and Forest Service rangers were content to let her do so.[16] Her actions relieved them of a responsibility that was beyond the realm of their expertise and that differed from the most important facets of their mission.

Clarkson's Indian Detours and the Frey's Frijoles Canyon Lodge laid the basis for Park Service development at Bandelier. Clarkson and the Freys shouldered most of the responsibility for visitors, and public interest grew as a result of their efforts. Their activities allowed travelers to see the plateau in modern terms and, more important, with twentieth-century comforts. Pinkley sought to augment that by changing the visitor's experience from emotional to educational in nature.

But in the months following the transfer, a visitor might never know that the Park Service administered the monument. The trail from the mesa ended at the Freys' lodge, and visitors drank from the pump near the porch when they arrived in the canyon. In the dry, dusty New Mexico summers, providing water had great symbolic significance. Here visitors were met, sheltered, and cared for following the often grueling descent from the mesa top. From the first drink of water, the lodge and its keepers remained the focus of visitors' attention. Pinkley had to make the Park Service presence more visible. He could not allow visitors to leave without learning that Bandelier was only one of a network of places that the NPS preserved for the public.

After the Park Service assumed control at Bandelier in February 1932, Pinkley pushed for a more substantial development program than had ever been contemplated in a national monument. He wanted to create facilities for administration and visitor service to parallel those in the major national parks. To serve his purposes, he needed an administration building with a custodian's office, a museum, and other developments, including all the necessities of modern life. As remote as Frijoles Canyon was during the 1930s, it had to become a community in the wilderness if Pinkley was to achieve his goals.

For development purposes, the Park Service acquired Bandelier at the right moment. It became part of the park system before Roosevelt transferred dozens of new park areas to the agency through Executive Order 6166, his 1933 measure to streamline the federal bureaucracy. When the federal emergency-relief system was established, Pinkley had already developed plans for Bandelier. As a result, the Park Service moved quickly. A CCC camp at Bandelier provided the necessary work force to build administrative and visitor facilities from scratch.[17]

The construction of a road into Frijoles Canyon was the most important feature of Pinkley's development program. Without a road, Bandelier was doomed to eternal inaccessibility. By the 1920s, travelers arrived at the canyon rim in comfort and wanted to reach the bottom just as easily. Visitors placed the premium on haste that characterizes modern America. The Indian Detours and the Frijoles Canyon Lodge made the canyon popular, but they could not counteract the inconvenience of walking or riding a horse or burro along the north mesa of the canyon, past the Tyuonyi overlook, and down the steep and foreboding trail to the bottom. Deterred by the thought of spending hours going down the trail, looking around the ruins, and the ominous prospect of climbing back up the steep canyon face, few made the trip. During the early 1930s, visitation at Frijoles Canyon lagged behind that at the nearby but less spectacular Puye ruins, where there was only a short climb to the top of the mesa. Automobile accessibility would increase visitation dramatically.

Local resistance to the road was strong. The colony of artists and writers who made Santa Fe into the "City Different" had a reflexive response that favored pure preservation. Pinkley referred to them as "mud hut nuts" and denigrated their perspective, but the opponents were an influential group. U.S. Senator Bronson Cutting, the owner of the *New Mexican*, rejected the idea of a road into the canyon, as did Edgar L. Hewett. Since the end of the 1920s, Hewett's perspective had again changed. Commercialized visitation offered little security for the ruins, and it fed the desires of the class of people whose activities Hewett feared. Jesse Nusbaum, a longtime resident of Santa Fe who was closely tuned to its idiosyncrasies and machinations, recognized the potent opposition. He sought to delay the road project until the NPS established a stronger presence in the canyon, in the hope that Santa Feans would be placated by an increase in responsibility commensurate with the increase in accessibility created by the road.[18]

Despite local opposition, the Park Service pursued its road. Pinkley argued that the road was essential. "We can't refuse 15,000 visitors admission," he explained to Horace Albright, "just because the Spanish didn't use automobiles 300 years ago: it just doesn't make sense." Too much depended on development to let local resistance slow implementation. Inspections at Bandelier after the transfer stressed the poor conditions. The trail into the canyon was an "actual barrier" for all but the most vigorous visitors, noted George Grant, a Park Service photographer. "The visitor," he opined in a clear enunciation of what would become the policy of the agency, "must be able to get his car close to the points of interest."[19]

From the perspective of the Park Service, the choice was easy. Without the road, Bandelier was no different from other Forest Service national monuments. With a road, it could become the most important park in Pinkley's Southwest, comparable to the Grand Canyon in its significance to visitation. The idea of a road to Frijoles Canyon easily won the sanction of agency leadership, particularly in a locale that had been the scene of a recent and still festering conflict with the USFS. "It would be unfortunate, indeed," Demaray stated in November 1932, "if we were to follow a no

more vigorous policy [regarding construction of the road] than was practiced by the Forest Service."[20] Little more than this direct comparison was
necessary to justify the highest priority for construction of the road.

Implementation of the plan quickly followed. Construction began in
November 1933, almost at the moment the CCC camp was installed at the
monument. On December 9, 1933, Evelyn Frey and Walter G. Atwell, the
Park Service engineer who oversaw the project, rode in the first car that
traveled down the unfinished trail.[21] The road to Frijoles Canyon was one
of Frank Pinkley's greatest triumphs. He now had the means to accommodate even the most sedentary visitor at a monument critically important to
the future of the southwestern national monuments group.

Construction of the road was the beginning of the development of Bandelier. As soon as the CCC camp filled with workers, Pinkley initiated new
projects from his wish list, and agency planners began to draw up a master plan for development. The chief planning problem at Bandelier was
finding adequate space in Frijoles Canyon for the facilities Pinkley
deemed necessary. He was determined to construct the administrative
area in a manner that would make Park Service facilities more important
than those of the concessionaire. Because the Freys' lodge was located at
the base of the foot trail, Pinkley wanted to use the new road into the canyon to bypass the lodge. This would alter the visitors' initial impression of
who was in charge in Frijoles Canyon.

The road to the canyon floor changed the orientation of the public. Entering the canyon from the southeast, the road offered the agency the opportunity to redesign visitor approaches to features on the floor, as well as
a greater measure of control of access to the ruins. The southeastern end
of Frijoles Canyon was the widest part of the mouth of the canyon. There
the creek began to angle away from the north wall toward the Rio Grande.
Ending the road in this area offered Pinkley the one place in the canyon
with ample space to construct the facilities he wanted. It also gave the
Park Service command of the entrance to the canyon. This meant that the
Park Service would become the ones who offered water at the end of the
new, more convenient trail.

Pinkley suggested that a combination administration building and museum, as well as a widened parking area, be located at the foot of the new
road in the southeast corner of the canyon. His plan ensured that tourists
would reach the Park Service before the ruins, as at Casa Grande. It also
offered much better protection, controlling access to the ruins. In addi-

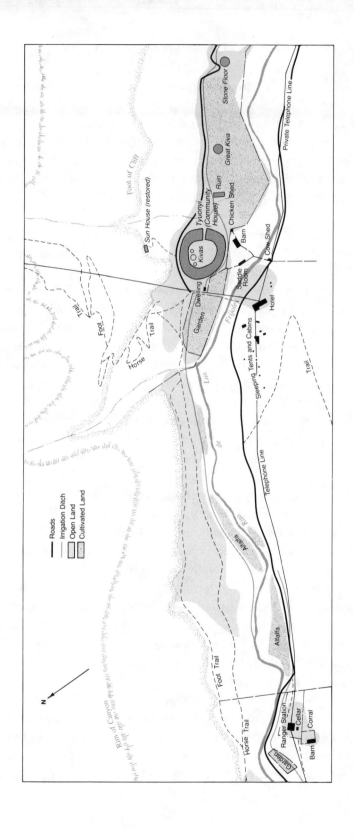

N

Rim of Canyon

Foot of Cliff

Trail
Foot
Horse Trail

Sun House (restored)

Garden
Dwelling

Tyuonyi
(Community
House)
Kivas

Ruin

Chicken Shed

Great Kiva

Stone Floor

Barn

Saddle Room

Cow Shed

Private Telephone Line

Frijoles

Los

de

Rito

Hotel

Sleeping Tents and Cabins

Trail

Telephone Line

Alfalfa

Rio

Alfalfa

Foot Trail

Horse Trail

Garden

Ranger Station

Cellar

Corral

Barn

— Roads
—— Irrigation Ditch
☐ Open Land
▧ Cultivated Land

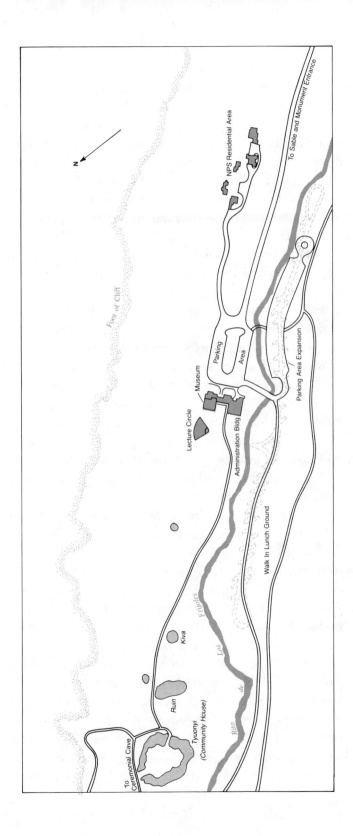

These two maps reflect the degree to which Park Service planning changed Frijoles Canyon and Bandelier National Monument. Prior to transfer of the monument, the canyon functioned as a homestead; after the construction of park facilities, it became a genuine destination for visitors.

tion, tourists would be forced to walk about one-quarter of a mile to the Tyuonyi ruins.

Pinkley's insistence created an uncomfortable situation in Frijoles Canyon. Like a conquering general, Pinkley was determined to dictate terms to his new subjects. They predated the arrival of the Park Service and were accustomed to the more flexible policies of the usfs. Pinkley sought to reshape Bandelier as he had the entire southwestern national monuments group, and his often dictatorial style caused friction.

Pinkley's ideas conflicted not only with the Freys but also with the practices of the Park Service's engineering branch, which was committed to the Mather-Albright ethic of visitor accommodation. Frank A. Kittredge, the chief engineer of the Branch of Engineering in San Francisco, thought that Pinkley's changes were self-serving and inappropriate. But Pinkley would not back down, even for his old friends in the engineering branch, and the planning process set the stage for a contest between the conflicting ideals of visitor service and park protection.

In an unusual situation, two avowed advocates of visitor accommodation disagreed, not about the principles of policy but about its implementation. Kittredge's position was defensive: visitors were used to the lodge, and the nps could build around it. Pinkley took the offensive. Accustomed to asserting his considerable power, he sought to supplant Frijoles Canyon Lodge. If the lodge interfered with the Park Service's ability to manage the monument, it would have to be moved to the administration area.[22] In Pinkley's view, concessionaires were less important than the presentation of the ruins in a professional fashion. The Freys would have to acquiesce.

It was no secret that Pinkley wanted Frijoles Canyon Lodge moved farther away from Tyuonyi. Although the Freys' operation was a success, Pinkley believed their facilities were inappropriate. The barns and outbuildings encroached on the ruins, and the lodge area was too close to the ruins for adequate protection. The house was constructed out of prehistoric stones from Tyuonyi. The entire canyon floor looked too much like a homestead to Pinkley, with fruit trees, a large garden, chickens and ducks in the canyon, and cattle grazing on the south mesa. As soon as the Emergency Conservation Work program at Bandelier was initiated, he asked for money to remove the Freys' fencing, barns, and outbuildings and vocally advocated more rigorous Park Service control of their activities. But cooler heads within the agency prevailed in 1933. The Park Service had to consolidate its position on the plateau, and moving the lodge was bad public relations. Pinkley had to wait to implement his plans.

A cost-conscious engineer, Kittredge held to the principle of accommodation established during the 1920s. This policy dictated a paved road all the way to the ruins. Compelling reasons supported Kittredge's point of view. Implementing his ideas would bring Bandelier in line with most of the other developed parks. It would assure that little future roadbuilding would be necessary. The important features of the monument were not going to change, engineers argued, and for once the Park Service had ample resources. Kittredge believed that the Park Service would continue to accommodate an increasingly sedentary public. If visitors were going to demand a road all the way to the Tyuonyi ruin, building an administrative area one-quarter of a mile away from the ruin was impractical and perhaps foolish.

Pinkley viewed the administration of archaeological ruins as an issue of protection, and he was not a man inclined to compromise. By controlling access through a gateway, Pinkley felt that the Frijoles Canyon ruins would be both accessible and protected. From his perspective, this was the chief obligation of the Park Service. He would not allow the demands of the public to be the sole factor in the formation of his policy.

Pinkley thought that Kittredge did not understand the issues in Frijoles Canyon. The engineer was unduly influenced by the view from the Tyuonyi overlook, Pinkley contended, and did not realize that road entry from the east end of the canyon would change the relationship between the visitors and the ruins on the canyon floor. Visitors would no longer descend the steep trail, except by choice; equally important, unable to see the semicircle of Tyuonyi from above, they would no longer instantly perceive it as the primary attribute of the canyon. The old trail made Tyuonyi seem like the only important ruin there. The road would provide a new orientation and emphasize other features in the canyon. The quality of the experience, Pinkley insisted, was best protected by keeping cars away from the ruins.[23]

The debate between Pinkley and Kittredge was a classic example of the preservation-use dichotomy embodied in the Park Service since its inception. Kittredge sought accommodation to facilitate use, but Pinkley advocated greater control and protection. By the early 1930s, both points of view had ample support within the agency, although as a result of the powerful influence of Horace M. Albright, the agency placed a higher priority on use than on pure preservation. But Pinkley's influence in the Southwest was vast, and he was so irascible that the agency frequently let him have his way so as to avoid conflict. The preservation-use dichotomy on the Pajarito Plateau was decided on the basis of personality rather than merit. Pinkley did as he pleased because no one wanted to fight with him about it.

Pinkley's stance also tied in to another controversy in the agency. The Mather-Albright accommodation edict had become onerous to many in the Park Service, and with the advent of New Deal programs, a counter-movement emphasizing strict preservation gained momentum. Pinkley won support from those who believed capital development had gone too far toward comfort. His extensive experience granted him sufficient authority and standing to contradict agency engineers and planners. In an odd irony, the man who had developed archaeological tourism in the park system became the standard-bearer for those who advocated the preservation of park areas over their use.

In the end, most of Pinkley's ideas for Bandelier were implemented. With Emergency Conservation Work labor and funding, the old lodge was torn down in the late 1930s, and a new one was constructed within the administration compound. Pinkley took great satisfaction in the removal of the Freys' buildings; in the 1980s, Evelyn Frey would wistfully remember the fruit orchards he tore out. Although for a brief period a portal allowed automobile traffic past the administrative compound in 1933–34, permanent roads beyond the main parking area were not built except for the campground road that led to the old lodge. For administrative purposes, the development offered the agency countless advantages. The compound served as a midpoint between the modern world and the prehistory of Frijoles Canyon, between accommodation and use, and as a barrier against the impact of future visitation. Containing more than forty buildings and the physical plant sufficient for a small city, the compound became the focus of life on the plateau.[24]

When the CCC camp at Bandelier was disbanded in 1940, it had been an important part of the transformation of the plateau. As a result of the camp, the Park Service increased its advantage on the plateau. Tourists found the accommodations in Frijoles Canyon extremely attractive, and the road achieved Pinkley's purposes. The many visitors recognized that they were visiting an NPS area, one of many in the southwestern national monuments group.

But as a result of the New Deal, another agency also influenced the plateau. The Soil Conservation Service (scs) initiated aerial photography of the entire region, purchased the depleted and damaged Ramón Vigil Grant from Frank Bond, and began soil- and watershed-protection projects on San Ildefonso and Santa Clara land, in García Canyon, and at other locations on the plateau. Although the service generally lacked its own land base, its cooperative programs with other agencies represented the highest objectives of the New Deal. The scs offered a new perspective and signaled a change in the direction of government policy toward the people of the area.

The Soil Conservation Service was a typical New Deal agency. It was designed to meet the needs of American agriculture with the scientific remedies of a modern society while teaching techniques that would prevent further destruction of land and assure prosperity. Beginning in 1933 as the Soil Erosion Service under the explosive and persuasive leadership of Hugh Hammond Bennett, the agency became a primary problem-solver as the southern plains began to blow away in the great dust storms of 1934. In 1935, it was transferred from the Department of the Interior to the Department of Agriculture and renamed the Soil Conservation Service.[25]

The agency became important in northern New Mexico as a result of the actions of John Collier, the Commissioner of Indian Affairs. After more than a decade as one of the most vocal critics of the Indian Service, Collier set out to alter its direction when he became commissioner in 1933. He had visited Taos Pueblo during the 1920s and saw in its communal structure a "Red Atlantis." This romanticized view of an idyllic subsistence community became the basis of Collier's policy, which he hoped would "recognize and respect the Indian as he is." His legislative program embodied these principles. Measures such as the Pueblo Relief Bill of 1933, which compensated pueblos for land lost to non-Indians, typified Collier's efforts. He also sought an end to the long-standing policy of assimilation, instead encouraging Native Americans to practice their religions and cultures, manage their own affairs, and develop viable subsistence economies.[26] If science could be harnessed in this cause, Collier would use it.

One program Collier developed toward this end was the Indian Land Purchase Program. The federal government acquired badly damaged land, an easy feat in northern New Mexico because of the prevalence of large land grants, and Collier received nineteen tracts, among them the

Ramón Vigil Grant. An agreement with Bennett put the Soil Conservation Service in control of the lands. The Indian ccc provided labor for the
implementation of programs. In an effort to recognize that the assumptions of a scientific society did not always square with the perceptions of
longtime natives in a multicultural, multiethnic environment, Collier
brought in social scientists. The Technical Cooperation–Bureau of Indian
Affairs (TC–BIA) unit was formed, with the human dependency team, as
the social scientists were labeled, attached to it. Soon after, the scs took
over the unit. Although in the majority of situations, programs of this nature were marginally successful, in northern New Mexico, the result was
the Tewa Basin Study, a three-volume report that looked not only at the
condition of Indians but at that of Hispanos as well.[27]

Collier's vision of freeing people through self-sufficiency was not limited to the first inhabitants of the continent. The Tewa Basin Study recognized serious problems in the socioeconomic structure of the region, the
greatest of which was the monopolization of the range and the sheep
economy by a few large landowners. Collier realized that the plight of
Hispanos differed little from that of Pueblo Indians. Chafing at the business practices of people like Frank Bond, Collier opposed the monopolization of the range by what he called "a handful of commercial interests."
The New Deal offered him a way to help the natives of the region successfully subsist without reliance on federal handouts.[28]

The result was a number of concerted efforts to evaluate the condition
of the land in the context of the values and practices of its people. Although the Vigil Grant had been purchased for Indian use, the Tewa Basin Study noted that in the valleys, Hispano families were closely integrated into the pueblos. Many families had lived in the same location for
longer than one hundred years, making them much more than squatters.
Area Hispanos needed the grant to augment the narrow resource base on
which they survived.[29]

By the 1930s, the grant was in abysmal condition. A half century of
commercial use had resulted in overcutting, overgrazing, and poor distribution of animals on the range. Much of the easily erodible soil had
washed away, and even immature timber was cut for firewood. A federal
range examiner called the situation a "fair example" of the fate of marginal
land in private ownership and stated that only regulatory controls and an
aggressive program of restoration could again make the land useful. By
the end of the decade, such programs had begun.[30]

By purchasing private land with federal emergency-relief administration money, Collier's program reversed the dominant current of land ownership. Since the 1880s, the plateau had been subjected to the whims of American society. The most clearly articulated ethos of that culture was that public land with the ability to sustain farming and ranching ought to be turned over to private citizens. Even in the twentieth century, when the idea of federal stewardship arose as a response to the general perception of the loss of the western frontier, the trend continued. The purchase of private land by a federal agency served as ironic counterpoint.

The return to federal ownership was new on the Pajarito Plateau. Although the purchase of land in the region for the various park attempts had been a frequent suggestion, it had never been given serious consideration. Nor had any private land ever been reserved, either within the boundaries of the pueblos or in the national forest or monument. The acquisition of the Vigil Grant—as necessary as it was, given the economic climate of the time, the condition of the land, and the belief that technology could reverse the impact of fifty years of overuse—was evidence that the government could rescue individual landowners no matter how poorly they treated their assets.

The sale to the federal government allowed Frank Bond to achieve a long-desired goal. Early in the century, he had learned the principle of trading land for scrip, and throughout the 1920s, while the national park controversy raged, Bond's attorney, William Powell of Albuquerque, sought to peddle the grant alternately to the NPS and the USFS. Pleading the poverty of his client, one of the richest men in northern New Mexico, Powell sought timberland from the USFS, cash from the NPS. Neither could afford his asking price. But the New Deal allowed the purchase of land made economically worthless by the practices of generations of owners.[31]

The acquisition tied in to the primary goal of the Soil Conservation Service: to show Americans that the development of new scientific techniques and hardier strains of plant species could not only halt the destruction of western land but also reverse previous damage. The success of the SCS was dramatic, particularly in areas like the dust bowl counties of western Kansas and Oklahoma, but in a fragile mountain ecosystem with people far removed from the sociocultural mainstream, the results were not as promising.

The Tewa Basin Study also provided the cultural background for programs on pueblo land. Evaluated under its auspices, Santa Clara and San Ildefonso were found to be in difficult situations. In 1937, the Santa Clara tribe owned 49,939 acres, including the area north of the Puye Mesa on the plateau. San Ildefonso contained 21,797 acres, about half of which were on the west side of the Rio Grande. The two tracts showed evidence of the effects of destructive land-use practices. Both had suffered moderate to heavy damage from large-scale erosion, usually on the gradients, although heavy timber on the Santa Clara land had limited the impact there. A large area of San Ildefonso needed to be totally reseeded, a solution with a cost termed "prohibitive" by F. D. Abbott, the TC-BIA range examiner. Changes in the patterns of use were necessary, both to further the lives of people in the pueblos and to protect the watershed of the region.

scs plans for the pueblos typified the approach of the federal resource bureaucracy of the 1930s, as well as its inherent limitations. The programs were designed with economic yield in mind, taking into account the condition of the land but discounting the cultures and traditions of the people who lived there. scs officials sought to counter destructive land practices by applying the best scientific knowledge. The scs would plant a restorative vegetative cover to prevent future erosion, using conservation knowledge and technology to recreate if not a cornucopia, at least a more dependable subsistence existence. The reward for the agency would be the modified behavior of people in the region. Although the Tewa Basin Study fostered awareness of the differences in cultures, talking about conservation remained easier than teaching it.

The solutions that conservation agencies presented were not sophisticated enough to address a long-term decline in the living conditions of the people of the region. Even though scs, TC-BIA, and usfs personnel were familiar with the Tewa Basin Study, the need for programs and education exceeded the remedies available. Federal examiners recognized the impact of industrialization and sought to counter it. In an ironic form of management, they used science to return the economic independence lost as a result of the advent of the market economy.

The programs offered detailed proscriptions for lands in the area. For San Ildefonso, the management plan suggested restoring high-quality forage cover and developing a stable livestock industry. This included eliminating animals from pueblo land that belonged to nearby Hispanos and creating a cooperative livestock association with education as its mission. For Santa Clara, less affected because it was more than twice the size of its neighbor, the plan was more scientific. At San Ildefonso, animals grazed throughout the year; at Santa Clara, the scs sought to design a conservation program to educate the pueblo in the most current techniques.

These recommendations showed how New Deal programs furthered the trend toward assimilation even as the Indian New Deal offered native peoples greater autonomy. The recommended changes conflicted with traditional practices, and Native Americans had little reason to trust any representative of the U.S. government. When the people of San Ildefonso were offered registered bulls for a minimal price, few were interested. Even when the pueblo had control of the Vigil Grant, the governor leased it to nearby Hispanos for their stock rather than follow suggestions to develop a cattle herd.[32] With the physical environment well worn and the breakdown of traditional culture in full swing, Native Americans and Hispanos did not see federal programs as a solution to their problems. By harnessing science—bringing in more specialists—the well-meaning Collier inadvertently defeated his own goals. Out of fear of change, suspicion, lack of knowledge, and absence of desire to adapt, the people took the advantages of the programs and ignored the changes they were asked to make.

If science could not measurably improve the situation of Native Americans on the plateau, there were other avenues. A larger land base temporarily solved questions of use. After the Vigil Grant was assigned to the scs, Collier began a campaign to acquire more land for San Ildefonso. Among the tracts he sought was an approximately eight-thousand-acre portion of the grant, beginning south of Mortandad Canyon and stretching toward Canyon del Buey. This area had religious and practical significance for the pueblo. It contained the prehistoric ruins of Navawi'i, the pueblo of the game trap, a site coveted by park advocates as early as 1900 and revered by the Pueblo Indians. It also offered economic possibilities, for there were a number of stands of timber and some large sections suitable for grazing. Acquisition would relieve some of the pressure on existing grazing land and help Collier create the kind of unalienated land base he believed the pueblo needed to break its reliance on Anglo institutions.

As always, jurisdictional disputes complicated the picture. The scs, which had administered the entire grant since its transfer from the Bureau of Agricultural Economics in October 1938, was located in the Department of Agriculture, and the Bureau of Indian Affairs, like the National

Park Service, was in Harold L. Ickes's Department of the Interior. In Ickes's view, Secretary of Agriculture Henry A. Wallace had stolen the scs in 1935. Ickes himself had made aggressive attempts to capture the Forest Service for the Interior Department and, at least once, had launched a frontal assault designed to blend the Departments of the Interior and Agriculture into a Department of Conservation headed by Ickes. By the end of the 1930s, Wallace had heard enough from Ickes. Land transfers from one department to another were unlikely in this climate.[33]

In no small part as a result of Ickes, Wallace expressed little desire to give the Vigil Grant to anyone in the Department of the Interior. On February 1, 1939, he transferred the 25,295 acres of the grant that were not in San Ildefonso's sacred area from the scs to the Forest Service. But Collier was able to circumvent the rivalry. He and Wallace had developed a working relationship early in Roosevelt's first term. They met frequently at the Cosmos Club in Washington, D.C., and in the spring of 1934, both visited the Southwest in search of land to inaugurate the Indian Land Purchase Program. Collier made a compelling case that the transfer of the sacred area to the pueblo would also help Hispanos in the region. More grazing land would be available for everybody, helping to restore a measure of dignity to the lives of the people of the Española Valley. Wallace heard Collier's plea with sympathy; the commissioner had tapped into a primary current of the New Deal. Rexford Tugwell, Undersecretary of Agriculture, also cooperated with Collier. Because of Wallace's respect for Collier and his programs at the BIA, Wallace willingly gave the commissioner what he requested. The sacred area was transferred to San Ildefonso Pueblo by Executive Order 8255 on September 18, 1939.[34]

Despite the long history of attempts to include the Vigil Grant in a national park, the Park Service was left out of the transfer of the grant. NPS-USFS and Ickes-Wallace rivalries played an important part in this omission, as did the favored status of the Park Service early in Ickes's tenure. The transfer left the NPS groping. When a bill came forward in the U.S. Senate to formally add the Vigil Grant to the Santa Fe National Forest, the Park Service fashioned a response. NPS officials recommended a "Jemez Crater National Park," an area of more than two million acres that would have eliminated the western section of the forest and a number of small towns such as Coyote and Gallina and would have included the Valles Caldera and the various pueblos in one national park. From this, NPS Director Arno B. Cammerer brought a proclamation to Ickes for the signature of the President that would have expanded Bandelier National Monument by more than seventy-five thousand acres, including the Vigil Grant and the Pajarito district of the Santa Fe National Forest. Roosevelt never signed it. Spurned by Wallace, the NPS made a final attempt to secure a contiguous national monument. Its failure confirmed the status quo.[35]

By 1940, the plateau belonged almost wholly to federal agencies. The Park and Forest services had their toeholds, and their competition continued. The addition of most of the Vigil Grant to the national forest left the NPS dissatisfied, creating conditions that could easily spark renewed conflict. With Collier's support, the pueblos had benefited. The transfer of the sacred area to San Ildefonso was a major triumph for Collier, the BIA, local Native Americans, and the liberal spirit embodied in the New Deal. Hispanos received a greater measure of attention than they had before, but the plateau was still a periphery. From Española to the Cañada de Cochiti Grant, the only privately owned areas were a few homesteads in García Canyon, the roughly forty family enterprises at the base of the Jemez Mountains, and the eight-hundred-plus acres of the Los Alamos Ranch School. The Ranch School was a powerful institution, dependent on the tuition of affluent parents from the East. Its concerns differed from those of the homesteaders, who watched as the government divided up the land around them. From the development of Frijoles Canyon to the addition of the Vigil Grant, the activities of the decade made cash crop farmers and ranchers anachronistic.

The appearance of the SCS was indicative of the future. It showed that there were areas of the West that were simply not productive enough on their own to support successful modern economic endeavors, places where technological solutions to economic problems did not exist. The SCS had sought to prove otherwise by making land responsive to the techniques of its inhabitants rather than trying to teach a more harmonious kind of interaction with the physical world. In some places, this approach worked wonders, most notably with commercial farmers. On the Pajarito Plateau, it made remote people living off marginal land more reliant on the infrastructure of American society. Even the most advanced technologies and programs of the time could not significantly improve life. As a result, the people of the plateau recognized that they were truly unimportant in the scope of larger society, and they became accustomed to federal support in a way that they had not previously expected.

John Collier's bold plans failed to rescue Indians and Hispanos on the Pajarito Plateau. Rather than derive permanent cultural and economic benefit from the New Deal, homesteaders and many of the people in the nearby valleys lost any remaining vestiges of the independence they had retained throughout the first third of the twentieth century. Their economic status improved temporarily, exposing them to a range of options not previously available and assuring a clamor when those opportunities disappeared. Even adding to the land base of traditional inhabitants did not help. Land in the region was destroyed, and the best efforts of federal agencies could not reverse patterns begun more than fifty years before. By the end of the 1930s, land was not the answer to the problems of independent family farmers in northern New Mexico. Applying preindustrial values in an age of monolithic institutions consigned farmers to a life of powerlessness outside of the mainstream.

The 1930s permanently changed the Pajarito Plateau and the West. Finally, U.S. governmental and social institutions had a firm grip on this remote region. The New Deal magnified the social, cultural, and economic dependence of the West, proving again that premises developed in humid climates led to failure in the semiarid world. Yet places like the plateau discovered a trade-off. As a result of the New Deal, many of the accoutrements of modern society reached the region. The process of integrating this remote place into the American mainstream had finally begun in earnest, but in an unusual fashion. Not economically valuable enough for the private sector, the Pajarito Plateau was subjected to the plans of the public sector. The various federal agencies with holdings in the region continued to squabble, unaware that they would soon face far more powerful opponents.

10

As Dorothy and her dog, Toto, hurry to safety in the movie *The Wizard of Oz*, a twister lifts them and their house into the sky and drops them in a faraway land called Oz. Spiraling downward, the structure lands atop the Wicked Witch of the East, killing her and initiating a celebration by a diminutive group of people called munchkins. Their joy puzzles Dorothy; she does not understand that in one unwitting action, she has obliterated the balance of power that existed in Oz before her arrival, divorced all that will follow from what came before, and inexorably altered the future.

With an impact no less great than that of Dorothy's arrival in Oz, a secret installation at Los Alamos created a permanent break between past and future on the Pajarito Plateau. The location of the research section of Project "Y" of the Manhattan Project—which developed the atomic bomb—on the plateau brought an alien concern with the full force of an institutional society and its federal government behind it, populated by people unlike those who had previously inhabited the region—Anglo, Hispano, or Native American. The values of these new Pajaritans, who came because they were ordered to, differed from those of their predecessors; unlike the fictional protagonist of *The Wizard of Oz,* they never had to adapt to the place they overwhelmed. Instead, they transformed the area physically and culturally to fit their specifications. Although they appreciated the beauty of the mountains and the graceful sunsets of the region, they were preoccupied, indeed obsessed, with a science that would have baffled Bandelier and Hewett. Colonists more than settlers, they and their keepers, the U.S. Army, imposed rigid order and reconstituted life in the region.

Nor was the experience of the plateau atypical. Throughout the West, the war remade western institutions—economic, social, cultural, and political—and laid the basis for vast change. Rather than function as a source for raw materials, the West became an amalgamation of economic colony and federally funded protectorate.[1] Like towns through which the railroads passed in the nineteenth century, places with war-based industries found their economic futures guaranteed, albeit with larger populations, new leadership, and different rules. Those areas that were not selected languished outside of the matrix of growth and continued on the road to oblivion.

Ironically, the very attributes that protected the Pajarito Plateau from the systematic colonization that engulfed much of New Mexico before the 1940s made it attractive for this secret project. Seeking a remote locale to hide those researching the possibility of creating the single most dangerous human weapon invented up to that time, federal and military officials wanted a place with minimal distraction and little chance of discovery or subversion. The Pajarito Plateau fit such requirements. It had never become thoroughly integrated into the economy of modern America, and in the 1940s, it remained as it had always been: remote, peripheral, and marginal to the mainstream. Although homesteaders and seasonal users were dependent on industrial society, the land they inhabited, the skills they knew, and the jobs they performed allowed them only marginal participation in the modern world. The region did not offer industrial society enough to justify development. Before the 1940s, the Pajarito Plateau failed the measure of importance in modern industrial society.

Precisely this failure made the area an attractive location for a research community. Federal authorities imported a culture of science and affixed it to an area that had been the province of preindustrial people. Possessed of the values and mores of scientific culture and completely divorced from the plateau as place, the scientists were themselves a dependent culture, imprisoned in a strange and remote place.

Even the New Deal and the resulting development could not change the reality that, like much of the West, the plateau was marginal. The agencies that conveyed a promise of federally financed prosperity paradoxically lost some of their significance in the government bureaucracy as a result of the very programs they implemented. Although both the Park Service and the Forest Service benefited greatly from the New Deal, the dam-builders and the highway constructors, such as the Bureau of Reclamation and the U.S. Army Corps of Engineers, were the real winners in the development programs of the 1930s. The scope of their activities overwhelmed that of their predecessors and resulted in resource-management agencies with vast constituencies and larger budgets. The Park Service and the Forest Service still dominated the plateau, but both reached the peak of their importance in the federal bureaucracy during the 1920s. Coupled with the new management bureaus, the agencies that sought to respond to crisis by modifying traditional practices—the Soil Conservation Service and the Grazing Service, for example—these passed-over agencies continued to dominate the plateau. The real power in the federal resource bureaucracy gravitated elsewhere.

As a result, the secret installation created a tremendous cultural and economic gap. Initially consisting of Quonset huts and military buildings, Los Alamos had been dropped into a world to which it bore no relation. Not only were the physicists immersed in the realm of science, concerned with a mission of supreme importance, and lonely and isolated in an aesthetically beautiful place, but they were also light years away from their predecessors in the way they perceived institutions, in their reliance on the sociocultural infrastructure, and in their level of integration into mainstream American society. They did not see the Pajarito Plateau as a place of sustenance—even those who loved it and hiked its canyons and mountains—for it did not sustain them as it had their predecessors. At best, the area surrounding the compound was a beautiful place for recreation; at worst, it was what stood between their dismal and isolated existence and the freedom they perceived in modern society.

The concerns of the scientists, their families, and the military personnel stationed there were not of the place but were of equations on their chalkboards and actions in faraway places. War and science, isotopes and processes, institutions and powers, were the foci of their lives. From another world, the people sequestered in this remote locale could see the land they inhabited only as a stage, its scenic mountains as backdrop.

The project and its overwhelming need for security took precedence over all other issues except the development of an atomic device. Physical barriers in the form of guarded checkpoints were notable additions to the topography of the region, as were fencing and high walls. Access to the facility was severely restricted: the people of Santa Fe did not know what happened on "the hill"; they knew only that the project was top secret. The installation at Los Alamos had no address except P.O. Box 1663, Santa Fe, and its residents possessed unsigned driver's licenses validated only by the military.[2]

Rivalry over land had been tense before Project Y began at Los Alamos, but barbed-wire fences had been rare and protective weaponry rarer. Although an array of people had fought for control of the plateau and its resources before the 1940s, all sought the economic or cultural value of the region. Those who planned the installation did so for other reasons, and the values and perceptions they brought removed the people who preceded them and made their perceptions anachronistic.

As a result of the Los Alamos installation, the Pajarito Plateau again became a crucible, but for a very different kind of science. The science of the land had given way to the science of its components. The physicists and specialists differed from people like Hewett and Bandelier, who were heirs to the Anglo-European exploring tradition of Humboldt and Hayden, King and Amundsen. The new scientists were much more than taxonomists and observers. They were empiricists. Yet what they studied was not the physical world around them but its essential composition. Their science was pure, theoretical. The only thing the physicists had in common with the anthropologists who had previously come to the region was the appellation "scientist." Their fields of inquiry and the times in which they made their discoveries were so different that, unlike their predecessors who tried to link past and present, the physicists destroyed any continuity between experience on the Pajarito Plateau before Project Y and subsequent actions. Physicists were not interested in the rewards of the physical world, be they archaeological or economic. Instead, an interior world, defined by the parts of the atom, preoccupied them, and a single purpose, the creation of a practical atomic weapon, became their sole horizon.[3]

The Pajarito Plateau offered a backdrop for life in Los Alamos but was of little necessity to that world. The developments of Los Alamos could have happened in the interior of Alaska or the West Texas desert. In the world of wartime Los Alamos, the plateau was only a distraction, an inter-changeable location important only to those who required extraordinary scenery while they thought and experimented.

The presence of the Los Alamos installation, the secrecy and urgency inspired by wartime conditions, and the gravity of the endeavor created a break in the continuity of human experience on the plateau. Institutions central to the modern world replaced the peripheral ones of homestead life. The plateau, a part of the industrial world for only sixty years, be-came subservient to people whose actions would shape the future of the world. The plateau as a place, and its past, were trivial in comparison.

But the 1940s, before the Los Alamos installation, had begun sleepily in northern New Mexico. Life continued, in a rhythm that mirrored the travel of the water in its deep arroyos. In a region far from many of the technological advances of the twentieth century, people lived as they al-ways had. As a result of the CCC, there were trails and roads and, in places, electricity, but such improvements did little to change the regime of life. The jobs created under federal programs were not permanent, and even had they been, they would not have insured prosperity. The end of the New Deal was solid evidence that Franklin D. Roosevelt meant what he said when he called federal relief a device for priming the pump of the American economy, not a replacement for traditional institutions.

The new facilities at Bandelier were emblems of the progress of the twentieth century. No other single entity on the plateau benefited from the New Deal as much as the monument. To residents of the region, the buildings, power plant, lights, and roads represented the best of modern life. The physical plant in the canyon gave many homesteaders their first real impression of the nature of life in cities and towns across the nation.

When the CCC camp in Frijoles Canyon was disbanded in 1940, an era ended. Its closure was a symbolic gesture as well, suggesting that the na-tion had passed the critical moment that required full-scale federal inter-vention on the local level. The nation again moved forward economically. The gross national product grew, and reattaining material standards es-tablished in the 1920s did not seem as distant a possibility as during the 1930s. The CCC became a representation of more pessimistic days, when individual initiative had been supplanted by group effort.

During the New Deal, the Park Service had lost ground to the federal agencies that used their money for massive construction projects. The Second World War completed the descent of the Park Service from the lofty position it had enjoyed during the first one hundred days of Roosevelt's initial administration in 1933. The energy directed at the federal emergency-relief programs instantly became part of the war effort. Land acquisition and maintenance issues seemed inconsequential in comparison with outside threats. War-related industries took precedence over all civilian projects, and during the bleak days of early 1942, when an invasion of the West Coast seemed imminent, recreation and spiritual enlightenment fell off the national list of priorities. The Park Service itself was moved to Chicago to make space for war-related activities in Washington, D.C. Even the most vocal advocate of the Park Service in Washington, Secretary of the Interior Harold L. Ickes, became concerned with other issues.

The southwestern national monuments group also lost a large portion of its power base during the late 1930s and early 1940s. The multitude of park units attached to the park system in the reorganization of 1933 created severe management problems in Washington, D.C. Agency officials decided that regional affairs and high-level agency business ought to be handled separately. In 1937, the Park Service divided itself into four regions. The creation of the hierarchical structure meant a different chain of command, and the southwestern national monuments group was affiliated with Region Three, which covered the Southwest.

Because of its proximity, the Region Three office in Santa Fe had a particularly strong impact on Bandelier National Monument. But Bandelier had been one of Pinkley's favorite projects, and he resented others trying to influence decisions that affected the monument. The future and the past came into conflict, and only Pinkley's death in 1940 ended these battles.[4]

But neither the Region Three office nor the southwestern national monuments group could prevent wartime conditions from changing the daily routine at Bandelier. As materials and money again became scarce, the monument returned to the obscurity from which the New Deal had rescued it. Visitation decreased as a result of gasoline and rubber shortages, and the agency had little money for maintenance. Like the custodians of the national monuments before the New Deal, the park fought a losing battle against wind, weather, and a position at the bottom of the list of government priorities.

During the first year of the Second World War, Bandelier receded into the background as quickly as it had become the focus of attention in the

Southwest. Once again, the monument was remote, the access developed during the 1930s a relic of the prerationing past. It became an outpost, albeit one with a telephone, buildings, and other amenities. Without visitors and laborers, auto tourists and development projects, Frijoles Canyon ceased to be a center of activity and returned to the state from which A. F. Bandelier had aroused it in 1880.

Quiet on the Pajarito Plateau did not last long. Fear that Hitler's Germany would construct an atomic bomb compelled similar efforts on the part of the United States. Buoyed by the presence of such refugee physicists as Albert Einstein—who in 1939, at the insistence of two other prominent European refugee physicists, Edward Teller and Leo Szilard, wrote Roosevelt and warned of the threat posed by German development of an atomic bomb—the American government planned an atomic device of its own.[5]

The initial steps involved funding research into a wide range of processes that sought to harness the power of the atom. A number of the most prominent universities in the United States, including the University of California-Berkeley, Massachusetts Institute of Technology, and the University of Chicago, were eager participants. As the effort progressed, industry was drawn into the process, with Du Pont and Eastman-Kodak among the leaders.[6]

But as research progressed, unanswered questions abounded. By May 1942, there were five processes from which sufficient fissionable material for a bomb could be produced. None of the five were guaranteed to succeed, and all were complicated and expensive. Yet the choice had to be made, and it fell to Roosevelt's designees, Vannevar Bush and Dr. James B. Conant. President of Harvard University, Conant was also the head of the S-1 Section—the atomic committee—of the Office of Scientific Research and Development, directed by Bush.

In May 1942, the S-1 Section met in Conant's office to make its decision. Among its members were three Nobel Prize laureates: Ernest Lawrence of the University of California, Arthur Holly Compton of the University of Chicago, and Harold Urey of Columbia University. In a stunning move, the committee decided to pursue all five processes, for they could not predict which would succeed and could not afford to be wrong. Bush received their recommendation and passed it upward through channels. Vice-President Henry A. Wallace, Secretary of War Henry L. Stimson, and Army Chief of Staff George C. Marshall all approved the plan and

sent it to the White House. The recommendation came back almost immediately, marked "OK, FDR."[7]

With impetus to proceed, the move to involve the best of American scientists—physicists and chemists, primarily—took shape. A dynamic,
brash, abrasive, demanding, determined colonel and soon-to-be briga-
dier general, Leslie R. Groves, was selected to guide the program. After
interviewing numerous scientists, he settled on J. Robert Oppenheimer of
the University of California-Berkeley to head this most secret of projects.

Oppenheimer was a surprising choice, and Groves encountered some
resistance. The scientist had left-wing connections, anathema to the military, but Groves, always a decisive figure, liked Oppenheimer's intel-
ligence and style. As he argued for a centralized location for all those
working on the project, Oppenheimer did not challenge Groves's position that compartmentalization—the principle that people involved
should know only what was necessary to perform their job—was essential. Groves was adamant about this issue, and Oppenheimer's agreement endeared the scientist to the general.

Groves's choice of Oppenheimer indirectly made the Pajarito Plateau a
candidate for the location of the secret, centralized laboratory designed to
invent an atomic bomb. The scion of an assimilated and wealthy German
Jewish family, J. Robert Oppenheimer was born and raised in New York.
Often ill, he was frail and spent his childhood at home. He became intrigued by science and nature. After graduating as valedictorian of the
Ethical Culture School in New York City, Oppenheimer was sent West for
the summer with a favorite teacher to Los Piños, a dude ranch in the Sangre de Cristo Mountains.

Six-foot-tall and irrationally thin, Oppenheimer was physically hardened in the vigorous climate of northern New Mexico. He explored both
the Sangres and the Jemez Mountains that summer, the latter on a pack
trip that started at the Boyds' guest house in Frijoles Canyon. He also visited Los Alamos Canyon and the ranch school, perhaps sensing the characteristics he shared with the younger students who studied at the
school.[8]

As Oppenheimer matured, New Mexico retained a symbolic significance for him. It had a spirituality that a man of his depth could appreciate. It also came to represent purity—a clean, uncluttered, sun-dried, and
wind-chapped place that embodied freedom and a lack of constraint. In
the years that followed, as Oppenheimer rose in the ranks of international

theoretical physics, his time in northern New Mexico remained a unique moment in his life. His appreciation of the desert played a crucial role in the siting of the secret installation.

Groves established a set of criteria for determining an acceptable location for the secret facility. Security was the top priority. Isolation from population centers assured control of access in and out of the facility. A good transportation network, adequate water, a moderate climate for year-round construction and outside experimentation, and a local labor force were other requirements. Groves also stipulated a location west of the Mississippi River and at least two hundred miles from any international border or the West Coast. He later recalled that the search focused on the Southwest.[9]

After an initial reconnaissance by Major John H. Dudley of the Manhattan Engineer District, two locations, Oak City, Utah, and Jemez Springs, New Mexico, were selected from a list that included sites in New Mexico, Colorado, and Utah. Dudley favored Oak City, but creating the laboratory there meant the eviction of more than thirty farm families and the expropriation of their farmland. These farmers, like many other southeastern Utahns, were Anglo-American Mormons, English-speakers. Whether this entered into the decision to forgo Oak City is unclear, but with the power of the Church of Jesus Christ of Latter-day Saints in Utah, such a siting could have inspired bad publicity.

With Oak City out of the question, Oppenheimer, Dudley, and Edwin McMillan, who was helping to start the laboratory, made an inspection tour of Jemez Springs on the morning of November 16, 1942. Oppenheimer was disappointed. The canyon felt gloomy and depressing to the man who once wrote a friend that his "two great loves [were] physics and desert country." The valley was long and thin, hemmed in on three sides by cliffs, and Oppenheimer worried that physicists would not want to move there.[10]

Displacement of the Native American population there also posed a problem. Jemez Pueblo had existed since before New Mexico entered the union. The people of Pecos Pueblo had moved to Jemez Springs in 1838, a full eight years before the arrival of General Stephen W. Kearny in Santa Fe signaled the beginning of the American era. As a result, the rights of the pueblo were protected under the Treaty of Guadalupe Hidalgo, and the condemnation proceedings planned to acquire land for the project might have been subject to legal challenge. In addition, with John Collier at the head of the Bureau of Indian Affairs, encroaching on the rights of the pueblo would surely engender opposition, national security notwithstanding. It would also draw attention to the secret facility.[11]

Groves cast the deciding vote. As Dudley and Oppenheimer argued, he arrived. "This will never do," Dudley recalled the general saying. Oppenheimer proposed the Los Alamos Ranch School area on the Pajarito Plateau as a nearby alternative. The men drove through the Valles Caldera, resplendent late in the fall, to Los Alamos mesa and found what they sought.[12]

Los Alamos mesa was a table-like expanse, created of the volcanic ash that had spewed from the Valles Caldera millions of years before. Fingerlike, it stretched from the base of the Jemez Mountains toward the Rio Grande. Its soft and erodible volcanic tuff surface belied a hard core beneath. And the view, of the entire Tewa world from Turtle Mountain—Sandia Peak—outside of Albuquerque to Blue Lake and the peaks near Taos and across the Rio Grande valley to the Sangre de Cristo Mountains and Lake Peak, was exquisite.[13]

To Groves, Dudley, Oppenheimer, and McMillan, the area had other advantages. Much of the land belonged to federal agencies, the Park Service and the Forest Service in particular, and the paucity of settlement posed fewer security problems than other comparable locations. Groves wanted an enclosed installation but had previously thought only of a bowl fenced at a higher elevation around its perimeter. A mesa allowed the inversion of Groves's plan.[14]

Besides Bandelier National Monument, there was only one other institution on the Pajarito Plateau. The Los Alamos Ranch School, founded in 1917, served upper-class America as a boarding school for boys with social or health problems. The climate in northern New Mexico made the school ideal for tubercular and asthmatic boys while the wilderness setting gave weak and sickly youngsters the opportunity to develop physically.

The school was an outgrowth of Ashley Pond's purchase of the Ramón Vigil Grant for the four Detroit businessmen in 1914. When the four men had become disgruntled with Pond's management, they made plans to sell the grant. Pond was left out in the cold, although because the owners had given him one-fifth of the property, he realized a financial profit at the expense of his dreams. In September 1916, Pond formed a partnership with Harold H. Brook, who had managed Pond's Pajarito Club. Brook still had financial difficulties resulting from the attempt of the Ramon Land

and Lumber Company to purchase the Vigil Grant, and the partnership offered him monetary advantages. He also owned a 540-acre tract of the Pajarito Plateau, an asset that attracted Pond's eye. The two planned a combination dude ranch and school at the site of Brook's Los Alamos Ranch.[15]

An unlikelier pair could not have been found, and their partnership was short-lived. Brook was tight-lipped and serious, a real bottom-line man. Pond, a dreamer, was impractical and full of ideas that were usually undercapitalized. From the beginning of the partnership, the men clashed constantly. Brook's health also deteriorated, the tuberculosis that had originally brought him to New Mexico worsening under stress. In December 1916, Brook sold his interest in the ranch to Pond for twenty thousand dollars and left the plateau to work with the Elephant Butte irrigation project in Doña Ana County in southern New Mexico.

Pond took over the combination ranch and school and ran it briefly in his own inimitable style. He eschewed formal instruction, believing that books were extraneous to real education. According to the 1917 promotional brochure, the school had a hearty disdain for "book-learning," with Pond subscribing to a philosophy of education by osmosis. He insisted that the boys would become both healthy and educated almost without realizing it as they were exposed to the climate and as they learned the things necessary for survival. The physical world around them was so spectacular, Pond contended, that the students would be filled with questions and never even notice the effort required for daily walks at an altitude of more than seven thousand feet.[16]

Pond was anything but a businessman, and under his care, the ranch faltered. He managed the school as he had the Vigil Grant, constantly spending more money than came in. Nor did his philosophy appeal to the parents of the students he courted. Although the school enrolled its first pupil, Lancelot Ingelsby Pelly, the son of the British counsul in Seattle, early in 1918, Pond "withdrew from active participation" in the school. After being told that he was too old to become a combat pilot, Pond went to France to join the American Red Cross. Destined not to fulfill his dream, he pursued other goals and finally earned a pilot's license at the age of fifty-eight.[17]

After Pond left, the Los Alamos Ranch School flourished. Before departing for France, Pond brought in a former Forest Service ranger, A. J. Connell, and Edward Fuller, the son of Philo C. Fuller, an affluent friend of Pond's family from Grand Rapids, Michigan. Connell insisted that if he was to be a part of the project, the institution was going to be either a dude ranch or a school, not both. The men decided on the school, Fuller provided the capital, and under Connell's dynamic directorship, the Los Alamos Ranch School became a center of activity in the region.[18]

Connell had arrived on the Pajarito Plateau in a roundabout way. In 1910, he left New York, where he was rumored to have been a decorator for Tiffany's, and lived briefly with his brother in Los Lunas, New Mexico. Shortly afterward, he began work as a forest ranger in the Gila National Forest in southwestern New Mexico and soon became the ranger in charge of the Panchuela District of the Santa Fe National Forest. Connell founded the first Boy Scout troop in the state in Santa Fe, bring him to Pond's attention.

Connell was a forthright, charismatic man who exuded concern from every pore, and his magnetism carried the school. Tall and blue-eyed, he ran his school on "Boy-Scout principles." His students came from the upper levels of the American social strata and included the future authors Gore Vidal and William S. Burroughs; Bill Veeck, the man who introduced midgets into major league baseball, the southwestern artist Wilson Hurley; and many others. Many of the boys found Connell inspirational and cherished their memories of the school. Most arrived a little out of sync with the world from which they came. Between Connell's paternal attentions and the rigorous outdoor life-style, they emerged physically and mentally prepared for the outside world. Those who graduated went on to colleges that fit their social backgrounds. By the early 1930s, Connell could brag in promotional brochures that his charges had been accepted into fifteen different schools, including Harvard, Yale, Princeton, Williams, and Colorado College. Some graduates were so impressed that they enrolled their own sons at birth, both to affirm their faith and to assure their sons a place.[19]

But there was another, more eccentric side to Connell. A lifelong bachelor, Connell often invited the teachers at his school to his room for a before-dinner drink. There the smell of burning incense and his maroon damask drapes and bedspread gave his staff a different impression from the image Connell presented to parents and students. He seemed to have a phobia about women and often contended that the worst thing that could happen to a boy was to have a mother. Connell actively discouraged the presence of women at the Ranch School, as if he feared that he would lose part of his androgynous protectorate if female influence intruded on his paradise in the mountains.[20]

On his arrival, Connell faced a dilemma. He wanted to attract students from the higher echelons of American society, but Pond's informal system of education had only limited appeal. Connell also stressed the physical side of the Los Alamos experience—his early brochures promoted the advantages of outdoor education for frail and unhealthy boys—but he recognized the need for formal academics. He developed a system that promoted close relationships between teachers and students. In the summer of 1918, after Pond left for France, Connell hired his first instructor, Fayette S. Curtis, Jr., a recent Yale University graduate with health problems of his own. Curtis came as much for the climate as the job, but the latter turned out to be quite a challenge. When Curtis arrived, he was shown the six students and told, "Here are the boys; now you make the school."[21]

Over the next eight years, until his death in 1926, Curtis did precisely that. He developed the school along the lines that Connell proscribed, implementing a rigid regime that kept the boys studying in the classroom during the mornings and doing outdoor ranch work or patrolling the grounds of the eight-hundred-acre ranch after noon. The school quickly grew, and in 1919, Curtis brought in Lawrence S. Hitchcock, another Yale graduate, to assist him. After Curtis died, Hitchcock succeeded him, leaving only when conscripted at the beginning of World War II.[22]

The Ranch School taught character and community responsibility and helped young men fit in with their peers. The boys learned teamwork and interaction, competing in sports like hockey and basketball. Connell stressed self-improvement over competition, asserting that he "never lost sight of the fact that sports were for the boys." He worked to build his students' self-esteem, and the rigorous programs he developed helped young men conquer feelings of inferiority and insecurity.[23]

The students also had the run of a spectacular outdoor world. They were surrounded by the beauty and splendor of the Pajarito Plateau, and most became avid outdoorsmen. Each was assigned a horse, and the boys could hunt, fish, and ride with their peers, learning to depend on each other. They also came to appreciate the sublime qualities of the region, and some developed a lifelong commitment to the school and the area.

The school and the homesteaders on the plateau soon developed an interdependent relationship. Bences González, a relative of a number of lo-

cal families, stocked the school store with many necessities, and homesteaders often came to purchase or trade. A closer relationship developed
between homesteaders and this institution of privilege than existed with
any of the federal agencies. Some homesteaders also offered services to
the school. Dick Boyd, an experienced horse-breeder, supplied the school
with new animals every year, often taking stock from the previous year in
trade. The Ranch School eventually employed more than forty people.
Ted Mather, who married Rosa Grant, the mother of O. O. Grant of the
Grant Ranch, kept horses for the school for nearly twenty years. Others
worked on the grounds or led camping and hunting trips.[24]

Like Frijoles Canyon, the Ranch School became an economic and social
center for the disjointed community of homesteaders. Their lives and
well-being became closely connected to it. With between ten and forty-
five young men each year, the school gave the plateau a vitality that residents were used to doing without. It also provided contact with the outside world, something that did not come easily during the winter.

By 1937, the school was a thriving enterprise. Forty-six students were
supervised by eight faculty members. The Edward Fuller Lodge, constructed in 1928, housed the dining room, and there were two additional
dormitory-like buildings and twelve smaller ones. The school also provided its own power and water. Like the ccc development in Frijoles
Canyon, the Los Alamos Ranch School was a self-contained community.

But when Oppenheimer, Groves, and Dudley made their decision,
they spoiled the idyllic community on the plateau. In October 1942, the
army began to acquire land for the secret installation. It appropriated
more than forty-five thousand acres from other government agencies, primarily the Forest Service, and made plans to purchase approximately
nine thousand privately owned acres.

The choice revealed a unique peculiarity about the federal view of the
Southwest. Even though Oak City and Jemez Springs had been ruled out
at least in part because of the need to acquire private land, this did not
protect the farmers and ranchers of the Pajarito Plateau. Most of the
homesteaders were Hispanos or poor whites. None had significant political influence. No homesteader on the plateau had since the departure of
Harold H. Brook in 1916. The federal acquisition of the Vigil Grant during
the 1930s meant that Frank Bond would not use his influence against the
project. Nor did the homesteaders have the formal network of the Mormons in Utah or the federal support of the Bureau of Indian Affairs, with

rights to land theoretically protected by the Treaty of Guadalupe Hidalgo. As had been the case since 1848, Hispanos occupied the bottom rung of Anglo society. Not as distinct in law as Native Americans, and despite nearly one-hundred-year-old promises, Hispanos did not receive formal protection. The military gobbled up their land.

Once the decision was finalized, acquisition style was heavy-handed. In a continuation of the pattern that the Santa Fe Ring and men like Thomas B. Catron had perfected at the end of the nineteenth century, Hispano land was taken by Anglos for purposes of their own. In this case, only the ostensible motive, the development of a weapon that would end the war, free the New Mexicans who had been captured in battle, and avenge those who perished, was different. National security replaced greed, but because of the need for secrecy, it was impossible to explain at the time. Anyone who challenged the government was labeled "unpatriotic," and some homesteaders were intimidated. One, Marcus Gomez, sold his ranchito for a paltry one thousand dollars, and many others felt that they were treated harshly.[25]

Only Connell turned the takeover to his advantage. He had more influence than anyone else in the region and resisted the takeover as much as he could. He understood how the government worked and used the position of his graduates, many of whom had become influential, to try to thwart the effort. His efforts came to no avail, and on November 20, 1942, Connell gave in. He requested that the government begin condemnation proceedings to protect himself against questions about his motives. He feared that the parents of his students would think he sold the school out from under them by choice. Connell also asked to be allowed to keep the school open until the end of the fall term. Versed in the ways of modern America and possessing influential friends, Connell played the hand he was dealt to the best of his ability. The government complied with his request, asking only that Connell remain quiet about the buyout.[26]

The transfer was not without friction. Army contractors began work around the school in early January 1943, before the army officially acquired the school, and they disrupted classes with blasting and heavy equipment. A contract employee took a dog belonging to one of Connell's staff to Santa Fe, where it was lost. The cavalier attitude of the contractors angered Connell. The army had begun work during January only by his leave, and he wanted to continue some semblance of a school. The army also requested the use of a cottage for its staff during January, a further imposition on Connell and the school. The demands seemed never-ending.[27]

What really angered Connell was the way the military tried to settle the purchase price of the school. Connell submitted papers that valued the land and the school at $500,000. The military expected to pay only $440,000 for all its acquisitions in the area. After four months, Connell received a settlement of $275,000. He became bitter, writing Lawrence S. Hitchcock, the former headmaster: "There are so many sides to the taking of Los Alamos. They stopped a going concern in the middle of its operations which could not be moved." The directors of the school thought it worth $400,000. At the end of the year, a federal court decided to split the difference, paying $335,000 and $7,884 in interest.[28]

But the Los Alamos Ranch School was finished, taking most of A. J. Connell's heart with it. He moved to Santa Fe and became director of the local Boys' Club but became ill late in 1943. Connell died of complications from pneumonia on February 11, 1944.[29] An era on the Pajarito Plateau was over, and the entire region would never again be the same.

With the acquisition of land in the region complete, Project Y administrators began to construct their own facilities. They planned an extensive if temporary community; most of the scientists required by the project had families and children. Roads, houses, waterlines, sewage disposal, and electrical power were all necessary. From a small, self-contained school with a population of less than two hundred, Los Alamos became the home of a secret installation that doubled in size every nine months until the end of the war. By then its population was three thousand.

Patriotic feelings helped account for the overwhelmingly positive response of scientists to Oppenheimer's invitation to come to the facility. The premier scientists, people like Hans Bethe, Enrico Fermi, and I. I. Rabi, knew what their task was, but many of the others knew only that they were asked to work on research within their area of expertise. Groves's insistence on the principle of compartmentalization ensured that many of the scientists could only guess at the real objective until they arrived at the barbed-wire fence that surrounded Los Alamos.[30]

The camp they found among the ponderosa pines, junipers, and cottonwoods of the Pajarito Plateau was neither attractive nor pleasant. Groves himself termed it "at best on the austere side." Tucked on the rim of the canyon across from Ashley Pond, overlooking the deep Pueblo Canyon, the entire place had a claustrophobic feel despite its extraordinary view. Armed guards stood vigilantly at the barred gates, and a dramatic watchtower silently attested to the ever present need for security. Entries and exits were controlled, and no one was really sure if the barriers existed to keep in the physicists, whom Groves regarded as prima donnas, or to keep out the rest of the world.

Life was hard within the confines of Los Alamos. Housing was generally abysmal and always in short supply. The technical area was built in a style labeled "modified mobilization." One-story and plain, without any distinguishing architectural features, these elongated rectangles with clapboard siding and shingled roofs served as the work area. Family housing was equally abominable. Except for the row of stone cottages that previously housed the ranch school faculty and had been reserved for the royalty of the world of science, most people lived in green, barracks-like, military-built, four-unit apartments. The water tower, a fixture in southwestern towns, was the only identifying feature of the community.[31]

For the scientists in particular, Los Alamos was not a real hardship. The project was like a reunion, for most of the top figures in each field were well acquainted with one another. Many had been at different universities; others had been hard to reach because of the war. They had professional camaraderie as well as common experience and background. Most were completely engrossed in their work. The plateau was just a setting. In reality, these extraordinary people lived in their minds.

Seth Neddermeyer, a thirty-six-year-old experimental physicist from the National Bureau of Standards, typified the breed. During a lecture by an ordnance expert, he conceived of a method to ignite an atomic bomb by implosion, a process discounted by most of his peers. Neddermeyer persisted and eventually was proven correct. This kind of commitment bordered on obsession. The extended work schedule of the scientists also reflected this, and even when they did not work, they could not escape the rigor of their task. Their work would end the greatest war of all time. Laxness on their part would be measured in lost human lives.[32]

Some scientists showed the strain. Richard Feynman, a brashly confident wizard in mathematics and an inveterate practical joker, forced numerous confrontations with security personnel over censorship of his letters. When his wife was ill in an Albuqerque hospital, Feynman wrote cryptic coded letters to her every day. The censors ordered him to stop. He continued to send his letters and received even more unusual ones. Some from his father were simply a progression of letters of the alphabet with dots and dashes interspersed. When Feynman was called in to explain, he claimed that he had requested his father to send him letters in code without a key so that he could pass the time by deciphering the system. He offered to unravel the code for the security people, a simple task for a man of his precocious talent. They were not amused. Feynman's practical jokes helped alleviate his boredom and frustration and gave him adversaries—the security division—on whom to focus.[33]

Life in Los Alamos was harder on families than on the scientists themselves. Families had few amenities, fewer amusements, and nothing like the research that occupied the scientists. Most of the spouses were not told of the secret of Los Alamos, and those who knew were forbidden to tell others. All faced the problems of trying to make a home and a life out of what was obviously a temporary situation. European refugees were very visible among the scientists, but adjusting to American military ways often entailed puzzling circumstances. When Enrico and Laura Fermi entered their three-bedroom apartment, they found three army cots stamped USED. They were shocked until they realized that the letters were the acronym for United States Engineering Detachment. But the Fermis were fortunate. They had a view of the Jemez Mountains, where Laura Fermi could see "the green tops slanting down against the sky, as in a three-panel picture by an old master. There were no man-made marks on the hill," she later wrote, "and I could call them mine."[34]

But that was about all the people of the hill could call their own. Everything else they had was military issue, and life easily became cramped and stifling behind the fence put up to ensure secrecy. As might be expected among largely young people with few other distractions, the population soared. Babies were everywhere, so much so that Groves demanded a halt. But he was ignored, and poignantly, Kitty Oppenheimer bore her second child in December 1944, after Groves's edict.[35]

There were other problems for the community. Epidemic disease was a threat. A rabid dog that bit several children set pet owners and parents against each other. A chemist died suddenly from some form of paralytic disease, sending shock waves through the community and causing physicians who feared an outbreak of poliomyelitis to implement a near quarantine. Santa Fe was declared off-limits, the schools in Los Alamos were closed, and parents were ordered to keep their children inside.

People made life bearable for the families in Los Alamos. "You'll always be in large groups here," Genia Peierls, the wife of the European scientist

Rudolph Peierls, told Laura Fermi, and it was true. The social life of the community revolved around raucous parties on Saturday nights, with the wildest parties held in the dormitories for single people. Technical Area grain alcohol and assorted liquors provided the impetus, and for the more sedate residents, square dancing became a passion. Eventually square dancers filled the meeting area in Fuller Lodge every Saturday night. Los Alamos reminded some of their college experiences.[36]

Sundays, the free day at the installation, completed the cycle of recreation that began on Saturday nights. A physicist used plastic explosives to clear the trees to make room for skiing, which offered a much-needed diversion. Outings were popular; Frijoles Canyon was a frequent destination for those with automobiles. Those with horses, headed by Oppenheimer, traveled the now silent trails developed from prehistory into the twentieth century. Fly-fishing was another pastime for some of the scientists, in particular Emilio Segre. Hans Bethe, an avid mountain-climber before he arrived in New Mexico, took advantage of the peaks of both the Sangre de Cristos across the Rio Grande and the Jemez Mountains to the west.[37]

Yet for the natives of the region, the installation meant only the opportunity to work at menial jobs, usually in construction and maintenance. Among the workers, those who stayed on the hill lived in corrugated Quonset huts without insulation, ensuring long cold nights at seven thousand feet. Busloads of Native Americans and Hispanos arrived daily to augment labor in the camp, the men to work in maintenance and construction, the women to serve as household help. Groves encouraged the latter, for he wanted the wives of the scientists to be involved in the project. Though such practices seemed typical at the time, the roots of the race-oriented class system that developed after the war became part of the fabric of the community from its inception.[38]

These experiences differed from those of the homesteaders. When the Roybals or Lujans fished, it was as much for food as for recreation. When Dick Boyd rode the trails of the Jemez Mountains, it was to report an accident, check on a neighbor, or go to town for supplies. When any of the homesteaders climbed a peak, it was in search of lost livestock. What was recreation to the physicists was an integral part of the daily life of the homesteaders. Pure recreation was a luxury that homestead life rarely allowed, and when it did occur, there was more often than not a purpose or urgency about it. Hunting was sport, but it was also necessary. It meant more and different food. When the people who struggled to make a living there sought to relax, they were more likely to lie down than to participate in activities so similar to the efforts required to survive.

This different sense of place was an integral part of the transformation of the Pajarito Plateau. Tourists had come to the area since before the beginning of the century, but they breezed over the landscape as they headed for other places. Delivered and conveyed by organizations and people catering to their comfort, they left little impact on the plateau. But a community of three thousand that drew its sustenance from elsewhere left an indelible imprint. Not only did their recreation leave its mark, but so did the more pressing needs of the installation and its people.

Groves economized on the needs of civilians at Los Alamos. The entire project was extremely expensive, and the only legitimate way he could keep costs down was to authorize as little as possible for civilian life in Los Alamos. The result was poor services, undependable electricity, a consistent run on housing, and frequent shortages of water. The installation was top priority, and its needs far exceeded those of the community on Groves's list of priorities. There was little left for extras.

Better roads to the plateau were one of the most important needs of the installation. Connell had resisted the coming of modern transportation. He had wanted his school as isolated from the surrounding world as possible. Nor did homesteaders have any need for auto roads. Few had automobiles. At the beginning of the 1940s, the only paved area on the plateau was the stretch from Frijoles Mesa to Frijoles Canyon. Most residents used horses for transportation, and the network of trails begun by the Anasazi and added to by sheepherders, homesteaders, federal agencies, and others still provided the primary avenue of transportation. Developing this system of trails into a network of roads that the machinery of a modern civilization could use was an arduous task.

The process of building roads encroached on the priorities of other federal agencies in the region, all of which were uninformed about the project. The staff at Bandelier often found themselves in conflict with Project Y. When Los Alamos began operations, Custodian Chester A. (Art) Thomas visited the installation to offer his cooperation. He found guarded barbed-wire gates and was rudely rebuffed. Surprised, he informed his superiors and left the camp alone. But Thomas knew that the access routes to the installation passed through the Otowi section, nearly twenty miles by road from Frijoles Canyon, and rumors that the army planned to build an extensive facility at Los Alamos abounded. Although Thomas did not want to obstruct the war effort, like everyone else, he was unaware of the importance of the installation. He was also determined to protect his park.

A shaky détente existed over the issue of road building. Groves's officers took an aggressive stance. Even before Connell vacated the Ranch School, the U.S. Army Corps of Engineers had planned a road through the detached Otowi section of the monument. Without permission, the military proceeded, and Thomas voiced opposition. The military planned to "shoot the whole cliff off in one blast," he contended. Thomas believed that if this occurred, the Otowi section would be irreparably damaged.[39]

Thomas and the Park Service pushed for some kind of formal agreement with the project. Obviously, Los Alamos was important. The secrecy surrounding the facility showed that. But the aggressive posture on the road issue threatened the Park Service, which resorted to the kind of bureaucratic maneuvering that had been so successful in its innumerable battles with the Forest Service. The Park Service was on the defensive; its officials needed to know what the demands of the army would be.

The situation became a standoff. In the course of numerous meetings, both sides expressed their position. Neither would relent. The representatives of Project Y could not take the Park Service people into their confidence. Many working in Los Alamos were not aware of the real purpose of the project. After almost three years of war, pronouncements that national security was at stake more often inspired ennui than enthusiasm. Military excess and the consistent pressure on Americans at home had begun to exhaust the nation. The Park Service had also faced the incessant demands of the war, and by 1944, its people were as suspicious as they were pliant. Los Alamos officials continued to resort to national security as their explanation, and with no explanation forthcoming, the Park Service protected its obligations. Repeatedly promised that the project would respect the monument boundaries, Thomas remained unconvinced. "Note that cooperation was promised," he informed his superiors, "but it will probably take a good deal of watching to gain compliance."[40]

Late in 1944, the two sides finally began to address the issues. The Corps of Engineers cleared a power line right-of-way through the northern tip of Otowi without Park Service permission. On one of his frequent visits, Thomas discovered a fifty-foot-wide clearing and two unauthorized buildings on monument land, as well as a surveying party setting up stakes to mark the location of poles to carry electric power lines. Thomas immediately threw them out of the monument and informed the Los Alamos commander, Colonel Whitney Ashbridge, that he must request permission before such projects began.

But repeated conferences did not improve communications between the two sides. After almost two years of random encroachment, M. R. Tillotson, the director of the Southwest Region of the Park Service, and Charles A. Richey, the superintendent of Southwestern National Monuments, did not believe representatives of the project. The cavalier attitude displayed by the project toward its neighbors affected relations. Major Frank W. Salfingere, who often served as the liaison between the project and its neighbors, was evasive about the concerns of the Park Service, and Tillotson was appalled by what he called "a continuation of the old army game of 'passing the buck.'"[41]

The conflict clearly illustrated that the balance of power had changed on the Pajarito Plateau. Used to being important participants, Park Service leaders responded as if they were in a position of power. But to the builders of Los Alamos, they were an inconsequential irritant, trivial in comparison with the project. Project Y leaders could evade and ignore, and no one except someone outside of the hierarchy, someone like Thomas, would challenge them. Higher officials like Tillotson were aware of the situation: "We realize that our opposition might not carry much weight," he noted late in 1944.[42] The secret installation had the real authority, and its leaders were only beginning to exert their cultural, economic, and political influence in the region.

Yet Los Alamos showed that its primary vulnerability was and would remain public opinion. Eventually, the Corps of Engineers backed down and found a location outside monument boundaries for the power line. Salfingere promised Thomas that when the two sides agreed on road issues, the Corps of Engineers would apply for special use permits. Yet this responsiveness was illusory.

Despite friction over the Otowi section, Park Service cooperation with the project was the rule rather than the exception. Housing remained one of the greatest needs of the secret installation, and in this, the Park Service could assist. The war had strained business at Frijoles Canyon Lodge, and without many visitors, the lodge became an attractive place to house scientists who were not allowed to speak with anyone outside their secret project. When the military requested permission to use the lodge in 1943, Evelyn Frey was more than glad to comply. In early June, fifty people moved into the canyon.

The canyon offered a respite from the bleak existence on the hill, as well as a much shorter commute than from other temporary housing areas located in Santa Fe or the Española Valley. The canyon and the architecture of its buildings had a warm feeling when compared with the drab huts of Los Alamos, and life there proceeded at a less intense pace. The spirituality of Frijoles Canyon infected Project Y personnel and allowed them a degree of relaxation and comfort unavailable farther up the road. Although having no idea what their visitors did, the Park Service staff abided by the stringent rules on secrecy. No other guests stayed overnight at the lodge, and no matter how curious they were, Thomas and his staff asked as few questions as possible. Interaction between staff and guests was minimal, as if the visitors were under some kind of quarantine. Two separate worlds revolved around the outpost in Frijoles Canyon.

The two worlds were so different that they often precluded common understanding. Colonel Ashbridge asked the Park Service to install horseshoe pits and other recreational amenities in the canyon. A graduate of the Ranch School, Ashbridge sought a similar atmosphere for the scientists. After fighting off the various requests of the concessionaire at the monument for more than a decade and battling the encroachment at Otowi, the Park Service had to once again explain its objectives. Agency policy and Ranch School–style recreation were irreconcilable, and the ever vigilant and increasingly impatient Thomas forbade such use.

When the secret of Los Alamos finally broke in August 1945, the people living near the installation were as astonished as everyone else. Most recognized that the old Ranch School housed a project of extreme importance, but few dreamed that its result would end the worst war in human history in a mass of flames, wholesale destruction, and death. The consensus had been that a secret project was going on in Los Alamos, with guesses as bizarre as submarine building and a home for pregnant WACs. When the news broke, Santa Feans claimed prior knowledge. "The 'I-Knew-It-All-The-Time Club' in Santa Fe has a vast membership," E. T. Scoyen of the Park Service sardonically remarked after he heard about Hiroshima. "No doubt many of our employees have already filled out membership applications." Yet, Scoyen asserted, no one really knew until the public announcement.[43]

For the Pajarito Plateau, the secret installation signaled a transformation. The plateau as it had been since the coming of the railroad in 1879
ceased to exist. What replaced it was socially and culturally different, a
place dependent in new ways on the institutions of modern America and
governed by people who were part of the American mainstream. The
magnitude and significance of the work done there created a world of cultural, psychic, and actual barriers that ever after separated modern life on
the plateau from the era before the siting of the secret installation.

In this sense, the arrival of the values of modern America spelled the
end of the cooperative ethos of pre-Spanish, *pobladore*, and homestead
life. Because these earlier peoples depended on fragile, marginal land for
sustenance, they had to cooperate to survive. With some exceptions,
most noteworthy the Texans who used the plateau in the 1880s and Buckman's little timber empire, a community ethic survived long after tools,
food, and amenities from outside spelled its demise elsewhere. The people who lived on the plateau had so little that they faced relatively little
pressure on their land. None could use it completely, and their existence
demanded interdependence. But the installation established formal, codified barriers that could not be transcended.

The Los Alamos facility also ended the ascendance of other federal
agencies in the area. The petty bickering between the Park Service and the
Forest Service dissolved with the decision to turn the installation into a
permanent scientific laboratory. The lands on which the usfs-nps conflict
had focused now belonged to the Los Alamos Scientific Laboratory, and
other than the point where the western boundary of the monument bordered the Santa Fe National Forest, the two agencies no longer controlled
adjacent territory. The existence of the facility diminished the mandate of
both agencies in the region. The size of the usfs constituency in the area
declined, and the nps could no longer argue that preservation was of primary importance on the plateau. Their traditional rivalry became muted;
faced with an overwhelming threat to their presence, the two agencies began to cooperate in ways that they previously had not.

In this, the plateau mirrored the rest of the West. The war became the
catalyst for the selection of areas that would be important in its aftermath.
Areas like the plateau found themselves transformed, their traditional
economies and cultural structures replaced. Populated by newcomers
and sustained by a federally supported economy, such places no longer
existed merely to produce raw materials. Instead, finished products, be

they airplanes, ships, or atomic science, made by newcomers to the region, became the basis of the economy of the newly created West. Areas omitted from war-related development were consigned to a place outside the mainstream, left to the historical vagaries of western experience.

This transformation divided the West and the plateau into two separate categories: areas with a future and those with only a past. In the twentieth century, land alone no longer equaled wealth. The formula was more complicated. Yet on peripheries like the Pajarito Plateau, few recognized this before the coming of the lab, and many western natives were economically and culturally displaced as a result of the transformations of the war. After the development of the atomic bomb, the plateau had a future tied to science, which became the basis for economic growth. Throughout the West, many places were still firmly locked into a crop-livestock economy.

The Los Alamos facility filled up any remaining open space on the plateau. Although only fifty-five thousand acres were handed to the Atomic Energy Commission, the influence of the installation on behavior and land use was far greater. Areas that had been grazed and home-steaded developed new functions, serving as barriers between the world outside and the secret research at Los Alamos. As a result, plant distribution changed; coupled with the effect of fire suppression, this increased the amount of combustible vegetation across the fifty-five thousand acres. In addition, seasonal use of any of that land was forbidden. Armed guards evicted trespassers. Livestock grazing was concentrated in other parts of the plateau. Besides NPS and USFS holdings, San Ildefonso Pueblo had charge of the sacred area between the Vigil Grant and the Otowi section. Farther to the north, the Santa Clara Reservation extended west to the Jemez Mountains. A few small plots of private land remained in García Canyon, south of Puye Mesa, but any hope the owners had of extending their holdings ended with the coming of the installation. After 1945, someone claimed every inch of the plateau, and no single entity could gain ground or influence without a loss to another.

But the Pajarito Plateau did not fade from the American imagination. After the atomic bomb became public knowledge, the region became a permanent part of a national consciousness. The very words *Los Alamos* came to represent the power of the United States and, conversely, the horror of exercising it. The name was so closely linked to the atomic bomb that Fermor Church, a teacher who tried to reopen the Los Alamos Ranch

School under the same name near Taos, later closed his school. The name bore too great a stigma for Americans who sought the best for their children.[44]

Modern science quickly superseded prehistoric ruins as the most prominent feature on the plateau. Proud of their victory over vicious enemies, Americans soon wanted to see the crucible from which their triumph had emerged. The Pajarito Plateau became the home of twin attractions, one prehistoric, the other so new and devastating that it was frightening, mysterious, and incomprehensible. Both were overwhelming, but in different ways. The old and the new were permanently juxtaposed as the facility at Los Alamos boomed and as the Pajarito Plateau became as easy to reach as Central Park and as modern as the tract housing that sprang up around the fringes of American cities.

The quiet place that had been the Pajarito Plateau no longer existed. It had been replaced by a culture that espoused the values of modern America and was sustained and nourished by modern American institutions. A community with far-reaching impact on the future of humanity became the heart and soul of life in the region. The effect was just as great on the immediate surroundings. Anasazi footpaths, silent for hundreds of years, echoed with the sounds of hikers and skiers, hunters and fishermen. Modern life had finally overtaken the past.

After the atomic bomb emerged from the facility at Los Alamos and the laboratory there became permanent, a completely new world developed on the plateau, one of barriers, instituted and institutionalized simultaneously with the establishment of the installation. Unlike previous efforts to regulate use of the region, the military took its isolation and security seriously. Archaeology and natural resources became secondary to the development of American weapons science. When Americans thought of the plateau ever after, the image of mushroom clouds over Hiroshima and Nagasaki and the crackling voices of the crew of the *Enola Gay* took precedence over the work of Edgar L. Hewett and everything else that preceded the splitting of the atom on the Pajarito Plateau.

11

✳ ✳ ✳ ✳ ✳ ✳ ✳ ✳ ✳ ✳ ✳ ✳ ✳ ✳ ✳ ✳

During a meeting to discuss the future of the Los Alamos installation in 1946, Norris E. Bradbury, Robert Oppenheimer's successor, pondered the unique predicament of life at the encampment. "It is curious," he remarked, "that the activity of the mesa should be dictated by its housing."[1] Even more strange was that the scientific installation, conceived, staffed, and supported from far away, could fall prey to the perennial problem of the Pajarito Plateau: no matter what kind of endeavor people began there, the resources of the region—be they timber, grass, or space—were too limited to sustain life at the level envisioned by those who anticipated a brighter future. Human aspirations exceeded capabilities, albeit in this case as a result of bureaucratic policy as much as natural insufficiency.

This restructuring typified the West in the decades following World War II. Only the firm hand of Norris Bradbury prevented urban sprawl in Los Alamos. Elsewhere, the West experienced the increased demands for housing, services, and resources, the growth of industries derived from the war, and the development of an economy with a permanently primed government pump. The most important parts of the economic

West became urban, spawning a rapid and dislocating pace of growth. The result was a restructuring of power in the West into hands that had not held it or had not been evident before the war.[2]

Similarly, the population and importance of the plateau grew after the secret installation became the Los Alamos Scientific Laboratory (LASL) and as the Atomic Energy Commission (AEC), formed in 1947, became the dominant federal agency in the region. The town of Los Alamos became the home of a growing population. To keep the extraordinary group of people assembled during the war, the Atomic Energy Commission sought to make Los Alamos into a typical American upper-middle-class community. Most of its residents concurred wholeheartedly, and this desire superseded all but the demand for scientific innovation. Federal agencies with long histories in the region were relegated to a lesser position and compelled to address use of their domain by the community.

One daunting consequence of the siting of the laboratory in Los Alamos was the emergence of a formalized world of barriers. When the installation began, no one except authorized personnel was allowed on its forty-five thousand acres. In the years that followed, the barriers required by the secret and dangerous work of the lab completed the process of delineation that had begun when Anglo speculators purchased the Ramón Vigil Grant in the 1880s. Although the plateau had not really been an open world for more than two decades, the region ceased to even offer the illusion that it resembled its past. It became a modern encampment, ordered by the cultural rules of an industrial society and the federal bureaucracy. Permanence magnified the gulf between past and present on the Pajarito Plateau.

For the two decades that followed the end of the Second World War, accommodating the residents of Los Alamos was the dominant current of AEC planning and, as a result, of life on the plateau. In many instances, this impinged on the domain and sensibilities of other agencies. Bureaucratic strife became a way of life in the region as the AEC asserted its power and as the Park and the Forest services battled to hold some measure of their previous position. This kind of strife was not new. Only in degree had the competitive situation escalated.

None of this was apparent at the end of the war. The dropping of the atomic bomb and the subsequent surrender of the Japanese sent a cathartic wave through the nation. For almost five years, Americans had delayed gratification and thought of the well-being of soldiers and sailors, prisoners of war and refugees. There was an explosion of celebration directly attributable to the research at Los Alamos. Across the country Americans went wild: in Los Angeles, people playing leapfrog on Hollywood Boulevard stopped traffic; thousands snake-danced in Salt Lake City in a driving rain; and in New York City, hats, bottles, torn telephone books, books, bolts of silk, and everything else handy became part of five thousand tons of celebratory litter. Since the repeal of Prohibition, there had been no other such outpouring of public enthusiasm. The war was over, and after quickly catching their breath, American leaders began to plan the arduous process of economic reconversion.

This was not an easy task. The war solved the economic problems left from the 1930s, but it also slowed the manufacture of most consumer goods. As a result, Americans had plenty of cash but little to purchase. Pent-up consumer demand permeated American society, including travel and leisure. Goods were available, but often only if a potential purchaser was willing to pay a price far above retail. But these premiums daunted few from savoring the physical glory of the continent that had inspired the nation that made the world safe for democracy. With money they had saved during the war and in the new automobiles for which they paid outrageous prices afterward, Americans wanted to see their land—particularly their national parks. Trains ceased to be a primary mode of transportation for park visitors; by the 1950s, more than 98 percent arrived in private automobiles.[3]

This set up a bifurcated threat to Bandelier National Monument. Even with the new physical plant, visitation in the 1930s and 1940s had not increased as rapidly as Park Service officials had hoped. The depression and the war had nearly halted recreational travel in the United States. But the end of the war, the many thwarted opportunities to rest, relax, and vacation, and the siting of nearby Los Alamos elevated the level of attention the plateau received from the American public. It also meant that Bandelier faced an incredible upsurge in visitors. Between 1945 and 1950, visitation increased from 10,689 to 47,059.[4]

The Forest Service faced similar circumstances. Its primary constituencies had been ranchers and timber companies, both of which had been badly hurt by the depression. Use of the national forest on the plateau for grazing had all but been eliminated by the siting of Los Alamos, leaving small timber companies the sole group of likely USFS constituents in the region. After the war, timber companies began to swing into action to fill the growing nationwide demand. The quantity of timber cut from USFS land in New Mexico more than doubled in the decade following the end of World War II, from 40,544,000 board feet in 1944 to 96,916,000 in 1956. Despite changing conditions within the agency, the USFS sought to continue the kind of close ties developed earlier.[5]

The siting of Los Alamos had decreased the importance of the Forest Service on the plateau. The USFS became a peripheral force as its territory was reduced in size and as the disputes between it and the NPS focused on the western boundary of the monument in the Jemez Mountains. While progressing toward a multiple-use doctrine for the national forests, the USFS retained its traditional focus on timber management. Without large tracts of marketable timber, the USFS turned to more productive holdings.

Paradoxically, the existence of the laboratory paralleled the interests of Native Americans. It created an isolated environment, removing much competition and many potential threats to the semitraditional economy in the pueblos of Santa Clara and San Ildefonso. The sacred area acquired by San Ildefonso Pueblo during the 1930s was surrounded by AEC and NPS land. The portion of the Santa Clara Reservation located west of the Rio Grande was similarly enclosed by USFS and AEC land. The installation at Los Alamos allowed the pueblos a measure of protection from the outside world. Stasis in landholding served the interests of the Native American community.

When the war ended, the future of Los Alamos was far from assured. The secret installation had served its purpose, and many of its top scientists, tired of the deprivation of life behind barbed-wire fences, sought to leave. Others developed an ex post facto moral revulsion to the practical results of their theoretical inquiry, and still others sought to parlay their wartime experience into careers in a variety of science-related fields in universities and industry. Most felt they had served their country and were entitled to pursue personal objectives.

The emergence of Norris Bradbury as a galvanizing leader rescued the installation and transformed it into a community with the possibility to become permanent. Groves, Oppenheimer, and Bradbury perceived that the nation would need Los Alamos. In their initial conception, the community would not change substantially. It would still be isolated and closed to the public. Oppenheimer had great confidence in Bradbury; he believed that Bradbury would continue his kind of leadership.

But Bradbury faced different conditions. His scientists were not the captives that Oppenheimer's had been. They could choose whether to stay or go. Bradbury understood that Los Alamos had to become more attractive to families as well as to scientists. After succeeding Oppenheimer, he developed a plan that stressed stimulating research, continuing weapons development, establishing a reasonable pay schedule, and most important, making the size of the laboratory conform to the available space and accommodations. All of these enticements were designed to keep Los Alamos a viable and therefore federally funded outpost of science.[6]

In a way, the predicament of Bradbury and the others who wanted to keep a scientific installation at Los Alamos mirrored a broader problem in American society. Many returning servicemen felt alienated and out of place, useless and used up in the postwar world. Their experiences had not prepared them for peace. This feeling was so widespread that it permeated the popular culture of the era; the stunning movie *Best Years of Our Lives* in 1946 was only the most poignant example.

Los Alamosans were in the same category as returning military personnel. They too had paid a high price, only to find that the expertise they had developed required adaptation to fit into the postwar world. But unlike ordinary servicemen and women, Los Alamosans who wanted to retain the insular qualities of the scientific camp had Norris Bradbury on their side. The plan he developed shaped the direction of unparalleled growth on the plateau.

Bradbury's insistence on facilities for the community became the catalyst for building a permanent infrastructure at Los Alamos. This contrasted with Groves's camp, in which nothing had ever worked well for civilians for long. After the future of the installation was secured with the formation of the AEC in 1947 and the permanent appointment of Bradbury, his maxim dictated that social growth and civilian amenities were to precede increases in the size of the work force at the lab. In 1945, Bradbury had three thousand workers and about eleven hundred places for them to live.[7] By sticking to his edict, Bradbury propelled growth at a rapid pace. To compete with universities and industry, the scientific installation had to grow. First, the region would have to be transformed.

The decision for permanence dictated clear terms. To attract top scientists and their families in peacetime, Bradbury had to offer the entire range of social services. After the war, schools, hospitals, adequate housing, and recreation became as important and exciting as "technically sweet" science. Los Alamos had to compete for its staff members. The wilds of New Mexico had to be adapted for the American upper-middle class. The plateau was rich in attractions from scenery to archaeology. Social and cultural institutions needed to follow.

A community with the amenities to compete with universities and industry ensured development at a level and pace never before attempted on the Pajarito Plateau. Despite its notoriety, the region remained remote, served only by New Mexico Highway 4. The loop to Los Alamos—both to the main gate and via the truck road—had been hastily constructed during the war. Both required upgrading. Housing remained a critical issue —in 1945, there were no more than five hundred family apartments and five hundred dormitory quarters in Los Alamos. Telephone service, a permanent and dependable supply of drinking water, and adequate sewage disposal facilities were other immediate necessities. Most problems could be solved by the application of technology, further emphasizing the independence of Los Alamos from the region itself. Despite limitations caused by developing services, the community grew rapidly, and its impact spread across the plateau.[8]

The first effect of the decision to continue at Los Alamos was a tremendous economic boost for the region. The Zia Company, the entity that managed the physical plant, offered numerous jobs. The economy of northern New Mexico had remained largely pastoral and agrarian, and American cities pulled many young people from rural areas. The jobs at Los Alamos paid excellent wages by the standards of the region and offered security. Hispanos, Native Americans, and Anglos from the nearby valleys found employment at the laboratory.

This perpetuated dependence on government funding, a process brought to the fore by the New Deal. Within a decade of the establishment of the lab, federal funding of Los Alamos provided the basis of the economy of the Española Valley. The best-paying jobs available to the people of the region were at the lab, and its existence inhibited economic diversification. With genuine economic opportunity available at Los Alamos, there was little need or desire to develop private enterprise that did not serve the lab or its people in some capacity.

What resulted was another form of the dependent economy that had characterized the region since its transfer to Anglo-American hands. Again an outside organization with little intrinsic relationship to the plateau provided most of the jobs and services in the region. Again people from the area were drawn by the promise of greater material prosperity, and again their integration into a system different from their own had high social cost and provided only a tenuous connection to the advantages of the modern world.

Working at the lab was a double-edged sword. The jobs there paid better than anything else in the region, but the work done by natives of the region was largely menial. Maintenance jobs abounded, as did openings for groundskeepers, laborers, helpers, and other similar positions. This category was informally reserved for Anglo, Hispano, and Indian residents of the area, leading to a situation where people of importance in local communities worked at demeaning and inconsequential jobs at Los Alamos. For example, Cleto Tafoya, the former governor of Santa Clara Pueblo, worked at the East cafeteria at the installation, illustrating that positions of honor and status in the valley had no meaning in Los Alamos.[9] The real money and prestige went to educated Anglos from elsewhere—either in scientific work or in management—and a distinct class structure emerged at Los Alamos. Although people from the valleys who worked at the lab were materially better off than their peers who did not, they were still second-class citizens on land that their families previously used for generations.

Yet without a permanent installation at Los Alamos, fewer young people could have remained in New Mexico. Los Alamos offered the best, and sometimes the only, steady work in this periphery. Opportunity in cities such as Los Angeles caused many of the most ambitious of young *norteños*, Spanish-speaking New Mexicans of the Rio Arriba region, to migrate after the Second World War. The loss of these people and their initiative would have been greater, and the sense of dislocation stronger and more widespread, without the installation. For many, being a second-class citizen at home was better than occupying the same role in the foreign environment of a large city.[10]

The Hispano and Native American people of the 1940s and 1950s faced a choice only slightly different from that of their grandparents two generations before. Again the institutions of mainstream America approached their region, offering material benefits in return for labor. Again the trade-off entailed accepting lesser status and pay than newly arrived Anglos while simultaneously experiencing a rise in standard of living. Again participation placed natives at the bottom of the socioeconomic ladder, in the least desirable jobs, while devaluing the psychic attributes of traditional culture.

Perhaps the primary difference between the generations was that by the middle of the century, few illusions remained for young Indians and Hispanos. For most, the cultural and social dignity associated with traditional ways of life was a dim memory, and the cash economy offered the best way to survive. Faced with three choices when they stayed in northern New Mexico—catering to the tourist trade, working at the lab, or low wages and unemployment—natives found Los Alamos to be the least of visible evils.

But issues of race and class were far from the forefront in the 1940s and 1950s. Growth was the dominant theme of the era, and the checks on it had little to do with social issues. In Los Alamos, rapid growth addressed glaring needs but occurred so quickly that the services provided were not dependable. A water crisis occurred in 1945 and 1946, as Leslie Groves had expected. Residents were asked to keep water in the refrigerator, turn off the shower while soaping, launder only once a week, and wash dishes only twice a day. As the crisis worsened, Los Alamosans had to refrain from daily showers. Despite the dry climate, the community became a more pungent place.[11]

Nor did the community or its residents have any legal standing. As late as 1948, the town had no cemetery, jail, or court, and as far as the legal machinery of either New Mexico or the United States was concerned, the residents had no formal status. Because the federal government had exclusive jurisdiction over the community, Los Alamos residents were not considered residents of the state and were not permitted to vote in its elections. At least in the view of state officials, Los Alamos was the equivalent of the District of Columbia.

The byzantine nature of New Mexico politics also affected the civil rights of Los Alamosans. Sandoval County, from which the parts of Los Alamos that had been private were taken, had its own political machine, and its officials feared the influence of a block of voters large enough to swing any election. During the war, residents had not actively sought the right to vote, recognizing that secrecy was paramount. But it was hard to sustain that perspective among civilians after the war. When Los Alamos residents tried to register at the Sandoval County Courthouse in Bernalillo, they were turned away.[12]

A legal system gradually emerged. The U.S. Commissioner's Court for Los Alamos held its initial session on Monday morning, July 8, 1946, outside the security fence surrounding the community. The community was closed to the public; federal law required that the commissioner's court be open to anyone. Judge Albert Gonzales, the U.S. commissioner for northern New Mexico, presided, providing one of the ironies of Los Alamos. In few other places in the United States did a Hispano sit in judgment of the offenses of upper-middle-class whites.

The drive for resident status in New Mexico also gained momentum. After long and intricate maneuvers, Los Alamosans became residents of the state of New Mexico in 1949. Atomic Energy Commission officials pushed for the idea of a separate county for Los Alamos, and Sandoval County political leaders, such as Joseph Montoya, supported the idea. In June 1949, Los Alamos County was created, further separating its future from the lives of the surrounding people. After the establishment of the county, Los Alamos was not only a cultural anomaly but also a political world of its own.[13]

Los Alamos gradually moved toward typicality. Military post leaders looking to boost morale published the first local newspaper, the *Los Alamos Times*, which printed its inaugural issue on March 15, 1946. Within months, General Leslie Groves authorized the development of a new large residential housing tract, and permanence seemed more likely. With a population of an average age around thirty years, the installation became a "town of dogs, babies, and bombs, in the order named." When the *Times* held a contest to name streets at the end of 1946, Canyon Boulevard, Trinity Street, and Central Avenue were among the choices. A post office and paved streets soon followed. Organizations like the Kiwanis Club began, and in the kind of juxtaposition that came to characterize Los Alamos, the newspaper advertised their gatherings next to reports of the meetings of major physicists. The strange mixture that was Los Alamos began to take permanent form.[14]

Despite the idyllic setting, the community had no aesthetic appeal. Los Alamos was ugly. It had been constructed in government-issue haste when materials were in short supply. Clapboard apartments and Quonset huts dominated the landscape, and bulldozers and earthmovers cut wide swaths across the mesa. Most buildings were duplexes, fourplexes, or apartments, hardly suitable enticements for the families of prominent scientists. During and after the war, the best homes in town were those that predated the installation. Fondly called "bathtub row" because they contained the only bathtubs in the community during the war, these wood-and-stone structures were the most comfortable housing around. Yet most people lived in conditions far less enjoyable and much less visibly appealing. In May 1946, more than 200 families lived in trailers and another 137 in a variety of wartime-constructed Quonset huts.[15] The community was as crowded as any urban slum, and the conditions were nearly as bad.

In keeping with Bradbury's edict, housing became the civilian priority at Los Alamos, but the result was little better in quality than that constructed in wartime. The first group of homes built after the war, the western area, lacked basements and insulation in the floors and had among their nefarious attributes poorly designed kitchens and plywood partitions between bedrooms. Throughout the late 1940s and the early 1950s, building was continuous. Much of it was hastily put together, prompting one critic to assert, "The whole damned town is built by the lowest bidder." The Mesa Club, a group of scientists' wives, took action and reviewed housing plans, but change was slow. The AEC built military-style housing; after the war, the people of Los Alamos sought civilian amenities. Yet even the rudimentary construction of the late 1940s decreased the number of scientists who left Los Alamos. It showed the commitment to provide services, and despite the hardships, a lot of exciting scientific work went on at the base of the Jemez Mountains.[16]

Housing remained a primary issue. The AEC sought the input of the community, only to learn that being responsive would not necessarily eliminate complaints. The people of the community became more vocal, but the military could never really satisfy them. There were too many restrictions on government construction. Neither side was happy until private construction was allowed in the late 1950s.[17] Then people could decide what features they wanted and pay for them, an ordinary feature of American life that must have seemed extraordinary to anyone who had been in Los Alamos since its founding.

By that time, there were alternatives to living in Los Alamos. Many of the employees of Zia Company lived in the nearby valleys, and after facing living conditions in Los Alamos, a trickle of physicists and other scientists followed them home. This gradually spread Anglo culture in ways that had not previously occurred. Affluent Anglos from "the hill," as Los

Alamos came to be known, living next door to Hispanos and Native Americans underscored the cultural impact of Los Alamos.

The spread-out living also led to a first on the plateau—traffic problems. The road to Los Alamos was merely an extension of Highway 4, which the U.S. Army Corps of Engineers had carved out with dynamite in 1943 and 1944. The only other entry was the truck road that had caused so much trouble with the Park Service. As the lab grew, the two-lane approach road could not accommodate the increase in traffic. Congestion was typical, particularly in the morning and in the evening. When a lanky wildlife biologist named Paul A. Judge, who had been on the front lines of conservation battles for two decades, became the superintendent of Bandelier in 1954, he and his family arrived by automobile. As they drove along Highway 4 between the Rio Grande bridge and the Los Alamos "Y" at about 4:30 P.M. on their way to the monument, Judge noticed a stream of cars coming down the hill, bumper to bumper. Surprised, he told his wife that he had never dreamed the monument had so many visitors. In reality, what Judge saw was the daily race home from Los Alamos to nearby communities.[18]

The founding of the first suburb of Los Alamos, the town of White Rock, attested to the need for housing. Located just northeast of the old bunkhouse in Pajarito Canyon and south of Navawi'i and the road from White Rock Canyon, the town began in 1949 as a lab-sponsored temporary housing project for construction workers. In dire situations, AEC, Zia Company, and LASL families all lived in this way-station community. The buildings were simple frame-construction, ranch-style structures, extremely small and poorly insulated. By the middle of 1950, 325 families resided there, and although the community was supposed to serve for five years, in 1956 some houses were still occupied. In 1961, three years after the last buildings in this "shanty town" were sold and hauled away, the new White Rock, a planned residential community, was initiated.[19]

Life in Los Alamos after the war remained as packed with pressure as ever. The escalation of the cold war, the Fuchs and Rosenberg trials, the pressure to stay ahead of Soviet scientists after the USSR debuted its atomic bomb in 1949, the continued need for entry and exit passes, and a number of fatal accidents contributed to making the laboratory an extremely stressful place to work. The tension in Los Alamos was stifling, and the lack of social amenities did not make life any easier. Getting away offered the only real relaxation. Close at hand and known for its serenity, Frijoles Canyon became a haven for those drained by the rigors of their world. Superintendent Fred Binnewies, at Bandelier from 1947 to 1954, recalled that he could feel workers "being renewed physically and mentally" during their visits.[20]

Yet the people of Los Alamos liked their situation. They saw themselves as wards of the military, and when they needed a service, they expected it to be provided. Military paternalism had convinced them that they would be accommodated. If there really were shortages, in the words of one resident, "it was up to the Army to get some of it and stop fussing." They were comfortable with their isolation and dependence. In response to the queries of consultants in 1951, representatives of the community articulated a preference for their enclosed community and outside sponsorship.[21] Los Alamos had developed the cocoon that has come to characterize the community.

By 1950, permanence was assured and a pattern of rapid growth established. Los Alamos had become a fixture, and its existence gave the Pajarito Plateau simultaneously fame and notoriety. The plateau had become the birthplace and home of the most threatening technology that human beings possessed. To knowledgeable Americans, the Pajarito Plateau had ceased to be the crucible of American archaeology and became instead the heart and soul of American atomic and nuclear science. This alone changed the plateau; it became a modern curiosity rather than a prehistoric one. Instead of connoting a romantic, nostalgic, or intellectual past, the place simultaneously represented the best and the worst of human endeavor.

The community also had a vast and previously unparalleled impact on the region. The census compiled in 1946, the first for the town, totaled 6,524, easily the largest permanent population in its recorded history and possibly the largest ever. By 1950, as many as 14,000 people lived on the plateau. Middle-class Anglo America not only reached the plateau but swallowed it. With money to spend, leisure time to enjoy, few amenities in Los Alamos, and a culture that already emphasized outdoor activity, the residents of Los Alamos took advantage of the hills and trails in unprecedented numbers. The natural and cultural resources of the region bore the brunt.[22]

Activity in the nearby monument and national forest reached a level that neither the Park Service nor the Forest Service had previously experienced. Both agencies designed their programs for specific constituencies, but Los Alamosans far surpassed previously targeted groups. Foresters had to address record numbers of hikers and campers instead of the timber companies and ranchers for whom they were best prepared. Bandelier, vulnerable with its limited space and facilities, was overwhelmed.

By the early 1950s, Bandelier had become a city park for Los Alamos and White Rock. Residents accounted for more than half the annual visits, an eventuality that those who designed the compound in the 1930s could not have foreseen. Instead of tourists for rangers to educate, Los Alamosans came to relax and enjoy a picnic. The limited size of the canyon compounded the confusion, as did the emphasis on education in the monument's original design. Long trails to the ruins, dotted with explanatory signs, contrasted with a cramped parking area on the east side of the barrier of buildings constructed to divide the prehistoric and modern worlds. The division of space ensured protection of the ruins from damage but made little allowance for recreational use of the canyon.

The local residents' view of the monument differed from that of the Park Service. After a few initial trips to the ruins, area residents became more interested in the picnic area than in the ruins. But overnight guests and daytime users shared a combined picnic area and campground. Day-long recreational trips from Los Alamos to Bandelier became prevalent as laboratory personnel came early and staked a claim to the shaded tables by the stream. Out-of-state visitors generally arrived later in the day and often found few available spaces to camp along the water. On weekends, the situation worsened. Locals picnicking near Frijoles Creek filled the campground, limiting the camping area for travelers from elsewhere. The Park Service faced a problem: local use impaired its ability to serve its traditional constituency.

Heavier use of the park system was not confined to Bandelier, but during the 1950s, the competition between different categories of visitors there was unique. Visitation increased exponentially at most Park Service areas after the war. Americans had more money, better mobility, and more leisure time. Facilities could not support demand, and overcrowding became common. Conditions deteriorated so badly that in the early 1950s, the noted author Bernard DeVoto suggested closing the national parks if they could not be properly maintained.[23] But the system remained devoid of urban parks.

Nor were overnight facilities for visitors available elsewhere on the plateau. Until well into the 1950s, Los Alamos remained a closed city. Only in 1957 did the first visitor without a permit, New Mexico Governor Edwin L. Mechem, enter the community. Ordinary travelers were not permitted to stay in town. Camping on laboratory land was also forbidden. Although the Frijoles Canyon Lodge could house some visitors, the nearest place where they could be assured of a room was Santa Fe, a little more than a one-hour drive from the entrance to Bandelier.

The Park Service faced a dilemma in management. The vast majority of its visitors sought recreation instead of interpretation. The growing numbers in Frijoles Canyon meant that in addition to mitigating their impact on the ruins, the Park Service also had to provide more recreational amenities. Traditional techniques no longer served the public at Bandelier.

There was no easy solution. Frijoles Canyon was an extremely small area, and the concentration of facilities at the southeastern end of the canyon made expansion in that direction—away from the ruins—impossible. The combined campground and picnic area bordered the canyon wall on one side and the creek on the other. Its northwesternmost point was within 650 feet of Tyuonyi, leaving little room for expansion there. Ruins and trails covered much of the remaining area. With limited space and with local residents visiting in unprecedented numbers, Frijoles Canyon became a major management problem.

During the 1950s, the Park Service was a development-oriented agency. Under the leadership of Conrad Wirth, who first entered the Park Service as an administrator of New Deal ECW projects, the agency sought to provide the facilities that Bernard DeVoto and others thought were lacking. Fortunately for agency leadership, a powerful lobby in Congress supported the park system. In 1956, a ten-year program called Mission 66, designed to renovate the park system in time for the fiftieth anniversary of the founding of the Park Service, began. Under its auspices, a development program that exceeded even that of the New Deal took shape, aided by a race in Congress to see who could provide the agency with the largest appropriation. New facilities—including visitor centers, campgrounds, roads, and other amenities—appeared at even the most remote park areas.[24]

Mission 66 had a tremendous impact on Bandelier National Monument. It provided the kind of funding that allowed the Park Service to redesign facilities to meet the demands of both constituencies. Out of the planning process that had become a trademark of the Park Service emerged a program addressing the primary problem at the monument: daily use and the consequent crowding of the canyon floor.

Overcrowding posed other potential problems. Despite the uneasy truce between the Forest Service and the Park Service, the two made excellent neighbors. Rarely did the nature of their uses cause conflict. Instead, attempts to acquire land were the source of their rivalry. As a result, park-forest boundaries were usually quiet. The battles took place at higher levels of administration. At Bandelier, there had been few disputes except acquisition battles. Since the founding of the monument in 1916, its northern boundary had been the rim of the north mesa of Frijoles Canyon, about two and half miles from the highway. After the NPS took over the monument, the boundary remained the same. But in August 1956, the Forest Service gave the AEC the area between the canyon rim and the highway. With the emphasis on growth and development in Los Alamos, this change in administration worried park officials.

During the 1950s, the Park Service solved problems by developing facilities. Mission 66 offered a powerful incentive, and officials developed a plan that, at a cost of five hundred thousand dollars, sought to create additional attractions on the Pajarito Plateau. The proposal included a development at Otowi with a visitor center and a range of recreational amenities.[25]

This forced an important question: were the parks sanctuaries of values and heritage or playgrounds? The NPS had to choose between implementing its congressionally sanctioned mandate or accommodating the increased demand created by conditions that postdated the mandate. The proposal meant diverting resources from the archaeological features of the monument in an effort to develop different kinds of use. Resistance in the agency was strong. One NPS official struck a responsive chord when he remarked, "Bandelier should be used as an archaeological area, not a playground." A counterproposal recommended a substantial increase in the fee charged to picnickers. Southwest Regional Director Hugh M. Miller, who sided with those who favored changing the fee structure, also suggested requiring reservations for the picnic area.[26] His suggestions strongly influenced the final Mission 66 plan for Bandelier.

The idea of developing a system of reservations for park use foreshadowed the future. Late in the 1970s, reservations became a normal part of a camping vacation in heavily used areas such as Yosemite National Park. As the national park nearest Los Angeles and San Francisco,

Yosemite faced the kind of urban demand encountered by Los Alamos more than two decades before. The problems of the Pajarito Plateau would soon spread.[27]

The most important part of the Mission 66 plan for Bandelier was the acquisition of Frijoles Mesa—the area between the north mesa of the canyon and New Mexico Highway 4. Although the monument bordered the national forest, there was no need for a buffer zone. The growth of Los Alamos, the pressure on the camping and picnic areas of the canyon, and the possibility of development on the mesa made its acquisition a priority for the NPS.

Frijoles Mesa would also provide the monument with a barrier to insulate Frijoles Canyon from the rapid growth of the technical areas and community of Los Alamos. The Park Service had been cognizant of the threat to the integrity of the monument since the incident in the Otowi section in 1944. After the war, both Jesse Nusbaum and Art Thomas alerted the regional office to the problems that extensive development of the Bandelier vicinity could present. Paul Judge was also concerned that local demand for housing and recreational land might impinge on the monument. The 3,846-acre addition offered a protective barrier for the ruins and could alleviate crowding in the canyon.[28] The tract was critical to NPS goals, but it remained in AEC possession.

After the Second World War, cooperation characterized NPS-AEC relations. The AEC offered little objection to the transfer of Frijoles Mesa. Since the mesa was four miles from Los Alamos at the closest point, the AEC perceived the area as a buffer zone for its testing facilities.[29] As long as the NPS agreed to limit development on the mesa, the local AEC office was willing to relinquish the tract. The Park Service agreed to AEC terms, and late in 1959, the Frijoles Mesa transaction was completed quickly and easily. On January 9, 1961, President Dwight D. Eisenhower formalized the transfer in Executive Proclamation 3388.

With Frijoles Mesa included in the monument, the Park Service could implement its plans to use the mesa to alleviate crowding in the canyon. Beginning in 1963, the old combination camping-picnic area on the canyon floor was reserved for day use while overnight campers were directed to the new campground atop the mesa. Los Alamosans could use the canyon in ever greater numbers, and the Park Service could still serve its primary constituency.

The Forest Service faced similar problems throughout the Southwest.

In Arizona and New Mexico, demand for recreational use of the national forests skyrocketed. The number of visits to southwestern forests increased from 813,000 in 1945 to 3,546,000 in 1955. This 340 percent increase without a comparable investment in resources strained the capability of the agency. Most of the facilities for visitors had been constructed during the New Deal. By the early 1960s, the foresters recognized that existing facilities were clearly inadequate.

On the Pajarito Plateau, the Forest Service faced an example of its regionwide problems. Visits to the Santa Fe National Forest increased from 48,200 in 1945 to 260,100 in 1955 and again to 5,758,200 in 1964, an even faster pace than in the region as a whole. The lab divided the western section of the forest, serving as a wedge between the Caja del Rio Plateau east of the Rio Grande, the Jemez Mountains and the vast area beyond to the west, and the Guajes Canyon area north of Los Alamos. The USFS experienced an onslaught not unlike that on Frijoles Canyon. Successful management required either creating separate administrative sections—an expensive proposition for a financially strapped agency—or making rangers responsible for vast areas, risking poor protection in an increasingly populated area.

Los Alamos was home to many outdoor enthusiasts. As early as 1944, a section of Pajarito Mountain had been converted into a ski area for enthusiasts from Los Alamos, and a dirt golf course had been installed. As the population grew after the war, so did its demands on the land surrounding Los Alamos. The number of hikers, riders, hunters, and other recreationists soared in the western portion of the Santa Fe National Forest.

During the 1950s, the Forest Service grappled with a changing mandate. *Multiple use* became the buzzword of the era as foresters extolled the virtues of managing resources for a variety of constituencies. Theoretically, recreation and other uses of forest land would be considered in agency policy, but in reality, multiple use only cloaked the long-standing emphasis on timber sales in more politically acceptable rhetoric. In the 1950s, as throughout the century, the Forest Service saw its primary responsibility as the management of timber resources.[30]

At the same time, staffing and appropriations for the national forests in the Southwest remained at pre–World War II levels. Many foresters who had served in the military discovered other careers after the war, and the GI Bill made possible their education. New jobs within the Forest Service were scarce. National priorities focused elsewhere. The Eisenhower administration curtailed plans to acquire new public lands, further limiting the growth of the agency. During this era, the Forest Service served as "a caretaker until better times."[31]

The result was a similar situation for both Park Service and Forest Service officials. Neither had the resources to address growth at this rate, and both applied temporary solutions to long-term problems. Before the 1950s, neither agency had experienced such a dramatic increase in demand in such a short time, and with growth increasing at an exponential rate throughout the forest and the park systems, responsiveness was limited. USFS and NPS programs simply tried to catch up to the demands of moment. There was little money or time to address the problems of the future.

With the changing mandate and the inexperience of Forest Service officials in recreation, the rise in use had a visible detrimental impact on the western portions of the Santa Fe National Forest. Although programs such as Operation Outdoors were implemented, adding an extra $830,000 to the recreation budget of the Southwest Region in its inaugural year of 1958, the Forest Service had difficulty meeting public demand. The emergence of winter sports, in particular downhill skiing, caused foresters to branch into another area of management, one that Gifford Pinchot's "Use Book" would not have recognized. With a limited budget for recreation, officials found themselves in a predicament.

The Santa Fe National Forest typified the situation. Nearby communities such as Santa Fe and Albuquerque forced USFS officials to address new demands in addition to traditional use, with a staff no larger than before the war. As a result, conditions declined, particularly in the Jemez Mountains, which remained isolated. The forest had few rangers on patrol, and as use increased so did the associated detrimental effects. Hikers and hunters left garbage, poaching occurred with rising frequency, thoughtless users dirtied the campgrounds, and unauthorized timber cutting and collecting increased.

Archaeological areas within the national forest also suffered. Many in the Los Alamos community became avid collectors of prehistoric pottery. Taking it from public land—AEC, NPS, or USFS—was a violation of the Antiquities Act of 1906, but no federal agency had sufficient staff to systematically enforce the law. Unaware or undaunted by the prospect of violating federal law, local residents took home whatever they found on their long hikes over the mesas and through the canyons of the region. All collectors learned to claim that they had found their artifacts on private land.

Younger Los Alamosans found their release in other, sometimes more destructive ways. The detached Otowi section of Bandelier was a prime location for the activities of young people. Unprotected, adjacent to the community, and yet far enough away for privacy and respite, it attracted the more ornery element in the town. In March 1960, Park Service inspectors termed its condition disastrous. People had driven vehicles of all kinds through the section, damaging vegetation and creating a vast "network of non-designated roads." Vandalism, pothunting, and target shooting were epidemic. The inspectors attributed the damage to the residents of Los Alamos.[32] The effect of the surrounding community on the Otowi section was already too great.

Otowi underscored an increasingly severe problem on the Pajarito Plateau. Although almost every tract of land had been included in one kind of reservation or another, much of the area had never been managed for human use. Otowi had been an administrative headache since its addition in 1932. Although it contained two important ruins, Otowi and Little Otowi, as well as a cave kiva with fourteenth-century drawings on a ceiling, an aboriginal animal trap, and other interpretable archaeological features, its distance from the Frijoles headquarters made Otowi difficult to protect. Nor did the NPS view Otowi as it did Frijoles Canyon. During the 1940s the military compromised much of the tract, building roads and installing service lines. After the war, recreational use turned to abuse, leading to a strong sentiment to release the area to the AEC if it could not be properly protected.

Relinquishing control of an archaeological area included in a monument that had been established to preserve such places pointed out the difficulties of managing an increasingly congested area. Preserving ruins in the face of all kinds of use was difficult in an urban setting. The Park Service faced a critical policy decision. Leaders had to choose between managing the archaeological resources within its domain, at a high cost, or bowing to expediency, narrowing its responsibilities, and protecting what it could to the best of its ability.

In the midst of the Otowi debate, NPS Director Conrad L. Wirth expressed interest in another tract of AEC land. Adjacent to the Frijoles Mesa tract, the Upper Crossing area, west of the "back gate" road to Los Alamos and mostly south of Highway 4, had been discussed only in private.

Since the AEC had been interested in acquiring Otowi for a long time, an exchange of lands was possible. But this quid-pro-quo proposal only complicated the decision on Otowi.

The relative values of two very different tracts of land had to be compared. One was a largely undeveloped natural area, the other a section of great archaeological value diminished by local encroachment. The needs of the AEC meant that the NPS had to, in Paul Judge's words, "decide how much, if any, of the Otowi Section" the NPS "would be willing to exchange for the Upper Frijoles area."[33]

There was no consensus in the Park Service about the exchange. A number of planners and land managers favored a trade, as did Superintendent Paul Judge. For Judge, the deal made sense. A wildlife biologist by training, he had spent his entire career in natural areas before coming to Bandelier. He had little experience with archaeological areas and focused on the natural features of the monument. In his view, the value of the upper canyon area far outweighed that of a compromised Otowi.[34]

The anthropologist Charlie Steen led the "keep Otowi" faction. Steen based his argument on the organic legislation that had established Bandelier, and he referred to the future of the site. "We do not need [its features] now—but two or three generations hence they may be quite valuable," he remarked.[35] No other federal agency had experience in archaeological management. Steen believed that turning the ruins over to the AEC was tantamount to agreeing that Otowi had no value. He positioned the needs of the future against expedience in the present.

Once again, a federal agency had to compare incommensurable values on the Pajarito Plateau. In this case, different factions in one bureau had to assess various management alternatives in the face of new influences on the area. The growth of Los Alamos called the question. In the end, advocates of the transfer won out. On May 27, 1963, after four years of debate, President John F. Kennedy issued Presidential Proclamation 3539, accomplishing the transfer.

All this maneuvering solved the problems of the moment, but none of it anticipated future growth. Although land exchange and Mission 66 programs improved conditions, both addressed the effects of overcrowding rather than its primary cause—the growth of Los Alamos, changing demographics, and the increasing mobility and affluence of American society. Capital development responded to overuse but could not anticipate it. Despite all the additional facilities, the number of people who wanted to live on and use the Pajarito Plateau was still more than the region could support without sustaining damage. The future could only become more crowded.

But the Park Service approach to land exchanges showed how completely the AEC and Los Alamos had come to dominate the region. Rather than attempt to administer an area with evident archaeological value and a unique interpretive feature, the agency chose to exchange it for an unaffected area outside of the flow of traffic that had developed in the region. In addition, the Park Service retained Tsankawi Mesa, a part of Otowi separated from the main portion by New Mexico Highway 4. It too was insulated from the influence of Los Alamos. More than any other specific case, the Park Service decision on Otowi showed how completely the balance of power had shifted. Had the battle for Otowi been against an agency of comparable strength and resources, even Wirth's development-oriented NPS would have fought with ardor. Obviously overpowered and lacking the resources to establish Otowi as an attraction, the NPS capitulated in a fashion it never would have if its adversary had been the USFS.

Los Alamos permanently controlled a large portion of the plateau, causing important changes in the physical environment of the region as well. Historically, humans and animals had used the area, and a lack of technology that could control fire had maintained a relatively stable balance of fire suppression and uncontrolled human-induced or natural burn. When the mountains blazed, there was little anyone could do. But because natural fire occurred with relative frequency, fuel loads remained low, and although fires were common, they were rarely a comprehensive threat. With the establishment of the monument and the national forest, the Forest and Park services practiced some fire suppression but were limited by the large area they had to protect and the meager resources available for that purpose.

The fire history of the Southwest was strikingly different from that of any other portion of the country. The diverse ecology of the region created a variety of fuel loads, and the long-standing human use of fire for cultural purposes created a complicated landscape. At the turn of the twentieth century, the Southwest was not virgin fire country. Instead, it had been subjected to human modification for more than one thousand years. Human use of fire in the region was augmented by a higher frequency of lightning-induced fire than anywhere else on the North American continent. These low-intensity blazes tended to last longer because of the extended dry summer season. Southwestern Native Americans from prehistory to the present used fire as a tool to shape the physical environment. Spanish explorers recognized and recorded this use, soon adapting what they learned to form their own relationship to fire. As a result, fire, though seemingly uncontrolled and wild in the Jemez Mountains and throughout the Southwest, in reality reflected a "preserved historical geography of fire" in the region.[36]

Until the beginning of the twentieth century, fire remained an important way for preindustrial peoples to influence their environment. Herders, whose propensity to start fires for economic and recreational purposes led to widespread occurrences of what scientists call "broadcast fire"—free-burning fire that responds to the natural conditions around it as it spreads over a broad area—were responsible for much of this change. A relatively constant cycle of regeneration of land for both aboriginal and agrarian-pastoral people resulted.[37]

The intervention of federal agencies altered the historical geography of fire in the Southwest. With a different approach—the principle of saving resources for future generations—and new objectives for the use of land, these advocates of conservation implemented programs that regulated not only the behavior of people toward the physical environment but also the degree to which human-induced and natural fire was allowed to shape the environment. Even with limited resources, both the Park Service and the Forest Service began aggressive fire-suppression campaigns during the 1920s.

The New Deal gave both agencies a better set of weapons to fight fires. Because emergency funding—New Deal money, not regular agency appropriations—financed fire-protection activity, both agencies could do a great deal more. In the Santa Fe National Forest, developing fire trails, fuel breaks, and the rest of the structure to fight fire on wild land took priority over everything except planting trees. These presuppression techniques helped reduce the chances of fire. Besides the work in Frijoles Canyon, the CCC also built a network of defenses against fire in the backcountry of the monument.

Fire-protection work made an excellent New Deal program for more than the obvious reason of need. With the multitude of CCC camps all over the West, federal officials needed programs that could be used interchangeably in different states, regions, and environments. One such program, developed by a young Lyndon B. Johnson in Texas, had CCC workers building picnic shelters along highways throughout the state. This, like the development of fire trails and other suppression mechanisms, was universally applicable in the forested but arid West.[38]

But New Deal programs were temporary, and afterward both the NPS and the USFS found their resources limited. The Los Alamos installation was the first entity in the region with the ability to consistently put out fires and to prevent others from starting. The possibility of an accident was never far from the minds of Oppenheimer and the other leaders during the war, and the installation had the resources to battle fire within the community or on surrounding lands. Protecting scientists against fire became a priority. As the plateau became more populated in the postwar era and as the danger of fire to larger numbers of people and secret experiments grew along with the demand on social services in Los Alamos, a pervasive fear of disaster caused a rigid, police-like insistence on prevention of every fire.

What marked Los Alamos as different was not its policy of fire suppression; it was the fear that the thought of fire inspired in the little community at the base of the Jemez Mountains. The water supply in Los Alamos was always a source of concern in the years after the war, and people in both the town and the laboratory felt vulnerable. In November 1946, water use exceeded supply by more than seventy-five thousand gallons every day. In addition, much of the installation was built of wood.[39] In a dry, windy area with little water, where unknown experiments with radioactive materials were conducted, the fear was easy to understand. A small fire could quickly become large, and its interaction with the facilities portended unknown catastrophes.

In the 1940s and 1950s, the Forest Service became the federal agency in the fore of fire protection. Fire-fighting technology improved vastly after the war, and cooperative efforts between the Forest Service and other federal agencies were common. One such venture, Operation Firestop, neatly fused the psychological and actual problems of the era. Fire protection had become urgent nationwide because of the specter of thermonuclear war. In Los Alamos, its immediacy was dictated by the research being conducted to support the American side of the conflict.[40]

A commitment to fire suppression on the LASL reservation compounded the effect of two decades of similar policy on the monument and forest land. The programs at LASL increased the efficiency of fire fighting across the plateau, for above all, this was a cooperative venture in which departmental rivalries past or present were set aside. As a result of the lab, comprehensive suppression of natural and human-induced fire on the plateau was the rule.

Fire suppression inspired environmental change on a scale similar to that caused by economic endeavors at the turn of the century. Not surprisingly, given the historical experience elsewhere in the Southwest, suppression and the termination of grazing resulted in greater density in forested areas. Ironically, these areas were populated by piñon and juniper, two drier, lower-elevation species that had climbed in elevation as a result of overgrazing and widespread timber cutting and had replaced the earlier ponderosa pine. In addition, forested areas had much denser and drier ground cover than before the era of intense suppression. This, in turn, resulted in the decay of grasslands, which were replaced by woody undergrowth. The suppression of fire limited the regenerative process of grassland; broadcast fire no longer regularly turned tracts of forest into new grassland. The consistent pattern of reburning—called a fire cycle—had been disrupted, resulting in a new ecological regime.[41]

This new stability was protected by the needs of the three federal agencies in the area. Neither the NPS, the USFS, nor the AEC could afford the effect of a major fire. The AEC and LASL were particularly vulnerable. As a result of the importance of LASL, its needs dominated life on the plateau, with the other agencies and their constituencies following the lead of the AEC. Fire would be suppressed at all costs on the Pajarito Plateau. This created a physical environment distinct from the ones that predated the 1940s. Fire suppression added a new stage in the historical geography of the region.

The changes in the physical geography of the plateau as a result of the needs of LASL mirrored a similar cultural transformation. Los Alamos, because of its national importance, was the overwhelming presence on the plateau for the two decades that followed World War II. A quiescent public and the company town that emerged made the AEC and its laboratory the dominant factor in politics, economics, geography, and environment. To keep its scientists happy, the government transformed its secret installation into a typical American suburb, with many of the same amenities created for similar migrants elsewhere in the West.

The other federal agencies, far less powerful than the AEC, could do little to resist. Both the Park and the Forest services found cooperation a bet-

ter approach than conflict. With cooperation, they might gain. By resisting, they would certainly lose. Their policies and decisions contributed to
the establishment of an AEC fiefdom on the plateau, a cloistered cocoon
that protected Los Alamos and created the insular world in which the
ideas that propelled the American side of the "arms race" could come to
fruition. Only a dramatic change in values could alter the direction of
growth on the Pajarito Plateau.

12

✳ ✳ ✳ ✳ ✳ ✳ ✳ ✳ ✳ ✳ ✳ ✳ ✳ ✳ ✳ ✳ ✳

The American cultural revolution was not nearly as gory as its Chinese counterpart. Only a very little bit of blood spilled in American streets, but the psychic and social impact of this transformation was as great as that of any series of events since secession and the Civil War. The traditional order in American society disintegrated under the weight of its own inconsistencies, leading to immense changes in social, cultural, and political behavior throughout the United States. Emerging from the civil rights struggle of the 1950s and codified in government policy during the administration of Lyndon B. Johnson, this shift in perception led to an increasingly individualist society, in which the members of an idealistic and affluent middle class defined their own values and goals and ceased to mindlessly accept the official pronouncements of their leaders. An iconoclastic spirit swept the nation; conformity seemed a vice.[1]

Like a similar period in the middle of the nineteenth century, when the abolition movement prompted an array of reform-oriented behavior in everything from diet to architecture, the cultural revolution inspired Americans to perfect not only their society but also themselves. The 1960s became an era of mass protest; from the march on Washington, D.C., in 1963 to events like the Woodstock, New York, music, art, and culture festival-in-the-mud in August 1969, people expressed their nonconformity in group action. By the early 1970s, the focus moved to the individual. Self-help books and assertiveness training gained a place on the American landscape, as did EST seminars and other programs directed toward solving intimate personality problems. A period of intense concern for the social good had been rapidly replaced by a preoccupation with the self—characterized by Tom Wolfe as the "Me Decade"—which seemed to overwhelm the actions of civil rights workers, Vietnam War protesters, and the array of socially conscious activists who had dominated the American stage.[2]

Wrapped up in both the socially aware and the self-indulgent phases of this era was a rebirth of the kind of environmental concern that had characterized the Progressive Era. Beginning with the Echo Park Dam controversy in the 1950s and peaking with the passage of the Wilderness Act in 1964 and the National Environmental Policy Act in 1970, the public gained new perspectives on environmental issues. Membership in environmental organizations increased astronomically; the Sierra Club alone went from 35,000 members in 1966 to 113,000 in 1970. Lady Bird Johnson's anti-litter campaign, so dramatically characterized for the first television generation by an Indian chief viewing a trash-strewn landscape with tears in his eyes, highlighted the wide dissemination of this cultural impulse. Earth Day, set aside on April 22, 1970, to acknowledge the fragility of the earth and the interrelationship between human beings and their planet, served to drive home the importance of the issue to the public at large.[3]

Yet the impetus behind this rise in environmental consciousness differed from that of previous conservation efforts. Conservation in the Progressive Era had been oriented toward the wise use and scientific management of natural resources. The prospect of scarcity frightened the people who became conservationists. Efficiency was their watchword. Preservation for aesthetic reasons was relegated to a lesser position in the cosmology of the greatest good for the greatest number. Progressive conservation embodied the concerns of a society beginning to find prosperity and preoccupied with the changes caused by rapid industrialization and urbanization. The 1960s and 1970s version reflected a different social situation. It had distinctly utopian characteristics, savoring the idea that the land could sustain the soul as well as the body. A much stronger emphasis on aestheticism and preservation emerged, as befitted an affluent society in which the most difficult challenges were internal rather than external.[4]

During the Progressive Era, conservationists looked to the government for direction and support. In the 1960s and 1970s, conservationists and the official bureaucracy became adversaries.

During this latter era, wilderness areas were the focus of the preservation movement. These preserves allowed a measure of competition between modern urban people and the physical environment, offering a link to the endeavors of earlier generations and providing an important rite of passage in a society with myriad ways to prove oneself but little public affirmation for such activity. To scale a mountain or to hike an arduous trail amid exquisite and seemingly pristine natural beauty needed no other affirmation. These were challenges that defined themselves, and their conquest was an end in itself.

This nostalgic vision did not differ greatly from that of the preservation wing of the conservation movement during the Progressive Era. In both, the emphasis on the relationship of the individual to the physical world superseded concerns of the moment. Besides the obvious benefits of beauty and serenity enjoyed in a trip to wild areas, this experience helped people forge a tie with an increasingly distant past. It allowed people to perceive that they hone the innate skills and attributes made dull as modern people vanquished primeval wild country and as machinery supplanted human resourcefulness.

The rapid development of sophisticated technologies opened the wilderness experience to growing numbers of Americans who sought to recreate in their own terms a semblance of the past. New materials such as Gore-Tex and other lightweight synthetic fibers reduced the need for physical strength for hikers; hiking boots that conformed to the foot made the experience more comfortable; and freeze-dried foods, however foul-tasting, eliminated the need to depend on the land. Tourists could cultivate the rugged outdoor look. Wilderness wear became fashionable, especially among college students. Even wilderness aficionados could be tourists. Dressed in clothes made by L. L. Bean, North Face, and Pendleton, they were supported by equipment constructed to minimize their difficulty.

The democratization of outdoor experience and its tie to a growing movement in American popular culture spelled significant changes in public attitudes about recreation. The wilderness was more symbolic than actual for most Americans, yet they embraced it as a concept as essential to American life as the family farm. Once again, an industrialized technological society saw its salvation in the untamed remnants of the wilds of the continent; once again, the cosmology of the outdoors had to be shaped to the psychic demands of an urban society.

The combination of the reawakening of environmental thinking and the growing outspokenness of the American public shattered the government-sponsored cocoon that the Pajarito Plateau had become. Federal agencies had always been vulnerable to public criticism, the AEC perhaps the most so. As the strongest and most influential entity in a sensitive area, the AEC was the first to be held responsible for any situation on the plateau. The Park Service, dependent on a national constituency and federal appropriations, was not far behind. The Forest Service was also a target; numerous groups thought the agency was not restrictive enough in its policies, and others saw its activities as federal interference in the destiny of the West. Once the American public began to question the rules and regulations that had legally and informally established the structure of American society, the hegemony developed by federal agencies on the plateau could not last long.

Los Alamosans had never been docile. During the war, General Leslie Groves regarded his physicists as an extraordinary pain in the backside. Subsequent federal administrators found that Los Alamosans were not shy about demanding services, but rarely did people from the hill challenge the direction in which the AEC leadership took the community. More typical were complaints that progress did not occur quickly enough. Nor were other federal agencies immune from the comments of Los Alamosans. Sensing the preeminence of the organization that ran the lab, the residents became accustomed to offering their perspectives on a range of issues.

During the 1960s, the Park Service fell from favor in the eyes of many of its supporters. Encouraged by the social current that convincingly argued that bureaucracy and government protected the status quo ahead of other objectives, advocates began to see the NPS as unresponsive and more concerned with bureaucratic maneuvering than preservation. After two generations of accepting the decisions of the agency, the very people that supported the Park Service questioned its policies.[5]

This created an ironic situation. For more than fifty years, the Park Service had relied on its friends to carry its case to Congress. Directors from Mather to George Hartzog, who served from 1964 to 1972, believed that a vocal public was the best advocate. By the late 1960s, the people from whom the Park Service most needed support were often openly critical of its policies. They questioned the priorities of the agency, testifying against its policies in hearings and writing vociferous editorials challenging its stance.[6]

The Wilderness Act of 1964 served as the catalyst for much of the discontent of the supporters of the Park Service. On September 3, 1964, President Lyndon B. Johnson signed the Wilderness Act into law in a simple ceremony in the Rose Garden. The signing belied the reality of nearly a decade of political maneuvering. Hubert H. Humphrey had first introduced such a measure in 1956, and in the ensuing eight years, it had gone through more than sixty revisions. The efforts of the Wilderness Society and the Sierra Club were instrumental in bringing the bill to passage, but the Park Service, preoccupied with its capital development program, Mission 66, offered little support. Howard Zahniser of the Wilderness Society and David Brower of the Sierra, two spearheads of the drive for protective legislation for wilderness, realized that they could not count on the NPS in this instance. Director Conrad L. Wirth and Brower had become verbal adversaries in the late 1950s, and their antagonism continued to permeate relations between the NPS and wilderness groups throughout the battle for passage. The signing in the Rose Garden served as a triumph for the wilderness movement, not the NPS.[7]

The legislation created an entirely new category into which to place reserved areas. Wilderness areas authorized by the bill were preserved, in perpetuity, from all forms of development, codifying the existing practice of the Forest Service in a formal system. Much of the opposition to the bill came from grazing, timber, and mining interests, all of which believed that permanently protected wilderness would hamper the development of the West. The individualist philosophy of the late nineteenth century lay dormant in the two decades following midcentury.

Whereas the reservation of new areas in a system of wilderness upset economic constituencies, the passage of the bill forced federal agencies into actions that they did not necessarily favor. Most of them administered areas that qualified under the terms of the Wilderness Act. The agencies were forced to ask whether their interests would be served by redesignating existing areas as wilderness areas. The symbolic connotations of wilderness were so strong that the public overwhelmingly supported the new category, even in western states. But it posed management problems for federal agencies.

The antigovernment climate of the late 1960s contributed to escalating tension on the Pajarito Plateau. Wilderness advocates responded negatively to what they regarded as the growing accommodationist tendency of the NPS; the Brower-Wirth rivalry formed much of the basis for continued suspicion. Since the Second World War, the NPS had become more cognizant of its bureaucratic survival. Its leaders knew that the economic growth of the West after the war would lead to greater demand on its resources. The Bureau of Reclamation and its ten-dam Colorado River Storage Project, even with the defeat of the Echo Park Dam, was a harbinger of the future. Development-oriented leaders and pragmatists in the agency recognized that the Park Service could not stop growth. What would surely be futile resistance could cost the agency much of its strong congressional support. Instead, agency leaders developed a strategy to try to control the impact of growth on NPS areas.[8] This policy raised the ire of wilderness groups, who, flushed with victory by the passage of the Wilderness Act, were eager to challenge what the tenor of the times told them was the flawed equivocation of a weak bureaucracy.

The Cochiti Dam proposal initiated a complicated sequence of events that ultimately divided the Park Service and its most avid supporters on the Pajarito Plateau. In the late 1940s, Congress, the U.S. Army Corps of Engineers, and the Bureau of Reclamation contemplated a flood-control dam near Cochiti Pueblo. The dam was originally designed to stop the seemingly annual flooding that threatened Albuquerque. In 1941 and 1942, disastrous floods had inundated portions of the city. As the community grew into the floodplain of the Rio Grande after the war, the strong chance of another such episode posed a threat to growth. The calamities attracted national attention, besmirching the positive image New Mexicans sought to put forward. Local leaders tired of damage to the city and its reputation while insurance agencies, including one owned by U.S. Senator Clinton P. Anderson, refused to underwrite locations that were annual candidates for inundation.

For political reasons, the original dam was conceived strictly as a flood-control mechanism. Neighboring Texas had existing claims on much of the water in the Rio Grande under the terms of the Rio Grande Compact, set up to adjudicate water rights along the river. In addition, a series of droughts in the late 1950s left New Mexico with a vast water debt. As long as the state remained several hundred thousand acre-feet in debt to Texas, no permanent pool could be constructed.[9]

Nevertheless, the idea for a dam had considerable support among the New Mexico congressional delegation. U.S. Senator Dennis Chavez was an original advocate, and his counterpart Clinton P. Anderson became a major supporter. Joseph Montoya, a U.S. representative who was swept into the senate in the Johnson landslide of 1964, was also a strong advocate. A native of Peña Blanca, a former mining town located near Cochiti Pueblo, Montoya saw the dam as the economic salvation of his home region. It was the sort of perquisite that western states sought after the war.

But major obstacles awaited advocates. Native Americans objected to heavy-handed treatment by federal agencies, most notably the U.S. Army Corps of Engineers and the Bureau of Reclamation. Neither had been sensitive to the Cochiti and Santo Domingo peoples before the 1950s, and the two agencies initially did little to promote a climate of trust. Compounding the problem, both pueblos resented the inundation of their best lands to further the growth of Albuquerque. Made suspicious by earlier cavalier treatment by federal agencies, private citizens, and legal machinery, the pueblos wanted safeguards.

The eventual compromise co-opted Cochiti Pueblo. At the request of the pueblo council, the deal gave the Indians control of the rights for all recreational facilities at the proposed dam, along with other important protection for the interests of the pueblo. The Corps of Engineers also agreed to construct facilities for visitors at no cost to the pueblo. It was a hard bargain to resist; Native Americans stood to receive revenue from each tourist who came to the lake, offering a source of income to an economically deprived group. Federal measures helped assuage Texas. In February 1963, Anderson initiated a bill, and with the support of New Mexico Senator Edwin Mechem and U.S. representatives Montoya and Tom Morris, the Cochiti Dam was authorized in 1964.[10]

The Park Service had objected to the project from its inception, but few in the energy bureaucracy paid any attention. The Corps of Engineers ignored the objections of the Park Service, as did the New Mexico State Engineer's office. The dam received much public support; the preservationist attitude of the Park Service seemed to belong to another era. This did not surprise NPS officials, who had spent the 1950s battling similar plans throughout the West. Adroitly, park officials sought to minimize damage by finding new options in response to the proposed dam. "If the [Corps of Engineers] wins out and the Cochiti Dam is built," read an unsigned NPS memo expressing the dominant sentiment in the agency, "we will have to do something with the south portion of the monument."[11]

Faced with encroachment, the Park Service fashioned a response. Besides granting an easement that allowed water to back up into the national monument, the Park Service also had to address the impact of recreational users who would arrive by water at the southern tip of the monument. Previously, reaching this area, the most difficult and remote portion of the monument, required either a horse ride or a two-day hike. The area contained numerous archaeological ruins—including the Cueva Pintada, a cave decorated with sixteenth-century pictographs—which had long been protected by their inaccessibility. With the finalization of plans for the dam, such vulnerable features were in clear danger.

The reality of being surrounded by entities more powerful than itself shaped the response of the Park Service. In the 1970s, a new master plan combined aggressive acquisition with visitor accommodation to counter the threat posed by recreational use of Cochiti Lake. The monument was to include both the Cañada de Cochiti Grant to the south and the headwaters of the Frijoles area, northwest of the western boundary of the monument. The Cañada de Cochiti Grant would become the location of a large development to accommodate the visitors who would arrive via the new Cochiti Lake—in short, would serve as a buffer similar to Frijoles Mesa. Various other new facilities for visitors were also included.[12]

A controversy erupted in response to NPS plans for the park. The new master plan inadvertently accelerated a dormant conflict based in the cultural revolution of the 1960s. As the American public became both more outspoken and more environmentally aware, a growing number of citizens who had previously been vocal supporters of the NPS now viewed the agency as stodgy and archaic. After passage of the Wilderness Act in 1964, the American environmental movement sought to apply a portion of its new power. The wilderness designation became a major issue at Bandelier. The terms of the act required the Park Service to evaluate all roadless areas of more than five thousand acres. Like many other park areas, Bandelier was reviewed. In 1970, the agency announced that the wilderness designation was not appropriate for Bandelier.

The zealous fervor of wilderness advocates persisted. Denied the primary perquisite of 1960s environmentalism by the federal agency that was supposed to preserve natural landscapes, many environmental groups reacted bitterly. The accommodationist aspects of the proposed NPS master plan became the focus of their animosity. The draft included provisions for a floating marina on the new lake, as well an unspecified means to connect the separate visitor facilities in Frijoles Canyon with those proposed for the southern tip of the monument. The prowilderness groups believed that the NPS sought an auto road between the two areas, an idea antithetical to their conception of the management of the back-country. From their point of view, the issue was very clear: a development at the southern end of Bandelier would destroy the remaining wildland in the area. A designated wilderness was necessary to protect the pristine character of the backcountry from callow intrusion.

A morality play developed, with wilderness advocates catering to the popular perceptions of the time. They defended the wild, they asserted, while the Park Service sought to please the sedentary public to win supporters for its budget. In their view, the NPS had become a short-sighted bureaucracy and had forsaken its mandate. Wilderness advocates believed they held the moral high ground and sought to make policy for the agency.

The wilderness supporters romanticized their cause at the expense of the Park Service. The agency's mission had always been bifurcated. Preservation and use, seemingly antithetical goals, had been part of the mandate and policy since 1916. Balance had always been difficult. Directors such as Mather, Albright, and Wirth erred on the side of use. Newton B. Drury, who directed the agency throughout the 1940s, was a rigid preservationist. In addition, the agency had always faced pressure from outside groups. In this case, environmentalists sought to mold the agency along lines more suitable to them. Politically realistic, potentially expedient, and serving a broad public, the NPS could not allow itself to bend to the will of any one of its many constituencies.

There were other reasons NPS officials opposed the wilderness designation. The idea was new, and its ramifications remained unclear. There had not yet been a wilderness established in an area reserved to protect archaeological features. Many NPS officials regarded the development of the southern end of the monument as a trade-off. It seemed clear that the lake would mean an increase in visitors to the previously inaccessible southern portion of the monument, whether it was a designated wilderness or not. As the entire history of reserved areas showed, passage of a law did not guarantee public compliance. The master plan permitted the

NPS to protect the wild areas of the monument with a permanent presence.

The Wilderness Act also limited the way in which wilderness areas could be used. The backcountry at Bandelier contained vast numbers of unexcavated prehistoric sites. The terms of the act specified that back-country excavations would have to be conducted without mechanized equipment. In an era when machinery played an important role in speed-ing up excavation and keeping down costs, this posed a significant ob-stacle.

From the NPS perspective, the wilderness designation limited manage-ment options. Officials sought to retain flexibility, and specific restrictions governing wilderness greatly limited their alternatives. According to park officials, the NPS had no intention of building a road in the backcountry, but, they averred, the public had to trust their professional judgment. Re-strictions imposed by the Wilderness Act took away their discretion.

The battle lines were distinct. The constituency that supported a wil-derness formed a private organization, the New Mexico Wilderness Study Committee (NMWSC), to monitor the Park Service and offer its own evaluation of all wilderness proposals within the state. In some cases, the NMWSC and the Park Service agreed; neither sought a designated wilder-ness for Chaco Canyon, for example. But at Bandelier, the NMWSC op-posed the Park Service, proposing the establishment of a 22,133-acre wil-derness that included the entire monument except for the area north of Frijoles Canyon.

The issue came to a head on December 18, 1971, in a public hearing at the Los Alamos Inn. Sixty-one people attended the meeting, of whom forty spoke. Another 174 letters were placed in the record, over-whelmingly supporting the idea of a wilderness. The New Mexico Wil-derness Study Committee led private organizations in opposition. Nor-man Bullard of the NMWSC expressed the view of the majority of the groups. He sought to protect the backcountry from "changing adminis-trative perceptions." Each of the private citizens who spoke opposed the no-wilderness recommendation of the agency, as did all who wrote let-ters. "Why invite another Yosemite?" wrote Steve Schum, the president of the University of New Mexico Mountaineering Club. "Anthropologists can research and develop ruins without using mechanized equipment." Echoing the sentiment of many, Elizabeth A. Jackson of Guilford, Con-necticut, wrote that wilderness was "the only way to preserve [Bandelier's] pristine state."[13] Many others stressed the compatibility of wilderness and archaeological management. Of the forty speakers in Los Alamos, fourteen supported the Wilderness Study Committee and its 22,133-acre proposal while an additional twenty-five supported the general idea of a wilderness in the Bandelier backcountry.

Bullard's comments pointed out the wide gulf that had developed between the NPS and other preservation groups. His choice of the phrase "changing administrative perceptions" reflected a lack of faith in the federal agency charged with preservation. Large segments of its public did not trust the Park Service, at least when it came to matters of wilderness, and the agency would have to find support for its proposal elsewhere.

The exuberance of some advocates cast doubt on the validity of some of their ideas. Unaware that the provisions of the act limited wilderness areas to undeveloped land, many wanted to add the Cañada de Cochiti Grant to the proposed wilderness. But prior human use had compromised its eligibility under the conditions set out in the Wilderness Act. Other advocates even suggested that the entire monument, including the developed portions of Frijoles Canyon and Frijoles Mesa, be declared a wilderness. The range of issues was broader than most of the respondents realized.

The result was a battle between a vocal constituency and its longtime ally, a battle made more contentious by the antigovernment tenor of the era. Both sides had valid points: a designated wilderness guaranteed a pristine backcountry in the future, and a lack of designation permitted flexible response. In their zeal, advocates sought to shape agency policy without clearly understanding its basis. The Park Service reacted too timidly in the face of the dam and underestimated the support for wilderness. It also failed to anticipate the demands of its traditional supporters. A long-standing alliance suffered as each side perceived malice in the actions of the other.

Resolution required compromise. In New Mexico, advocates of wilderness had strong support. The new designation and its appeal to vocal and visible interest groups made wilderness an attractive option. Compared with what seemed to be an ordinary, dull bureaucratic plan, wilderness received considerable backing. In response to the public pressure, NPS officials reconsidered. In August 1972, the agency recommended a wilderness area of 21,110 acres for Bandelier. To the cheers of the environmental community and many within the agency, the wilderness area was established in 1976.[14]

As if to justify its original position, the Park Service was determined to manage the proposed wilderness in conjunction with the planned development. NPS officials sought to dispel notions of the incompatibility of the two objectives. Despite the designation of a wilderness at Bandelier, the agency excised only the most blatantly threatening features—the floating marina and the proposed "connection" between Frijoles Canyon and the Cañada de Cochiti Grant—from the final master plan for the monument. The accepted program authorized a wide range of management goals, allowing the Park Service to retain flexibility. It seemed that a compromise had been reached.

The possibilities that had spurred the uproar failed to materialize. The recreational bonanza at Cochiti Lake never developed. Despite growing nationwide enthusiasm for outdoor sports, Cochiti Lake did not lure large numbers of middle-class Americans. The location imposed too many restrictions for most vacationers. The lands on which homesites were located were pueblo trust lands and could be sold only with permission of the Bureau of Indian Affairs. The BIA offered only long-term leases for land and homes; outright purchase was not permitted. To Americans looking for vacation property, this prospect was daunting. Jurisdiction presented another problem. Tribal law governed the community, providing one more obstacle for potential owners. No-wake zoning of the lake, which limited the use of powerboats, also made the area less attractive to recreation seekers. After a long slow descent, the company that managed the lake padlocked its doors in 1984 and filed for bankruptcy.[15]

The Forest Service fared no better with the wilderness constituency. The Roadless Area Review and Evaluation (RARE I & II) processes of the 1970s further highlighted the differences between federal agencies and a growing segment of the public. RARE I, the initial stage in evaluating national forest land for inclusion in the national wilderness system under the Wilderness Act, began in 1973, but it was an incomplete, slow process that frustrated both preservation advocates and those who wanted to develop national forest land. In 1977, the Forest Service came out with its RARE II proposal, designed to speed up the review process and evaluate all national forest land in the United States.[16]

Although a solid idea in principle, RARE II offended wilderness advocates in the West. The emphasis of the Forest Service on multiple use—the doctrine of balancing a number of different kinds of uses of national forest land—angered the wilderness community, as did the quantitative nature of the assessment of roadless areas. The Forest Service used a formula that assigned numeric values in four categories to each roadless tract of more than five thousand acres. On that basis, the USFS placed the areas in one of three categories: instant wilderness, further review, or unsuited for wilderness designation.

Despite the efforts of the Forest Service to involve the public, wilderness advocates found the process unsatisfactory. Organizations like the New Mexico Wilderness Study Committee regarded multiple use as a euphemism for development. Environmentalists believed that the RARE II process was designed to move quickly to placate timber, grazing, and mining interests and that the quantitative measurement system was a threat to equitable assessment of the aesthetic value of wildland.[17]

This backlash against the Forest Service differed from that directed at the Park Service. The idea of protected wild areas in the federal system had begun in the Forest Service, which had protected the vast majority of them before 1964, but the utilitarian emphasis that dated from the founding of the agency ensured an adversarial relationship with wilderness advocates. The Park Service had disappointed the wilderness movement in the 1950s, but by the early 1970s, it had again begun to seem responsive. From the national to the local level, wilderness advocates generally did not regard the Forest Service as either friends or allies.

The Park Service favored the goals of RARE II but found the selection process cumbersome and ineffective. By the middle of the 1970s, the idea of wilderness had gained a strong position in the Park Service. Sensitive to public opinion, the NPS recognized the advantages of such a popular idea. Officials made their peace with the wilderness movement as greater numbers of natural scientists reached management positions in the agency. More sensitive to ecological concerns than their predecessors, the new leaders took steps toward ensuring the position of wilderness in their agency. In addition, the upheaval of the 1960s produced a new generation of park rangers, many of whom were trained in fields such as ecology and who became avid supporters of wilderness. As wilderness areas ceased to be perceived as management liabilities in the park system, NPS officials sought the designation. But in the Southwest, where Park and Forest service holdings often abutted, relations remained rancorous, and the evaluation process caused numerous problems. As they had for more than two generations, the agencies saw different qualities in the same tracts.[18]

Typically, the Pajarito Plateau became the scene of a comparison of different perspectives. In the proposal for the western half of the Santa Fe National Forest, the USFS reviewed two areas near Bandelier—the St. Peter's Dome area west of the Bandelier Wilderness and the Caja del Rio area, east of the Rio Grande—as well as a number of other sections in the Jemez Mountains, for inclusion in the national wilderness system. To the Park Service and the prowilderness community, the areas close to the monument offered important additions to the Bandelier Wilderness. The NMWSC strongly advocated a recommendation of instant wilderness for both of these regions, as well as many of the areas in the Jemez.

The Forest Service had existing wilderness areas in the Santa Fe National Forest. One, the 41,132-acre San Pedro Parks Wilderness, dated from 1964, the year of the passage of the Wilderness Act. Located in the far northwestern corner of the forest—northwest of Jemez Springs, north of the Rio Puerco, and south of Gallina—the wilderness lacked substantial economic potential. Also in 1964, 167,416 acres in the Sangre de Cristo Mountains became the Pecos Wilderness. Split between the Carson and Santa Fe national forests, the Pecos Wilderness became one of the most heavily used in the nation. When addressing wilderness, the Forest Service was in familiar if not completely comfortable territory.

Yet the USFS remained true to its original value system. The RARE II administrator, Zane G. Smith, admitted that the review was "skewed toward the commodity side" and that the decisions of the USFS reflected this perspective. In places with sparse stands of economically valuable trees or without easy access for trucks to haul timber, the agency favored wilderness. When competing economic interests existed, utilitarian use generally won out. But the law required that each roadless area be evaluated, even though some seemed compromised. For example, a natural-gas pipeline road on the south boundary of the Caballo tract, next to Los Alamos, damaged the area's quality as a potential wilderness. The tract failed the minimum statutory tests for designation. RARE II required a review of this kind of area, but critics charged that such action provided evidence that the Forest Service conspired against the concept of wilderness.

The Forest Service faced a dilemma. Many of its roadless areas were high-mountain sections that were difficult to log. These were the best candidates for wilderness, for they were the most inaccessible. Conversely, they were the most remote from people—who wanted accessible wilderness. As a result, few areas on the Pajarito Plateau fit the concept of the usfs. Little of the region had not been affected by human beings. The agency's focus on multiple use and prior patterns of use in the area determined that the usfs proposals were generally mountaintops and unique features with little apparent economic value.

In this, the wilderness regions were only vaguely different from the national parks established in the late nineteenth and early twentieth centuries. The early parks were selected from lands for which no one could find profitable economic use at the time. It was not that places like Yosemite, Yellowstone, Mount Rainier, Glacier, and Grand Teton did not have economic value.[19] But their economic value was limited by the market conditions of the time, by transportation, by better, more easily accessible resources, and by other similar concerns. Their extraordinary features made them good candidates for park status.

There was an ecological drawback to the selection process. Like the parks of a century before, the wilderness areas were more alike than different in character. They had become islands of preservation, diminished in integrity as the character of the lands around them changed. In addition, such a wilderness system would have primarily scenic value. More accessible lands at lower elevations would be altered, leaving the wilderness areas as a representation of a limited natural world.

During the RARE II process in northern New Mexico, these premises governed the planning of the Forest Service. The bulk of its proposed acreage was adjacent to the Pecos Wilderness, the only area in the forest where the usfs perceived that aesthetic values superseded economic ones. In contrast, the wilderness values of areas closer to valuable resources or competing agencies did not impress the Forest Service. Most of the proposals were small; the high-elevation areas of the Jemez were exquisite canyons or mountaintops, no larger than fifteen thousand acres. Only one area in the mountains, a tract that combined archaeological features, an escarpment, and desert arroyos, was larger—and it was only fifty thousand acres. "Wood-hauler rut roads" crisscrossed the Caja del Rio section, the next largest at twenty-nine thousand acres, and Cochiti Lake and White Rock Canyon separated it from the Bandelier Wilderness. The Forest Service valued the wild character of the Dome section even less. Of the fourteen areas within the forest assessed by the formula, the Dome section rated the lowest.[20]

Again incommensurable comparisons had to be made. Although the aesthetic qualities of the areas did not meet the criteria of the Forest Service, wilderness advocates saw a permanently protected biota that transcended jurisdictional boundaries. A series of areas in the Jemez would serve as a savings account against future change. In particular, the two tracts next to Bandelier inspired support. The wilderness groups saw them as an extension of the original idea. For the Park Service, further designation would affirm its decision at Bandelier and offer the guarantee that the wilderness area within the monument would not be damaged by the development of its watershed.

In June 1978, the Forest Service debuted the Draft Environmental Impact Statement of RARE II for the Santa Fe National Forest. Despite the negative appraisals, the document included a number of areas on the Pajarito Plateau. With the exception of 129,500 acres next to the Pecos Wilderness Area in the Sangre de Cristos, the remaining proposals were for small areas, closely fitting the idea that these areas were of little economic value at that time. The two areas close to Bandelier—the 15,000-acre St. Peter's Dome tract and the 9,000-acre Caja del Rio area—were recommended. The Park Service also supported these two areas.[21]

When the final Forest Service RARE II plan for the Santa Fe National Forest emerged in early 1979, the wilderness constituency was outraged. The Forest Service sought to designate only 6,000 acres of the Dome area as wilderness, slicing 75 percent of the total wilderness acreage that the draft proposal had recommended. Even the ever popular Pecos Wilderness suffered. Only 55,000 acres of the original 129,500-acre addition were added. Despite the fact that the 50,260-acre Chama River Canyon Wilderness Area had been established the year before, the decision of the Forest Service did little to reconcile the differences between federal agencies and the wilderness constituency on the Pajarito Plateau.

RARE II also had national repercussions. Earlier in the process, a coalition of the most important conservation and environmental groups, including the Wilderness Society, the Sierra Club, Friends of the Earth, and the National Audubon Society, recommended wilderness designation for thirty-six million of the sixty-two million acres reviewed by the Forest Service. The final proposal designated slightly more than fifteen million acres, less than one-fourth the acreage reviewed. It seemed to many that the usfs had capitulated to development interests. The coalition labeled the proposal "an acute disappointment."[22]

The battle over wilderness on the Pajarito Plateau showed how fragile relations had become in the region. In a short time span, the Park Service found itself with a new conception of its mission, one that squared with the goals of the vocal group that had recently castigated it. This rebuilt alliances that had collapsed, and strengthened the nps against a traditional rival. The crowded situation pushed the Park Service toward preservation more quickly on the plateau than elsewhere in the nation.

Other developments in northern New Mexico encroached on the isolated world of Los Alamos and the Pajarito Plateau. Among the cultural changes of the era was an increased emphasis on the position of minorities. Riots in American cities showed the previously placid that issues of race, class, and economics had to be addressed. In New Mexico, this translated into attempts by Hispanos to play a meaningful role in the political, cultural, and economic life of the state. Left out since the American army captured Santa Fe in 1846, Hispanos began an assault on the status quo during the 1960s. Much of their animosity focused on the loss of land to Anglos and federal agencies.

Beginning in the mid-1960s, Hispanos in New Mexico began to assert their historic rights to land. New Mexico provided a rare opportunity to challenge the system. The Treaty of Guadalupe Hidalgo guaranteed the rights of former Mexican citizens and their descendants in the areas annexed by the United States after the Mexican War, but in many parts of the Southwest, Anglo-American migrants so numerically overwhelmed Spanish-speakers that there was no legitimate way to enforce the provisions of the treaty, had anyone cared to. California served as an example; within a decade of the discovery of gold, the Hispanic presence had been obliterated by waves of miners. In the Rio Arriba region of northern New Mexico, however, Hispanos remained equal to if not larger than the Anglo population. The peripheral economic value of the region, its out-of-the-way location, and the continued growth and strength of Hispanic culture made the region less attractive to Anglos than other parts of the West. As a result, when Hispanos tired of their position at the bottom of the socioeconomic ladder, a position assigned them by the Anglo world, a substantial number with legitimate historic claim safeguarded by official documents could contest 120 years of inequitable treatment.[23]

The Alianza Federal de Mercedes—the Federal Alliance of Land Grants —was headed by a forty-year-old son of a sharecropper, an evangelist-turned-revolutionary named Reies Lopez Tijerina, who embodied the hopes of Spanish-speaking New Mexicans. Tijerina had marched on Washington with Dr. Martin Luther King, Jr., in 1963 and, in the same vein, envisioned a populist crusade that would free land from the hold of oppressors, individual or systemic. Yet there were major differences between King and Tijerina, the most important of which was that Tijerina saw violence as a necessary part of the struggle. Beginning in 1966 and reaching a high point on June 5, 1967, the Alianza made concerted efforts to "liberate"—in the phrase of the time—land grants transferred from Hispano to Anglo hands. In one instance, Alianza members placed two USFS rangers on trial on a land grant that had become the property of the Forest Service; in another, they raided the Rio Arriba County Courthouse in Tierra Amarilla, wounding one police officer and kidnaping another and a UPI reporter.[24]

This kind of unrest was divorced from the world that surrounded Los Alamos. Los Alamos and White Rock had become bedroom communities, predominantly Anglo and complete with a golf course and Kentucky bluegrass lawns that required daily watering. Their architecture was suburban and bland, from Anywhere, U.S.A. It looked as if the tornado that had carried Dorothy to Oz had also deposited the two communities on the plateau. Even the transfer of land had been orderly; the military had coerced homesteaders in the 1940s, but the ubiquitous citing of national security seemed to justify its behavior. The issues of Los Alamos were those of a white-collar company town. The hill and its high-paid technical staff were a cultural millennium away from the turmoil along the Rio Grande.

Yet Los Alamos was not as removed from the conditions that spurred the Alianza as many of its residents would have liked to suppose. Although LASL was a major provider of employment for Hispanos and although the wages they received were excellent by the standards of northern New Mexico, Los Alamos had a built-in class system that relegated Hispanos and Indians to its lower levels. The nature of white-collar work in Los Alamos required scientific education, and the vast majority of people in this work were white males who had received their training outside of New Mexico. Natives of the region filled lower positions, many in construction, maintenance, food service, and other similar areas. They often competed with each other for what the most embittered among them referred to as scraps off the white man's table. A few rose to supervisory positions, but generally in fields that did not demand Ph.D.-level training in science.

Nor was this phenomenon exclusive to Los Alamos. At Cochiti Dam, Indians received preferential hiring treatment for available construction jobs. As a result, members of the two pueblos, Cochiti and Santo Domingo, made up the minority proportion of the work force at the dam, effectively freezing out equally needy Hispanos from U.S. Senator Joseph Montoya's hometown of Peña Blanca. This kind of situation fed the issues of the time and created competition and hard feelings among those scrambling for the crumbs of material prosperity.

In essence, the emergence of Los Alamos in the postwar era grafted an upper-middle class on an economic region that lacked a strong traditional middle class. The result resembled economic distribution in the third world, with a small, affluent, largely white upper-middle class and numerous poorer nonwhites seeking to serve them. Los Alamos County was more than 80 percent Anglo. In the two counties that surrounded it, Sandoval and Rio Arriba, Hispanos and Indians made up more than 80 percent of the population in 1970. In Los Alamos, the median family income in 1970 was $15,273, the highest standard of living in the state. Together, the median incomes of Sandoval and Rio Arriba, perennially among the poorest, were slightly more than two-thirds of that in Los Alamos. The cost of living was so high in Los Alamos that even the highest-paid nontechnical workers continued to live in the valleys. Had those who could have afforded it decided to move, they would have found a foreign, white-bread culture that would have made them feel like outsiders. An important truth remained: workers from the valleys were economically dependent on Los Alamos, but no matter how hard they worked, they would not attain the level of affluence of the scientific community.

This placed valley residents who worked at the lab in an awkward social position in the late 1960s and the 1970s. Although their economic position was generally better than that of their neighbors, they were regarded in varying degrees as *vendidos*, or sellouts. Too few in number to constitute a strong middle class, such workers remained trapped between the increasing militance of Hispanos and their own psychic and material aspirations in the Anglo world of Los Alamos.

Those material aspirations had genuine advantages. Jobs at the lab were another form of pioneering the cash economy, bringing the benefits of the outside world home. Cash money gave the people of the region access to goods they could not have previously afforded. It also created economic security that rippled throughout families as the extended network of kinship made the results of one worker's labor available to many. Increases in income gave people a greater measure of control over their lives, and distance from abject poverty modified traditional life-styles with new material advantages, in some cases paving the way toward more comprehensive assimilation. Income at least partially enfranchised people of the region; it gave them new economic independence, a greater measure of control over their interaction with the modern world, and material means and role models to protect their interests.[25]

Yet an ongoing issue for nonwhites in the region and across the nation resurfaced. There was an all-or-nothing feel to the late 1960s and early 1970s, an immediacy that demanded personal and cultural fidelity. To waver was to sell out. Indians and Hispanos confronted a question that their grandparents would have recognized. They could participate in a world that rewarded them materially but consigned them to second-class status, or they could remain apart, seeking the kind of cultural integrity that militants advocated in this era but simultaneously risking poverty and the myriad shortcomings it guaranteed. The dilemma these people faced was largely the same one their ancestors had encountered at the turn of the century; the choices the younger generation made were politically charged and seemingly more extreme.

For Los Alamosans, highly educated denizens of an extremely sophisticated version of the company town, the situation posed a paradox. The lab was good to its people, but the science it offered challenged the values of its scientists. Race and class animosities were less visible, since scientists regarded the lack of Hispanos in scientific positions as a function of educational level rather than systemic disorder. Los Alamosans soon earned the reputation of being liberal about all the wrong things—social issues as opposed to the great moral issues such as the Vietnam War, that faced American society. Los Alamos developed a self-indulgent attitude reminiscent of the upper-middle class, critics charged, an attitude made possible by its economic dependence on the weapons industry.

During the 1970s, a gradual opening of the psychic barriers in Los Alamos occurred, although economic and cultural limits remained. By the early 1980s, Los Alamos schools admitted the children of people who lived in the valley and worked at the lab, an important step toward assuring some semblance of equality of opportunity. In some cases, Hispanos advanced to positions of significant responsibility, but largely in non-technical areas. Although some critics, following the tone of the times, called such advances tokenism, in reality they portended a gradual lessening of race and class distinction. The status quo remained, but small cracks in the wall of systematic exclusion had begun.

Ultimately, differences in perspective were overshadowed by the looming possibility of natural or man-caused disaster in the region. By the middle of the 1970s, all kinds of fires had been suppressed on the plateau for more than forty years. The vast increase in density of ground cover and the almost total halt of the natural cycle of ecological replacement increased the likelihood of a major fire. Testing at the LASL compounded the general uneasiness of the people of Los Alamos and the rest of the plateau. Although federal agencies in the region did an excellent job of suppressing fires, the fire history of the region and its unique geography suggested that such successes could not last forever. All of those fears came to fruition late on the afternoon of June 16, 1977, when a spark from a cigarette, a motorcycle engine, or a chainsaw smoldered in a pile of leaves on the Mesa del Rito in the national forest and grew into the largest fire on the Pajarito Plateau in the twentieth century.

This catastrophe—known as La Mesa fire—was a major environmental disaster. The spread of the fire was terrifying. Hot, dry, windy weather and a dense fuel load in the area of ignition fed the fire, which spread quickly. Within an hour and one-half of the initial siting at about 4:00 P.M., the fire had covered more than fifty acres. It spread from the Mesa del Rito area into the monument by midnight on June 17, penetrating as far as Escobas Mesa in the western section of the monument. By noon on June 18, the fire had crossed State Highway 4, headed toward Los Alamos. Each day, it gobbled vast tracts of forest, gaining in strength and intensity from the fuel it consumed. Weather worsened the situation for the next few days as winds revived the fire a number of times when it had seemed to lose intensity. By June 21, intermittent thunderstorms began to slow the fire; officials declared it contained, in what was conservatively estimated at fifteen thousand acres, at 3:00 P.M. Two days later, heavy rain and cool temperatures continued, and at 4:00 P.M. that afternoon, the fire was considered under control.

The damage was devastating. Raging for a week, the fire destroyed more than twenty-three thousand acres of the plateau, including more than ten thousand acres of timber in the northwestern portion of Bandelier and an additional five thousand acres in the adjacent national forest and on LASL land. The families who lived in Frijoles Canyon had been evacuated early in the fire. Cinders and burning ash fell in White Rock. Some of the technical areas south of Los Alamos were threatened by the blaze. Wood-shingled roofs there were hosed down constantly in an effort to prevent them from igniting. There had been many small fires on the plateau since the establishment of Los Alamos, but never one that went out of control so quickly and burned such a large area.

Every available human resource joined against the fire. Fire-fighting crews from the lab, the Park Service, the Forest Service, and a host of other federal, state, and local agencies threw in together to face the threat. Enlisted to stop its progress were 1,370 people, nine bulldozers, twenty-three ground tankers, five helicopters, and five air tankers. Fire fighters swung their Pulaskis—a combination mattock and ax—in two twelve-hour shifts around the clock in the heavy smoke; many slumped exhausted at the end of their shift, only to rise again in the morning and repeat the battle.[26]

The fire traveled an enormous distance, growing in concentric circles each day, beginning in the national forest and spreading on the east to within about three miles of Frijoles Canyon. Only the most vigorous efforts and complete commitment of resources prevented the fire from reaching the technical areas southeast of Los Alamos, and for at least a day, the town itself was in danger. As the threat to modern life on the plateau diminished, Pajaritans all considered themselves lucky.

The fire became an educational experience for the various federal agencies in the region. The burned areas were filled with subsurface prehistoric ruins, and quick thinking by Park Service officials allowed scrutiny by archaeologists who preceded the fire-fighting bulldozers. This plan came about almost serendipitously. On his way to visit an archaeologist friend at the Park Service regional office on Old Santa Fe Trail in Santa Fe, Milford R. Fletcher, the head scientist for the NPS in the Southwest, looked up and saw smoke. He told Cal Cummings, an NPS official responsible for cultural resources, that the situation demanded that archaeologists go ahead of the construction of fire lines. Archaeologists could locate buried sites and direct the bulldozers away from them. Cummings, Superintendent John D. Hunter of Bandelier, and Santa Fe National Forest Supervisor Cristobal Zamora agreed; Cummings found and scheduled volunteers, and Fletcher provided supervision. Nearly forty archaeologists worked in front of the bulldozers during La Mesa fire.[27]

The fire cleared the way for greater cooperation in the management of cultural resources. Before 1977, the Park Service, the Forest Service, and the LASL operated their programs independently. The agencies had different objectives, and often their work seemed antithetical. The fire promoted new cooperation and awareness for everyone in the region. But there were tense moments. In one case, Fletcher turned off a USFS bulldozer, telling its driver: "We don't care if the trees burn. They'll grow back. Ruins won't." Nor was the idea a complete success. Although archaeologists recorded sites and guided fire fighters away from ruins during the initial construction of fire lines, they often were not present during subsequent widening. More than 40 percent of archaeological sites surveyed showed signs of damage. Nonetheless, 60 percent were not affected, a measure of the success of the program, and veterans of the fire remembered that shared objectives superseded occasional conflicts.[28]

The fire also gave the Park Service a new way to address one of its most persistent problems in the region: the presence of feral burros. This nonnative species had spread across the plateau early in the twentieth century. Peggy Pond Church remembered them in White Rock and Guaje canyons in the 1920s. In 1940, approximately twenty were sited at Bandelier, leading to plans to eliminate them. In 1946, rangers shot sixty-five burros, and burro eradication became NPS policy. Programs between then and 1977 met with intermittent success. In the fall of 1964, the Park Service hired the Los Alamos County Sheriff's Mounted Patrol to hunt burros. Despite confident predictions, they caught few animals. The rough terrain of the backcountry thwarted the mounted hunters. Trapping agile burros in open canyons and mesas while on horseback was not an easy task.[29]

The passage of the Wild Horse and Burro Act of 1971 complicated the management of burros on federal land. The law protected wild horses and burros on Bureau of Land Management and Department of Agriculture (USFS) land. The number of burros on the national forest near Bandelier increased, particularly in the piñon-juniper habitats they favored, and since the fenced boundary had many breaks, and burros did not recognize federal jurisdiction, some crossed into the monument. There burros were exotics; on forest land, they were protected species. The Park

Service, unable to stop the entry of the burros from the forest, had to contend with a growing herd in the backcountry.

The burros became a political problem. NPS lands were exempt from the jurisdiction of the Wild Horse and Burro Act. NPS policy that mandated the removal of exotic animals from park areas offended animal advocacy groups.[30] The animals were "cute," in the popular parlance, and seemed harmless. But park employees suspected that the burros were responsible for much damage to the backcountry. Erosion there had increased to an estimated thirty-six tons of soil per acre per year, an astonishingly high rate that threatened unexcavated archaeological sites. NPS officials needed a strategy that would remove the burros and not hurt the agency's public image. For regional office and park staff, the burro issue became a no-win situation. No matter what the NPS did, portions of its constituency were sure to resent it.

Between 1974 and 1977, the Natural Resources Division of the Southwest Region spent $130,000 on burro research and removal. In the process, the Park Service removed 130 burros, but research showed that the agency barely held its own. The proximity of the protected burro herds on Forest Service and Bureau of Land Management land and the imperfect fencing on the western and southern boundaries of the monument allowed a constant ingress of burros. The animals also proved to have an astonishing rate of reproduction, doubling their population every four years. The Park Service was unable to win the battle, and what had been an issue became a crisis.[31]

The fire provided an opportunity to substantially reduce the burro population at Bandelier. The animals became easier to find, since they were more exposed and much of their cover had been destroyed. If the Park Service could destroy one hundred burros, it would nearly eliminate burros from the monument. The idea was approved, and a crew of experienced people who had worked at Bandelier and knew its topography was recruited. During the week of the fire, they shot sixty-six burros.[32]

But an intemperate remark cost the Park Service some public support. During the fire, a reporter spoke with Resource Manager Roland Wauer about the burro-eradication program. He asked if shooting the animals bothered park rangers. Wauer acknowledged the difficulty of the job but also asserted that Park Service people were professionals who understood that unpleasant tasks were part of their obligation. Besides, he remarked casually, "our people don't suffer from the Bambi complex." The press seized on the remark, which made headlines in a number of western newspapers. The public image of the Park Service suffered.[33]

Eradication programs bothered animal advocacy groups such as the Fund for Animals, Inc. (FFA). An association devoted to protecting wild and domestic animals, the Fund for Animals believed there was a better way to solve the problem. Nor were its members strangers to the burro issue. When burros had become a problem at the Grand Canyon National Park, the organization proposed a solution that led to the successful capture and removal of many of the burros, which were then put up for adoption. The project solved the burro problem at the Grand Canyon and attracted favorable media attention.

Flushed with success, the Fund for Animals offered to try similar tactics at Bandelier. In May 1983, two cowboys from Bishop, California, arrived at the monument. In the company of a backcountry ranger, they tried to rope burros and caught one. They then tried to catch the burros in a foot snare, a trap hidden in small hole into which they hoped the burros would walk. They caught only a few more. After two weeks, the two cowboys withdrew.

The Fund for Animals then brought in Dave Erickson, the Arizona cowboy who had been responsible for the success at the Grand Canyon. He used dogs to hold the burros at bay while his crew roped the animals. This novel approach netted more burros than previous efforts, but even with increased success, the removal of burros from Bandelier was an arduous process. The closed box canyons within the Grand Canyon made catching burros there a relatively easy task. Pilots chased the animals up the canyon until the burros ran out of room. Trapped against a three-sided canyon, the animals were easy to capture. But as the Los Alamos County Sheriff's Mounted Patrol had discovered in their vain attempt to trap burros in 1964, the canyons of Bandelier were open-ended. The agile animals easily eluded their would-be captors.

But Erickson had a deal with the FFA, and he sought to fulfill his contract. Soon the burro corral on Frijoles Mesa began to fill. There was only one problem: most of the animals in the corral were tan with a dark cross running down their spine and across their shoulders. They were unlike any other burros ever found on the Pajarito Plateau and were not at all similar to the larger black animals previously seen at Bandelier. Many at the monument believed the burros were "ringers," but at the height of tourist season, park rangers could not stay with Erickson as closely as they had with the California cowboys.

Plenty of circumstantial evidence supported the feeling that the burros were imported. One park staff member arose at 2:00 A.M. and waited all night on Highway 4 in the hope of catching a truckload of burros on their way to the corral on Frijoles Mesa. Another observed one of Erickson's horse trailers coming to the park late one evening but did not realize its significance until too late. The staff member also spoke on the phone with Erickson, who was in his motel room, around 11:00 P.M. on an evening before burros appeared in the corral. Since the animals were there by 5:00 A.M., Erickson had supposedly caught between fifteen and eighteen burros in unfamiliar country, along miles of backcountry trails, in the dark, in less than six hours. No one succeeded in proving that Erickson brought his own burros, but the circumstantial evidence abounded.

Nevertheless, the origin of the burros was not an issue for the Park Service. The transaction between the FFA and its contractor did not involve the agency. Shortly afterward, Fund for Animals officials asserted that the twenty-nine burros the FFA had captured, including at least sixteen termed controversial, were the last in the monument. Claiming its work completed, the Fund for Animals left Bandelier, giving tacit approval to agency programs to reduce the burro population. The Park Service continued its eradication policy, shooting an additional twenty-two burros. The park also received money to fix the fence along the western boundary next to the protected burro range on the national forest, limiting further entry. By the end of 1983, there were few burros left within the monument.[34]

La Mesa fire of 1977 also offered untold opportunities to better understand the role of fire in shaping ecosystems. Before the blaze, the historic role of natural fire in the region had never been closely studied. Subsequent research showed how fire had maintained a stable ecosystem in the region before suppression. Every five to fifteen years, natural fires had cleared different areas on the plateau. Over time, this pattern created a mosaic of burned areas, leading to collections of trees of different age classes. In a ponderosa pine environment like that of the plateau, this kind of burning led to a healthy ecosystem. By 1900, however, overstocking of the range had created de facto fire suppression, which the practices of federal agencies institutionalized.

Among federal agencies, the Forest Service had always taken the lead in fire prevention and fire fighting. It had the largest area to administer, a mandate that stressed conservation of resources, and the longest history of active planning and prevention. By the 1970s, USFS fire policy had passed through a number of stages as the agency responded to the prevailing types of fire and the resources available to battle them. State-of-the-art policy regarded fire as biology and sought to modify fuel loads by a system of prescribed burning. Scientists understood that the accumulated fuel loads of a long period of suppression presented a real danger to natural resources. The idea of a controlled, human-induced fire to clear out such areas gained credence.

Fire policy in other federal agencies had traditionally been derived from that of the Forest Service. When the Park Service had begun to develop its first systemwide fire policy late in the 1920s, the man it hired as national fire officer, John Coffman, came from the Forest Service. During the 1950s and 1960s, the USFS took the lead in a number of joint fire-prevention ventures with federal agencies such as the Department of Defense. Although the role of the Forest Service diminished in the 1970s, other federal agencies continued to follow the lead of the USFS, albeit slowly.[35] Forest Service policy had long been the guide for national fire standards, and other agencies reflexively looked to the USFS. The Park Service moved swiftly in some of its most threatened areas. By 1977, some natural parks such as Yellowstone and Sequoia had controlled-fire programs in place. These programs generally allowed natural fires to burn within predetermined boundaries. If the fires exceeded certain prescribed conditions, then the Park Service would respond. Otherwise, the fire simply burned on with careful monitoring.

Despite a growing body of scientific evidence to support controlled burning, people who had fought fires all their lives still resisted the idea. Fire had always been anathema—particularly in the arid Southwest—and a program that allowed fires to burn unchecked violated every principle they knew. Yet the scientists had considerable influence. A generational split occurred within the ranks of federal agencies, often pitting older, experienced managers against younger scientists. But the time for reactive fire suppression as the dominant mode of response had ended, and following the lead of the USFS, other agencies developed new programs. On the Pajarito Plateau, this meant a significant change in policy. In the spring of 1977, Regional Director John Cook approved a controlled-burn program for La Mesa area. La Mesa fire started the month before the program was scheduled to begin.

La Mesa fire highlighted an important reality for federal agencies. It revealed a degree of interdependence that had previously existed but had never been acknowledged, changing the tone of interaction on the plateau. When the agencies faced an important problem, the similarities between them far outweighed the differences in their management policies. To battle such a vast conflagration required cooperative effort and pooled resources. In an era during which their leadership was questioned and the public ceased to be quiescent, federal administrators from a variety of agencies found that they needed to rely on one another in a way never previously acknowledged. On the Pajarito Plateau, La Mesa fire served as a symbol of that interdependence.

By the end of the 1970s, federal agencies on the Pajarito Plateau recognized their vulnerability to public opinion and began to manage land in a less autocratic fashion. They responded to the queries and demands of the various communities in the region and shaped policy to suit the needs of these various groups. No longer did federal administrators offer edicts that a docile public followed; instead, they fashioned policies that negotiated a narrow path between a number of volatile and contradictory constituencies.

This change led to greater cooperation among the administrators of different agencies as they realized that each of their decisions affected fellow officials in other agencies and that they all faced a fickle public likely to erupt against them at any moment. Unlike earlier groups on the plateau, the people of Los Alamos were affluent, educated, and used to having an impact on the world they inhabited. Nor were they dependent on agencies like the Park and the Forest services for their livelihood. Administrators could not safely ignore such a powerful interest group. They were compelled to respond not only to its needs but to those of peer groups as well.

The American cultural revolution reshaped not only the social mores of the nation but the very way Americans and their government interacted. After the Second World War, Americans had accepted the pronouncements of their leaders and administrators, feeling that challenging the decisions made by official representatives was inappropriate. Beginning with the civil rights movement and culminating with the resignation of

Richard Nixon in the Watergate scandal in 1974, the public took a more jaundiced view of leaders and a less passive role in social affairs. This spread even to remote areas like the plateau, where Los Alamos and its educated, affluent, and influential residents had already transformed the region. The cynicism that grew out of the questioning of American values fueled the desires of the vocal public to affect the decisions of federal administrators. Conversely, these criticisms from residents of a bedroom community drew federal administrators and agencies together as they faced what sometimes seemed to them arbitrary attacks from uninformed people.

The result was not the end of federal hegemony in the region but instead its reconstitution as a more inclusive ethic. Rather than repel this vocal public so interested in their decisions, federal officials included them in the decision-making process. Systematic exclusion had ceased to be an effective mode of management in social affairs in the United States. Federal management still reigned supreme on the plateau, but it had become more flexible and responsive, although far from compliant. Although this cooperation created peace in the region, it also dramatically slowed the speed of decision making.

By the end of the 1970s, the Pajarito Plateau had become crowded. Space there was finite, and despite their good intentions and well-thought-out plans, federal administrators faced a seemingly permanent pattern of growth with limited space and resources. Everyone in the region wanted more, but there was only so much land and so much money.

13

✳ ✳ ✳ ✳ ✳ ✳ ✳ ✳ ✳ ✳ ✳ ✳ ✳ ✳ ✳ ✳ ✳

The rapid growth of the plateau in the 1960s and 1970s propelled it toward an impending crisis. Space in the region had always been finite. The boundaries that created limits were unconquerable and impossible to negotiate. The resources of the region—its usable space, water, sewage, even its miles of roads—were also finite. The demand for space, services, and comfort, however, seemed infinite. The lab required more services, and more visitors came every year. Very simply, the plateau was full.

As a result, the gains of any one group were offset by the losses of another. The plateau entered a stalemate, enmeshed in a form of gridlock more generally associated with Manhattan Island. Yet environmental gridlock was every bit as paralyzing. Any action that anyone sought to implement necessitated a negative response from at least one other equally well-entrenched entity. To proceed with a plan, an agency needed consensus, an elusive concept when a variety of groups had interests to protect. Managers felt beleaguered, trapped by swirling powers that overwhelmed their own. Bandelier Superintendent John D. Hunter best described their feelings when he addressed a town meeting in White Rock in June 1985. The monument, he told the audience, was "an island besieged by external threats."[1]

As the one agency in the region charged with preservation, the Park Service seemed most vulnerable to conditions engendered by the hardening of positions. Its designated task was to protect its areas from growth and change, to preserve them as relics of times and places gone by. Other agencies could adapt their mandates to changing conditions, but stasis was a part of the NPS mission. Pressure on the lands surrounding the park threatened not only the image of the agency but also its ability to maintain the support of its many constituencies.

This sensitivity was a result of the American cultural revolution. Beginning in the 1960s, the conservation movement in the United States took a more holistic approach to preservation. Its concerns stretched beyond the protection of the park system and into the beautification of ordinary landscapes. The concept of the biota or ecosystem gained credence, and environmentalists and professionals began to regard park boundaries as artificial constraints. This perspective translated into concern for lands beyond the borders of park areas.

The new current of thinking took on unprecedented importance during the Carter administration. In 1976, Director Gary E. Everhardt declared that the most severe threats the system faced were external. By 1980, this position was agency policy. Documents such as the *State of the Parks 1980* report to Congress focused on commercial enterprises and industrial development outside park boundaries, interests with the potential to affect the national park system. The Park Service began to develop ways to identify and counteract the broadening range of threats. This issue rose to the top of the agenda of the agency, and individual parks and monuments stepped up responses.[2]

On the Pajarito Plateau, myriad interests posed problems that, though historically rooted, also reflected the balance of power and the conflicting interests of the region. The demands of the population of Los Alamos impinged on the values of every area outside the Department of Energy (DOE) jurisdiction. The various federal agencies in the area confronted a powerful and, during the first years of the Reagan administration, noticeably callous DOE. Conversely, the position of Native American groups improved as a result of increasing sensitivity to their plight by individual administrators within the federal system. Private landowners and indus-

trial concerns that sought to develop economic potential found a quagmire with roots that long preceded their arrival. By the middle of the
1980s, the whirlpool of competing interests, each of which had the ability
to affect the future of the region, swirled in a stalemate.

The residents of Los Alamos were both the source of much of the contention as well as the most vocal advocates of protecting the plateau. The
permanence of Los Alamos and its continued growth created a paradoxi-
cal situation. The needs of the community put considerable pressure on
the resources of the plateau, but the highly educated, civic-minded citizens of the town also valued an intangible ingredient called "quality of
life," an important measure of success for upper-middle-class Americans
in the 1980s. Although the people of the town valued the resources of the
region, their use diminished the very attributes they prized.

This predicament typified life in the Sun Belt during the first half of the
1980s. Cities such as Austin, Dallas, and Houston in Texas, Phoenix and
Tucson in Arizona, and others faced similar problems. In Austin, a five-
year boom at the beginning of the 1980s was propelled by the common acceptance of the principle that Austin was a wonderful place to live. Its
rapid growth quickly created the kind of traffic, housing, and environmental problems that the new carpetbaggers had sought to leave behind.
The attributes that attracted people to the community were demolished
by the growth necessary to serve those who sought such amenities. The
pattern continued across the region.

The DOE and LASL, which became the Los Alamos National Laboratory
(LANL) in the early 1980s, exacerbated the tensions. Since the late 1940s,
the DOE had gradually divested itself of more than 60 percent of the land it
administered in the region. Officials in other agencies hungrily awaited
excess DOE land. Between 1945 and 1980, the Forest Service received
29,593 acres, the Park Service 6,483, and Los Alamos County 5,196, while
an additional 4,018 acres were sold to private owners. In some cases,
there were fights for the land. The Forest Service opposed returning
27,000 acres of AEC surplus to San Ildefonso in the late 1960s. Despite conflict, agencies became accustomed to the largess of the lab. By the early
1980s, the LANL stabilized at about 28,000 acres, almost half its postwar
high. The flow of land ceased, and the Park Service, the Forest Service,
the pueblos, private businesses, and other interests faced increased competition for any available space.[3]

These factors made an ordinarily complicated situation even more complex. Los Alamos had a unique timbre of life, a style all its own. Yet its individuality grew out of conflicting factors. Los Alamos was an enclave of scientific America located in a more traditional world. The average level of education in the community was unusually high. The relative inaccessibility of the town and its outdoor-oriented culture contributed to many residents' dissatisfaction about the comparatively few cultural amenities available in Los Alamos County. The long commuting time between the hill and Santa Fe also frustrated local residents. Social change and development offered the promise of new experience while simultaneously threatening to destroy the insular world of Los Alamos.

Little was new about this conflict over the use of space. Again, the people of the Pajarito Plateau had to weigh the relative merits of incommensurable values, of the tangible and intangible benefits each change might bring. A number of different interest groups had plans for any tract that came open, and deciding which use would take priority involved an intricate tangle of public, private, aesthetic, economic, and quality-of-life issues.

The question of the development of the old Girl Scout retreat called Camp Evergreen or Westgate, a fifty-acre tract in the Jemez Mountains, at the outset of the 1980s typified the nature of the problems within the community and the threats the growth of Los Alamos presented to the stability of the plateau. As the population of the plateau grew, so did the demands on the limited space of the region. New residents needed housing, utilities, sewer lines, and other services. As the area available for development in and around Los Alamos diminished, remaining sections attracted everyone on the plateau—from potential developers to the Park Service and the Forest Service.

Camp Evergreen had a history of recreational use. In 1967, the Sangre de Cristo Girl Scout Council acquired the tract from the AEC and used the two structures on the property as the basis for a summer camp and retreat. In the ensuing decade, the Girl Scout camp was a frequent target of vandals. The safety of the Girl Scouts became an issue, and with no effective way to protect their charges, the leaders made plans to sell the tract. They surmised that it held promise for small-scale development.[4]

A prime piece of land on the Pajarito Plateau rarely appeared on the market, but when one did, it commanded a high price. The Sangre de Cristo Girl Scout Council had acquired the land without any resistance in the late 1960s. But in the 1980s, there was strong demand for such a property.

Before either the Park Service or the Forest Service became aware that the land was for sale, private parties arranged to purchase it. In October 1980, a group calling itself "Westgate Families" delivered a down payment of $25,000, out of a total selling price of $275,000. The partners planned a high-density development in the area. They sought to rezone the tract.[5]

The land bordered on both NPS and USFS lands. Opposing the development, the agencies approached the national offices of the Girl Scouts of America and made efforts to work with state and local government to restrict uses of the land. Park officials even scheduled a meeting to express their disapproval. But despite its concern, the Park Service had no legal standing to prevent either the rezoning attempt or the project. Since the land fell outside of park boundaries, agency policy limited vigorous opposition.[6]

With seemingly token resistance, the partners carried their project forward. On January 14, 1981, they asked the Los Alamos County Planning and Zoning Commission to rezone the 50-acre tract from wilderness and recreation status to 13.2 acres of residential and agricultural and 36.6 acres of planned development at 3.5 units per acre. The county commission scheduled public hearings on the issue.

The people of Los Alamos faced a problem. The community needed the housing, but the development was a threat to the quality of life in Los Alamos. Although the partners claimed to want to "preserve the integrity of the area," local residents were suspicious of their plans. The sale of the Camp Evergreen property also affected the plans of the Los Alamos Ski Club to expand its ski runs. At the suggestion of the USFS, the skiers had purchased a 40-acre tract of wilderness along the Jemez River in the hopes that its value would equal that of a 150-acre parcel of forest land the skiers coveted. But the $275,000 price of Camp Evergreen had driven up the value of land on the plateau, and a new appraisal of the relative worth of the two tracts left the skiers with a shortfall of approximately $350,000. This inadvertent complication of a matter of considerable local interest inspired antipathy, and the editorial pages of the *Los Alamos Monitor* were filled with antidevelopment letters.[7]

The lack of response from the NPS and the USFS thrust Los Alamosans into the forefront. At a time when the leadership of the Department of the Interior unequivocally favored the development of public land in the West, park officials kept out of the fray as Westgate became the most important local development issue of 1981. Local people took the lead in opposing the project. After considerable public scuffling and a number of legal challenges, the rezoning issue landed on a referendum ballot. On June 30, 1981, the public turned back the zoning changes proposed for the Westgate tract. Each of the three ballot issues failed by an average of about 4 percent, out of a total of fifty-two hundred votes. The ballot temporarily terminated the development plans of the Westgate Families.[8]

During the following years, the community of Los Alamos continued to battle over the development. Westgate Families pressed its case and, over time, won concessions from both the city and the county. In August 1984, the tract cleared the final zoning hurdle, and the county permitted a density of 3.5 units per acre over the entire fifty-acre tract. The owners announced that they hoped to begin construction during the spring of 1985. But after they received final clearance for utilities on the tract, Westgate Families sold the tract to Paul Parker, a local developer. The Forest Service then sought to acquire the tract by an exchange of land, and Parker delayed his plans to see what the foresters would offer. Throughout 1986, the USDA Forest Service searched for an appropriate exchange, but found none. Parker remained patient. Efforts to negotiate the exchange continued, but by 1991, little progress had been made.[9]

Again, resolution of an issue on the plateau bypassed questions of value and was determined by political clout and manipulation. The quality-of-life issue that had been juxtaposed with the need for housing was subsumed as developers sought profit from the tract. None of the potential builders had any commitment to the concept of development. Instead, the Westgate tract was a commodity, to be parlayed in the most advantageous way possible. Although not guilty of the excesses of people like Thomas B. Catron, the owners of the land had similar motives.

Yet the primary issue, reconciling the needs of the Los Alamos community with those of its neighbors on the plateau, remained. Los Alamos County would grow, and to a certain degree, everybody else would remain defenseless against such growth. The Native American community used its historic presence and its location along the only approach road to Los Alamos to strengthen its position. The Park Service decided its best defense was to make Bandelier a visible asset to the unique life-style of Los Alamos. Park officials hoped to rely on local people to point out the sensitivity of the values of the park and resist efforts that threatened to destroy the unique character of the region.

Interest in a new road from Santa Fe to the plateau area also pitted progress against protection of the region. New Mexico Highway 4 provided the only access from Santa Fe to the plateau. From Pojoaque to the Rio Grande, the road was only two lanes; from the river to the Los Alamos Y, it was only three. As commuting to Los Alamos became standard for many, congestion on the road increased. The thirteen-mile trip from the "Y" to the four-lane U.S. Highway 84/285 often turned into thirty-five minutes of stop-and-go traffic. Local wags who worked on the hill referred to their trek as the "Frijoles 500." Particularly in the evenings, bumper-to-bumper traffic down the hill became the rule. For people who sought easier travel to the plateau, a shorter road had considerable allure.

The idea of a direct route from Santa Fe to the plateau was not an innovation. Earlier roads to the region were the result of individual enterprises. Most were built without the benefit of road-grading equipment and other technological advances of the twentieth century. They were often roundabout routes that went from one specific feature to another. Early in the century, road construction was limited by a lack of equipment and the dictates of the railroad in the valley. After the Chili Line ceased to operate in 1941, advocates clamored for a direct road from Santa Fe. The growth of the lab increased the intensity of demands.

The original modern road, which Harry Buckman had built to facilitate his timber cutting, wound up White Rock Canyon. It stretched from the town of Buckman on the east side of the Rio Grande in Cañada Ancha to the Buckman sawmills in Water Canyon. Early travelers to the monument followed its course. In 1912, the trail was extended from Water Canyon to the north rim of Frijoles Canyon to accommodate the Selig movie company. After the post office in the town of Buckman was closed in the early 1920s, the Los Alamos Ranch School had its own post office, and the emphasis shifted away from the trail that Buckman had constructed. The school received an easement from the Forest Service to build a road between the crossing and the school, and soon there were two ways to take an automobile to the plateau. The Ranch School road was the antecedent of New Mexico Highway 4, which began in Pojoaque and finished at the school. Yet both roads were unpaved, cumbersome, and rutted and often discouraged travel to the region.[10]

When the Park Service made efforts to acquire Bandelier, officials perceived that new roads would increase visitation. The roundabout trip across the Otowi Bridge encouraged sentiment for a shorter route between Santa Fe and the plateau. During the early 1930s, Jesse Nusbaum reported that the construction of a direct road from Santa Fe to the vicinity of Bandelier had become likely. Nusbaum suggested that its path follow the old Buckman road, eliminating mileage from the Otowi Crossing–Ranch School route and shortening the trip to Frijoles Canyon. Persistent rumors were all that ever came of this effort.[11]

The creation of Los Alamos also affected the chances of a road. The military cut its own road, which became known as the Los Alamos spur or truck road, through the Otowi section. Although the establishment of the lab brought substantial capital development, its secrecy considerably dimmed prospects for a public road. During and after the Second World War, the manned security gate symbolized Los Alamos. Officials wanted to make access to the area as difficult as possible. The amount of acreage controlled by the lab also limited available locations for an additional road. But as traffic congestion on Highway 4 increased during the 1970s, so did talk of a new road.

In the early 1980s, the New Mexico State Highway Department outlined three possible routes from Santa Fe to the Los Alamos area. The southernmost of these, called the Montoso Peak route, proposed a 2,900-foot bridge across the Rio Grande; the bridge would join the existing Highway 4 at Los Alamos Technical Area-33 (TA-33), adjacent to the northeast boundary of Bandelier. The middle route, the Potrillo alternative, would meet the existing Highway 4 loop south of the town of White Rock. The northernmost route, titled the Buckman Road, would roughly follow its namesake and pass between the detached Tsankawi section of the monument and the town of White Rock. Each was significantly shorter than the existing road.

The proposals offered other benefits besides decreased distance. Each option provided better access to recreational areas, and the reduction of traffic congestion would decrease the frequency of accidents on both the new road and its predecessor. The new options also allowed the lab to avoid transporting hazardous waste along winding roads in populated areas. Yet the project seemed likely to divert business from establishments along U.S. Highway 84/285, and questions of air, noise, and sight pollution merited consideration.[12]

None of the routes made everyone happy. The Montoso Peak and Buckman Road proposals posed difficulties for the Park Service. Both would affect the park, and Superintendent John Hunter viewed them "with some alarm." The Montoso Peak route also threatened the Forest Service. The proposal divided national forest lands into two distinct parcels and divided the Caja (Del Rio Grant) Wild Horse Territory, separating approximately one thousand acres from the remainder of the designated area. Santa Fe National Forest Supervisor Maynard T. Rost worried that the road would encourage people to use an area largely reserved for feral animals and that new kinds of use would threaten the integrity of the area.[13]

Rost expressed legitimate concerns. Previously, whenever a tract of land had been divided by a road, the character of one of the sections had been altered dramatically. Otowi offered the clearest example. The construction of the truck spur in the 1940s was a prelude to a gradual encirclement of the portion west of Highway 4. In time, the impact of the road—including noise, litter, power lines, and eventually the Clinton P. Anderson Meson Physics Accelerator—destroyed the cultural and aesthetic value of that portion. Rost correctly recognized the threat and sought to prevent it.

Residents of White Rock held a different view. The one alternative that the Park and Forest services did not protest, the Potrillo route, did not please townspeople. Many thought it would bring too much traffic into their small community, adding a variety of hazards to their lives. The new road was a necessity, but from the local point of view, a route north of White Rock offered the best alternative.[14]

In a world of limited space, it came as no surprise that the interests of the Park Service, the Forest Service, and the people of White Rock were at odds. Since the Park Service sought to protect the values of the monument, a road that impinged on either the main portion or the detached Tsankawi section was unacceptable. The foresters also had obligations to fulfill. The people of White Rock wanted the advantages of shorter travel time to Santa Fe but did not want their community turned into a freeway exit. A resolution would require compromise and, in all likelihood, some dissatisfaction on all sides.

During the fall and winter of 1985–86, public support for the road grew in Los Alamos County. Petitions in favor of the road circulated, and some businesses, including the Los Alamos Credit Union, allowed advocates to solicit signatures on their premises. In 1986, Congress appropriated thirty-two million dollars for the project, to be matched by eight million dollars from the state. Local residents believed that a direct route would be built in the near future. Late in 1989, a complicated exchange of land involving San Ildefonso, the highway department, and the Forest Service was under way, but the road still seemed a decade away. In the interim, San Ildefonso permitted the widening of the road across the valley, noticeably decreasing traffic congestion.[15]

Many advocates did not appear to have considered the long-term consequences of an additional road to Los Alamos. Seduced by the convenience of a shorter trip to Santa Fe, they failed to recognize that the new road could have a profound effect on life on the hill. The culture of Los Alamos was predicated on its isolation. With only one viable way both in and out, the town remained sheltered. Those who valued the quality of life above all else thought that shorter travel would change the tight-knit feeling of community that characterized Los Alamos. The desirability of real estate in Los Alamos County would decrease, with slower increases in property values likely. The social problems that were endemic throughout the nation could also become more evident in Los Alamos. "They don't know what they have up there," one long-time resident of the plateau growled, "but they sure won't like it when it changes."[16]

But the needs of the LANL remained paramount on the plateau, and the Department of Energy continued to dominate the region. Providing for the lab was its main function, and at times this objective posed problems for other federal agencies. In one typical instance, a DOE joint venture with the Public Service Company of New Mexico (PNM) and Union Geothermal Company of New Mexico presented a complicated matrix of problems at the end of the 1970s. The three entities agreed to develop a fifty-megawatt demonstration plant to illustrate the uses of geothermal power. Union Oil of California, the parent company of Union Geothermal, held a lease for geothermal rights on the Baca Location, and the companies located a project near Redondo Creek, about twenty miles from Los Alamos and sixty from Albuquerque.[17]

The construction of the plant presented traditional problems, including noise, increased traffic, and other intrusions. The possibility of sulfur dioxide emissions and the resulting potential for acid rain also concerned other agencies. The NPS and the USFS recognized that the plant could damage their holdings. The three sponsoring entities wielded significant power in New Mexico, and on private land, the companies faced fewer strictures than on federal land. The DOE had a track record, dating from the 1940s, of paying only lip service to such complaints. Faced with an obvious threat, other agencies could only request that the planners respect their values; they had no way to influence James P. (Pat) Dunigan, the owner of the Baca, or the DOE, the PNM, and Union Geothermal.

The transmission of power from the plant posed another kind of threat. A pipeline was to terminate at Technical Area-3 (TA-3) in Los Alamos, about two miles north of the back gate road from Los Alamos and Highway 4. The PNM and the DOE surveyed a number of possible routes, but with strictures imposed by Dunigan, they focused on routes that approached Los Alamos from the southwest.

The alternative they selected crossed national forest and monument lands, leaving both the Park and the Forest services in a difficult position. Dunigan favored a route that went south from Redondo Creek across federal land and approached TA-3 from the southwest. For the PNM, the southern route had additional advantages. Much of the geothermal capability of the Jemez region centered around Redondo Creek. PNM officials believed that when new sources of power generation materialized, this route would prove safe and economical. The cost of the power line averaged one hundred thousand dollars per mile, and the eighteen-mile route was the shortest alternative. Beginning in November 1978, the PNM explored the possibility of a right-of-way through the national forest and Bandelier.[18]

The two agencies believed that the reasoning of the PNM was specious. Although the PNM claimed to have tried to avoid damages to the environment and the visual effect when it considered routing alternatives, officials felt their concerns were being ignored. The Park Service termed the proposed route the most environmentally damaging of the options. Values of significance to the PNM differed from those of importance to the two agencies; among the advantages of the route cited by the PNM was that transmission lines would be hidden from the "sensitive" Pajarito Mountain Ski Area outside of Los Alamos.[19] The PNM sought the path of least resistance, recommending routes based on a principle of inverted opposition. The most desirable routes were those that imposed on the least powerful constituencies. From that point of view, the NPS and the USFS were the least important entities on the plateau.

The Park Service responded more aggressively than did the USFS. But as officials sought to counter the direct threat, the timing of the proposal left them vulnerable to charges of extremism. Domestic energy sources were a primary national concern in the late 1970s, and geothermal power offered a "clean," nonpolluting alternative. Most environmental groups supported the principle of power sources that did not pollute; thus, they could not protest the power line too vociferously without the risk of being perceived as out of the mainstream. This limited the effectiveness of the usual cadre of NPS supporters. Park Service officials also worried about resisting. They feared that Congress and others would perceive the NPS position as obstructionist. Yet the agency needed a clearly defined position very quickly. If there was a delay, the DOE and the PNM would circumvent the NPS and approach the Department of the Interior, leaving the agency little say in the final siting of the transmission line.[20]

The PNM committed itself to the one route before thoroughly considering others. Its Environmental Impact Statement was an incomplete document that did not reflect the impact of the transmission lines or the range of available alternatives. One option through the Jemez Valley seemed viable, but the PNM expressed little interest in it. When the PNM announced that it had chosen the forest-monument route because of the visual effect of a transmission line in the valley, Park Service officials suspected that opposition by owners of summer homes and the fact that the alternative crossed Native American land accounted for the sudden aesthetic sensitivity of the PNM.[21] Again, the path of least resistance seemed to govern PNM decision-making.

The lack of sensitivity NPS officials perceived hardened their resolve. In a show of strength, the Park Service held its ground. After the agency reviewed the preliminary environmental analysis of the project, Wayne B. Cone, the acting regional director, informed the Department of Energy that the transmission line failed to meet any of the conditions previously established for right-of-ways through park areas.[22] The highest echelon of the Park Service supported the controversial regional decision.

Ironically, the project died for other reasons. The geothermal reserves of Redondo Creek did not generate enough power to make the project economically feasible. In the face of NPS resistance and marginal production potential, the PNM and the DOE relented. They capped the well at Redondo Creek and terminated the project. Less a political victory for the NPS than an economic statement by the PNM, the DOE, and Union Oil, the resolution of the Redondo Creek issue offered no precedent for solving the problems of environmental gridlock.

Environmental issues were far from settled on the plateau. The DOE soon initiated another test site at Fenton Hill, about twenty miles west of

Los Alamos in the Jemez Mountains. Instead of trying to harness natu-
rally produced steam, DOE engineers drilled deep holes to hot, dry rock
formations deep below the surface. Under pressure, cold water was
pumped into the holes, creating steam as it came into contact with the
rock. A pressure system forced the steam up another hole, where it drove
a turbine. In 1986, the plant produced a portion of the power required by
the communities of the Jemez and had the potential to offer more.[23]

Although Fenton Hill remained the extent of geothermal development
in the vicinity of the Pajarito Plateau, its presence meant that the issue of
transmission lines had only begun to be addressed. The final Environmental Impact Statement for the geothermal program at Redondo Creek
had included provisions for the construction of a new 345-kilovolt power
line to Los Alamos. When the program died, the PNM sought other alternatives for power transmission corridors.

In 1985, the Ojo Line Extension program again pitted the various entities of the plateau against each other. Early in the 1970s, the PNM and the
Plains Electric Generation and Transmission Cooperative had determined
that they needed to expand the 345-kilovolt transmission system to meet
the increasing demand of northern New Mexico. Originally, the two companies planned a line from the Ojo Caliente Station to Norton Station, between Santa Fe and Los Alamos, and on to the Bernalillo-Algodones Station outside of Albuquerque. The prospect of a geothermal plant whetted
the appetite of the two power companies. By the early 1980s, they decided
that they could wait no longer to begin the new line. They installed a 345-
kilovolt line between the Bernalillo-Algodones and Norton locations.
They also sought an additional line across the Pajarito Plateau and the
Jemez Mountains.[24]

Two possible routes for the extension of the Ojo line existed. One followed the path of the earlier line through the Española Valley to the Norton Station and bent back north at an angle toward Los Alamos. The other
bypassed the Ojo Station, departing from Coyote directly across the
Jemez Mountains toward Los Alamos and continuing to Norton Station in
a direct line. In the cramped confines of the region, each proposal found
advocates and detractors. Characteristically, a power struggle ensued, igniting the kind of incommensurable comparison that dated from the
1920s. In the modern era, expedience rather than economics opposed aesthetic and cultural values. Initially the Bureau of Indian Affairs, the Park
Service, the Forest Service, the U.S. Fish and Wildlife Service, the New

Mexico Department of Game and Fish, the Sierra Club, and a local environmental group, Save the Jemez, all favored the valley route. The DOE, the LANL, and Los Alamos County favored the mountain route. The two sides quickly became polarized.[25]

Concerns about the mountain route focused on the environmental impact of the transmission line. The project included transmission towers that were thirteen stories high, a serious threat to the vistas of the Jemez Mountains. The line would also affect archaeological sites. The valley already had one high-voltage power line, argued activists such as Tom Ribe, a local free-lance writer. Combining the lines would spare thousands of acres of mountain wildland. The Park Service concurred, suggesting that the Coyote–Los Alamos route would present a threat to the concentration of archaeological sites along the corridor.[26]

In contrast, the DOE, the LANL, and Los Alamos County presented economic and technical reasons for favoring the mountain route. The shorter distance between Coyote and Los Alamos made it desirable for Los Alamos. Although their reasons were less compelling than those of their opponents, the DOE and the LANL wielded considerable power. With the support of those in the valley who wanted the power line located as far from them as possible, it seemed they would prevail no matter what kind of resistance arose.

The Draft Environmental Impact Statement for the project aroused the opponents of the mountain route. The Park and the Forest services took the lead, with James Overbay, the acting regional forester, informing the BIA that the study by the PNM lacked objectivity. Concerns of the Park and the Forest services were similar, but environmental groups wondered if the project was necessary. Some contended that the statement rejected viable alternatives for no reason. Others believed that the proposal was the result of faulty strategy on the part of the PNM. Everyone expected the final Environmental Impact Statement to offer a more balanced perspective.[27]

When the final statement appeared in August 1986, critics of the mountain route were outraged. The final copy barely addressed the concerns of the opponents. John Hunter at Bandelier labeled it "an absolute disaster," and other opponents of the project loudly expressed their disapproval. After an interlude, the state of New Mexico filed a suit against the mountain route. Early in 1987, opponents were optimistic about their chances to defeat the proposal. "I think it's going to be beat," one remarked in February of that year.[28] By the early 1990s, the Ojo Line Extension was dormant.

DOE and LANL projects also threatened to disturb the relative balance of power in the gridlocked region. The election of Ronald Reagan in 1980 and the subsequent initiation of the Strategic Defense Initiative program, the defensive missile shield proposal of the 1980s, made the LANL even more significant, for federal scientific organizations were expected to handle much of the research in the "Star Wars" program. Its importance and power made the DOE less sensitive to the concerns of other agencies, and during the mid-1980s, the department planned projects that did not bode well for the cultural values of the region.

The two most evident were the Overblast Program, designed to test the effect of artillery noise on human hearing, and a proposed firing range near Tsankawi in Los Alamos Canyon. Both threatened Bandelier and the Santa Fe forest, for although their physical effect was confined to DOE land, the noise from both projects would carry through the clear air and possibly disrupt wildlife, visitors, and anyone else seeking the spirituality of the plateau and surrounding mountains.

Both projects were well into the planning stages when DOE officials first approached the two agencies. Typically, the Park Service felt the greatest threat. The Overblast Program was scheduled for Technical Area-49 (TA-49), adjacent to the monument. It would detonate between thirty and one hundred explosive blasts each weekday for up to three years. Its proximity meant that the noise would be audible on Frijoles Mesa and most likely in Frijoles Canyon and would also echo in the mountains. The firing range would be visible from Tsankawi, and anyone in the vicinity would hear the sound.[29] But Los Alamos officials did not understand the concern of park officials. The two agencies brought different value systems to the question, and communicating became difficult. Without an understanding of aesthetic and cultural values, the DOE ignored the Park Service.[30]

As was usual on the plateau, the two organizations were locked in a conflict of incommensurable values. To a degree, their perspectives were mutually exclusive. The Park Service valued the aesthetic merits of the peace and serenity of Bandelier. The cold logic of the DOE did not include intangible concepts in its quantitative analysis. DOE officials measured the noise within the park and found that it fell within the range their graphs designated as acceptable. Yet to the Park Service, levels acceptable to the DOE presented a clear nuisance in a park designed to preserve the prehistoric past. The DOE simply ignored challenges to its position and proceeded. Because of its vast influence, the DOE expected an easy victory.[31]

But the DOE had not considered the effects of public opinion. In November 1985, Tom Ribe, who had earlier challenged the mountain route of the Ojo Line Extension, published similar articles detailing the struggle in both the *High Country News* and the *Santa Fe New Mexican*. LANL officials made a number of insensitive comments, and their callous attitude awakened preservationist sentiment in Los Alamos and Santa Fe, prompting an editorial against the project in the *New Mexican*. Sandi Doughton-Evans of the local newspaper, the *Los Alamos Monitor*, began to pursue the story. Local and regional environmental groups also responded. When NPS Director William Penn Mott visited Bandelier late in 1985, he added his opposition. In the following months, the issue generated so much attention that the DOE cancelled both projects. Carrying the debate to the public provided a powerful way to resist the occasional insensitivity of the DOE.[32]

But public opinion could also work against the Park and the Forest services. In 1987, both agencies faced public opposition to their plans. A quiet effort by the Park Service to create a large national park in the region was inadvertently sabotaged by vocal advocates. Before the agency could put together an effective plan, Save the Jemez debuted a proposal for a national park even larger than those contemplated early in the century. Publicity inspired opposition before the NPS could organize support, and the remote possibility of acquiring lands in the region again disappeared.[33]

The Forest Service faced similar problems with its management plan for the Santa Fe National Forest. In hearings and written comment, the public attacked the priorities of the agency. Foresters claimed that they planned for recreational and aesthetic demand, but increasingly sophisticated quantitative analyses of their activities showed that their practices remained economically inefficient and skewed toward use. Policy demanded efficiency of federal agencies, and when timber sales lost money, the utilitarian emphasis of the agency made little sense. The reputation of the USFS suffered in the aftermath of the 1960s, and many regarded the Forest Service as misguided. To them, the forest plan offered additional ammunition. USFS contentions failed to placate opponents.[34]

As the pressure on the resources of the region increased, conflicts spread to previously remote areas. The Caja del Rio section of the forest, east of the Rio Grande and across from Bandelier, was an example. Undeveloped, the area had a large designated wild horse and burro territory. Although harvesting wood was permitted there, the Forest Service restricted permits to limit the effect of human intrusion on feral animals. In 1985, officials came under pressure to open the area for more wood cutting.

Stands of piñon caught the attention of New Mexicans. Preservationists were upset at the destruction of the increasingly rare pine and the possibility that cutting would damage the view from Bandelier. Dorothy Hoard, a resident of Los Alamos and a veteran of the NMWSC, approached Maynard T. Rost to voice her displeasure. After her intervention, Rost added to the revised draft of the Environmental Impact Statement for the forest a recommendation for the protection of the visual quality of areas adjacent to Bandelier.[35]

Each federal agency with a stake in the region had the ability to affect the uneasy tranquillity of the plateau. Each had its mandates and congressionally assured rights, many of which overlapped. As a result, changes in anything from appropriations and policy to the weather could initiate controversy.

By the mid-1980s, rainfall had done exactly that. Heavy winter snows, monsoon-like rainfall, and the vagaries of western water law conspired to place two different kinds of management values in conflict. In this instance, the Park Service and the U.S. Army Corps of Engineers found that the overlap between them had become untenable. The problems centered on the permanent pool at Cochiti Dam. In the enabling legislation, the Corps of Engineers had acquired an easement that allowed water to flood approximately 270 acres of Bandelier. For a decade, the easement had not been an issue. But in 1979, when runoff backed up into Bandelier and reached an elevation of 5,388 feet, well within the legal limits set by Congress and about 60 feet above the level of the river before the dam, it became a public concern.

The array of water regulations in the arid Southwest further complicated the situation. The Rio Grande Compact of 1937 set up a commission to regulate water use along the river. Its members—New Mexico, Colorado, and Texas—developed an intricate system to divide the resources of the river. The terms of the compact granted the extra runoff to farmers below Elephant Butte, most of whom were in Texas. But the Rio Grande Compact Commission could not release the extra water from Cochiti because the courts had not established the rights of farmers in the Middle

Rio Grande Conservancy District, between Cochiti and Elephant Butte. As a result, the commission asked Congress to limit the flow of water through the district between July 1 and November 1 of each year to fifteen hundred cubic feet of water per second (cfs), the traditional amount tapped by farmers in the middle district. With as much as eighty-three hundred cfs entering the northern reservoirs, and only five thousand cfs leaving before July 1 and fifteen hundred leaving between July 1 and November 1, Cochiti and Abiquiu dams filled beyond capacity. The portions of Bandelier nearest the Rio Grande were inundated.[36]

For Park Service officials, the 1979 flooding was a reality they had long dreaded. In the 1950s, they had recognized the potential of damage from the easement. But the tenor of the 1950s supported wholesale economic development, and officials recognized how precarious their objections were. Throughout the decade, dam projects sprouted along western rivers. The billion-dollar Colorado River Storage Program and the construction of the Glen Canyon Dam typified the era. The Park Service lacked compelling grounds to oppose the easement. In the late 1950s, the Cochiti Dam underwent a transformation from flood control to multipurpose dam with an emphasis on attracting tourists to northern New Mexico. As the economic benefits of the dam became increasingly clear, the Park Service position became untenable.[37] The Corps of Engineers received its easement. The flooding in 1979 was only a precursor of a more severe threat.

During the summer of 1985, the Corps of Engineers announced plans to use its easement and flood the lower reaches of Capulin, Alamo, and Frijoles canyons in Bandelier. A warm spell in April, causing an unusually high amount of snowmelt early in the year, prompted the decision. By early May, Elephant Butte and Caballo reservoirs in southern New Mexico had reached 90 percent of capacity, the highest levels in forty-three years. The level of water in the southern reservoirs threatened to flood a portion of the town of Truth or Consequences, five miles from the Elephant Butte Dam. Additional water, stored in the Cochiti and Abiquiu reservoirs, backed up into Bandelier.[38]

The creeping rise of the water throughout May and June posed serious environmental problems. When the water receded, the inundated areas became, in the words of a Park Service resource manager, an "aesthetic mess." A bathtub ring of drowned vegetation remained, and natural recovery might take four to five years. Tree species like juniper and ponderosa pine were particularly vulnerable. If inundated for more than several weeks, they were unlikely to recover. Among the ponderosa pines that were threatened was a group of 450-year-old trees that provided winter roost for about twenty-five bald eagles. Whether the eagles would return after the flooding became an issue.[39]

The date of July 1 loomed especially large for the NPS. Many of the threatened areas could survive inundation for a few weeks. But if the water stored in Cochiti did not go over the dam before July 1, the terms of the compact held the water there until November 1, after the end of the irrigation season in central New Mexico. This protected the interests of farmers below the Elephant Butte and Caballo reservoirs but threatened natural resources in the canyons of the Rio Grande.

Throughout late May and early June, water continued to back up into the canyons. By early June, it reached within two vertical feet of the Kiva House ruin, and the hiking trails along the Rio Grande washed away. The Park Service watched in dismay. "We hate to see it," Chief Ranger Kevin McKibbin told the press, "but there's not much we can do about it. Our hands are tied."[40] Congress had decided the issue during the 1960s, and the Park Service had nowhere to go with its complaints.

The flooding of Bandelier in 1985 attracted local, regional, and national interest. A vocal portion of the public expressed outrage. In a symbolic gesture of opposition, a bucket brigade went to Cochiti Dam to throw buckets of water over the top of the dam. Phone calls lit up the switchboard at the monument, many asking if the ruins in Frijoles Canyon were underwater. The *New York Times* ran a feature on the issue, as did the *Denver Post*, the *Philadelphia Inquirer*, and a number of other major daily newspapers.[41] Although some of the excess water was released from the dam, the lower reaches of the monument remained flooded.

Even after 1985, the Corps of Engineers retained its easement. By June 8, 1987, high water was estimated to reach 5,444 feet above sea level, more than 120 feet higher than the level of the river before the construction of the dam. Despite public outcry at local, regional, and national levels, the law allowed the flooding of the monument. The dam offered one of the first cases of actual overlap between groups that managed the Pajarito Plateau.

The flooding was only a precursor of future collisions. Looming in the distance was the greatest challenge of all: the question of Native American water rights. Since the *Winters* v. *United States* decision in 1908, Native

American water rights had been clearly distinguished in law. Unlike rights granted under the doctrine of prior appropriation—the ethos of "first-in-time-first-in-right" most common throughout the West—Indian rights were guaranteed by the federal government. The western principle of "use-it-or-lose-it" did not apply to Native American water. In addition, water controlled by Native Americans could be diverted to nonriparian lands. In short, Indian water belonged to Indians, who retained greater control over its disposition than did others. After the 1963 U.S. Supreme Court decision in *Arizona* v. *California*, which allotted five bands of Native Americans with agricultural traditions as much water as necessary to grow crops on all their practically irrigable land, Native American claims to water became an important part of the matrix of growth.[42]

Beginning with *The State of New Mexico ex. rel. S. E. Reynolds, State Engineer* v. *R. Lee Aamodt et al. defendant*, commonly known as the *Aamodt* case, the courts have been asked to determine pueblo claims to water. Yet the combination of waters in the Rio Grande was fully appropriated when the suit began, meaning that any increase in the amount of water the pueblos were guaranteed assured curtailment of the existing rights of someone else, usually their Hispano neighbors in the Rio Grande Valley. Adjudication was politically charged, with evident winners and losers. It pitted two economically impoverished groups in the region against one another, with typical consequences.

As they had at the turn of the century, Native Americans found themselves in a better position than their Hispano neighbors. Once again, two nonwhite groups at the bottom of the socioeconomic scale were placed in competition. With the support of the Justice Department, the four northern pueblos filed a suit based on the *Arizona* v. *California* decision that supported granting Native Americans water rights for all "practically irrigable acreage" in their holding. The Northern Pueblo Tributary Waters Rights Association asked for the prior and paramount right to irrigate more than twenty-one thousand acres north of the accounting station for the Rio Grande Compact at Otowi Bridge. This awoke Hispanos and Anglos in the valleys, who started their own organization, the Pojoaque Valley Irrigation Association, but who found themselves without the federal support guaranteed the pueblos. Although the Hispanos and Anglos seemed the likely losers in *Aamodt*, they clung to their position. Relations between the pueblos and their longtime neighbors deteriorated. Although Pete Domenici, the U.S. senator from New Mexico, tried to initiate arbitration in 1983 after seventeen years of posturing, the difference between the perspectives was too great. Once again, to the joy of the lawyers and no one else, the issue went back to the courts.[43]

Even though Los Alamos typically remained apart from the *Aamodt* controversy, it was not immune to the phenomenon. Beginning in the mid-1980s, the *Jemez* case posed a threat to Los Alamos. By the end of the decade, the case had entered an early phase of what looked to be a long battle as attorneys began to wage legal warfare over the commodity most essential for the future of any group, project, or community in the West. In Los Alamos, the scenario was different. In it, a powerful Anglo entity with federal support battled Native American interests.

Gridlock over water rights poses great threats. It is the only evident issue that can pierce the armor surrounding modern society on the plateau, the only situation in which interests with no ties to the region and fealty to other worldviews—in this case, the idea of justice—can genuinely affect the plateau. The impact of adjudication of water is obvious. Ultimately, either less water will be available for towns like Los Alamos or the water that is available will cost more. Either result will greatly change the entire Southwest. Not surprisingly, there is no hurry to resolve such cases.

The situation on the plateau is a microcosm of the problems facing the American West. The limited space on the Pajarito Plateau and the needs of various constituencies have established a matrix of conflict. Balancing the interests of a variety of groups remains a complicated scenario. Many of the groups worry about the security of their position in the region; only the lab has little to fear—as long as water-rights cases are not adjudicated. The smaller agencies, compromised and vulnerable, feel that constant vigilance and occasional Machiavellian politicking are their salvation. They and the DOE recognize that public opinion is the way to slow the impact of the lab. As a result, the Park Service, the pueblos, and to a lesser degree, the Forest Service, have sought to carry out their battles as public issues. Los Alamos and the DOE have developed a studied insensitivity, hiding under the cloak of national security and making projects public only after spending large sums of money. As issues have become subject to public debate, the DOE has created a capacity to influence the public. It too has developed master planning and public relations. Throughout the 1980s, a stalemate existed. But as the Pajarito Plateau becomes more crowded and as more people seek to live, work, and play there, the problems will continue to escalate.

The lesson of the Pajarito Plateau is not its problems per se. The real story is in the exponential increase in the capability of human beings to affect their physical environment. In a preindustrial world, the attributes of the Pajarito Plateau limited its usefulness. It was decidedly not a Neo-Europe. Unattractive economically because of its limited productivity, remote location, and arid climate, the region had little to offer preindustrial Europeans. As a result, competition for its resources was minimal. The land seemed abundant, and to a small pastoral community, it was. There was no need or cultural reason for formal barriers. Only the application of industrial technology could change the subsistence realities of the plateau.

But harnessing a remote periphery like the Pajarito Plateau required more than technology, a market economy, and systems of transportation. The railroad, the ultimate technological innovation of the nineteenth century, linked the plateau to the burgeoning world of industrial America, but for nearly sixty years, the impact of the place on the people who came outweighed the reverse. The appearance of federal agencies served as a transitory step. Their officials sought to manage the region in accordance with scientific standards while relying on Washington, D.C., for resources. The results were uneven. With the establishment of the Los Alamos installation, activities on the plateau no longer depended on its physical and cultural resources. Independent of geographical and environmental constraints, growth was limited only by the willingness of federal officials to support the lab. Only when the plateau and its inhabitants became important enough to mainstream America to fund every facet of their existence could the most technologically advanced society on the planet successfully colonize this remote periphery.

The consequences were not as positive as Americans like to think when they view the progress of their civilization. The bedroom communities of Los Alamos and White Rock failed to develop any substantial relationship to the rest of the region. Their sustenance came from elsewhere. Although this situation guaranteed a significant measure of economic prosperity in the region, it also created a grafted-on cultural structure and placed overwhelming demands on the physical environment. Decisions for the future were made independent of the region as anything but a backdrop. As homes were built, each required more and more of the comforts of modern society. More space became urban; less unrestricted open area remained.

One of the most basic premises of modern society is that technology can and will solve economic and social problems; a less clearly articulated corollary is that cultures use environments to the best of their ability. Technology exponentially increases capability, counteracting disadvantages and often making something out of nothing. In the modern industrial world, this principle has become a given, the basis for life in consuming societies. Yet the implication of this never-ending race to expand, create more goods, and develop larger markets is a world increasingly altered to suit the whimsical desires, not the needs, of human beings.

Because Los Alamos and all its subareas have no direct relationship to the plateau, no one questioned the growth. Instead, people assumed that such progress was natural and that humans would find a way to overcome the limits of the physical environment, a point of view generally sustained by American culture. This outlook posits that ingenuity and technology will provide answers to any sociocultural or economic problem. Yet technological solutions to all classes of questions pose problems in and of themselves. Not the least of these on the Pajarito Plateau is how to create more usable space in a finite area with legitimate geographic, cultural, and legal boundaries.

By the end of the 1980s, the question had barely been addressed, much less resolved. The increasing pressure for a variety of uses throughout the decade had only accelerated the pace of technological progress. Possible water restrictions, new roads, new sources of electricity, and geothermal energy all seemed to set the stage for a great conflict of values. Even though economically marginal, the Pajarito Plateau had shown great resilience when faced with human endeavor. Yet the land and its resources seemed to be approaching a limit, one that spurred increasing reliance on outside sources and that was caused and shaped by that reliance. In the 1980s, the plateau reached gridlock in spatial terms; in the 1990s, gridlock of services may follow.

What has happened is devastatingly simple. The carrying capacity of the region, the maximum permanently supportable load of people and their accoutrements, has been approached.[44] Technology and industrial society dramatically increased the carrying capacity of the Pajarito Plateau, but even with funding that is derived from outside, systems of delivery that do not rely on the physical resources of the plateau, and an economy that has little to do with the region, limits remain that cannot be transcended. Ironically, intangible quality-of-life issues that juxtaposed life in Los Alamos with that in major universities or in industry revealed that the limits were near. Even though technological enhancements could offer the shell of modern living—roads, VCRs, schools, and theaters—in the minds of residents, that was not always enough. Even more, these amenities had a price beyond their dollar value. Demand for them could irrevocably alter the nature of life on the plateau.

Gridlock itself is a representation of maximum use, even with technological modification. The rapid development of the plateau changed people's perception of its attributes. After the war, residents of Los Alamos clamored for growth. By the 1980s, they sought to limit and manage it. Although in raw economic terms the physical carrying capacity remained much greater, its psychic equivalent was close at hand. For growing numbers of residents, the benefits of further development of the plateau do not equal the intangible value of the attributes that will be changed. When people of the region are asked to make incommensurable comparisons, increasingly they favor aestheticism disguised as the status quo.

A system that allows these decisions to be made suggests a growing balance between considerations of aestheticism and development. There will be no "Bandelier Acres" commercial housing development on the rim of Frijoles Canyon because even in Los Alamos, such a use would be considered inappropriate. Crowding of roads means more than outgrowing the existing infrastructure. It indicates that cultural values dictate a fundamental limit to expansion. It was and is always possible to build a new road, more direct and less bumpy, but it is not always culturally desirable. A limited solution such as a widened road, which symbolically puts a de facto cap on growth, may be more acceptable. In a world of limits, where every action has ripples of effects, decisions of capital growth cease to be purely material. Instead, they revolve around a constellation of sociocultural, political, and economic values, reshaping the pace and nature of environmental and cultural change.

This does not mean that the Pajarito Plateau will not continue to grow. It only posits that future growth cannot occur uncontested. As the noose of limits tightens around Los Alamos, issues of land use and its impact will become more fractious and hotly contested. With more at stake and with threats looming larger, federal agencies, businesses, and individuals will work to protect their interests. There will be less room—psychic and physical—to accommodate compromise. In the end, raw power and public opinion will determine outcomes, but the strife caused in the process will leave open wounds and irreconcilable scars.

This is the lesson of the Pajarito Plateau writ large. The nature of technological societies diminishes space. Actual distance becomes figuratively smaller as goods, services, ideas, and accoutrements flow to peripheries, creating islands of privilege at the end of long roads. The disadvantage is that local space becomes more diminutive as areas farther and farther away from fragile centers can be sustained from the core. This diffusion spreads across a landscape of people who expect the benefits of living at the core. Ironically, this spread encroaches on the world outside the realm of technology and systems of delivery, a world not yet caught up in the swirl or not previously dedicated for other purposes, pulling it into the modern world. The result is conflict, when various groups in a limited area—and ultimately, all areas are limited in size—have to harness a small space made more diminutive for their own purposes. American society lacks mechanisms for unbiased comparisons of tangible and intangible resources, of economic and quality-of-life issues. Such concepts barely enter our lexicon. A gently buffed version of might-makes-right, often acted out through the use of political and economic power, is the usual source of resolution.

The history of the Pajarito Plateau is the future of the American West. The region passed from periphery to administrative colony. After being "rescued" from oblivion by an infusion of federal funding, it finally became a federal protectorate, administered and managed for a specific purpose unrelated to its cultural or natural history. The science of the land gave way to the science of its components, and split-level houses soon followed. The economy of the region depends on the lab. Without it, the choices are narrow: either the abject poverty of the rural West, or the degrading colonialism of the tourist industry, which is more demeaning than extractive resource industries because it packages identity as well as natural resources.

What makes the Los Alamos area different from most of the rest of the West is its importance in a larger arena. Most other areas of the West are as dependent as the plateau, yet their significance to the U.S. government does not approach that of Los Alamos. As a result, western leaders cannot legitimately expect the kind of federal support that the DOE gives Los Alamos. The decline in the oil and gas industry and the collapse of the Sun

Belt in the late 1980s articulated this point as the nadir in the boom-bust cycle again reoccurred. This, coupled with the failure of western savings and loan institutions that had invested in boom-inflated real estate only to face the bust, again revealed the fundamental weakness of the western economy. Without federal entities and government contracts in defense and other industries, the West would be even more dependent, even more locked in to the boom-bust cycle and its inevitably painful low points.

Yet westerners have not responded with an understanding of the problems they face. Instead, they seek technological panaceas to solve problems of aridity, limited economic resources, and poor and badly distributed infrastructures. Movements like the Sagebrush Rebellion, anachronistic in its emphasis on grazing land, timber, and mining, illustrate the lack of comprehensive western response to the realities of the postindustrial world. The lessons of Los Alamos and the plateau, both positive and negative, are still overwhelmed by the mythic West and its unquestioning belief in the power of individuals rather than institutions.

Unlike the West of the American imagination, the Pajarito Plateau is not a story of unmitigated failures or unbroken successes. Instead, the story of the plateau is about the perceived value of a place and its adaptation to fulfill the desires of successive groups of inhabitants. Changes in needs and demands, the removal of the characteristics that made the region a periphery, and linkage to a powerful outside society altered its utilization and consequently the lives of its people. There were winners and losers and those who broke even, but no one remained unaffected. The institutions and accoutrements of twentieth-century American culture overwhelmed what came before. The price was dependence, ironically on the very entities powerful enough to comprehensively reshape the region.

The history of the Pajarito Plateau provides a barometer of problems and responses in the modern world. Much of the plateau today looks untrammeled by humanity. Piñon and juniper abound, testimony to the spread of lower-elevation plants to higher altitudes as well as to the ability of lab security to enforce antigrazing edicts, and archaeological ruins still dot the south faces of nearly every mesa. Yet the visual landscape is deceiving. The land has been heavily used, harnessed and transformed by the stages of use that occurred in the region. In fact the lush, untrammeled look is a result of the creation of a world of barriers, made possible by the needs and patterns of use of a technological society. As the amount of open space in the United States decreases, resources such as water become more scarce, and the attributes of technological society make the remaining resources seem more diminutive. Without realistic mechanisms to solve the problems that hurried change inherently creates, other previously isolated parts of the nation face a brutal and dislocating process of rapid integration into the mainstream. The story of the Pajarito Plateau is a harbinger of an ominous future in the West.

On a blustery February day in 1987, a car turned onto New Mexico Highway 4 at the Pojoaque junction and traversed the valley on the way to the Otowi bridge. The towns drifted by beyond the windshield, first Pojoaque, Jacona, and Jaconita, then El Rancho, and later San Ildefonso Pueblo. The road was two lanes, but markers showing where it would be widened were strewn along the sections east of the pueblo boundary. Moving over the rolling hills of the pueblo and down to the bridge, the car crossed over into a land special to the two travelers.

They were different, these two men. One was tall and craggy, face lined from a lifetime in the southwestern sun. He wore cowboys' clothes, a fleece-lined denim jacket free of the nametags of designer clothing makers, boots covered with the residue of hard outdoor work. The younger man was shorter and muscular, radiant with excitement, sometimes too eager. He dressed in flannel, denim, and boots, but his taste in clothes, like his knowledge of the place, was acquired, not native.

Their car climbed to the plateau that they both knew so well in very different ways. The older man said he had been born there, long before Los Alamos and the Park Service, he chuckled, even before the road. He had spent the better part of his life in its environs, growing up, learning to ride, shoot, and rope, working for the Forest Service or on Frank Bond's cattle ranch in the Valle Grande. The younger man had come to the plateau as an adult, after college and graduate school, seeking to understand its essence. He had studied its history, anthropology, archaeology, and geology, had read the original documents, and had even learned its geography by traversing as much of the plateau on foot and by horseback as the security division of the Los Alamos National Laboratory would allow.

The two men shared their plateaus that day. They were different, these two and their worlds, and the point of interaction between them was the essence of this place. The older showed the younger where landmarks of his day had been; the younger tried to explain the changes that had occurred. Even in his own ears, his words often sounded hollow, the explanations of a society and its actors to a person directly affected by the change. Little remained from the worlds that had come before except that designated as a memorial to the past. Many places were off-limits because of the laboratory; still others had been covered by undergrowth and trees, visually obliterated by the passage of time.

As the sun set behind the Jemez Mountains, the two men climbed Tsankawi Mesa and walked past the caves that so fascinate adventurous visitors. They stopped at the mesa's very point. Below them opened the Rio Grande valley. To the east, the Sangre de Cristo Mountains had taken on a wine-colored evening hue. The mountains near Taos shimmered to the north, and Sandia Peak was visible in the twilight far to the south. The two could share this experience, no matter how different their comprehension of this place, American society, or anything else. The dimming rays of the sun in that place made them both understand better the words of the other.

NOTES

CHAPTER 1

1. Alfred W. Crosby, *Ecological Imperialism: The Biological Expansion of Europe, 900–1900* (Cambridge: Cambridge University Press, 1986), provides the foundation for this argument. Crosby's earlier work, *The Columbian Exchange: Biological and Cultural Consequences of 1492* (Westport, Conn.: Greenwood Press, 1972), addresses these issues in the conquest of the Americas.

2. Robert H. Lister and Florence C. Lister, *Those Who Came Before*, (Tucson: University of Arizona Press, 1983), 1–41; Richard Woodbury, "Prehistory: Introduction," in Alfonso Ortiz, ed., *The Handbook of North American Indians*, vol. 9, (Washington, D.C.: Smithsonian Institution, 1979), 22–31; Cynthia Irwin-Williams, "Post-Pleistocene Archaeology, 7000–2000 B.C.," in ibid., 31–42; Richard B. Woodbury and Ezra B. W. Zubrow, "Agricultural Beginnings, 2000 B.C.-A.D. 500," in ibid., 43–60; Robert P. Powers, "Draft Archeological Research Design for a Sample Inventory Survey of Bandelier National Monument" (Division of Cultural Research, National Park Service Southwest Region, Santa Fe, November 7, 1986); and Frances Joan Mathien, "The Bandelier Survey Project: Archeological Background" Division of Cultural Resources, National Park Service, Southwest Region, Santa Fe, (second draft, January 24, 1986).

3. Woodbury and Zubrow, "Agricultural Beginnings, 2000 B.C.-A.D. 500," 43–60; Linda S. Cordell, "Prehistory: Eastern Anasazi," in Ortiz ed., *Handbook of North American Indians*, vol. 9, 131–51; Lister and Lister, *Those Who Came Before*, 1–41.

4. Roy A. Gallant, *The Ice Ages* (New York: F. Watts, 1985), 39–53; Henry F. Dobyns, "Practical Approaches to Riparian Resource Management: An Educational Workshop" (D'Arcy McNickle Center, Newberry Library, Chicago, May 9, 1989); Craig D. Allen, "Changes in the Landscape of the Jemez Mountains, New Mexico" (Ph.D. diss., University of California, Berkeley, 1989), 11; Lister and Lister, *Those Who Came Before*, 1–41; Powers, "Draft Archeological Research Design," 21–62. See also W. W. Hill, *An Ethnography of Santa Clara Pueblo New Mexico*, ed. Charles H. Lange (Albuquerque: University of New Mexico Press, 1982), 296; Woodbury, "Prehistory: Introduction," 22–31; Charles H. Lange, "Relations of the Southwest with the Plains and Great Basin," in Ortiz, *Handbook of North American Indians* 9:203; Sandra Edelman, "San Ildefonso Pueblo," in ibid. 9:312. Adolph Bandelier, *The Delightmakers* (New York: Harcourt Brace Jovanovich, 1971), offers a fictional account of prehistoric life in Frijoles Canyon on the plateau.

5. Urs Bitterli, *Cultures in Conflict: Encounters Between European and Non-European Cultures, 1492–1800*, trans. Ritchie Robertson (Stanford: Stanford University Press, 1989), 20–51, provides a remarkable analysis of the ways and means of cross-cultural contact over a three-hundred-year period.

6. Peter Wood, *Black Majority: Negroes in Colonial South Carolina from 1670 through the Stono Rebellion* (New York: W. W. Norton and Co., 1974), 70–91.

7. Elizabeth A. H. John, *Storms Brewed in Other Men's Worlds: The Confrontation of Indians, Spanish, and French in the Southwest, 1540–1795* (Lincoln: University of Nebraska Press, 1975), 87, 90, 92–99; Marc Simmons, *New Mexico: A History* (New York: W. W. Norton and Co., 1977), 66–75; Joe Sando, "The Pueblo Revolt," in Ortiz, *Handbook of North American Indians* 9:194–97.

8. David J. Weber, *The Mexican Frontier, 1821–1846: The American Southwest under Mexico* (Albuquerque: University of New Mexico Press, 1982), 180–81.

9. Halka Chronic, *Roadside Geology of New Mexico* (Missoula, Mont.: Mountain Press Publishing Co., 1987), 150–59, 220–23; Daniel Sawyer and Stephen C. McElroy, "Survey of the Ramón Vigil Grant" (Bureau of Land Management, Santa Fe, April 2–6, 1877), 101:584–88.

10. Edgar L. Hewett, Junius Henderson, and Wilfred William Robbins, *The Physiography of the Rio Grande Valley, New Mexico, in Relation to Pueblo Culture*, Bureau of American Ethnology Report no. 54, (Washington, D.C.: Government Printing Office, 1913), 17.

11. There are numerous archaeological studies of the Pajarito Plateau, beginning with those done by Edgar L. Hewett and continuing until the present. Observers throughout the twentieth century have noted that the largest of the prehistoric pueblos on the Pajarito Plateau were located between Frijoles Canyon and Puye Mesa. The Vigil Grant alone includes Tschirege, the largest of the pueblos, as well as Navawi'i, Big Otowi, Little Otowi, Tsankawi, and many

others. Edgar L. Hewett, *The Pajarito Plateau and Its Ancient People* (Albuquerque: University of New Mexico Press, 1938), remarked on this. Even archaeological maps of the region follow this track; see the "Archaeological Map of the Proposed Cliff Cities National Park," Proposed National Park File o-32, "Cliff Cities," pt. 2, Record Group (RG) National Archives (NA). The map was drawn by William B. Douglass in 1914 to support the efforts of the Santa Fe Chamber of Commerce to establish a national park in the region. For a comprehensive picture of the archaeology of the Pajarito Plateau, see Powers, "Draft Archeological Research Design," and Mathien, "Bandelier Survey Project." See also David G. Noble, *Ancient Ruins of the Southwest: An Archaeological Guide* (Flagstaff: Northland Press, 1981), 122–28, and Marjorie Bell Chambers, "Technically Sweet Los Alamos" (Ph.D. diss., University of New Mexico, 1974), 30–43. Chambers's dissertation chronicles the politics of the Vigil Grant.

12. Chambers, "Technically Sweet Los Alamos," 1–29; the insightful accounts of Peggy Pond Church, "Trails over Pajarito" (manuscript, Los Alamos Historical Society) and *The House at Otowi Bridge* (Albuquerque: University of New Mexico Press, 1960), discuss Vigil's homestead and locates it outside the grant. A map in the Ramón Vigil Grant File, L. Bradford Prince Papers, New Mexico State Records Center and Archives, Santa Fe (hereafter cited as NMSRCA), confirms the location.

13. Richard Nostrand, "The Century of Hispano Expansion," *New Mexico Historical Review* 62 (October 1987): 361–86; Allen, "Changes in the Landscape," 145; Frances L. Swadesh, *Los Primeros Pobladores: Hispanic Americans of the Ute Frontier* (Notre Dame: University of Notre Dame Press, 1974), 15–28; Thomas D. Hall, *Social Change in the Southwest, 1350–1880* (Lawrence: University of Kansas Press, 1989).

14. John R. Van Ness, "Ecology and Subsistence in the Uplands of Northern New Mexico and Southern Colorado," in Charles L. Briggs and John R. Van Ness, eds., *Land, Water, and Culture: New Perspectives on Hispanic Land Grants* (Albuquerque: University of New Mexico Press, 1987), 141, 158–61.

15. Paul Kutsche, ed., *The Survival of Spanish-American Villages* (Colorado Springs: Colorado College, 1979), 3–55; Swadesh, *Los Primeros Pobladores*, 133–59; William E. deBuys, *Enchantment and Exploitation: The Life and Hard Times of a New Mexico Mountain Range,* (Albuquerque: University of New Mexico Press, 1985), 193–98.

16. Albert J. Abbott to Rodger Abbott, January, 12, 1948, Archive, Bandelier National Monument; see also Ida Patton Abbott, "An Account of a Trip to Frijoles Canyon, June 20–24, 1907," Miscellaneous Diaries and Journals, no. 38, NMSRCA. Albert Abbott visited Frijoles Canyon with two graduates of the Carlisle Indian School, John and Cyrus Dixon, who worked for the Forest Service. They gave Abbott the name of C. De Baca, reporting that he had recently left.

During a conversation with Hal Rothman and Bandelier Museum Curator Virginia Robicheau on October 24, 1985, Mrs. Evelyn C. Frey, the Bandelier concessionaire from 1925 until 1981, also confirmed the presence of Hispano families in Frijoles Canyon. Mrs. Frey's husband, George, investigated the remains of the structure during the 1920s, and Mrs. Frey recalled that he told her the house had a basement. In a November 16, 1964, letter to Homer Pickens, Dick Boyd, Sr., intimated that the home belonged to the Pino family. He recalled that they came up every summer from La Cienega, near Santa Fe. In an interview with Hal Rothman and Virginia Robicheau on November 14, 1985, Richard Boyd, Jr., of Chama, New Mexico, confirmed his father's recollection. He believed that his family purchased their lodge in Frijoles Canyon from the Pinos, although documentary evidence suggests otherwise. The Bandelier National Monument Library has the original tape and transcripts of the conversation. The best guess is that both C. De Baca and the Pinos inhabited the structure at different times, C. De Baca before 1906 and the Pinos between then and about 1919.

17. Allen, "Changes in the Landscape," 94–95, 145–49.

18. Stephen J. Pyne, *Fire in America* (Princeton: Princeton University Press, 1983), is the best explanation of the role of fire as a catalyst for change in the natural environment. David Romero's testimony in *Sanchez* v. *Fletcher* explains Hispano patterns of use in the period before 1880. It is located in the L. Bradford Prince Papers, Ramón Vigil Grant File, NMSRCA.

19. Sawyer and McElroy, "Survey of the Ramón Vigil Grant," 101:584–88. Archaeologists have studied the Pajarito Plateau since before 1900. Edgar L. Hewett did a significant amount of excavation in the region before 1915. Unfortunately, much of it was never published. A number of Hewett's publications, however, pertain to the region. Among the most important of these is *Antiquities of the Jemez Plateau, New Mexico*, Bureau of American Ethnology Report no. 32 (Washington, D.C.: Government Printing Office, 1906).

20. Crosby, *Ecological Imperialism*, 279. Robert A. Caro, *The Years of Lyndon Johnson: The Path to Power* (New York: Random House, 1981), 9–32, chronicles similar circumstances in the hill country of Texas.

21. Teralene S. Foxx and Gail D. Tierney, *Status of the Flora of the Los Alamos National Environmental Research Park: A Historical Perspective* (Los Alamos: Los Alamos National Laboratory, 1984), 2–4, estimates the carrying capacity of the Vigil Grant; Aldo Leopold, "Grass, Brush, Timber, and Fire in Southern Arizona," *Journal of Forestry* 22 (1924), is perhaps the seminal article on the effect on ecosystems; David R. Harris, "Recent Plant Invasions in the Southwest of the United States," in Thomas R. Detwyler, ed., *Man's Impact on the Environment* (New York: McGraw-Hill, 1971), looks at the impact of replacement plants in arid environments; R. R. Humphrey, "The Desert Grassland," *Botanical Review* 24 (1958), 198–217, addresses similar questions; Pyne, *Fire in America,* comprehensively

discusses fire suppression and interdiction; and John York and William Dick-Peddie, "Vegetational Changes in Southern New Mexico during the Past Hundred Years," in William G. McGinnies and Bram J. Goldman, eds., *Arid Lands in Perspective* (Tucson: University of Arizona Press, 1969), and Frederick R. Gehlbach, *Mountain Islands and Desert Seas: A Natural History of the U.S.-Mexico Borderlands* (College Station: Texas A&M University Press, 1982), provide models for assessing vegetational and faunal change in the Southwest. Many thanks to Bill deBuys for his assistance in sorting out a preponderance of scientific sources.

22. deBuys, *Enchantment and Exploitation*, 217; Nostrand, "Century of Hispano Expansion," 372–81.

CHAPTER 2

1. Robert G. Athearn, *The Denver and Rio Grande Western Railroad: Rebel of the Rockies* (Lincoln: University of Nebraska Press, 1977), 93–98.

2. Howard R. Lamar, *The Far Southwest, 1846–1912: A Territorial History* (New Haven: Yale University Press, 1966), 136–70; Malcolm Ebright, "New Mexican Land Grants: The Legal Background," and Robert J. Rosenbaum and Robert W. Larson, "Mexicano Resistance to the Expropriation of Land Grants in New Mexico," in Briggs and Van Ness, *Land, Water, and Culture*, 15–66, 269–312; Athearn, *Denver and Rio Grande*, 96–98. See also John A. Gjevre, *The Chili Line: The Narrow Rail Trail to Santa Fe* (Española: Rio Grande Sun Press, 1969), 1–12.

3. Birge Harrison, "Española and Its Environs," *Harper's Magazine,* May 1885 (reprinted separately under its original title by Las Trampas Press, Española, New Mexico, in 1966), 1–2. After passenger trains entered New Mexico in the 1880s, railroad companies sought to bring the Southwest to the attention of the American public. Harrison's article was part of the process.

4. Victor Westphall, *Mercedes Reales: Hispanic Land Grants of the Upper Rio Grande Region,* (Albuquerque: University of New Mexico Press, 1983), 110–21, 193–216; Ebright, "New Mexican Land Grants," 16–66. The question of the transfer of land grants in the old Mexican North has provoked much scholarship. The work of the Center for Land Grant Studies has contributed greatly to the discussion. John R. Van Ness and Christine M. Van Ness, eds., *Spanish and Mexican Land Grants in New Mexico and Colorado* (Manhattan, Kans.: Sunflower University Press, 1980), is an excellent collection of essays on the subject. Some fine case studies exist: G. Emlen Hall, *The Four Leagues of Pecos* (Albuquerque: University of New Mexico Press, 1984), is an outstanding example. The January 1982 issue of the *New Mexico Historical Review* was devoted to land-grant scholarship; Malcolm Ebright, G. Emlen Hall, and Bruce T. Ellis contributed significant articles to the edition. For an additional view of the tenor of the times in New Mexico, see

Victor Westphall, *The Public Domain in New Mexico* (Albuquerque: University of New Mexico Press, 1965), and *Thomas Benton Catron and His Era* (Tucson: University of Arizona Press, 1973). Along with Stephen B. Dorsey, Catron was a leader in the "Santa Fe Ring," the members of which acquired large land grants in northern New Mexico for their cattle operations. Leonard Pitt, *The Decline of the Californios: A Social History of Spanish-Speaking Californians, 1846–1900* (Berkeley: University of California Press, 1971), 83–129, 148–91, shows the process by which Spanish-speaking Californians were divested of their lands. In New Mexico, Hispanos were not as outnumbered by Anglos as in California, and they resisted in a number of ways. See David J. Weber, *Foreigners in Their Native Land: Historical Roots of the Mexican American* (Albuquerque: University of New Mexico Press, 1973), 208. See also Robert Rosenbaum, *Mexicano Resistance in the Southwest: The Sacred Right of Self-Preservation* (Austin: University of Texas Press, 1982), 98–124.

5. Most current scholarship has relied on Chambers, "Technically Sweet Los Alamos," giving 1879 as the date of the transfer from Vigil to Hayes. Further research shows this to be incorrect. The testimony in *Sanchez* v. *Fletcher* discusses Hayes's actions as the owner of the grant before 1879. These are located in the L. Bradford Prince Papers, Ramón Vigil Grant File, NMSRCA. In addition, General Land Office documents show both that Hayes owned the grant during the Sawyer-McElroy survey in 1877 and that he was out of the country at the time. His absence was the basis of his protest, which, when disallowed, bound Smith and Sheldon to the boundaries drawn by Sawyer and McElroy. See "Copy of Notes of Court Decision, Ramon Vigil Survey, case no. 38, April 16, 1883," Report #38, file #30, Ramón Vigil Grant, 49–59, NMSRCA.

6. L. Bradford Prince Papers, Ramón Vigil Grant File, NMSRCA. See also Church, *Otowi Bridge*. Chambers, "Technically Sweet Los Alamos," 35, gives clear evidence of Vigil's advanced age. File H542C, Ramón Vigil Grant, Los Alamos Historical Society, contains copies of all the documents from the Hayes transactions. Ironically, when Hayes purchased the Vigil Grant, Vigil did not have a patent. It was finally granted in 1898.

7. Hall, *The Four Leagues of Pecos*, 171–97; see also deBuys, *Enchantment and Exploitation*, 171–92.

8. Lamar, *Far Southwest*, 143–55; Robert W. Larson, *New Mexico's Quest for Statehood, 1846–1912* (Albuquerque: University of New Mexico Press, 1968), 141–46.

9. "Copy of Notes of Court Decision, Ramon Vigil Survey, case no. 38, April 16, 1883," Report #38, file #30, Ramón Vigil Grant, 49–59, NMSRCA. Part of the reason that Atkinson lost the case can be attributed to the Democratic victory in the presidential election of 1884 and the appointment of reform-minded Territorial Governor Edmund Ross.

10. Joseph A. Stout, Jr., "Cattlemen, Conservationists, and the Taylor Grazing Act," *New Mexico Historical Review* 55 (October 1970).

11. "Testimony of Juan Vigil Montes, Alejandro Montes E. [*sic*] Vigil, and David Romero," in *Sanchez* v. *Fletcher*, L. Bradford Prince Papers, Ramón Vigil Grant File, NMSRCA. One Hispano, Delores Gonzales, reportedly kept one hundred head of cattle on the grant during the Texans' stay, but the difference in scale between his ownership and that of his neighbors suggests that Gonzales misunderstood the question in the testimony in the *Sanchez* v. *Fletcher* case.

12. "Testimony of Juan Vigil Montes," in *Sanchez* v. *Fletcher*, L. Bradford Prince Papers, Ramón Vigil Grant File, NMSRCA.

13. The transcripts of depositions in the *Sanchez* v. *Fletcher* case, taken in 1902–4, discuss Hispano reticence to challenge Texans. The L. Bradford Prince Papers, Ramón Vigil Grant File, NMSRCA, contain the original documents. Ralph Emerson Twitchell, *Leading Facts of New Mexican History*, 2 vols. (Cedar Rapids, Iowa: Torch Press, 1912), 2:83, chronicles the murder of Antonio José Chavez.

14. Chambers, "Technically Sweet Los Alamos," 38; "Testimony of Juan Vigil Montes," in *Sanchez* v. *Fletcher*, L. Bradford Prince Papers, Ramón Vigil Grant File, NMSRCA.

15. Transcripts of Bences Gonzales interview, April 21, 1948, Los Alamos Historical Society; "Moses Gomez . . . Los Alamos Pioneer," *Los Alamos Monitor,* September 24, 1970; Melissa Adams, "Resident's Kin Homesteaded in García Canyon," *Los Alamos Monitor* June 5, 1977. In its Homestead Collection, the Los Alamos Historical Society has maps that show the location and date of patent for each of the homesteads. García Canyon is now part of the Santa Fe National Forest. Visitors to the canyon can still see homestead structures, including a house built from prehistoric cut blocks.

16. This information is synthesized from an array of natural science sources. These include Allen, "Changes in the Landscape," 95–97; Neil E. West and Nicholas S. Van Pelt, "Succession Patterns in Pinyon-Juniper Woodlands," in *Proceedings—Pinyon-Juniper Conference* (Washington, D.C.: U.S. Department of Agriculture, 1987), 43–53; Foxx and Tierney, *Status of the Flora*.

17. Chambers, "Technically Sweet Los Alamos," 30–34; H. S. Buckman to L. Bradford Prince, April 14 and September 3, 1900, in *Sanchez* v. *Fletcher*, L. Bradford Prince Papers, Ramón Vigil Grant File, NMSRCA. See also Gjevre, *Chili Line*.

18. H. S. Buckman to L. Bradford Prince, September 6, 1900, L. Bradford Prince Papers, Ramón Vigil Grant File, NMSRCA. Accounts have long suggested that Buckman spent forty thousand dollars to build the road to the plateau. His letters use this figure in an attempt to elicit sympathy. In his testimony in *Sanchez* v. *Fletcher*, James Loomis, Buckman's former foreman, recounts the cost as six thousand dollars. This is more plausible. Loomis was present during the con-

struction, and unlike Buckman, he did not seek sympathy when he made his comments. Buckman's total investment may have approached forty thousand dollars.

19. The question of scrip is an important one that scholars have only begun to address. The organic legislation for forest reserves (national forests) included the forest lieu provision; see *United States Statutes at Large* (1897–99), 30, 36. Harold K. Steen, *The United States Forest Service: A History* (Seattle: University of Washington Press, 1976), 34–36, discusses the Sundry Civil Bill and refers to the forest lieu provisions; William Greever, "Two Arizona Forest Lieu Land Exchanges," *Pacific Historical Review* 19 (May 1950): 137–50, addresses individual cases, as does deBuys, *Enchantment and Exploitation*, 196–97.

20. Transcripts of testimony from the *Sanchez* v. *Fletcher* case, L. Bradford Prince Papers, Ramón Vigil Grant File, NMSRCA; the Ramon Vigil file in the N. B. Laughlin Papers, NMSRCA, also contains valuable information.

21. Weber, *Foreigners in Their Native Land*, 208. See also Rosenbaum, *Mexicano Resistance*, 98–124; Rosenbaum and Larson, "Mexicano Resistance," 291–95.

22. Weber, *Foreigners*, 208. On the sociocultural nature of western violence, see Richard White, "Outlaw Gangs of the Middle Border: American Social Bandits," *Western Historical Quarterly* 12 (October 1981): 387–408.

23. Rosenbaum and Larson, "Mexicano Resistance," 291–95. For a more comprehensive view of populism in New Mexico, see Robert W. Larson, *New Mexico Populism* (Boulder: Colorado Associated University Press, 1974).

24. Testimony in *Sanchez* v. *Fletcher*, L. Bradford Prince Papers, Ramón Vigil Grant File, NMSRCA. For the tenor of the times, see Westphall, *Public Domain in New Mexico*, and idem, *Mercedes Reales*.

25. Larson, *New Mexico's Quest for Statehood*, 143–44, 194–98; Lamar, *Far Southwest*, 138–54; Twitchell, *Leading Facts* 2:502–7.

26. Ebright, "New Mexican Land Grants," 34–50.

27. Testimony in *Sanchez* v. *Fletcher*, L. Bradford Prince Papers, Ramón Vigil Grant File, NMSRCA.

28. Ibid. See also deBuys, *Enchantment and Exploitation*, 171–92, for an in-depth chronicle of this process for one village.

29. John R. McFie to L. Bradford Prince, February 1, 1905, L. Bradford Prince Papers, Ramón Vigil Grant File, NMSRCA. Twitchell, *Leading Facts* 2:507, has a brief biography of McFie.

30. Dick Boyd, Sr., to Homer Pickens, November 16, 1964, File H14, Bandelier National Monument Library, Bandelier National Monument.

31. Richard L. White, *The Roots of Dependency: Subsistence, Environment, and Social Change among the Choctaws, Pawnees, and Navajos* (Lincoln: University of Nebraska Press, 1983), 212–314, offers the best look at the process of making subsistence cultures dependent. White's look at the Navajos in the twentieth

century offers a parallel to the experience of Hispanos in northern New Mexico. Many of the same factors affected both groups, and the difference in reactions of the groups allows readers considerable insight. deBuys, *Enchantment and Exploitation*, 215–16, discusses changes in rainfall in northern New Mexico between 1905 and 1920.

32. White, *Roots of Dependency*, xiii–xix, 315–22; deBuys, *Enchantment and Exploitation*, 196; Frank Bond, "Memoirs of Forty Years in New Mexico," *New Mexico Historical Review* 21 (October 1946): 342–43.

CHAPTER 3

1. Charles H. Lange and Carroll L. Riley, eds., *The Southwestern Journals of Adolphe F. Bandelier, 1880–1882* (Albuquerque: University of New Mexico Press, 1966), 165.

2. Ibid., 165.

3. For biographical information on Bandelier, see ibid., 1–67; Frederick W. Hodge, "Bandelier Obituary," *American Anthropologist* 16 (1914): 349–58; Hiram Bingham, "Bandelier Obituary," *Nation* 98 (March 26, 1914): 328–29; Gordon R. Willey and Jeremy A. Sabloff, *A History of American Archaeology* (London: Thames and Hudson, 1974), 42; Beatrice Chauvenet, *Hewett and Friends: A Biography of Santa Fe's Vibrant Era* (Santa Fe: Museum of New Mexico Press, 1983), 16–21; C. W. Ceram, *The First American: A Story of North American Archaeology* (New York: Harcourt, Brace, Jovanovich, 1971), 64–67.

4. Curtis M. Hinsley, Jr., *Savages and Scientists: The Smithsonian Institution and the Development of American Anthropology, 1846–1910* (Washington, D.C.: Smithsonian Institution Press, 1981), 103.

5. Roderick Nash, "The American Cult of the Primitive," *American Quarterly* 18 (1966): 517–37; T. C. McLuhan, *Dream Tracks: The Railroad and American Indian, 1890–1930* (New York: Harry N. Abrams, 1985), 8–41.

6. Florence C. Lister and Robert H. Lister, *Earl Morris and Southwestern Archaeology* (Albuquerque: University of New Mexico Press, 1968), 4–10.

7. Harrison, "Española and Its Environs," 39–42.

8. Lister and Lister, *Earl Morris*, 4–15, 19; Sherman S. Howe, "My Story of the Aztec Ruins" (Farmington, N.M.: The Basin Spokesman, 1955); Frank McNitt, *Richard Wetherill: Anasazi Pioneer Explorer of Southwestern Ruins* (Albuquerque: University of New Mexico Press, 1966), 32–37.

9. Willey and Sabloff, *American Archaeology*, 43–48.

10. Hinsley, *Savages and Scientists*, 83; Robert W. Rydell, *All the World's a Fair: Visions of Empire at American International Expositions, 1876–1916* (Chicago: University of Chicago Press, 1984), 2–8.

11. Hinsley, *Savages and Scientists*, 116–17, 139–40, 147–55. See Wallace Stegner, *Beyond the Hundredth Meridian* (Boston: Houghton Mifflin Co., 1954), for the best account of Powell's life. For an interpretive account of Powell, see William H. Goetzmann, *Exploration and Empire: The Explorer and the Scientist in the Winning of the American West* (New York: Alfred A. Knopf, 1966), 531–34.

12. Hinsley, *Savages and Scientists*, 181–82.

13. Ibid., 191–92, masterfully adapts Richard Slotkin's work to establish this context.

14. Willey and Sabloff, *American Archaeology*, 59; Goetzmann, *Exploration and Empire*, 355–576, chronicles the various surveys.

15. Hinsley, *Savages and Scientists*, 193–207.

16. Hal Rothman, *Preserving Different Pasts: The American National Monuments* (Urbana: University of Illinois Press, 1989), 11–14; Ronald F. Lee, *The Antiquities Act of 1906* (Washington, D.C.: National Park Service, 1971), 10–16.

17. Douglas Cole, *Captured Heritage: The Scramble for Northwest Coast Artifacts* (Seattle: University of Washington Press, 1985), 74–164, 286–311, shows in detail this process in the Northwest; Rothman, *Preserving Different Pasts*, 6–30.

18. McNitt, *Anasazi*, 32–33; Rothman, *Preserving Different Pasts*, 18–19.

19. McNitt, *Anasazi*, 54–57; Rothman, *Preserving Different Pasts*, 17, 19, 25. For more on the exposition itself, see Rydell, *All the World's a Fair*, 38–71.

20. Rydell, *All the World's a Fair*, 38–63; Hinsley, *Savages and Scientists*, 108–12. In contrast to Rydell and to a lesser degree Hinsley, Robert A. Trennert, "Fairs, Expositions, and the Changing Image of Southwestern Indians, 1876–1904," *New Mexico Historical Review* 62 (April 1987), contends that southwestern Indians were generally not involved in the degrading events at the fair.

21. Hinsley, *Savages and Scientists*, 138–40.

22. Rothman, *Preserving Different Pasts*, 74–81.

23. Chauvenet, *Hewett and Friends*, 28–30.

24. Hewett, *Pajarito Plateau*, 14. Hewett wrote this and another book, *Ancient Life in the American Southwest* (Indianapolis: Bobbs-Merrill, 1930), late in his career, long after he had ceased his research in the plateau area. Both books revive the kind of descriptive archaeology that the work of A. V. Kidder and Nels C. Nelson had long since superseded. Jesse Nusbaum gives Naranjo's Indian name as "K'hapóa" in Rosemary Nusbaum, *Tierra Dulce: Reminiscences from the Jesse Nusbaum Papers* (Santa Fe: Sunstone Press, 1980), 50.

25. Chauvenet, *Hewett and Friends*, 38–47; James Taylor Forrest, "Edgar Lee Hewett," in Clifford Lord, ed., *Keepers of the Past* (Chapel Hill: University of North Carolina Press, 1965), 145–46; Lansing B. Bloom, "Edgar Lee Hewett: His Biography and Writings to Date," in Donald Brand and Fred E. Harvey, eds., *So Live the Works of Men* (Albuquerque: University of New Mexico Press, 1939), 13–20.

26. For an in-depth look at the life of Richard Wetherill, see McNitt, *Anasazi*. McNitt's account, however, is heavily biased in Wetherill's favor.

27. Forrest, "Edgar Lee Hewett," 145–46; Bloom, "Edgar Lee Hewett," 13–20.

28. For more on the Progressive worldview, see T. J. Jackson Lears, *No Place of Grace: Antimodernism and the Transformation of American Culture, 1880–1920* (New Haven: Yale University Press, 1983), and Robert Crunden, *Ministers of Reform* (New York: Basic Books, 1982). See also Robert Wiebe, *The Search for Order* (New York: Hill and Wang, 1968), and Samuel Hays, *Conservation and the Gospel of Efficiency* (Cambridge: Harvard University Press, 1959).

29. Hays, *Conservation*, 19, 141–46, 256–60.

30. E. Louise Peffer, *The Closing of the Public Domain: Disposal and Reservation Policies, 1900–50* (Stanford, Calif.: Stanford University Press, 1951); Elmo R. Richardson, *The Politics of Conservation: Crusades and Controversies, 1897–1913* (Berkeley: University of California Press, 1962); Hays, *Conservation*, 1–4, 55–59, 155–60; and Donald C. Swain, *Federal Conservation Policy 1921–1933* (Berkeley: University of California Press, 1963), 63–79, all present pieces of the history of the Department of the Interior.

CHAPTER 4

1. McNitt, *Anasazi*, 188.

2. Rothman, *Preserving Different Pasts*, 54–55, discusses the idea of the temporary withdrawal; Peffer, *Closing of the Public Domain*, 108–32, places this issue in context.

3. Alfred Runte, *National Parks: The American Experience*, 2d ed. (Lincoln: University of Nebraska Press, 1987), 33–47.

4. Binger Hermann to James D. Mankin, October 12, 1899, and Richard Rathbun to Hermann, December 22, 1899, 0-32, Cliff Cities or Pajarita, RG 79, NA; Edgar L. Hewett, "New Mexico Normal School," *Report of the Governor of New Mexico to the Secretary of the Interior, 1900* (Washington, D.C.: Government Printing Office, 1901), 106–7. See also Thomas L. Altherr, "The Pajarito or Cliff Dwellers' National Park Proposal, 1900–1920," *New Mexico Historical Review* 60 (July 1985): 271–94.

5. James D. Mankin report to Commissioner of the General Land Office Binger Hermann, December 4, 1899, Proposed National Park File 0–32, "Cliff Cities," RG 79, NA (hereafter cited as "Cliff Cities").

6. On the issue of Indian assimilation, see Brian Dippie, *The Vanishing American: White Attitudes and U.S. Indian Policy* (Middletown, Conn.: Wesleyan University Press, 1982), and Frederick Hoxie, *A Final Promise: The Campaign to Assimilate the Indians, 1880–1920* (Lincoln: University of Nebraska Press, 1984).

7. Mankin report, December 4, 1899, "Cliff Cities." The "Pajarito" name would become characteristic of the park proposals that Hewett orchestrated.

8. J. D. Mankin to Binger Hermann, March 3, 1900, "Cliff Cities."

9. Duane Hampton, *How the U.S. Cavalry Saved the National Parks* (Bloomington: Indiana University Press, 1971).

10. Edgar L. Hewett to Binger Hermann, October 26, 1900, "Cliff Cities."

11. Ibid., March 29, 1901, "Cliff Cities"; House Committee on Public Lands, *H. R. 13071*, 56th Cong., 2d sess., December 21, 1900, H. rept. 2427; "Washington Column," *New York Times*, January 27, 1901.

12. Steen, *Forest Service*, 33.

13. John J. Cameron, "The Proposed Cliff Cities or Pajarito National Park," circa 1935, "Cliff Cities."

14. Beulah B. Corbett to University of New Mexico, School of Archaeological Research [*sic*], Santa Fe, May 27, 1962, File H2215, Bandelier National Monument Library. Information about homesteading on the Ramón Vigil Grant can be found in the Homestead Collection at the Los Alamos Historical Society.

15. Altherr, "Cliff Dwellers' National Park Proposal," 279. The *Santa Fe New Mexican*, March 2, 4, May 20, and August 23, 1902, show examples of the attitude of homesteaders.

16. Binger Hermann to Santa Fe Register and Receiver, July 31, 1900; Commissioner of the General Land Office to Arno B. Cammerer, November 10, 1938; Cammerer to General Land Office, March 15, 1939; all in "Cliff Cities."

17. Harry Field, "The Account of a Visit to the Bandelier National Monument Vicinity in 1900 by Harry Field," undated, File H14, Bandelier National Monument Library. Quotations in the following three paragraphs are from Field's account. Field spent more than a week at Buckman's sawmill in Pajarito Canyon. His account describes one of his day trips, using it as an example for others. Although he most probably visited Frijoles Canyon, the trip he recounts does not describe Frijoles. He indicated that the ruins were next to a dry creek bed, which he believed to have once been perennial. Though his description is vague, Otowi (Pueblo) and Mortandad canyons both approximate Field's account.

18. Edgar L. Hewett to J. D. Mankin, April 29, 1901, "Cliff Cities."

19. Special Agent S. S. Mathers to General Land Office Commissioner, July 11, 1901; W. B. Childers to Mathers, July 14, 1901; Mathers to Commissioner, July 15, 1901; Mathers to Commissioner, July 24, 1901 (two letters), and July 26, 1901; all in "Cliff Cities."

20. George T. Cole to S. S. Mathers, July 30, 1901, and Mathers to Commissioner, July 31, 1901, "Cliff Cities."

21. S. S. Mathers to Commissioner, July 31, 1901, "Cliff Cities."

22. Archaeological depredation was such an issue that L. Bradford Prince kept a file of news clippings on the subject. His earliest clippings date from the 1890s;

as late as 1910, Prince was adding new accounts to his files. The collection is included in the L. Bradford Prince Papers, NMSRCA.

23. Hinsley, *Savages and Scientists,* 231–56; Chauvenet, *Hewett and Friends,* 42, 46.

24. Hinsley, *Savages and Scientists,* 238, 248–52. For a description of the old Department of the Interior building, see Horace Albright as told to Robert Cahn, *The Birth of the National Park Service: The Founding Years, 1913–1933* (Salt Lake City: Howe Brothers Press, 1985), 4, 60–61.

25. *Santa Fe New Mexican,* March 2 and 4, 1902, microfilm collection, Museum of New Mexico History Library, Santa Fe.

26. "The Pajarito Cliff Dwellers National Park," *Santa Fe New Mexican,* May 20, 1902.

27. Hays, *Conservation,* 10–22; Rothman, *Preserving Different Pasts,* 9–17.

28. Rothman, *Preserving Different Pasts,* 35–41; Lee, *Antiquities Act,* 1–35, discusses the role of the Records of the Past Society in detail.

29. Rothman, *Preserving Different Pasts,* 37.

30. Ibid., 35–49.

31. Clinton J. Crandall to Commissioner of Indian Affairs, May 22, 1903, "Cliff Cities."

32. Rothman, *Preserving Different Pasts,* 24–30, 57–58; McNitt, *Anasazi,* 198–207. These two perspectives on Holsinger's activities differ greatly.

33. Marc Simmons, "History of the Pueblos since 1821," in Ortiz, *Handbook of North American Indians* 9: 214–15; W. W. Hill and Charles Lange, eds., *Ethnography of Santa Clara Pueblo,* 312–13; Marta Weigle, ed., *Hispanic Villages of Northern New Mexico: A Reprint of Volume II of 1935 Tewa Basin Study with Supplementary Materials* (Santa Fe: Lightning Tree Press, 1975), 42–44; S. J. Holsinger, "Report on the Proposed Pajarito National Park," "Cliff Cities."

34. Holsinger, "Report on the Proposed Pajarito National Park," "Cliff Cities."

35. Rothman, *Preserving Different Pasts,* 40–43.

36. Ibid.

37. House Public Lands Committee Hearing, January 11, 1905, "Cliff Cities"; Twitchell, *Leading Facts* 2:543–44; Westphall, *Thomas Benton Catron,* 276–300.

38. House Public Lands Committee Hearing, January 11, 1905, "Cliff Cities."

39. Rothman, *Preserving Different Pasts,* 37–40, 42–43.

40. Executive Order 80218, July 29, 1905, *United States Statutes at Large;* Steen, *Forest Service,* 71–78; Edwin A. Tucker and David Gillio, eds., *The Early Days: A Sourcebook of Southwestern Region History, Book 1* (Albuquerque: USDA Forest Service, 1989), 1.

41. Edgar L. Hewett, "Anthropological Miscellania: Preserving Antiquities," *American Anthropologist* 7 (1905): 570.

42. Rothman, *Preserving Different Pasts,* 37–38, 42–48.

43. Cameron, "Pajarito National Park," "Cliff Cities."

CHAPTER 5

1. Keith L. Bryant, Jr., *History of the Atchison, Topeka & Santa Fe Railway* (Lincoln: University of Nebraska Press, 1974), 109–22; Alfred Runte, *Trains of Discovery: Western Railroads and the National Parks* (Flagstaff: Northland Press, 1984), 5–36. For information about tuberculars in the Southwest, see Billy M. Jones, *Health-Seekers in the Southwest, 1817–1900* (Norman: University of Oklahoma Press, 1967).

2. Rothman, *Preserving Different Pasts*, 54–73.

3. The Act of June 11, 1906, is an important and largely overlooked piece of legislation. Few historians have commented on it, yet almost every forester from the time period refers to it as the cause of a major shift in the responsibilities of individual rangers. The law made arable land within national forests available to homesteaders, thus sponsoring a dependent constituency for the infant Forest Service.

4. Chauvenet, *Hewett and Friends*, 38–47, 50–51.

5. Ibid., 71–74; T. C. McLuhan, *Dream Tracks*, 16–46. See also the Edgar L. Hewett Papers, Box 22, Museum of New Mexico History Library. For population figures for Santa Fe, see Jerry I. Williams and Paul E. McAllister, *New Mexico in Maps* (Albuquerque: Technology Application Center, University of New Mexico, 1979), 104.

6. Arrell M. Gibson, *The Santa Fe and Taos Colonies: Age of the Muses, 1900–1942* (Norman: University of Oklahoma Press, 1983), 30–49; Keith L. Bryant, Jr., "The Atchison, Topeka, and Santa Fe Railway and the Development of the Santa Fe and Taos Art Colonies," *Western Historical Quarterly* 9 (October 1968): 437–54.

7. Willey and Sabloff, *American Archaeology*, 42–88. See also Ceram, *First American*, 57–87; Gordon R. Willey, *Portraits in American Archaeology: Remembrances of Some Distinguished Americanists* (Albuquerque: University of New Mexico Press, 1988), 3–27.

8. Ceram, *First American*, 67–69; Nusbaum, *Tierra Dulce*, 1–23, 43–45.

9. Willey and Sabloff, *American Archaeology*, 42–88; Lister and Lister, *Earl Morris*, 1–15. Hewett's correspondence with Charles Lummis in August and September 1907, Braun Research Library, Southwest Museum, Los Angeles, indicates clearly his emphasis on artifacts and his disregard for permit regulations.

10. McNitt, *Anasazi*, 218. For accounts of the various fairs, see Rydell, *All the World's a Fair.*

11. See the Edgar L. Hewett Papers, Box 22, Museum of New Mexico History Library, for copies of his permits. Hewett to Lummis, August 31, 1907, Braun Research Library, Southwest Museum, Los Angeles.

12. Edgar L. Hewett, *Excavations at Puye, 1907*, and *Excavations at Tyuonyi, 1908* (Santa Fe: School of American Archeology, 1909); *Fifth Annual Report of the School*

of American Archaeology, 1911–1912 (Santa Fe: School of American Archaeology, 1912), 259–62.

13. Willey and Sabloff, *American Archaeology,* 60–61.

14. deBuys, *Enchantment and Exploitation,* 235–54, gives the clearest picture of the Hispano view of the USFS; William D. Rowley, *U.S. Forest Service Grazing and Rangelands: A History* (College Station: Texas A&M University Press, 1985), 22–95. See also Elliott S. Barker in Tucker and Gillio, *Early Days,* 149.

15. In its Homestead Collection, the Los Alamos Historical Society holds a map of the various homesteaders and the location of each claim; Elliot S. Barker in Tucker and Gillio, *Early Days,* 146–47.

16. George White, unpublished manuscript, undated. The manuscript belongs to Jim and Linda Goforth of Los Alamos, to whom I am grateful for permission to use this information.

17. deBuys, *Enchantment and Exploitation,* 197–200; Sarah Deutsch, *No Separate Refuge: Culture, Class, and Gender on an Anglo-Hispanic Frontier in the American Southwest, 1880–1940* (New York: Oxford University Press, 1987), 13–40, is a brilliant treatment of the ramifications of the market economy. For an interesting if idiosyncratic view of this issue, see Grace Pritchett, *The Road Goes This Way and That Way* (St. Paul, Minn.: Braun Press, 1981). It is the story of an Anglo schoolteacher in a Hispano community in the first decades of the twentieth century.

18. Gail D. Tierney and Teralene S. Foxx, "The Botanical History of the Romero Site" (unpublished partial draft in possession of the author); Bences Gonzales interview with the author, April 21, 1948; Phyllis Briscoe, "Patriarch of the Pajarito Plateau" (unpublished manuscript, Los Alamos Historical Society); Deutsch, *No Separate Refuge,* 9–10. Stanley Crawford, *Mayordomo: Chronicle of an Acequia in Northern New Mexico* (Albuquerque: University of New Mexico Press, 1988), shows the importance of the acequia to the social life of Hispano villages.

19. Albert J. Abbott to Rodger Abbott, January 12, 1948, Archive, Bandelier National Monument. See also Ida Patton Abbott, "An Account of a Trip to Frijoles Canyon, June 20–24, 1907," Miscellaneous Diaries and Journals, no. 38, NMSRCA.

20. Information about Harold H. Brook can be found in Los Alamos Historical Society, File H542L. Included is an annotated collection of his letters and some information from his wife's brother, Price R. Cross, of Rome, Georgia; when interviewed in 1948, Bences Gonzales asserted that among Brook's holdings was a section that had belonged to his wife's family but that was lost when they could not afford the taxes.

21. Ibid.

22. Harold H. Brook to Edgar L. Hewett, November 11, 1909, Edgar L. Hewett Papers, Museum of New Mexico History Library. Brook was later able to return Hewett's favor. During the existence of the Ramon Land and Lumber Company,

one of Brook's tie gangs found a trunk that had been stolen from Hewett. Although the valuables were gone, Hewett's field notes from a summer of research remained. Brook promptly returned them, for which Hewett was very grateful. See Page Otero, New Mexico Mounted Police to New Mexico Territorial Governor George Curry, September 11, 1908, New Mexico Mounted Police, Letters Sent, Microfilm Roll 92, frames 382–383, NMSRCA; Hewett to Curry, September 7, 1908, Governor's Office, Letters Received, Roll 167, NMSRCA; Brook to Hewett, May 10, 1910, Edgar L. Hewett Papers, General Correspondence File, 1910, Museum of New Mexico History Library.

23. Runte, *National Parks*, 33–48.

24. Secretary of the Interior Richard A. Ballinger to GLO Commissioner Fred Dennett, December 8, 1909; Ballinger to Secretary of Agriculture James Mason, December 8, 1909; Mason to Ballinger, December 11, 1909; Assistant Secretary of Interior Eric C. Finney memorandum, attached to Mason's December 11, 1909 letter; all in 0-32, Pajarito, RG 79, NA.

25. Rothman, *Preserving Different Pasts*, 76–80. For more on Douglass, see Stephen C. Jett, "The John Wetherills and the 'Pre-Discovery' of Rainbow Natural Bridge" (paper, International Conference on Parks and Culture, Mesa Verde National Park, December 17–20, 1988). For more on Cummings, see Willey, *Portraits*, 3–27.

26. Chauvenet, *Hewett and Friends*, 75; Curtis M. Hinsley, Jr., "Edgar Lee Hewett and the School of American Research in Santa Fe, 1906–1912," in David J. Meltzer, Don D. Fowler, and Jeremy A. Sabloff, eds., *American Archaeology Past and Future: A Celebration of the Society for American Archaeology, 1935–1985* (Washington, D. C.: Smithsonian Institution Press, 1986), 217–33. See also Joan Mark, *A Stranger in Her Native Land: Alice Fletcher and the American Indians* (Lincoln: University of Nebraska Press, 1988), 298–308.

27. Fred Dennett to Secretary of the Smithsonian W. D. Walcott, October 19, 1910, "Cliff Cities."

28. Crandall to Commissioner of Indian Affairs, July 11, 1910, "Cliff Cities." Crandall's contentiousness in this case typified the man, according to Thomas L. Altherr, who has seen his personal letters in a private collection.

29. Ibid.

30. Simmons, "History of the Pueblos," and Marjorie Lambert, "Pojoaque Pueblo," in Ortiz, *Handbook of North American Indians* 9:214–15, 325; Hoxie, *Final Promise*, ix–xiv, 147–88, 239–44; Francis Paul Prucha, *The Great Father: The United States Government and the American Indians*, abridged ed. (Lincoln: University of Nebraska Press, 1984), 273–75; U.S. President, Executive Order 80218, July 29, 1905, included Puye in the Santa Clara Reservation (executive order in Clifford L. Lord, ed., *Historical Records Survey* (Wilmington, Del.: Michael Glazier, 1981), 1:178.

31. Assistant Commissioner of Indian Affairs F. H. Abbott to Secretary of the Interior, October 13, 1910, and Fred Dennett to W. D. Walcott, October 19, 1910, "Cliff Cities." Abbott's letter uses the exact phrases that Crandall attributed to Hewett in July 1910.

32. W. D. Walcott to Fred Dennett, October 26, 1910, and Dennett to Walcott, October 28, 1910, "Cliff Cities."

33. See Ramón Vigil Grant File, N. B. Laughlin Papers, NMSRCA; "Notes from an Afternoon with Peggy Pond Church, August 14, 1984" (Los Alamos Historical Society). See also Edgar L. Hewett Papers, Box 24, Museum of New Mexico History Library, for information about the Ramon Land and Lumber Company. deBuys, *Enchantment and Exploitation*, 226–28, discusses the Santa Barbara Tie and Pole Company, as does Gjevre, *Chili Line*. See also Chambers, "Technically Sweet Los Alamos," 30–43. Though generally an outstanding study, Chambers's dissertation occasionally uses, without corroboration, the dates given by oral history interviewees. In 1984, one of Chambers's main respondents, Peggy Pond Church, informed Los Alamos Historical Society Archivist Linda Aldrich that when she spoke to Chambers during the early 1970s, she "didn't know what [she] was talking about." Much of what Church knew she had learned from research rather than memory; as a result, despite the fact that she lived her early life on the plateau, her credibility as an uncorroborated source is much better for the era after the founding of the Los Alamos Ranch School. By then, she was an adult.

CHAPTER 6

1. Larson, *New Mexico's Quest for Statehood*; Richard Melzer, "New Mexico in Caricature: Images of the Territory on the Eve of Statehood," *New Mexico Historical Review* 62 (October 1987): 335–60.

2. Cameron, "Pajarito National Park," "Cliff Cities," 18. See also Catron Papers, Box 222, Museum of New Mexico History Library. For the documents pertaining to Arizona's attempt to get its first national park after statehood, see 0-32, Proposed National Park File, Papago Saguaro, RG 79, NA.

3. Cameron, "Pajarito National Park," "Cliff Cities," 18–19. For information about Abbott's appointment, see *Santa Fe New Mexican*, February 11, 1916.

4. Rydell, *All the World's a Fair*, 1–8; Runte, *National Parks*, discusses the national parks as an explication of the same cultural impulse.

5. Rydell, *All the World's a Fair*, 208–33; Chauvenet, *Hewett and Friends*, 97–108.

6. Chauvenet, *Hewett and Friends*, 97–108; Nusbaum, *Tierra Dulce*, 53.

7. Runte, *Trains of Discovery*, 36–59; Chauvenet, *Hewett and Friends*, 97–108.

8. Hinsley, "Edgar Lee Hewett," 217–33; Gibson, *Santa Fe and Taos Colonies*, 3–

85. For an account of American attitudes toward the cultural and natural past, see Roderick Nash, *Wilderness and the American Mind*, 3d ed. (New Haven: Yale University Press, 1983).

9. Chauvenet, *Hewett and Friends*, 109–20, gives a narrative account of this question.

10. Ibid., 113–15.

11. Ibid., 114–16.

12. Ibid., 118–20; Hinsley, "Edgar Lee Hewett," 217–33. See also Curtis M. Hinsley, Jr., "Bibliographic Note," *History of Anthropology Newsletter* (1982), and *Ninth Annual Report of School of American Archaeology, 1916* (Santa Fe: School of American Archaeology, 1916), 3–9.

13. Chauvenet, *Hewett and Friends*, 118–20.

14. Commissioner of the General Land Office Clay Tallman to Undersecretary of the Interior A. A. Jones, April 4, 1914, "Cliff Cities."

15. Robert Shankland, *Steve Mather of National Parks*, 3d ed. (New York: Alfred A. Knopf, 1970), 100–106; Runte, *National Parks*, 98–104; John Ise, *Our National Park Policy: A Critical History* (Baltimore: Johns Hopkins University Press, 1961), 185–93.

16. G. H. Van Stone to A. A. Jones, May 5, 1914, "Cliff Cities."

17. Edgar Hewett to A. A. Jones, April 3, 1914, "Cliff Cities."

18. Chauvenet, *Hewett and Friends*, 85–86, and Willey and Sabloff, *American Archaeology*, 72, cover Hewett's work in Mexico from different perspectives.

19. Santa Fe Chamber of Commerce to A. A. Jones, April 4, 11, May 9, 1914, "Cliff Cities."

20. Ashley Pond was quite a promoter, and the *Santa Fe New Mexican*, April 9, 1914, carried a story about the purchase of the Vigil Grant. See microfilm of *Santa Fe New Mexican*, role #91, Museum of New Mexico History Library. See also the accounts of Peggy Pond Church, Ashley Pond's daughter. Included among these are "Trails over Pajarito," an unpublished manuscript in the Los Alamos Historical Society. For a marginally different account, see Malcolm Ebright, "Los Alamos: An Undetected Forgery and a Priest Speculator" (unpublished manuscript, NMSRCA), 21–25, which presents a different original asking price, fifty thousand dollars. The *Santa Fe New Mexican*, July 25, 1914, confirms Muller as the culprit, referring to him as "Fritz," but an assessment of Loughran's work on the case shows that Cartwright was behind the attempted swindle.

21. Church, "Trails over Pajarito."

22. The insightful accounts of Peggy Pond Church—"Trails over Pajarito" and *Otowi Bridge*—cover this aspect thoroughly.

23. Secretary of Agriculture D. F. Houston to Chairman, Senate Public Lands Committee, Henry C. Myers, April 29, 1914, "Cliff Cities."

24. William B. Douglass to New Mexico Representative Harvey B. Fergusson,

May 9, 1914, "Cliff Cities"; *Albuquerque Morning Journal,* June 9, 1914.

25. Douglass to Fergusson, May 9, 1914, "Cliff Cities"; *Albuquerque Morning Journal,* June 9, 1914.

26. Tallman report to Secretary of the Interior, July 1, 1914, "Cliff Cities."

27. Assistant Secretary of the Interior Bo Sweeney to Henry C. Myers, October 7, 1914, "Cliff Cities."

28. See Hal Rothman, "Conflict on the Pajarito: Frank Pinkley, the Forest Service, and the Bandelier Controversy, 1925–1932," *Journal of Forest History* 29 (April 1985): 68–77. See also Arthur C. Ringland, "Conserving Human and Natural Resources" (Oral interview by Amelia Fry, Regional Oral History Office, Bancroft Library, Berkeley 1970), 95–98, and Arthur C. Ringland to Bandelier Superintendent Linwood E. Jackson, July 24, 1972, File H14, Bandelier National Monument Library.

CHAPTER 7

1. Franklin A. Waugh, *Recreation Uses on the National Forests* (Washington, D.C.: Government Printing Office, 1918), 13–17.

2. William B. Douglass in the *Santa Fe New Mexican,* February 7, 1916, copy located in Edgar L. Hewett Papers, s-24, 6, Museum of New Mexico History Library.

3. *Santa Fe New Mexican,* December 15, 1915.

4. deBuys, *Enchantment and Exploitation,* 171–92. For a lively fictional account of these issues, see John Nichols, *The Milagro Beanfield War* (New York: Holt, Rinehart, and Winston, 1974).

5. Douglass in the *Santa Fe New Mexican,* December 15, 1915, and Harold H. Brook rebuttal, *Santa Fe New Mexican* January 9, 1916, Edgar L. Hewett Papers, s-24, 6, Museum of New Mexico History Library.

6. Interview with Richard Boyd, Jr., of Chama, New Mexico, by Hal Rothman and Virginia Robicheau, November 14, 1985, Bandelier National Monument Library. For more on Bond, see deBuys, *Enchantment and Exploitation,* 188–97; Frank Bond, "Memoirs of Forty Years in New Mexico," *New Mexico Historical Review* 21 (1946): 340–49; Frank H. Grubbs, "Frank Bond: Gentleman Sheepherder of New Mexico, 1883–1915," *New Mexico Historical Review* 35, no. 3 (July 1960): 169–99.

7. Frank H. Grubbs, "Frank Bond: Gentleman Sheepherder of New Mexico, 1883–1915," *New Mexico Historical Review* 35, no. 4 (October 1960): 305; deBuys, *Enchantment and Exploitation,* 190; Herbert W. Gleason Report to the Secretary of the Interior and the National Park Service, 1919, Archive, Accession #595, Bandelier National Monument. Gleason attributes the rating of Bond's stinginess to

William Boone Douglass. Ironically, Frank Bond purchased the Vigil Grant, and Douglass tried to persuade him to donate that land for the park in 1919. Bond predictably was not interested.

8. Weigle, *Hispanic Villages*, 213–22; deBuys, *Enchantment and Exploitation*, 204–6; Deutsch, *No Separate Refuge*, 21–23; Edward N. Wentworth, *America's Sheep Trails* (Ames: Iowa State College Press, 1948), 607.

9. Harold H. Brook Letters, File H542L, Los Alamos Historical Society; Allen, "Changes in the Landscape," 272–75; Alvar W. Carlson, "New Mexico's Sheep Industry, 1850–1950: Its Role in the History of the Territory," *New Mexico Historical Review* 44 (January 1969): 25–49; William N. Denevan, "Livestock Numbers in Nineteenth-Century New Mexico and the Problem of Gullying in the Southwest," *Annals of the Association of American Geographers* 57 (1967): 691–703.

10. Interview with Richard Boyd, Jr., of Chama, New Mexico, by Hal Rothman and Virginia Robicheau, November 14, 1985, Bandelier National Monument Library; Benjamin M. Read to G. W. Bond and Brothers, February 23, 1901, and Frank Bond to Benjamin Read, March 12, 1901, Frank Bond Papers, Item #59, Special Collections, Zimmerman Library, University of New Mexico. See also Deutsch, *No Separate Refuge*, 21–23.

11. Interview with Richard Boyd, Jr., of Chama, New Mexico, by Hal Rothman and Virginia Robicheau, November 14, 1985, Bandelier National Monument Library; *Santa Fe New Mexican*, April 2, 1918; Bond & Nohl Company, Annual Statement to Stockholders, Year Ending January 30, 1909, and Year Ending December 31, 1918, Frank Bond Papers, Item #59, Special Collections, Zimmerman Library, University of New Mexico.

12. From the *Santa Fe New Mexican*, circa February 15, 1916, Edgar L. Hewett Papers, s-24, 6, Museum of New Mexico History Library.

13. Ibid.

14. Edgar L. Hewett, "The Proposed National Park of the Cliff Cities," *El Palacio* 3 (April 1916).

15. "Douglass Has Sizzling Reply to Opposition to National Park," *Santa Fe New Mexican*, April, 1916, "Cliff Cities."

16. William B. Douglass and his doings have been the source of much controversy. deBuys, *Enchantment and Exploitation*, 16, 24, shows Douglass's drawings of Chacoma; Herbert W. Gleason, "Report to the Secretary of Interior and the National Park Service, 1919" (Archive, Bandelier National Monument), places Douglass at Ojo Caliente excavating in 1919; and Douglass has been generally vilified for trying to take credit as the first Anglo to see Rainbow Bridge.

17. Conversation with E. J. Ward by James Godbolt et al., November 11, 1967, Los Alamos Historical Society; Richard Boyd (Sr.) to "Homer" (Pickens), November 16, 1964, File H14, Bandelier National Monument Library.

18. Grace Spradling Ireland, "Diary of a 1917 Trip to Bandelier National Monu-

ment," miscellaneous bound files, Bandelier National Monument Library.

19. Ibid.

20. Neil Judd, "1910 in El Rito de Frijoles," *El Palacio* 69 (Fall 1962): 138–41.

21. Ireland, "1917 Trip," 23.

22. Ibid.; Judd, "El Rito de Frijoles," 138–40; Allen, "Changes in the Landscape," 152–54; Evelyn Frey, the Bandelier concessionaire, told the author during their October 24, 1985, conversation that there were mountain lions in Frijoles Canyon until the 1930s. She reports that her husband used to say, "Used to be lots of lions; now, lots of people." Elliot Barker in Tucker and Gillio, *Early Days*, 145–49, supports that contention, as do the exploits of Homer Pickens, who is noted for shooting five mountain lions in one day.

23. Richard Boyd (Sr.) to "Homer" (Pickens), November 16, 1964, File H14, Bandelier National Monument Library.

24. Governor W. E. Lindsey to Secretary of the Interior Franklin K. Lane, November 21, 1917, "Cliff Cities."

25. William B. Douglass to Franklin K. Lane, February 26, 1918, and Acting Commissioner of Indian Affairs Charles Burke to Joseph Cotter, January 25, 1919, "Cliff Cities."

26. Stephen T. Mather telegram, January 30, 1919, and Horace M. Albright telegram, February 1, 1919, "Cliff Cities."

27. Herbert W. Gleason to Stephen T. Mather, June 15, 1919, and William B. Douglass to Horace M. Albright, June 15, 1919, "Cliff Cities."

28. Herbert W. Gleason to Stephen T. Mather, June 15, 1919, "Cliff Cities."

29. Ibid.

30. Stephen T. Mather to Edgar L. Hewett, May 20, 1916, Edgar L. Hewett Papers, Box 6, Museum of New Mexico History Library.

31. Herbert W. Gleason, "Report to the Secretary of Interior and the National Park Service, 1919," Archive, Bandelier National Monument. See also Nusbaum, *Tierra Dulce*, 21.

32. Gleason, "Report to the Secretary of Interior"; Albright to William B. Douglass, June 25, 1919, "Cliff Cities"; "Minutes of an Open Meeting of the Santa Fe Chamber of Commerce," June 24, 1919, Santa Fe Chamber of Commerce Papers, Box 145, Museum of New Mexico History Library.

33. William B. Douglass to Horace M. Albright, July 4, 1919, "Cliff Cities." See also *Santa Fe New Mexican* editorial, June 25, 1919, ibid.

34. The Park Service–Forest Service rivalry has garnered much attention in recent years. Though there have long been partisan perspectives, scholars have now begun to address the rivalry in more scholarly terms. See Ben Twight, *Organizational Values and Political Power: The Forest Service Versus the Olympic National Park* (University Park: Pennsylvania State University Press, 1983), for one view. For another, see Hal K. Rothman, " 'A Regular Ding-Dong Fight': Agency Cul-

ture and Evolution in the NPS-USFS Dispute, 1916–1937," *Western Historical Quaterly* 20 (May 1989): 141–61.

35. Stephen T. Mather to Herbert W. Gleason, August 9, 1919, "Cliff Cities."

36. Ibid.

37. Ibid.

38. Arthur E. Demaray to Arno B. Cammerer, November 29, 1919, "Cliff Cities."

39. Ise, *Our National Park Policy*, 296–97.

40. *Santa Fe New Mexican*, December 12, 1921, "Cliff Cities"; Edgar L. Hewett to A. A. Jones, June 21, 1919, Edgar L. Hewett Papers, Box 44, Museum of New Mexico History Library.

41. *Santa Fe New Mexican* editorial, December 14, 1921, "Cliff Cities."

CHAPTER 8

1. Chauvenet, *Hewett and Friends*, 163–73.

2. Willey and Sabloff, *American Archaeology*, 91–93; Lister and Lister, *Earl Morris*, 1–23; George W. Stocking, Jr., "The Santa Fe Style in American Anthropology: Regional Interest, Academic Initiative, and Philanthropic Policy in the First Two Decades of the Laboratory of Anthropology, Inc.," *Journal of the History of the Behavioral Sciences* 18 (1982): 3–19.

3. For a complete account of Stephen T. Mather, his policies, and his years as director of the Park Service, see Shankland, *Steve Mather*. Nusbaum, *Tierra Dulce*, 21–23, reveals Jesse Nusbaum's view of Hewett.

4. For a complete account of Frank Pinkley and his administration, see Rothman, *Preserving Different Pasts*, 108–44.

5. Hal Rothman, "Second-Class Sites: The National Monuments in the Park System during the 1920s," *Environmental Review* 10 (Spring 1986): 45–56.

6. Rothman, *Preserving Different Pasts*, 108–21.

7. Miscellaneous correspondence, Edgar L. Hewett Papers, Box 44, Museum of New Mexico History Library.

8. Arno B. Cammerer to Edgar L. Hewett, February 1, 14, 1923, Edgar L. Hewett Papers, Box 44, Museum of New Mexico History Library.

9. Edgar L. Hewett to Robert S. Yard, August 4, 1923, "Cliff Cities."

10. Ibid.

11. By the late 1920s, the leaders of the Forest Service had begun to realize that competition with the NPS would require that they too develop a recreational policy. Elements in the USFS began to agitate for such a policy in the early 1920s, but it took until 1929 for the development of the L-20 regulations. As part of its counterattack, the USFS took to calling the NPS approach to land management "single-

use," to differentiate it from their own broad-based commercial resource development. Like many other similar jabs by both sides, this one fell well short of the mark. See Steen, *Forest Service*, and Sally K. Fairfax and Samuel T. Dana, *Forest and Range Policy* (New York: McGraw-Hill, 1980), for more.

12. R. S. Yard to John Oliver La Gorce, August 26, 1924, "Cliff Cities."

13. Ise, *Our National Park Policy*, 273–76; Albright as told to Cahn, *Birth of the National Park Service*, 174–75.

14. Ibid.

15. United States Forest Service, "Memorandum for the Members of the Coordinating Committee on National Parks and Forests," attached to Acting Forester L. F. Kneipp to Mather, July 10, 1925, "Cliff Cities."

16. Ibid.

17. Robert D. Baker, Robert S. Maxwell, Victor H. Treat, and Henry C. Dethloff, *Timeless Heritage: A History of the Forest Service in the Southwest* (Washington, D.C.: United States Department of Agriculture, 1988), 49–59. For a summary of efforts to regulate grazing on the Santa Fe National Forest, see Forest Service Division of Range Management, General Correspondence, 1905–52, Boxes 617–20, RG 95, NA; Tucker and Fitzpatrick, *Men Who Matched the Mountains*, 43; David Clary, *Timber and the Forest Service* (Lawrence: University of Kansas Press, 1986), 67–93.

18. Jesse L. Nusbaum confidential report to Director Stephen T. Mather, September 10, 1925, "Cliff Cities." Nusbaum wrote this nineteen-page indictment of the Forest Service immediately after the incident described. No comparable USFS response to the meeting in Santa Fe exists, but Nusbaum reveals enough childishness, intransigence, and pettiness for both sides.

19. Albright as told to Cahn, *Birth of the National Park Service*, 174–75, 177–84; Ise, *Our National Park Policy*, 271–85; Rothman, "Conflict on the Pajarito," 68–77; Robert Righter, *Crucible for Conservation: The Creation of Grand Teton National Park* (Boulder: Colorado Associated University Press, 1982), 35–38.

20. Jesse L. Nusbaum to Stephen T. Mather, September 10, 1925, "Cliff Cities."

21. Los Alamos Historical Society (LAHS), *When Los Alamos Was a Ranch School* (Los Alamos: Los Alamos Historical Society, 1974), 7–22; Roland A. Pettit, *Los Alamos: Before the Dawn* (Los Alamos: Pajarito Publications, 1972), 47–50.

22. Jesse L. Nusbaum to Stephen T. Mather, September 10, 1925, "Cliff Cities."

23. Rothman, "NPS-USFS Dispute," 141–61. For a perspective of the evolution of recreation in the national forests, see William C. Tweed, *A History of Outdoor Recreation Development in National Forests, 1891–1942* (Clemson, S.C.: Clemson University, Department of Parks, Recreation, and Tourism Management, n.d.), 1–15.

24. Wanda (Lee) Worrell interview with Hal Rothman at Bandelier National Monument, June 27, 1985. Mrs. Worrell was born on the Valle Grande in a home-

stead cabin and grew up in the region. She pointed out that the settlers on the farmland west of Frijoles Canyon had little contact with or even interest in the ruins, for archaeology was so commonplace that it was almost invisible. Her only memory of visiting Frijoles Canyon was when her mother went to the ranger station to bear a child in the winter of 1926. The telephone, in case of complications, was the main attraction. Worrell also said that when Valle residents made their semiannual trips to Santa Fe, they did not traverse the Pajarito Plateau. Instead, they traveled via Peña Blanca or Bland. When Worrell returned to the region after the construction of Highway 4, she came from the south and still used the old Forest Service roads. By the 1950s, it was quite an experience.

25. Jesse L. Nusbaum to John Morrow, September 12, 1925, "Cliff Cities."

26. Jesse L. Nusbaum to Stephen T. Mather, September 10, 1925, "Cliff Cities."

27. Ibid.

28. Jesse L. Nusbaum to John Morrow, September 12, 1925, and Assistant Director Arno B. Cammerer memo for the files, December 3, 1925, "Cliff Cities."

29. Rothman, "NPS-USFS Dispute," 141–61.

30. Jesse L. Nusbaum to Horace M. Albright, March 20, 1928, Series 6, Bandelier National Monument File 12–5, RG 79, NA. The announcement appeared in the March 3, 1928, *Santa Fe New Mexican*, and Nusbaum attached a clipping of the article to his bitter and despondent letter.

31. Minutes of the Eighth Meeting of the Coordinating Commission on National Parks and Forests, December 8, 1925, and Jesse L. Nusbaum to Stephen T. Mather, September 10, 1925, "Cliff Cities."

32. Arthur Ringland to Edgar L. Hewett, March 25, 1927, "Cliff Cities."

33. Frank Pinkley to A. E. Demaray, "Report on the Bandelier National Monument," May 23, 1927, Series 6, Bandelier National Monument File 12–5, RG 79, NA.

34. Horace Albright to Stephen T. Mather, June 8, 1927, "Cliff Cities."

35. Edgar L. Hewett to Arno B. Cammerer, January 17, 1928, and Stephen T. Mather to Hewett, January 24, 1928, "Cliff Cities."

36. Jesse L. Nusbaum, Roger W. Toll, and M. R. Tillotson, "The Bandelier National Monument and the Proposed Cliff Cities National Park," November 26, 1930; Arno B. Cammerer to Horace M. Albright, December 3, 1930; Albright memo, January 2, 1931; all in "Cliff Cities."

37. Clark Wissler to Director, February 10, 1931; Jesse L. Nusbaum to Stephen T. Mather, September 10, 1925; Arno B. Cammerer memo for the files, February 12, 1931; Roger W. Toll to Director, December 3, 1931; all in "Cliff Cities."

38. H. C. Bryant memo for the files, February 26, 1931, and United States Forester Major R. Y. Stuart to Horace Albright, November 10, 1931, "Cliff Cities." There was a two-year period during which Albright and Stuart corresponded on

the Bandelier issue. With Park Service assurance that it would remain a national monument, by early 1932, Stuart was more than glad to turn Bandelier over to the NPS. Executive Proclamation 1991, February 25, 1932, *United States Statutes at Large*, L. 47 Stat. 2503, accomplished the transfer. For more on leadership succession in both agencies, see Rothman, "NPS-USFS Dispute," 141–61.

39. Barry Mackintosh, *Interpretation in the National Park Service: A Historical Perspective* (Washington, D.C.: National Park Service, 1986), 5–18; C. Frank Brockman, "Park Naturalists and the Evolution of National Park Service Interpretation through World War II," *Journal of Forest History* 22 (January 1978): 24–43; Rothman, *Preserving Different Pasts*, 119–39.

40. Horace M. Albright to Stephen T. Mather, March 3, 1928, "Cliff Cities."

41. H. C. Bryant memo to the Director, March 25, 1931, "Cliff Cities."

42. Arthur E. Demaray memo to Horace M. Albright, June 8, 1931, "Cliff Cities."

43. Jesse L. Nusbaum to Horace M. Albright, March 18, 1932, Nusbaum's File, Bandelier National Monument Files, National Park Service Southwest Region Interpretation Library, Santa Fe.

CHAPTER 9

1. William E. Leuchtenberg, *Franklin D. Roosevelt and the New Deal* (New York: Harper and Row, 1963), remains the standard work on the New Deal; Richard Lowitt, *The New Deal and the West* (Bloomington: Indiana University Press, 1984), focuses on the impact of Roosevelt's policies in the West.

2. deBuys, *Enchantment and Exploitation*, 215–33; Donald Worster, *Dust Bowl: The Southern Plains in the 1930s* (New York: Oxford University Press, 1979), 310–16; Suzanne Forrest, *Preservation of the Village: New Mexico's Hispanics and the New Deal* (Albuqerque: University of New Mexico Press, 1989), 103–50.

3. Gerald D. Nash, *The American West in the Twentieth Century: A Short History of an Urban Oasis* (Albuquerque: University of New Mexico Press, 1973), 185–86; Deutsch, *No Separate Refuge*, 162–99; deBuys, *Enchantment and Exploitation*, 231–54. In the summer of 1988, Maria E. Montoya performed more than fifty oral histories with people who participated in the CCC camps and lived or worked in the Pajarito Plateau region. This immensely valuable collection allows a view into the thoughts and feelings of Hispanos and Anglos who experienced the depression and the New Deal. The collection is located at the National Park Service Southwest Region Interpretation Library.

4. Clary, *Timber and the Forest Service*, 94–110.

5. Two volumes produced by the National Park Service cover its development during the 1930s. Harlan D. Unrau and G. Frank Williss, *Administrative History:*

Expansion of the National Park Service in the 1930s (Denver: National Park Service, 1983), and John C. Paige, *The Civilian Conservation Corps and the National Park Service: An Administrative History,* (Denver: National Park Service, 1985) address changes in the agency as a result of New Deal programs. See also Clary, *Timber and the Forest Service,* 96, and Steen, *Forest Service,* 196–221. Twight, *Organizational Values and Political Power,* covers the NPS-USFS rivalry over Olympic National Park.

6. Tucker and Fitzpatrick, *Men Who Matched the Mountains,* 161–71; Clary, *Timber and the Forest Service,* 94–110; Steen, *Forest Service,* 196–221.

7. Clary, *Timber and the Forest Service,* 94–95; Pyne, *Fire in America,* 264–77, 365–66.

8. Donald C. Swain, "Harold Ickes, Horace Albright, and the Hundred Days: A Study in Conservation Administration," *Pacific Historical Review* 34 (November 1965): 455–65. See also Albright as told to Cahn, *Birth of the National Park Service.*

9. Rothman, "Conflict on the Pajarito," 68–77.

10. United States Forest Service, "Memorandum for the Members of the Co-ordinating Commission on National Parks and Forests," attached to Acting Forester L. F. Kneipp to Stephen T. Mather, July 10, 1925, "Cliff Cities"; Steen, *Forest Service,* 152–61, 209; and Fairfax and Dana, *Forest and Range Policy,* 131–34, 155–57, all contain background for USFS policy. See also Alison T. Otis, William D. Honey, Thomas C. Hogg, and Kimberly K. Lakin, *The Forest Service and the Civilian Conservation Corps: 1933–1942* (Washington, D.C.: USDA Forest Service, 1986), 29–33.

11. McLuhan, *Dream Tracks,* 41–45; D. H. Thomas, *The Southwestern Indian Detours: The Story of the Fred Harvey/Santa Fe Railway Experiment in "Detourism"* (Phoenix: Hunter Publishing Co., 1978).

12. Scrapbook, R. Hunter Clarkson Papers, NMSRCA; McLuhan, *Dream Tracks,* 41–45; *Indian-detours: Off the Beaten Path in the Great Southwest* (Santa Fe: Courier Cars, 1938), collection of the author. Even the federal government promoted travel in New Mexico during the 1930s. *New Mexico: A Guide to the Colorful State* (Albuquerque: Coronado Cuarto Centennial Commission, 1940), reissued as *The WPA Guide to 1930s New Mexico* (Tucson: University of Arizona Press, 1989), contains guides to car trips, including ones to Bandelier and the Pajarito Plateau.

13. Rothman, "Second-Class Sites"; Hal Rothman, "Forged by One Man's Will: Frank Pinkley and the Administration of the Southwestern National Monuments, 1923–1932," *Public Historian* 8 (Spring 1986).

14. Evelyn Frey, November 1985 interview with Hal Rothman and Virginia Robicheau. Mrs. Frey has long accounted for her presence in Frijoles Canyon by insisting that the Forest Service gave her and her husband a ninety-nine-year lease in 1925. In the 1980s, no one could recall seeing the actual document. Correspondence between the author and USDA Forest Service Archaeologist David Gillio in

1988 indicates that such a lease would have gone against policy even in the 1920s. One possible explanation for the unusual lease is that Evelyn Frey's father worked for the USFS and remained close to that agency. For more on George Cecil, see *Early Days in the Forest Service* (Missoula: United States Forest Service, 1944), 37–41. A Los Alamos resident, Dorothy Hoard, informed the author that Mrs. Frey's sister claims to have the original permit in her possession.

15. Evelyn Frey, November 1985 interview with Rothman and Robicheau. See also Hal Rothman and Virginia Robicheau interview with Richard Boyd, Jr., in Chama, New Mexico, November 14, 1985, Bandelier National Monument Library.

16. Evelyn Frey, November 1985 interview with Rothman and Robicheau.

17. Unrau and Williss, *Administrative History*; Hal Rothman, *Bandelier National Monument: An Administrative History* (Santa Fe: National Park Service, 1988), 65–94; Frank Pinkley to Arthur E. Demaray, November 18, 1932, Series 7, Bandelier National Monument File 12–5, RG 79, NA; Rothman, "Forged by One Man's Will," makes clear Pinkley's objectives.

18. Jesse L. Nusbaum to Horace M. Albright, November 7, 1932, and Frank Pinkley to Albright, October 8, 1932, Series 7, Bandelier National Monument File 12–5, RG 79, NA.

19. Frank Pinkley to Horace M. Albright, October 8, 1932, and George Grant, "Report on the Bandelier National Monument," November 20, 1932, Series 7, Bandelier National Monument File 12–5, RG 79, NA.

20. Arthur E. Demaray to Jesse L. Nusbaum, January 18, 1932, and Frank Pinkley to Hunter Clarkson, May 23, 1933, Series 7, Bandelier National Monument File 12–5, RG 79, NA.

21. Arthur E. Demaray to Jesse L. Nusbaum, November 18, 1932, Series 7, Bandelier National Monument File 12–5, RG 79, NA.

22. See "CCC Work Accomplished under Supervision of National Park Service [at Bandelier National Monument] from November, 1933, to June 30, 1939," Bandelier National Monument File 207, Administration: Reports, General, Federal Records Center, Denver, Colorado; Laura Soulliere Harrison and Randy Copeland, *Historic Structures Report: CCC Buildings, Bandelier National Monument* (Denver: National Park Service, 1984), 22–55. See also *Southwestern National Monument Monthly Report* (December 1933), 19, Bandelier National Monument Library; Frank Pinkley to Director Arno B. Cammerer, November 6, 1933, and Frank A. Kittredge to Pinkley, September 11, 1934, Bandelier National Monument File 600, Lands, Roads, Buildings, and Trails, Federal Records Center, Denver, Colorado.

23. Frank Pinkley to Field Headquarters, San Francisco, September 28, 1934, Bandelier National Monument File 600, Lands, Roads, Buildings, and Trails, Federal Records Center, Denver, Colorado.

24. See "ccc Work Accomplished," Bandelier National Monument File 207, Administration: Reports, General, Federal Records Center, Denver, Colorado.

25. Sandra S. Batie, "Soil Conservation in the 1980s: A Historical Perspective," *Agricultural History* 59 (April 1985): 107–23.

26. Kenneth R. Philp, "John Collier, 1933–1945," in Robert M. Kvasnicka and Herman J. Viola, eds., *The Commissioners of Indian Affairs, 1824–1977* (Lincoln: University of Nebraska Press, 1979), 273–82; Dippie, *Vanishing American,* 297–336; Prucha, *Great Father,* 274–77, 311–25; John Collier memo to Harold L. Ickes, May 4, 1939, Series 7, Bandelier National Monument File, 602, RG 79, NA.

27. Andrew R. Cordova, "Effect of Government Land Purchases on the Tax Structure of Three New Mexico Counties," *New Mexico Business Review* 8 (January 1939): 3–10; Forrest, *Preservation of the Village,* 132–35; Lawrence C. Kelly, "Anthropology in the Soil Conservation Service," *Agricultural History* 59 (April 1985): 136–47. For more on soil conservation activities on the Navajo reservation, see Donald L. Parman, *The Navajos and the New Deal* (New Haven: Yale University Press, 1976), 36–43, 81–94.

28. John Collier memo to Secretary of the Interior Harold L. Ickes and Secretary of Agriculture Henry Wallace, December 30, 1936, and Collier memo to Ickes, May 4, 1939, copies in Series 7, Bandelier National Monument File, 602–01, Boundary Extension, RG 79, NA.

29. Weigle, *Hispanic Villages,* 52–54.

30. J. A. Rodriguez, "Erosion Problem Area Survey, #9 Ramón Vigil Grant," United States Forest Service, M, Plans, Soil Erosion Survey, January 2 and January 8, 1940, copies in the Los Alamos Historical Society; USDA Soil Conservation Service, *Annual Report Region No. 8, 1936–37* (Washington, D.C.: Government Printing Office, 1938), 119; Allen, "Changes in the Landscape," 161.

31. William H. Powell to Arthur F. Ringland, January 18, 1929; Ringland to Powell, January 27, 1929; Powell to Stephen T. Mather, February 1, 1928; Arthur E. Demaray to Powell, February 7, 1928; Mather to Powell, April 13, 1928; all in "Cliff Cities."

32. F. D. Abbott, "Range Management Plan for San Ildefonso Pueblo Grant and Indian Reservation," April 12, 1937, and "Range Management Plan for Santa Clara Pueblo Grant and Indian Reservation," March 15, 1937, TC-BIA, SCS, USDA, Albuquerque, Records of the Soil Conservation Service, RG 114, NA; Indian Land Research Unit, *Tewa Basin Study* (Washington, D.C.: Office of Indian Affairs, 1935), 1:57–59.

33. Richard Polenberg, *Reorganizing Roosevelt's Government: The Controversy over Executive Reorganization, 1936–1939* (Cambridge: Harvard University Press, 1966), 100–122; Swain, "Harold Ickes, Horace Albright, and the Hundred Days," 455–65; Rothman, "NPS-USFS Dispute," 141–62; Ise, *Our National Park Policy,* 352,

439–40; Irving Brant, *Adventures in Conservation with Franklin D. Roosevelt* (Flagstaff, Ariz.: Northland Press, 1988), 73–74; Harold L. Ickes, *The Secret Diary: Volume I, The First Thousand Days, 1933–1936* (New York: Simon and Schuster, 1954), 21–23, 52, 250, 350, 364–65, 534–35; Albright as told to Cahn, *Birth of the National Park Service*, 282–88, 303–20.

34. Kenneth R. Philp, *John Collier's Crusade for Indian Reform, 1920–1954* (Tucson: University of Arizona Press, 1977), 122–23; U.S. President, Executive Order 8255, September 18, 1939.

35. Regional Geologist Charles N. Gould, "Report on the Proposed Jemez Crater National Park," Series 7, 0–35, Jemez Crater, RG 79, NA.

CHAPTER 10

1. Gerald D. Nash, *The American West Transformed: The Impact of the Second World War* (Albuquerque: University of New Mexico Press, 1985), is the best work on the impact of the war on the West. See also Nash, *American West in the Twentieth Century*, and Michael P. Malone and Richard W. Etulain, *The American West: A Twentieth-Century History* (Lincoln: University of Nebraska Press, 1989).

2. Richard Rhodes, *The Making of the Atomic Bomb* (New York: Simon and Schuster, 1986); Stephane Groueff, *The Untold Story of the Making of the Atomic Bomb* (Boston: Little, Brown, and Co., 1967); Richard G. Hewlett and Oscar E. Anderson, Jr., *Volume I, A History of the United States Atomic Energy Commission: The New World, 1939–1946* (University Park: Pennsylvania State University Press, 1962); David Hawkins, *Project Y: The Los Alamos Story, Part I: Toward Trinity* (Los Angeles: Tomash Publishers, 1983), and Edith C. Truslow and Ralph Carlisle Smith, *Project Y: The Los Alamos Story, Part II: Beyond Trinity* (Los Angeles: Tomash Publishers, 1983).

3. For the best examples of the history of American scientific exploration and the attitudes of scientists and explorers, see Goetzmann, *Exploration and Empire*, and idem, *New Lands, New Men: America and the Second Great Age of Discovery* (New York: Viking Penguin, 1986). Daniel J. Kevles, *The Physicists: The History of a Scientific Community in Modern America* (New York: Vintage Books, 1977), shows the evolution of empirical science in the person of the practitioners of physics.

4. Ronald A. Foresta, *America's National Parks and Their Keepers* (Washington, D.C.: Resources for the Future, 1984), discusses the evolution of agency policy after 1933. See also Rothman, *Preserving Different Pasts*, for an account of the evolution of the national monuments, agency policy, and the impact of the reorganization of 1933. See Harrison and Copeland, *Historic Structures Report*, and Rothman, *Bandelier National Monument*, for more details on the effect of these

changes on Bandelier National Monument in particular. Rothman, "Forged by One Man's Will," covers Pinkley's role. Much of the information about Pinkley can be found in Series 6, Casa Grande File, RG 79, NA.

5. Groueff, *Untold Story,* 10; Rhodes, *Atomic Bomb,* 303–8; James W. Kunetka, *City of Fire: Los Alamos and the Atomic Age, 1943–1945,* rev. ed. (Albuquerque: University of New Mexico Press, 1979), 20–21.

6. Groueff, *Untold Story,* 54–63; Kunetka, *City of Fire,* 36.

7. Groueff, *Untold Story,* 11–13.

8. Rhodes, *Atomic Bomb,* 119–27.

9. Ibid., 449–50; Leslie R. Groves, *Now It Can Be Told: The Story of the Manhattan Project* (New York: De Capo Press, 1975), 63–67; Kunetka, *City of Fire,* 13–14; Groueff, *Untold Story,* 64–67.

10. Rhodes, *Atomic Bomb,* 450–51; Groves, *Now It Can Be Told,* 66–67; Kunetka, *City of Fire,* 10–15; Groueff, *Untold Story,* 64–66.

11. For the story of Pecos Pueblo, see Hall, *Four Leagues of Pecos,* 31–67; Joe Sando, "Jemez Pueblo," in Ortiz, *Handbook of North American Indians* 9:423; and for a view of Collier's role in strengthening the Bureau of Indian Affairs, see Lawrence C. Kelly, *The Assault on Assimilation: John Collier and the Origins of Indian Policy Reform* (Albuquerque: University of New Mexico Press, 1983).

12. Kunetka, *City of Fire,* 14–15; Rhodes, *Atomic Bomb,* 450–51; Groueff, *Untold Story,* 64–67.

13. Chronic, *Roadside Geology of New Mexico,* 150–59; Pettit, *Before the Dawn,* 5–19, and idem, *Exploring the Jemez Country* (Los Alamos: Pajarito Publications, 1975), 9–12; Rhodes, *Atomic Bomb,* 450–51. Alfonso Ortiz, *The Tewa World: Space, Time, Being, and Becoming in a Pueblo Society,* (Chicago: University of Chicago Press, 1969), defines the physical and spiritual boundaries of the Pueblo Indian world.

14. Rhodes, *Atomic Bomb,* 450–51.

15. Transcript of interview with Bences Gonzales, April 21, 1948, Los Alamos Historical Society; Price R. Cross to Margaret Wohlberg, September 8, 1977, File HS 42K, Los Alamos Historical Museum; Notes by Peggy Pond Church, File HS 42C, Los Alamos Historical Museum; Pettit, *Before the Dawn,* 47–48; Church, *Otowi Bridge,* 7.

16. The Los Alamos Historical Society contains copies of the Los Alamos Ranch School brochures; see also LAHS, *Ranch School* 9.

17. Church, *Otowi Bridge,* 7; Pettit, *Before the Dawn,* 47–55; LAHS, *Ranch School,* 10–11.

18. Church, *Otowi Bridge,* 9; Church, "Trails over Pajarito."

19. LAHS, *Ranch School,* 10–20; Pettit, *Before the Dawn,* 49–54.

20. Church, "Trails over Pajarito"; Church, *Otowi Bridge,* 7–10; Pettit, *Before the Dawn,* 54.

21. LAHS, *Ranch School,* 12; Church, "Trails Over Pajarito."

22. Pettit, *Before the Dawn,* 54–55.

23. LAHS, *Ranch School,* was published to commemorate a 1973 reunion of Ranch School graduates, even though the institution had been defunct for more than thirty years. The booklet brims with talk of the development of character and other attributes that Connell stressed.

24. Hal Rothman and Virginia Robicheau interview with Richard Boyd, Jr., in Chama, New Mexico, November 14, 1985, Bandelier National Monument Library.

25. Recollections of Hispanos who felt that they were treated poorly in the takeover have become part of public currency since the 1970s. Many of these have appeared in the *Los Alamos Monitor.* See Anne Poore, "Tour Starts Off with Mystery: Is It Gomez or Montoya Ranch?" *Los Alamos Monitor,* June 6, 1983, and "Marcus Gomez . . . Los Alamos Pioneer," *Los Alamos Monitor,* September 24, 1970.

26. A. J. Connell to War Department, November 20, 1942, and Henry Stimson to Connell, December 1, 1942, Los Alamos Ranch School Papers, Los Alamos Historical Society. See also Pettit, *Before the Dawn,* 58, and LAHS, *Ranch School,* 20–22.

27. A. J. Connell to Lt. Col. J. M. Harmon, December 26, 1942; Harmon to Connell, December 29, 1942; Connell to Harmon, January 2, 1943; all in Los Alamos Ranch School Papers, Los Alamos Historical Society.

28. A. J. Connell to Lawrence S. Hitchcock, May 5, 1943, L. S. Hitchcock Papers, Los Alamos Historical Society.

29. Connell's obituary is in the *Santa Fe New Mexican,* February 12, 1944.

30. Groueff, *Untold Story,* 42–179; Groves, *Now It Can Be Told,* 140; Rhodes, *Atomic Bomb,* 454–55, 460–61.

31. Rhodes, *Atomic Bomb,* 459–60; Groves, *Now It Can Be Told,* 165–66.

32. Rhodes, *Atomic Bomb,* 459, 465–67; Groves, *Now It Can Be Told,* 157–58.

33. Kunetka, *City of Fire,* 99; Groueff, *Untold Story,* 203.

34. Laura Fermi, *Atoms in the Family: My Life with Enrico Fermi* (Chicago: University of Chicago Press, 1954), 207; Phyllis K. Fisher, *Los Alamos Experience* (Tokyo: Japan Publications, 1985), 37–38.

35. Fermi, *Atoms in the Family,* 208; Rhodes, *Atomic Bomb,* 567; Fisher, *Los Alamos Experience,* 50.

36. Fermi, *Atoms in the Family,* 209; Rhodes, *Atomic Bomb,* 565–67.

37. Rhodes, *Atomic Bomb,* 564–68; Fermi, *Atoms in the Family,* 209.

38. Fisher, *Los Alamos Experience,* 43–45; Groves, *Now It Can Be Told,* 165–66.

39. C. A. Thomas to M. R. Tillotson, February 8 and February 18, 1943, File H14, Bandelier National Monument Library.

40. C. A. Thomas to M. R. Tillotson, October 20, 1944, and Tillotson confiden-

tial memo for the Director, October 21, 1944, File H14, Bandelier National Monument Library.

41. M. R. Tillotson confidential memo for the Director, October 21, 1944, File H14, Bandelier National Monument Library.

42. Ibid.

43. E. T. Scoyen, memo for the files August 7, 1945, Series 7, RG 79, NA; Groves, *Now It Can Be Told*, 151–52.

44. "Los Alamos School Still Goes On," *Santa Fe New Mexican*, August 11, 1945; "Famed Alamos School Closes, A-Bomb Held Partly to Blame," *Santa Fe New Mexican*, February 9, 1946.

CHAPTER 11

1. Kunetka, *City of Fire*, 205.

2. Malone and Etulain, *American West*, 120–34; Nash, *American West Transformed*, 201–16.

3. Eric Goldman, *The Crucial Decade—and After: America, 1945–1960* (New York: Random House, 1956), 4–5, 12–15; Bernard DeVoto, "The National Parks," *Fortune* 35 (June 1947): 120–21; Runte, *National Parks*, 156–61.

4. Rothman, *Bandelier National Monument*, 155.

5. Clary, *Timber and the Forest Service*, 151–52; Baker, Maxwell, Treat, and Dethloff, *Timeless Heritage*, 60–61, 83–86.

6. Kunetka, *City of Fire*, 191–94, 202–6, 755–56, Rhodes, *Atomic Bomb*, 766–70; Hewlett and Anderson, *The New World*, 625–26. Donald A. Strickland, *Scientists in Politics: The Atomic Scientists Movement, 1945–46* (West Lafayette, Ind.: Purdue University Studies, 1968), discusses one response of scientists to the horror of the atomic bomb. Chambers, "Technically Sweet Los Alamos," 159–63, suggests that the decision for permanence was made during the war and that even General Leslie Groves approved.

7. Chambers, "Technically Sweet Los Alamos," 168.

8. Ibid.

9. Fern Lyon and Jacob Evans, eds., *Los Alamos: The First Forty Years* (Los Alamos: Los Alamos Historical Society, 1984), 46.

10. Author's conversation with Adrian Bustamante and Federico Sánchez, Dallas, Texas, Summer 1986.

11. Chambers, "Technically Sweet Los Alamos," 175–80; Groves, *Now It Can Be Told*, 66, remembers: "We also found—which did not surprise me—that it was almost impossible to control the use of water by the residents. This was not so much because they were not under military discipline as because they were

twentieth-century Americans and they are always prodigal in their use of water."

12. Chambers, "Technically Sweet Los Alamos," 208–13.

13. Ibid., 212–60, is an excellent account of the process of enfranchising the citizens of Los Alamos.

14. Lyon and Evans, *First Forty Years,* 49, 56–57, 63; Chambers, "Technically Sweet Los Alamos," 192.

15. Chambers, "Technically Sweet Los Alamos," 195; Church, *Otowi Bridge,* 5–9.

16. Chambers, "Technically Sweet Los Alamos," 197–99; Lyon and Evans, *First Forty Years,* 70.

17. Chambers, "Technically Sweet Los Alamos," 203.

18. Paul Judge interview by Hal Rothman and Virginia Robicheau, May 1986, Bandelier National Monument Library.

19. Chambers, "Technically Sweet Los Alamos," 240; Lyon and Evans, *First Forty Years,* 71; Peggy Corbett, "White Rock 'Temporary,'" *Los Alamos Monitor,* October 31, 1971, p. 4; "White Rock . . . Modern Ghost Town on the Plateau," *LASL Community Affairs News,* (March 1959), 4. The author can attest to the lack of insulation and comfortable features in original housing constructed for White Rock. When the buildings were declared excess to AEC needs, the Park Service moved a number of them to Bandelier for use as temporary housing. There the author lived in one for six months in 1985.

20. Charlie Steen memo to the Regional Director, July 26, 1960, File L1417, Bandelier National Monument Library.

21. Chambers, "Technically Sweet Los Alamos," 178–79, 361–62.

22. Ibid., 185, gives 7,000 as the population for 1946; Lyon and Evans, *First Forty Years,* offers the 1946 census figure.

23. Bernard DeVoto, "Let's Close the National Parks," *Harper's* 207 (October 1953): 49–52.

24. Foresta, *America's National Parks,* 49–57; Conrad L. Wirth, *Parks, Politics, and the People* (Norman: University of Oklahoma Press, 1980), 237–84.

25. Thomas J. Allen to Conrad L. Wirth, August 9, 1960, File L1417, Bandelier National Monument Library.

26. Leslie P. Arnberger memo for the files, May 31, 1961; John J. Burke to Thomas J. Allen, June 21, 1961; Allen to Conrad L. Wirth, March 6, 1962; all in File L1417, Bandelier National Monument Library. See Runte, *National Parks,* 160–61, for a discussion of the sanctuary-playground issue.

27. Runte, *National Parks,* 262–65, discusses the implementation of a reservations policy; Richard Reinhardt, "Careless Love: The Pitfalls of Affection in the Incomparable Valley of Yosemite," *Wilderness* 52 (Summer 1989): 17–26.

28. Regional Director Hugh M. Miller to Director Conrad L. Wirth, July 29, 1958, and Superintendent Paul Judge to Miller, July 9, 1958, File L1417, Bandelier National Monument Library.

29. Ben Thompson, Chief of Recreation and Resource Planning, memo for the files, March 6, 1959, File L1417, Bandelier National Monument Library.

30. Clary, *Timber and the Forest Service,* 151–53; Baker, Maxwell, Treat, and Dethloff, *Timeless Heritage,* 131–37; Pyne, *Fire in America,* 264.

31. Baker, Maxwell, Treat, and Dethloff, *Timeless Heritage,* 59.

32. George Von Der Lippe and Edward J. Widmer, "A Field Report on the Uncontrolled Use of the Otowi Section of Bandelier National Monument," March 4, 1960, Bandelier National Monument Files, National Park Service Southwest Region Interpretation Library.

33. E. T. Scoyen memo to Regional Director, Region 3 [Southwest], July 29, 1959, and Paul Judge to Regional Director, Region 3, August 4, 1959, File L1417, Bandelier National Monument Library.

34. Leslie P. Arnberger memo to the Regional Director, July 18, 1960; Jerome Miller memo to the Regional Director, July 25, 1960; George Kell memo to the Regional Director, July 26, 1960; all in File L1417, Bandelier National Monument Library.

35. Charlie Steen memo to the Regional Director, July 26, 1960, File L1417, Bandelier National Monument Library.

36. Pyne, *Fire in America,* 514–16.

37. Ibid., 518–20.

38. Caro, *Lyndon Johnson,* 347–48; Pyne, *Fire in America,* 360–71; Baker, Maxwell, Treat, and Dethloff, *Timeless Heritage,* 53–57.

39. Chambers, "Technically Sweet Los Alamos," 176–77.

40. Pyne, *Fire in America,* 283–89; Baker, Maxwell, Treat, and Dethloff, *Timeless Heritage,* 116.

41. Allen, "Changes in the Landscape," 250–59.

CHAPTER 12

1. In recent years, the politics and culture of the 1960s have been under great scrutiny. Among the worthy sources are William O'Neill, *Coming Apart: An Informal History of the 1960s* (New York: Quadrangle New York Times Book Co., 1971), Todd Gitlin, *The Sixties: Years of Hope, Days of Rage* (New York: Bantam Books, 1987), and James Miller, *Democracy Is in the Streets: From Port Huron to the Streets of Chicago* (New York: Simon and Schuster, 1987).

2. The era of reform between 1815 and 1860 is best documented in Ronald Wal-

ters, *American Reformers, 1815–1860* (New York: Hill and Wang, 1978), and Alice Felt Tyler, *Freedom's Ferment: Phases of American Social History from the Colonial Period to the Outbreak of the Civil War* (New York: Harper and Brothers, 1962). Tom Wolfe's essay "The Me Decade and the Third Great Awakening" in *Mauve Gloves and Madmen, Clutter and Vine, and Other Stories, Sketches, and Essays* (New York: Farrar, Straus, and Giroux, 1975), 126–66, sheds light on the character of the early 1970s.

3. Nash, *Wilderness and the American Mind*, 316–20; Samuel P. Hays, *Beauty, Health, and Permanence: Environmental Politics in the United States, 1955–1985* (New York: Cambridge University Press, 1987), 52–53; Stephen G. Fox, *John Muir and His Legacy*, 250–90, 313–17.

4. Hays, *Conservation*, 1–5, provides the best summary of the attitudes of the Progressive conservation movement. Hays's later work, *Beauty, Health, and Permanence*, clearly articulates the sentiments of the most recent era.

5. Foresta, *America's National Parks*, 96–99; Richard A. Baker, *Conservation Politics: The Senate Career of Clinton P. Anderson* (Albuquerque: University of New Mexico Press, 1985), 106.

6. Foresta, *America's National Parks*, 93–128; Runte, *National Parks*, 197–208, addresses changes in management.

7. *Wilderness* (Spring 1989), 3–11; Nash, *Wilderness and the American Mind*, 220–26; Baker, *Conservation Politics*, 100–104, 108, discusses the rivalry between Conrad L. Wirth and David Brower and Howard Zahniser. Wirth explains his actions, albeit lamely, in his *Parks, Politics, and the People*, 360–61.

8. Nash, *Wilderness and the American Mind*, 209–19.

9. Michael E. Welsh, *U.S. Army Corps of Engineers: Albuquerque District, 1935–1985* (Albuquerque: University of New Mexico Press, 1987), 139–42.

10. Regional Director to Conrad L. Wirth, November 20, 1958, and Acting Director, NPS, to Secretary of the Interior, October 21, 1963, File L2419, Park Files, Bandelier National Monument Library. See also "Anderson Introduces Bill to Obtain Two-Mile by One-Mile Cochiti Lake," *Santa Fe New Mexican*, February 6, 1963; "Bill Would Create Recreational Lake," *LASL Community Affairs News*, February 14, 1963; Welsh, *U.S. Army Corps of Engineers*, 139–52.

11. Unsigned memo of March 3, 1960, from Regional Planning Office to Paul Judge, File D18, Bandelier National Monument Library; Welsh, *U.S. Army Corps of Engineers*, 143.

12. 1971 Draft Master Plan and 1973 Final Master Plan, File D18, Bandelier National Monument Library.

13. Norman Bullard to Linwood E. Jackson, January 15, 1972; Steve Schum, University of New Mexico Mountaineering Club, to Jackson, Bandelier Superintendent, December 18, 1971; Elizabeth A. Jackson to Linwood E. Jackson, Janu-

ary 2, 1972; all in File D18, Proposed Wilderness Hearing, Park Files, Bandelier National Monument Library. These letters are representative of a much larger collection.

14. "Wilderness Recommendation," August 1972, File D18, Bandelier National Monument Library.

15. Welsh, *U.S. Army Corps of Engineers*, 160–62; Hal Rothman conversation with Bandelier Superintendent John D. Hunter, June 29, 1985; and Michael C. Robinson, "The Relationship between the U.S. Army Corps of Engineers and the Environmental Community," *Environmental Review* 13 (Spring 1989): 1–41.

16. USDA Forest Service, RARE II: *A Quest for Balance in Public Lands* (Washington, D.C.: U.S. Government Printing Office, 1978); "RARE II: Questions and Answers," File L7619, Bandelier National Monument Library. See also M. Rupert Cutler, "National Forests in the Balance," *American Forests* (May 1978), and *Western Wildlands: A Natural Resource Journal* 5 (Summer 1978).

17. *New Mexico Wilderness Newsletter*, July 1978, presented the objections to RARE II proposals in New Mexico. See also Denise Tessier, "Time for Decision Nears on State Wilderness Areas," *Albuquerque Journal*, August 13, 1978; *Wilderness Report* (September 1978), 1–2, (October 1978), 2, (November 1978), and (December 1978).

18. John Lissoway, telephone conversation with Hal Rothman, February 20, 1987.

19. Runte, *National Parks*, 33–64, covers the "worthless lands" thesis, which I have modified, and the idea of monumentalism.

20. Tim Mahoney, "RARE Draft EIS Sparks Heavy Input by Conservationists," *Wilderness Report* 15 (September 1978); USDA Forest Service, "RARE II: Santa Fe National Forest," (no publication information available).

21. John Hunter to Regional Director, July 31, 1978, and David S. Wright, Assistant Director, to Regional Directors, July 10, 1978, copy in File L7619, Bandelier National Monument Library.

22. David Crosson, "RARE II Results Final: 'An Acute Disappointment,'" *High Country News*, January 12, 1979.

23. Weber, *Foreigners in Their Native Land*, provides a view of this situation in the words of the dispossessed; Hall, *Four Leagues of Pecos*, shows one method of disenfranchising Native American and Hispano landowners; Arnoldo De León, *They Called Them Greasers: Anglo Attitudes towards Mexicans in Texas, 1821–1900* (Austin: University of Texas Press, 1983), addresses similar issues in Texas; Manuel P. Servin, *An Awakened Minority: The Mexican-Americans*, 2d ed. (Beverly Hills, Calif.: Glencoe Press, 1974), and Manuel A. Machado, Jr., *Listen Chicano: An Informal History of the Mexican American* (Chicago: Nelson Hall, 1978), offer insights into the perspective that inspired the awakening of Spanish-speaking Americans.

24. Peter Nabakov, *Tijerina and the Courthouse Raid* (Albuquerque: University of New Mexico Press, 1969), is the best chronicle of the actions of Tijerina and his supporters.

25. Williams and McAllister, *New Mexico in Maps*, 68–72; Welch, *U.S. Army Corps of Engineers*, 157; Dorothy Hoard to the author, September 3, 1990.

26. Teralene Foxx, ed., *Los Alamos Fire Symposium, Los Alamos, New Mexico, October 6–7, 1981* (Los Alamos: Los Alamos National Laboratory, 1984), 3–6.

27. Dr. Milford R. Fletcher, conversation with the author, August 21, 1986; Senior Archaeologist Cal Cummings to Chief Anthropologist, WASO, January 24, 1986, copies in possession of the author.

28. Dr. Milford R. Fletcher, conversation with the author, August 21, 1986; Diane Traylor, "Effects of La Mesa Fire on Bandelier's Cultural Resources," in Foxx, *Los Alamos Fire Symposium*, 97.

29. John R. Morgart, "Burro Behavior and Population Dynamics" (Master's thesis, Arizona State University, 1978), 5–11; Dorothy Hoard to the author, August 3, 1990.

30. John Lissoway, interview with the author, August 17, 1986, and telephone conversation with the author, February 17, 1987. See also Michael Wolfe, "The Wild Horse and Burro Issue, 1982," *Environmental Review* 7 (Summer 1983): 179–92. Wolfe offers a summary of the impact of the Wild Horse and Burro Act on federal lands.

31. The Park Service commissioned a number of reports on the burro situation at Bandelier. Besides Morgart's, these include Roland H. Wauer, "Feral Burro Control Program for Bandelier," and David Koehler, "Preliminary Reconnaissance Report—Feral Burro Ecological Impact Project." These reports and a number of others are available in the National Park Service Southwest Region Interpretation Library. See also interview with Milford Fletcher, August 21, 1986.

32. John Lissoway, telephone conversation with the author, February 17, 1987; Dr. Milford R. Fletcher, conversation with the author, August 21, 1986.

33. Bandelier Superintendent John D. Hunter, conversation with the author, June 29, 1985; Chief Ranger Kevin McKibbin, conversation with the author, June 30, 1985; Resource Manager John Lissoway, conversation with the author, January 22, 1986; Dr. Milford R. Fletcher conversation with the author, August 21, 1986.

34. John Lissoway, telephone conversation with the author, February 20, 1987.

35. Pyne, *Fire in America*, 261, 290–91, 298; Allen, "Changes in the Landscape," 250–55.

CHAPTER 13

1. Superintendent John D. Hunter, quoted in J. W. Schomisch, "White Rock Wants Bypass out of Town," *Santa Fe New Mexican,* June 28, 1985. For a broader picture of the issues facing the park system in the 1980s, see "Parks under Pressure: Three Aspects of the Problem," *Wilderness* 52 (Summer 1989).

2. Foresta, *America's National Parks,* 225–28, 232–35.

3. Donald M. Kerr, "Lab's Plans—What Effect on Housing Resources?" *Los Alamos Monitor,* June 22, 1980, p. 4; Ben Neary, "Los Alamos, Pueblo Trying to Cut Deal for Road," *Albuquerque Journal,* June 4, 1989, c1–2.

4. "Girl Scout Camp Will Turn into Three Homes," *Los Alamos Monitor,* October 19, 1980.

5. Evelyn Vigil, "Camp Evergreen Sold to Local Partnership," *Los Alamos Monitor,* November 18, 1980; Russell D. Butcher, npca Southwest Regional Representative, to John D. Hunter, October 25, 1980, File l3215, Bandelier National Monument Library.

6. Tom Lucke to "Roger," October 20, 1980, and John D. Hunter memo for the files, December 30, 1980, File l3215, Bandelier National Monument Library. See also Charmian Schaller, "Evergreen Rezoning Bid Rekindles Conflict," *Los Alamos Monitor,* January 10, 1981.

7. Westgate Families, letter to the Editor, *Los Alamos Monitor,* January 25, 1980; Clifton Swickard, letter to the Editor, *Los Alamos Monitor,* March 31, 1981.

8. The referendum became a headline issue in Los Alamos. See the *Los Alamos Monitor* for the weeks preceding June 30, 1981.

9. John Lissoway, telephone conversation with the author, February 17, 1987.

10. Reconstructing the building of the roads to the Pajarito Plateau required much historical legwork. The papers of L. Bradford Prince contain letters from Harry Buckman, describing his efforts. The papers are located at nmsrca in Santa Fe. A number of diaries that detail travel routes to the Pajarito Plateau exist. The best of these were written by Grace Spradling Ireland and Ida Patton Abbott, the wife of Judge A. J. Abbott. The Bandelier National Monument Library contains copies of both in its vertical file. The Los Alamos Historical Society possesses much information about the Ranch School and its roads under the "Los Alamos Ranch School" headings. See also the *Santa Fe New Mexican,* May 10, 1912, and Williams and McAllister, *New Mexico in Maps,* 144.

11. See Nusbaum's File, National Park Service Southwest Region Interpretation Library, for details. See also Thomas, *Southwestern Indian Detours,* and Athearn, *Denver and Rio Grande.* Thomas's book is of marginal value to scholars.

12. New Mexico State Highway Department, "Public Involvement Meetings: The Santa Fe–Los Alamos Corridor," copy in File l7619, New Road, Bandelier National Monument Library.

13. John D. Hunter to Regional Director Robert Kerr, October 10, 1984; Draft of Hunter's comments to the public involvement meeting in White Rock on June 27, 1985; Forest Supervisor Maynard T. Rost to Thomas Scanlon of H.W. Lochner, Inc., June 14, 1985; all in File L7619, Bandelier National Monument Library.

14. Schomisch, "White Rock Wants Bypass."

15. Neary, "Deal for Road."

16. Interview by the author of a longtime Los Alamos resident who requested anonymity, Summer 1986.

17. James Metzger, Mountain Research West, Inc., to John D. Hunter, September 22, 1978, File L7619, Bandelier National Monument Library.

18. PNM-DOE, "Draft Preliminary Environmental Analysis," May 16, 1979.

19. Wayne Eckles, PNM, to Regional Director John Cook, February 2, 1979, File L7619, Bandelier National Monument Library.

20. John Cook to John D. Hunter, February 21, 1979, File L7619, Bandelier National Monument Library.

21. Ibid.

22. Wayne Cone to Ray Brechbill, DOE, March 30, 1979, and Acting Director Ira J. Hutchinson to Cristobal Zamora, November 8, 1979, File L7619, Bandelier National Monument Library.

23. Jon Bowman, "LASL to Drill Deeper for 'Hotter' Well System," Los Alamos Monitor, March 6, 1979, copy in File L7619, Bandelier National Monument Library; John Hunter, interview with the author, November 10, 1986; John Lissoway, telephone conversation with the author, February 17, 1987.

24. PNM, "Ojo Line Extension Project Newsletter," August 3, 1985.

25. "Brief for Sotero Muniz on OLE Project," File L7621, Ojo Line extension, Bandelier National Monument Library.

26. Thomas Ribe, "A Proposed Powerline Jolts New Mexico," High Country News, March 31, 1986, p. 6; Thomas Ribe to the Editor, Los Alamos Monitor, November 8, 1985; John D. Hunter to Robert Kerr, October 31, 1985, File L7621, Bandelier National Monument Library.

27. PNM, "Ojo Line Extension Project Newsletter," December 4, 1985; Eldon G. Reyer, Associate Director, Planning and Cultural Resources, Southwest Region, to Vincent Little, Area Director, Albuquerque Office, Bureau of Indian Affairs, August 15, 1985; James Overbay to Little, August 16, 1985; Reyer to Little, January 17, 1986; all in File L7619, Bandelier National Monument Library.

28. Bureau of Indian Affairs, "Final Environmental Impact Statement: Proposed Ojo Line Extension" (Washington, D.C.: Bureau of Indian Affairs, 1986); John D. Hunter, interview with the author, November 10, 1986; Craig Allen, telephone conversation with the author, February 6, 1987.

29. John D. Hunter to Harold Valencia, May 10, 1985; Hunter to Eloy Nuñez,

Chief, Project and Facility Management Branch, DOE, June 3, 1985; Hunter to Regional Director Robert Kerr, June 17, 1985; Valencia to Hunter, June 21, 1985; Hunter to Eldon G. Reyer, July 23, 1985; all in File L7621, Bandelier National Monument Library.

30. John D. Hunter to Robert Kerr, June 17, 1985, and Harold Valencia to Kerr, September 5, 1985, File L7619, Bandelier National Monument Library.

31. Robert Kerr to Harold Valencia, October 22, 1985, and John Lissoway memo, September 18, 1985, File L7619, Bandelier National Monument Library.

32. Tom Ribe, "Weapons Research Harasses Monument," *High Country News*, November 11, 1985, p. 6; idem, "Bandelier Officials Worry about Noise from Lab Projects," *Santa Fe New Mexican*, November 10, 1985, B-6; Editorial, "Bandelier No Place to Test Explosives," *Santa Fe New Mexican*, November 14, 1985. See also John D. Hunter to Robert Kerr, November 14, 1985; Harold Valencia to Kerr, February 14, 1986; Russell D. Butcher to Hunter, March 3, 1986; Butcher to W. L. Thompson, LANL, March 3, 1986; Janet E. Schmitt to Hunter, February 20, 1986; all in File L7619, Bandelier National Monument Library.

33. Draft Bill, "To Establish a Jemez Mountains National Park in the State of New Mexico and for Other Purposes" and "A Save the Jemez Draft Legislative Bill to Create a Jemez Mountains National Park: Background Information," January 27, 1987, both in possesssion of the author; Sandi Doughton-Evans, "National Park Proposed in Jemez," *Los Alamos Monitor*, February 5, 1987; Scott Sandlin, "National Park Sought for Jemez Mountains," *Albuquerque Tribune*, February 5, 1987; Rene Kimball, "Environmentalists Seek Jemez National Park," *Albuquerque Journal*, February 6, 1987; Ben Neary, "Locals Oppose Proposal for Jemez National Park," *Rio Grande Sun*, February 19, 1987; Rene Kimball, "Rep. Richardson Criticizes Jemez Park Plan," *Albuquerque Journal*, February 19, 1987; Faye Davis, "Opposition to Jemez Park Will Persist," *Albuquerque Journal*, March 25, 1987.

34. USDA Forest Service, "Santa Fe National Forest Plan" (USDA Forest Service, Southwestern Region, Albuquerque, 1987); "Environmental Impact Statement, Santa Fe National Forest Plan" (USDA Forest Service, Southwestern Region, Albuquerque, 1987); "Public Comments and Forest Service Response to the Revised DEIS, Proposed Santa Fe National Forest Plan" (USDA Forest Service, Southwestern Region, Albuquerque, 1987), 5:1–3; Sandi Doughton-Evans, "Settlement Requires FS to Protect Sites," *Los Alamos Monitor*, March 4, 1986; Dyan Zaslowsky, "Hired Gun: Randal O'Toole, Forestry Economist, Takes Aim at the Forest Service," *Harrowsmith* 3 (January/February 1988): 45–53; and Randal O'Toole, *Reforming the Forest Service* (Washington, D.C.: Island Press, 1988).

35. Dorothy Hoard to Laura Loomis, Boundary Projects Coordinator, NPCA, September 9, 1985, and Hoard to Forest Supervisor Maynard T. Rost, February 15, 1986, File L7619, Bandelier National Monument Library.

36. Iver Peterson, "Big Spring Runoff, New Water Battle," *New York Times*, June 13, 1985.

37. Regional Director to Director, November 20, 1958, File L30, Park Files, Bandelier National Monument. For the stories of Echo Park and Glen Canyon, see Nash, *Wilderness and the American Mind*, 202–19, 228–37. See also William deBuys, "Cochiti: The Dam That Got Away," *Audubon Magazine* (June 1977), 121–23.

38. Sandi Doughton-Evans, "Bandelier Canyons Will Be Flooded," *Los Alamos Monitor*, May 10, 1985; Nolan Hester, "Reservoir's Storage Rate to Double," *Albuquerque Journal*, May 14, 1985.

39. J. W. Schomisch, "River Threatening Indian Ruins," *Santa Fe New Mexican*, May 17, 1985; Sandi Doughton-Evans, "Bandelier Flooding to Affect Eagles," *Los Alamos Monitor*, May 22, 1985.

40. Kevin McKibbin quoted in *Santa Fe New Mexican*, June 17, 1985.

41. Sandi Doughton-Evans, "Protesters Speak Out on Flooding," *Los Alamos Monitor*, June 20, 1985; Mike Leary, "Fight over Water Threatens a Park," *Philadelphia Inquirer*, June 17, 1985; "Water Threatens Bandelier Treasures," *Denver Post*, June 23, 1985.

42. Western water is the most complicated issue in the future of the West. Historians and attorneys have begun to produce what will become one of the most voluminous sets of documentation in American history. In the late 1980s, nineteen separate cases were in the process of adjudication, nine of those in New Mexico. The future will become only more crowded with cases. For an introduction to questions of the Winters Doctrine and Native American water rights, see Norris Hundley, Jr., "The Dark and Bloody Ground of Indian Water Rights: Confusion Elevated to Principle," *Western Historical Quarterly* 9 (October 1978): 455–82, and idem, "The 'Winters' Decision and Indian Water Rights: A Mystery Reexamined," *Western Historical Quarterly* 13 (January 1982): 17–42. For the comprehensive assessment of water in New Mexico, see Ira G. Clark, *Water in New Mexico* (Albuquerque: University of New Mexico, 1987). See also Lloyd Burton, "American Indian Water Rights in the Future of the Southwest," in Zachary Smith, ed., *Water in the Future of the Southwest* (Albuquerque: University of New Mexico Press, 1989), 153–78.

43. There is an apocryphal story concerning the *Aamodt* case. A young attorney, full of enthusiasm, inquires about the location of files for the case. Everyone in his law office laughs. One takes him to a warehouse in a shady part of town, turns the key, and lets the young man into a twenty-four-foot-square building packed with papers. "It's a fire hazard," he remarks, "enjoy yourself." Volumes of material on the *Aamodt* case do exist. For a brief overview, see Clark, *Water in New Mexico*, 659–63; F. Lee Brown, *Water and Poverty in the Southwest* (Tucson: University of Arizona Press, 1987), 65–72, 180–83; Charles T. Dumars, Marilyn

O'Leary, and Albert E. Utton, *Pueblo Indian Water Rights: Struggle for a Precious Resource* (Tucson: University of Arizona Press, 1984). For a view of water and oligarchy in the West, see Donald Worster, *Rivers of Empire: Water, Aridity, and the Growth of the American West* (New York: Pantheon Books, 1985).

44. William R. Catton, Jr., *Overshoot: The Ecological Basis of Revolutionary Change* (Urbana: University of Illinois Press, 1982), 17–53. See also Bill McKibben, *The End of Nature* (New York: Random House, 1989), 47–94, and Garrett Hardin, "The Tragedy of the Commons," *Science* 162 (December 13, 1968): 1243–48.

BIBLIOGRAPHIC ESSAY

✳ ✳ ✳ ✳ ✳ ✳ ✳ ✳ ✳ ✳ ✳ ✳ ✳ ✳

A number of works had specific and general influence on this book. The most important of these were Alfred W. Crosby, *Ecological Imperialism: The Biological Expansion of Europe, 900–1900 A.D.* (Cambridge: Cambridge University Press, 1986); Richard White, *The Roots of Dependency: Subsistence, Environment, and Social Change among the Choctaws, Pawnees, and Navajos* (Lincoln: University of Nebraska Press, 1983); and William E. deBuys, *Enchantment and Exploitation: The Life and Hard Times of a New Mexico Mountain Range* (Albuquerque: University of New Mexico Press, 1985). Each of these had profound impact on my thinking; they helped establish a framework within which I have tried to place this project.

The field of southwestern history has become crowded with excellent work in recent years. Alfonso Ortiz, ed., *The Handbook of North American Indians*, Volume 9 (Washington, D.C.: Smithsonian Institution, 1979), is an excellent place to begin. Other useful works include Elizabeth A. H. John, *Storms Brewed in Other Men's Worlds: The Confrontation of Indians, Spanish, and French in the Southwest, 1540–1795* (Lincoln: University of Nebraska Press, 1975); Jack D. Forbes, *Apache, Navajo, and Spaniard* (Norman: University of Oklahoma Press, 1960); David J. Weber, *The Mexican Frontier, 1821–1846: The American Southwest under Mexico* (Albuquerque: University of New Mexico Press, 1986); and Howard R. Lamar, *The Far Southwest, 1846–1912: A Territorial History* (New Haven: Yale University Press, 1966). For the history of New Mexico, Marc Simmons, *New Mexico: A History* (New York: W. W. Norton and Company, 1977), is an excellent source.

The number of important works about New Mexico's Hispano community has also grown in recent years. Frances L. Swadesh, *Los Primeros Pobladores: Hispanic Americans of the Ute Frontier* (Notre Dame: University of Notre Dame Press, 1974), and Paul Kutsche, ed., *The Survival of Spanish-American Villages* (Colorado Springs: Colorado College, 1979), offer perspectives into the nature of life in Hispano communities. Sarah Deutsch, *No Separate Refuge: Culture, Class, and Gender on an Anglo-Hispanic Frontier in the American Southwest, 1880–1940* (New York: Oxford University Press, 1987), is a brilliant look at the nature of cross-cultural interaction in a marginal environment. Suzanne Forrest, *Preservation of the Village* (Albuquerque: University of New Mexico Press, 1989), provides a look into Hispanic life as well. David J. Weber, *Foreigners in Their Native Land: Historical Roots of the Mexican American* (Albuquerque: University of New Mexico Press, 1973), and Robert Rosenbaum, *Mexicano Resistance in the Southwest: The Sacred Right of Self-Preservation* (Austin: University of Texas Press, 1982), show some of the consequences of the collision of cultures.

The question of the transfer of land grants in the old Mexican north has provoked much scholarship. Charles L. Briggs and John R. Van Ness, eds., *Land, Water, and Culture: New Perspectives on Hispanic Land Grants* (Albuquerque: University of New Mexico Press, 1987), is an excellent collection of insightful essays. The work of the Center for Land Grant Studies has contributed greatly to the discussion. John R. Van Ness and Christine M. Van Ness, eds., *Spanish and Mexican Land Grants in New Mexico and Colorado* (Manhattan, Kans.: Sunflower University Press, 1980), adds an important dimension to the study of the field. Some fine case studies exist: G. Emlen Hall, *The Four Leagues of Pecos* (Albuquerque: University of New Mexico Press, 1984), is an outstanding example. The January 1982 issue of the *New Mexico Historical Review* was devoted to land-grant scholarship; Malcolm Ebright, G. Emlen Hall, and Bruce T. Ellis contributed significant articles to the edition. Victor Westphall, *Mercedes Reales: Hispanic Land Grants of the Upper Rio Grande Region* (Albuquerque: University of New Mexico Press, 1983), *The Public Domain in New Mexico* (Albuquerque: University of New Mexico Press, 1965), and *Thomas Benton Catron and His Era* (Tucson: University of Arizona Press, 1973) all provide important contributions. Leonard Pitt, *The Decline of the Californios: A Social History of Spanish-Speaking Californians, 1846–1900* (Berkeley: University of California Press, 1971), shows the process by which Spanish-speaking Californians were divested of their lands.

The history of archaeology and anthropology is only beginning to attract attention. The basic source is Gordon R. Willey and Jeremy A. Sabloff, *A History of American Archaeology* (London: Thames and Hudson, 1974). Curtis M. Hinsley, Jr.,

Savages and Scientists: The Smithsonian Institution and the Development of American Anthropology, *1846–1910* (Washington, D.C.: Smithsonian Institution Press, 1981), is the best book about the role of anthropology and archaeology in late-nineteenth-century America. Robert W. Rydell, *All the World's a Fair: Visions of Empire at American International Expositions, 1876–1916* (Chicago: University of Chicago Press, 1984), provides excellent contextual analysis of the role of anthropological sciences as American society coped with the ramifications of industrialization. Douglas Cole, *Captured Heritage: The Scramble for Northwest Artifacts* (Seattle: University of Washington Press, 1985), is an important look at the consequences of the rise of anthropology and archaeology and the emphasis on collecting artifacts.

Edgar L. Hewett's personal bibliography relating to the Pajarito Plateau is extensive. The most important archaeological studies he published date from the early 1900s. These include *Antiquities of the Jemez Plateau, New Mexico*, Bureau of American Ethnology no. 32 (Washington, D.C.: Government Printing Office, 1906), *Excavations at Puye, 1907*, and *Excavations at Tyuonyi, 1908* (Santa Fe: School of American Archaeology, 1909). Hewett's best-known works occurred much later in the 1930s, when he published *The Pajarito Plateau and Its Ancient People* (Albuquerque: University of New Mexico Press, 1938), and the more general *Ancient Life in the American Southwest* (Indianapolis: Bobbs-Merrill, 1930). Hewett remains without a substantive biography. Beatrice Chauvenet, *Hewett and Friends: A Biography of Santa Fe's Vibrant Era* (Santa Fe: Museum of New Mexico Press, 1983), is a beginning, but the Hewett who emerges there is far from the complex man who dominated southwestern archaeology for more than three decades.

The history of federal agencies plays an important role in this book. Alfred Runte, *National Parks: The American Experience* 2d ed., rev. (Lincoln: University of Nebraska Press, 1987), is the definitive history of American attitudes about the national parks. Runte also addresses park policy in some detail. Ronald A. Foresta, *America's National Parks and Their Keepers* (Washington, D.C.: Resources for the Future, 1984), is the best book on modern park policy. Harold K. Steen, *The United States Forest Service: A History* (Seattle: University of Washington Press, 1976), is the best general history of the Forest Service. For an outstanding critique of USFS history and policy, see David Clary, *Timber and the Forest Service* (Lawrence: University of Kansas Press, 1986). For the activities of the Forest Service in the Southwest at the turn of the century, see Edwin A. Tucker and George Fitzpatrick, *Men Who Matched the Mountains: The Forest Service in the Southwest* (Albuquerque: U.S. Department of Agriculture, 1972). A more comprehensive collection on the same subject is Edwin A. Tucker and David Gillio, eds., *The Early Days: A Sourcebook of*

Southwestern Region History, Book 1 (Albuquerque: USDA Forest Service, 1989). The best account of the U.S. Army Corps of Engineers in New Mexico is Michael E. Welsh, *U.S. Army Corps of Engineers: Albuquerque District, 1935–1985* (Albuquerque: University of New Mexico Press, 1987). For the best account of John Collier's activities, see Lawrence C. Kelly, *Assault on Assimilation: John Collier and the Origins of Indian Policy Reform* (Albuquerque: University of New Mexico Press, 1983). Lawrence C. Kelly, "Anthropology in the Soil Conservation Service," *Agricultural History* 59 (April 1985): 136–47, is the best research into the activities of the TC-BIA.

The West in the twentieth century has begun to attract the interest of scholars. Michael P. Malone and Richard W. Etulain, *The American West: A Twentieth-Century History* (Lincoln: University of Nebraska Press, 1989), is the best general history. The work of Gerald D. Nash has helped define the history of the region in this century. His *The American West Transformed: The Impact of the Second World War* (Albuquerque: University of New Mexico Press, 1985), is the best work on the impact of the war on the West. See also Nash, *The American West in the Twentieth Century: A Short History of an Urban Oasis* (Albuquerque: University of New Mexico Press, 1973), and *World War II and the West: Reshaping the Economy* (Lincoln: University of Nebraska Press, 1990).

The scientific history of the installation at Los Alamos has become an important part of the story of the Second World War. It has been chronicled in numerous places, as has the history of the personalities who inhabited the laboratory in the mountains. By far the best source for information about Los Alamos is Richard Rhodes, *The Making of the Atomic Bomb* (New York: Simon and Schuster, 1986). Despite a number of lapses chronicled by Barton Bernstein in "An Analysis of 'Two Cultures': Writing about the Making and the Using of the Atomic Bomb," *Public Historian* 12 (Spring 1990): 83–107, Rhodes synthesized many other accounts in his definitive and readable work. Other important sources include Stephane Groueff, *The Untold Story of the Making of the Atomic Bomb* (Boston: Little, Brown, and Company, 1967); Richard G. Hewlett and Oscar E. Anderson, Jr., *Volume I, A History of the United States Atomic Energy Commission: The New World, 1939–1946* (University Park: Pennsylvania State University Press, 1962); David Hawkins, *Project Y: The Los Alamos Story, Part I: Toward Trinity* (Los Angeles: Tomash Publishers, 1983), and Edith C. Truslow and Ralph Carlisle Smith, *Project Y: The Los Alamos Story, Part II: Beyond Trinity* (Los Angeles: Tomash Publishers, 1983), explain the history of the physics involved in the bomb. For life in Los Alamos itself, see James W. Kunetka, *City of Fire: Los Alamos and the Atomic Age, 1943–1945,* rev. ed. (Albuquerque: University of New Mexico Press, 1979). Firsthand accounts also abound. Among the best are Leslie R. Groves, *Now It Can Be Told: The Story of the Manhattan*

Project (New York: De Capo Press, 1975); Laura Fermi, *Atoms in the Family: My Life with Enrico Fermi* (Chicago: University of Chicago Press, 1954); and Phyllis K. Fisher, *Los Alamos Experience* (Tokyo: Japan Publications, 1985).

Yet like any book about a specific place, this one involved asking unusual questions. The collections of the Los Alamos Historical Society, the Museum of New Mexico History Library, the New Mexico State Records Center and Archives, the Laboratory of Anthropology in Santa Fe, Bandelier National Monument, the Interpretation Library of the Southwest Regional Office of the National Park Service in Santa Fe, and the Special Collections of the Zimmerman Library at the University of New Mexico all provided answers. In the modern era, newspaper articles, interviews, and journal and magazine articles helped fill numerous gaps. The public documents of various federal agencies and state and local entities helped provide an outline of the most recent issues. Interviews with a wide range of people, from old-timers like Homer Pickens, Paul Judge, and Richard Boyd to employees of the Park Service, the Forest Service, and the Los Alamos National Laboratory to Los Alamos residents, all helped give me an insider's view of many issues. Their contributions were essential to this study.

One often overlooked source for histories such as this is the place itself. I spent more than two years living on the plateau and made numerous trips to the region before, during, and after writing this book. I hiked its canyons and mesas, viewed it from airplanes, cars, foot, and horseback, visited well-hidden archaeological ruins, and played softball in the shadow of its mountains. I came to know its landscapes, the signs of the changing seasons, the sound of elk bugling in the mountains, and the smell of storms blowing in. The people of the region, native and transplanted, became my friends. When I wrote about the places in this book, I could see them in my mind's eye. If I have been able to reflect even a part of the character of the place—its rhythms, history, and feel—it is because of the time I spent there and the people willing to share their experiences and perceptions with me.

INDEX

✳ ✳ ✳ ✳ ✳ ✳ ✳ ✳ ✳ ✳ ✳ ✳ ✳ ✳ ✳ ✳

Abbott, Albert, 95

Abbott, F. D. (TC-BIA range examiner), 202

Abbott, F. H. (Assistant Commissioner for Indian Affairs), 103

Abbott, Ida Patton, 95, 138

Abbott, Judge A. J., 95–96, 100, 104, 107, 120, 122, 125, 136, 138, 140, 189–90

Abiquiu Dam, 304

Alamo Canyon, 304

Albright, Horace M., 141–42, 144, 159–61, 165–66, 168–73, 184, 192, 196–97, 266

Albuquerque, 18, 66, 216, 250, 263–64, 296, 299

Alianza Federal de Mercedes, 275

American Anthropological Institute, 81

American Anthropologist, 43, 81

American Antiquarian, 43

American Antiquities, An Act for the Preservation of, 71–72, 80–81, 84, 89, 98, 114, 154, 250

American Museum of Natural History, 170

Ancho Canyon, 138

Anchor Ranch, 63

Anderson, Sen. Clinton P., 263–64

Andrews, Willam H., 80

Archeological Institute of America, 78, 81, 86, 100, 112

Arizona v. California, 306

Ashbridge, Col. Whitney, 228–29

Atchinson, Topeka, and Santa Fe (AT&SF) Railroad, 22–23, 84, 86–87, 104, 110, 129

Atkinson, Henry, 26

Atomic Energy Commission (AEC), 231, 234, 237, 241–43, 247–48, 250–53, 256–57, 261, 289

Atwell, Walter G., 193

Austin, Mary, 142, 144

Baca Location #1, 130, 144, 155–56, 296–97

Bandelier, Adolph F. A., 40, 49, 58,

Bandelier, Adolph F. A. *(cont.)*
76–77, 95, 111, 122, 208, 210, 213
Bandelier National Monument, 2, 11,
125, 136, 139, 142, 144, 147–48, 158,
175, 205, 212, 216; proclamation of,
122; and proposal for four national
monuments, 133; and national park
proposal (1920s), 165–67; transfer to
NPS, 170–73; and CCC development,
181, 184–87, 189–93, 196–98; conflict
with Project Y, 226; threats to, 235,
243–48, 250, 252; and development
plans, 265–69
Bandelier Wilderness Area, 271–73,
279–80, 282–83, 287, 292–94, 297,
300–305
Barnes, Will C., 120, 122, 125–26, 144–
45, 165
Baum, Rev. Henry Mason, 71–73, 76–
77, 79, 81
Bennett, Hugh Hammond, 199
Bernalillo–Algodones Station, 299
Bethe, Hans, 222, 225
Binnewies, Fred, 244
Bishop, W. C., 27–31, 36, 64
Bland, N. M., 14, 66, 92
Boas, Franz, 47, 112
Bond, Frank (GLO Chief Clerk), 100
Bond, Frank (rancher and landowner),
24, 38, 64, 128–34, 140, 143–44, 146,
155, 161, 174, 199–201, 220
Bond & Nohl, 130
Bourke, John, 45
Boyd, Dick, 140, 220, 225
Boyd, John and Martha, 140, 189, 214
Boyd Ranch, 164
Bradbury, Norris E., 233, 236–37, 242
Brook, Harold A., 96–98, 103–4, 117,
119, 125, 127–28, 130, 216–17,
220
Brookings Institute, 173

Buckman, Harry S., 31–34, 36–37, 63–
67, 90, 104, 138, 230, 293
Buckman, N.Mex., 31–32, 36–37, 66,
137, 139, 293
Bullard, Norman, 267–68
Bureau of American Ethnology, 43,
47–48, 59, 68, 77, 81, 87, 111. *See also*
Bureau of Ethnology
Bureau of Ethnology, 41, 43–45. *See
also* Bureau of American Ethnology
Bureau of Forestry, 76
Bureau of Indian Affairs, (BIA), 73, 79,
102–3, 105, 107, 113–14, 119, 141–
42, 149, 172–73, 199, 203–5, 216,
220, 269, 299–300
Bureau of Land Management, 280–81
Bureau of Reclamation, 177, 209, 263–64
Burroughs, William S., 218
Bush, Vannevar, 213

C. de Baca, Pacifico, 15, 95
Caballo Reservoir, 304–5
Caballo tract, 271
Caja del Rio Plateau, 249, 271–73, 302
Caja (Del Rio Grant) Wild Horse Terri-
tory, 295
Cameron, Sen. Ralph Henry, 161
Cammerer, Arno B., 153, 155, 157, 170,
173, 204
Camp Evergreen, 290–91
Cañada Ancha, 293
Cañada de Cochiti Grant, 11, 62, 64,
205, 265, 268–69
Canyon del Buey, 203
Canyon de San Diego, 156
Capulin Canyon, 304
Carlsbad Caverns, 154, 157
Cartwright, Hiram B., 104
Carson National Forest, 92, 271
Casa Grande Ruin Reservation, 45, 57,
153, 193

Catron, Sen. Thomas B., 26, 34–35, 78, 90, 107–9, 113, 118, 120, 127, 131–33, 135, 141–42, 148, 221, 292

Cebolleta Grant, 36

Cecil, George H., 189

Ceremonial Cave, 190

Chaco Canyon, 6, 48, 56, 72–73, 79, 87–88, 107, 168, 267

Chacoma Peak, 136

Chama River Canyon Wilderness Area, 273

Chapin, Roy, 116, 130

Chapman, Kenneth, 86

Chavéz, Don Antonio Jose, 28

Chavéz, Sen. Dennis, 264

Childers, William B., 66

Chili Line, 23, 31, 86, 137, 293

Church, Fermor, 231

Church, Peggy Pond, 280

Civilian Conservation Corps (CCC), 177, 180–83, 191, 193, 198, 211, 220, 254–55

Clarkson, R. Hunter, 186, 190

Cliff Cities, 62, 108, 132, 135, 142, 144, 158

Clinton P. Anderson Meson Physics Accelerator, 295

Cochiti Dam, 263–64, 276, 303–4

Cochiti Lake, 265, 272, 305

Cochiti Pueblo, 8, 40, 263–64

Coffman, John, 284

Cole, George Townsend, 66–68, 89, 113, 136

Cole, Sen. Cornelius, 66

Collier, John, 199–201, 203–6, 215

Colorado River Storage Project, 263, 304

Columbian Exposition of 1893, 46–47, 53, 59, 88

Committee on the Study of Educational Problems in National Parks, 170

Compton, Arthur Holly, 213

Conant, Dr. James B., 213

Cone, Wayne B., 298

Connell, A. J., 161–62, 217–19, 221–22, 226–27

Cook, John, 284

Coordinating Committee for National Parks and Forests, 161–62, 167

Coyote, N.Mex., 204, 299–300

Crandall, Clinton J., 72–75, 100–103

Cuba, N.Mex., 18, 90, 159

Cueva Pintada, 265

Cummings, Bryon, 87, 99

Cummings, Cal, 279

Curtis, Fayette S., Jr., 219

Cushing, Frank Hamilton, 45, 47–49, 56

Cutting, Bronson L., 111–13, 192

Davenport, John, 189

Dawes Act of 1887, 101

Demaray, Arthur E., 172, 192

Dennett, Fred, 99, 103

Denver and Rio Grande (D&RG) Railroad, 11, 22–24, 137

DeVoto, Bernard, 245–46

Dorman, Harry, 110–13, 132

Doughton–Evans, Sandi, 302

Douglass, William B., 99–104, 108, 113, 115, 118–20, 126–27, 131–37, 141–48, 155, 171

Dudley, Major John H., 215–16, 220

Dunigan, James P. (Pat), 297

Duran, Jose Francisco, 34

Echo Park Dam, 259, 263

Einstein, Albert, 186, 213

Elephant Butte, 303–5

Elephant Butte irrigation project, 217

El Palacio, 134, 136

El Rito de los Frijoles, 11, 32, 40, 49, 75, 95, 104

Emergency Conservation Work, 177, 182, 196, 198, 246

Emergency Fire Fighters, 182

Erickson, Dave, 282–83

Escobas Mesa, 278

Española, 23–24, 30, 32, 37, 42, 63–64, 72, 78, 91, 104, 128, 130, 142, 155, 180, 205

Española Valley, 13–15, 23–24, 30, 92, 129, 204, 228, 238, 299

Everhardt, Gary E., 288

Fall, Sen. Albert B., 148

Fenton Hill, 298–99

Fergusson, Erna, 186

Fergusson, Rep. Harvey B., 108, 118

Fermi, Enrico, 222, 224

Fermi, Laura, 224–25

Fewkes, Jesse Walter, 45, 56, 77

Feynman, Richard, 223–24

Field, Harry, 65–66, 164, 187

Fiske, Eugene A., 34–36

Fletcher, Alice, 100

Fletcher, George, 26–27, 31–34

Fletcher, Milford, 279–80

Forest Homestead Act, 85

Fred Harvey Company, 160, 186, 188–89

Frey, Evelyn, 193, 229

Frey, George and Evelyn, 189–91, 193, 196, 198

Friends of the Earth Society, 273

Frijoles Canyon, 11–13, 15, 18, 29, 40, 60, 63–64, 75–76, 80, 89, 95–96, 100, 103–4, 107, 120, 137–41, 146–47, 155, 160, 163–64, 166–68, 171, 185, 187, 189–93, 196–98, 205, 210, 213–14; and Manhattan Project, 225–26; and Los Alamos Scientific Laboratory, 244–49, 251, 254; and Cochito Lake, 266–69, 271, 304–5; and La

Mesa fire, 279; and roads, 293–94; and Overblast Program, 301; and area growth, 310

Frijoles Canyon Lodge, 189, 191, 196, 198, 228–29, 246

Frijoles Creek, 245, 265

Frijoles Mesa, 226, 248, 251, 265, 268, 282–83, 301

Frost, Max, 69–70

Fuller, Edward, 217–18

Fuller Lodge, 96, 220, 225

Fund for Animals, Inc. (FFA), 282–83

Gallina, N.Mex., 204, 271

García, Juan Luis, 30

García Canyon, 30, 199, 205, 231

General Land Office (GLO), 12, 16, 26, 51, 54–56, 58, 60–62, 66–70, 73, 76, 79, 81, 89, 97–99, 102–4, 107, 114–15, 119, 136, 156

Glacier National Park, 114, 272

Gleason, Inspector Herbert W., 107, 142–47

Gloff, Henrietta, 186

Gomés, Donaciano, 63

Goméz, Marcus, 221

Gonzales, Bences, 94, 219

Gonzales, Juan (Aguaono), 49

Gonzales, Judge Albert, 241

Gonzales, Pedro Goméz y, 29, 62

Gonzales, Severo, 29, 94

Grand Canyon National Park, 147, 154, 156, 160, 168–69, 192, 282

Grand Teton National Park, 161, 272

Gran Quivira (Salinas) National Monument, 153–55

Grant, George, 192

Grant, O. O., 220

Grant, Rosa, 220

Graves, Henry, 146, 170

Gray, David L., 116

Gray, Paul R., 116
Greeley, William, 158, 162, 170, 181
Grinnell, George Bird, 158
Groves, Leslie R., 214–16, 220, 222–27, 236–37, 240–41, 261
Guadalupe Hidalgo, Treaty of, 21, 215, 221, 274
Guaje River, 133
Guajes (Guaje) Canyon, 12, 26, 249, 280

Harrison, Birge, 42
Hartzog, George, 261
Harvey, Fred, 110
Hayden, Carl, 106, 210
Hayes, Father Thomas Aquinas, 24–26, 34–36
Hemenway, Mary, 45
Hermann, Binger, 58, 60, 62
Hewett, Cora Whitford, 49
Hewett, Edgar L., 174, 192, 208, 210, 232; young life of, 49–56; and initial national park efforts, 58–60, 62, 64–69, 71–72, 74–83; rise to prominence as an archaeologist of, 85–89; range of influence of, 95–104, 107–17; and establishment of Bandelier National Monument, 120, 122–23, 126; and battles for control of Pajarito Plateau, 130–37, 139, 142–45, 148; and changing nature of American archaeology, 148–58; and 1920s park proposal, 162, 167, 169
Hinojos, Alfred, 35
Hitchcock, Ethan Allen, 78
Hitchcock, Lawrence S., 219, 222
Hoar, Sen. George Frisbie, 45
Hoard, Dorothy, 303
Hodge, Frederick Webb, 111
Holmes, Oliver Wendell, 45
Holmes, William Henry, 47–48, 68–69, 77, 87

Holmquist, Adela, 157
Holsinger, Special Agent S. J., 73–75
Hopper, Willam M. "Mack," 96
"Hot Shots," 183
Hough, Walter, 77
Houston, D. F., 118–20, 123, 127
Hunter, John D., 279, 287–88, 294, 300
Hurley, Wilson, 218
Hyde, Fred and Talbot, 87

Ickes, Harold L., 181, 184, 204, 212
Indian Civilian Conservation Corps, 200
Indian Detours, 186–91
Indian Land Purchase Program, 199, 204
Ireland, Grace Spradling, 138, 139–40, 164

Jemez Crater National Park, 204
Jemez Forest Reserve, 80–81, 97, 145, 183
Jemez Mountains, 1, 11, 13–14, 18, 26, 29, 37, 62–63, 75, 91–92, 103, 130, 133, 136, 187, 189, 205, 214, 216, 224–25, 231, 236, 242, 249–50, 254–55, 271–73, 290, 299–300
Jemez National Forest, 90, 99–100, 108, 120, 159, 171
Jemez National Monument, 133
Jemez Pueblo, 215
Jemez Springs, N.Mex., 215, 220, 271
Johnson, Claudia A. "Lady Bird," 259
Johnson, Lyndon B., 176, 255, 258, 262, 264
Johnston, Don P., 118, 145
Jones, Sen. A. A., 114, 116, 141–42, 148
Jose, Juan, 40
Joy, Henry B., 116
Judd, Neil, 87, 107, 139–40
Judge, Paul A., 243, 248, 252

Kearney, Gen. Stephen W., 215
Kelsey, Francis W., 77, 100, 113
Kidder, Alfred V., 87, 107, 152, 156
King's Canyon National Park, 60
Kittredge, Frank A., 196–97
Kiva House, 305
Kneipp, Leon F., 162, 164–65
Koshare Tours, 186
Kroeber, Alfred, 152

Laboratory of Anthropology, 162, 173
Lacey, Rep. John F., 58, 60, 69, 71–72, 75, 78, 80–81, 98
La Cienega, 14–15, 63
Lafayette (Acadia) National Park, 147, 156
"La Floresta," 90, 127, 131
La Fonda Hotel, 186–87
La Gorce, John Oliver, 158
La Mesa fire, 278–80, 283, 285
Lamy, Archbishop Jean Baptiste, 24
Lane, Franklin K., 122, 133, 141, 143
Langley, Samuel P. 69
Las Trampas, N.Mex., 25, 128
Las Vegas, N.Mex., 33, 35, 50
Lee, Willis T. 157
Laughlin, Napoleon B., 104
Lawrence, Ernest, 213
Leopold, Aldo, 160
Lindsey, Gov. W. E., 141
Lodge–Rodenberg Bill, 76–77, 81, 86
Loomis, James, 63
Los Alamos, 1, 12, 207, 209–11, 216, 222–24, 226–53, 261, 274–76, 278, 285–86, 288–92, 294, 296–97, 299, 302, 307–11
Los Alamos County, 241, 276, 289–90, 292, 295–96, 300
Los Alamos County Planning and Zoning Commission, 291

Los Alamos County Sheriff's Mounted Patrol, 280, 282
Los Alamos Credit Union, 295
Los Alamos Inn, 267
Los Alamos Monitor, 291, 302
Los Alamos National Laboratory (LANL), 3, 289, 296, 300–302, 308. *See also* Los Alamos Scientific Laboratory
Los Alamos Ranch, 96
Los Alamos Ranch School, 159, 161–62, 165, 171, 205, 214, 216–20, 222, 227, 229, 231, 293
Los Alamos Scientific Laboratory (LASL), 230, 234, 243, 255–57, 275–80, 287, 289. *See also* Los Alamos National Laboratory
Los Alamos Ski Club, 291
Los Piños, 214
Loughran, Patrick, 104
Louisiana Purchase Centennial Exposition, 88, 109
Lowrie, Ed, 173
Luján, Martin, 28
Lummis, Charles F., 84, 111

McDonald, Gov. William, 118
McDougal, Robert G. (Archie), 103
McElroy, Stephen E., 16–17, 23, 26
McFie, Judge John R., 36
McGaffey, A. B., 104
McGee, W J, 69
McKibbin, Kevin, 305
McMillan, Edwin, 215–16
Madden, Rev. G. S., 66–68, 89, 113, 136
Manhattan Project, 3, 207, 209–10
Mankin, J. D., 58–62, 66
Martin, Eben W., 78
Mather, Stephen T., 122, 127, 141–44,

146–48, 153–56, 158–63, 166, 168–
69, 171, 196, 198, 261, 266

Mather, Ted, 220

Mathers, S. S., 66–67, 136

Matthews, Washington, 45

Mechem, Edwin L. 246, 264

Mendoza, Viceroy don Gaspar Domingo de, 12

Mesa Verde National Park, 76–77, 79–
81, 114, 116, 160, 162, 168

Middle Rio Grande Conservancy District, 179, 303–4

Miller, Hugh M., 247

Mindeleff, Victor and Cosmos, 77

Mission 66, 246–48, 252, 262

Montezuma Castle, 73, 189

Montoya, Crestino, 28

Montoya, Joseph, 241, 264, 276

Mooney, James, 47

Moran, Thomas, 41

Morgan, Lewis Henry, 40

Morley, Sylvanus G., 87, 116

Morris, Earl H., 87

Morrow, John, 157–58, 164, 166

Moses, William, 63

Mott, William Penn, 302

Mount Rainier National Park, 57–58,
60, 272

Muller, Frederic "Fritz," 117

Museum of New Mexico, 86, 100, 110–
12, 133–34

Naranjo, Santiago, 142–45

National Environmental Policy Act,
259

National Geographical Society, 157

National Parks Association, 155–56

National Park Service (NPS), 122, 124,
126–27, and initial attempts at a national park, 141–50; and 1920s effort
to establish a national park, 153–74;
and New Deal programs, 177, 181–
82, 184–85, 189, 191–93, 196–98,
201; and New Deal era land acquisition, 203–5; and Project Y, 209, 211–
12, 216, 227–31; and post–war
changes, 234–35, 243–48, 250–56;
and development of Bandelier, 261–
71; and RARE II, 273–74; and La
Mesa fire, 279–81; and burro eradication, 281–85; and threats to park
areas, 287, 289, 291–92, 294–97,
299–305

Natural Resources Division of the
Southwest Region, 281

Navajo National Monument, 99–100,
135

Navawi'i, 12, 60, 65, 80, 104, 142, 146,
203, 243

Neddermeyer, Seth, 223

Nelson, Nels C., 152, 156

New Deal, 175–78, 180–84, 198–201,
203–6, 209, 211–12, 238, 246, 249,
254–55

New Mexico Department of Game and
Fish, 300

New Mexico Federation of Women's
Clubs, 137

New Mexico Lumber Company, 92

New Mexico National Parks Association, 127, 132, 135, 137

New Mexico Normal School, 50, 86, 111

New Mexico State Engineer's Office, 264

New Mexico State Highway Department, 294

New Mexico Wilderness Study Committee (NMWSC), 267–68, 270–71,
303

Nordenskiold, Gustav, 46

Northern Pueblo Tributary Waters
Rights Association, 306

Norton Station, 299

Nusbaum, Jesse L., 86–87, 162, 164–
    67, 169, 171–73, 192, 248, 293–94

Oak City, Utah, 215, 220
Ojo Caliente, 136, 142
Ojo Caliente Station, 299
Ojo Line Extension program, 299–302
Operation Firestop, 255
Operation Outdoors, 250
Oppenheimer, J. Robert, 214–16, 220,
    222, 225, 233, 236–37, 255
Oppenheimer, Kitty, 224
Ortiz, Ambrosio, 35
Otero, Gov. Miguel A., 35, 78, 86, 111
Otowi, 75, 80, 134, 136, 142, 147, 155,
    165, 168, 171, 226, 228–29, 231, 247–
    48, 251–53, 295
Otowi bridge, 14, 293–94, 306
Overbay, James, 300
Overblast Program, 301

Packard Motor Car Company, 116
Painted Cave, 120
Pajarito Canyon, 12, 27–29, 64, 117,
    138, 243
Pajarito Club, 117, 216
Pajarito Mountain, 249
Pajarito Mountain Ski Area, 297
Pajarito National Park, 59, 72–73, 77–
    83, 132–33, 144, 148–49, 156–57
Pajarito Plateau, 28–29, 68, 71, 73, 75,
    77, 85–86, 89, 91, 93–94, 96–100,
    104, 107–8, 113, 115–16, 118–19,
    122–25, 127, 129–30, 133–37, 142,
    145, 147–52, 155, 157–61, 167–69,
    174–75; and New Deal, 177–79, 181,
    183–84, 201; and Indian Detours,
    186, 188; and Frank Pinkley, 198;
    and Soil Conservation Service, 205–
    6; and Manhattan Project, 207–11,
    213–14, 216, 222, 226, 228–29; and

Harold Brook, 217; and Los Alamos
    Ranch School, 218–19; and Los Al-
    amos Scientific Laboratory, 231,
    233–34, 238, 244, 247–49, 251–53,
    256–57, 261; and Wilderness Society,
    263; and RARE II, 271–74; and La
    Mesa fire, 278, 284–85; and area
    growth, 286–88, 290, 307–12; and
    energy, 299; and Cochiti Dam, 305
Palace of the Governors, 111
Panama–California Exposition, 109
Panama–Pacific International Exposi-
    tion, 109
Papago Saguaro National Monument,
    107
Parker, Paul, 292
Parkman, Francis, 45
Partido, 128–30
Partido del Pueblo Unido, El, 34
Peabody Museum, 43, 47, 87
Pecos, N.Mex., 10, 25, 152
Pecos Pueblo, 25, 215
Pecos Wilderness Area, 271–73
Peierls, Genia, 224
Peierls, Rudolph, 225
Peña, Antonio Domingo (Weyima), 48
Peña Blanca, 264, 276
Pepper, George W., 87
Philadelphia Commercial Museum,
    134
Phillips, B. S., 104
Pinchot, Gifford, 170, 181, 250
Pinkley, Frank "Boss," 153–54, 167–
    69, 171, 174–75, 184–86, 189, 191–
    93, 196–98, 212
Pipe Spring National Monument, 189
Plains Electric Generation and Trans-
    mission Cooperative, 299
Pojoaque, 91–92, 180, 293
Pojoaque Pueblo, 75, 102
Pojoaque Valley, 8, 13–15, 23–24, 30

Pojoaque Valley Irrigation Association, 306

Pond, Ashley, 116–17, 159, 162, 216–19

Pooler, Frank, 159, 162

Powell, John Wesley, 41, 43–45, 48, 56, 68–69, 77, 87

Prince, Gov. L. Bradford, 34–36

Progressivism, 53, 70, 90, 166, 185, 259–60

Project Y, 3, 207, 210, 222, 226, 228–29

Public Service Company of New Mexico, (PNM), 296–300

Pueblo Canyon, 13, 222

Pueblo Rebellion of 1680, 10

Pueblo Relief Bill of 1933, 199

Putn·.m, Frederic Ward, 43, 47, 87

Puye Mesa, 13–14, 89, 202, 231

Puye National Monument, 172

Puye Ruins, 30, 41–42, 60, 62, 64, 75, 79–81, 100–104, 107, 108, 115, 133, 141, 143–44, 147, 155–56, 165, 168, 171–74, 181, 187, 192

Quintana, Benigno, 29–30

Rabi, I. I., 222

Ranch of the Ten Elders, 95–96

Rathbun, Richard, 76

Ramon Land and Lumber Company, 104, 117, 138, 216–17

Ramón Vigil Grant, 12–13, 15–16, 19, 22–27, 29–32, 34, 36–37, 50; and James Loomis, 63; and park proposal, 64; and G. T. Cole, 66–67; and Pajarito Plateau park proposal, 75–76, 80–81; and Jemez Forest reserve, 80; and timber, 90; and Puye ruins, 103; and Ramon Land and Lumber Company, 104; and Detroit owners, 116–18, 216; sold to Frank Bond,

130; and Pajarito national monument, 133; and Gleason, 144, 146; and Edgar Hewett, 156; and Henry Temple, 165; and Soil Conservation Service, 199–201, 203–4; and Santa Fe National Forest, 204; and Bandelier National Monument, 205; and Ashley Pond, 217; and Los Alamos Scientific Laboratory, 231–32, 234

Reagan, Ronald, 288, 301

Records of the Past Society, 71–72, 76, 81

Redondo Creek, 296–99

Rhoads, Charles J., 172–73

Ribe, Tom, 300, 302

Richards, W. A., 76, 82

Richey, Charles A., 228

Ringland, Arthur, 120, 125–26, 165, 167

Rio Arriba, 15, 23, 31–33, 239, 274–75

Rio Arriba County, 276

Rio Grande (river), 10, 13–14, 16, 18, 23, 31, 36, 75, 137, 193, 202, 216, 249, 263, 275, 293–94, 302, 305–6

Rio Grande bridge, 243

Rio Grande Compact, 303, 306

Rio Grande Valley, 1, 11, 13, 20, 23–25, 90, 216

Rio Puerco, 13, 18, 90, 271

Roadless Area Review and Evaluation (RARE I & II), 269–73

Roads, planning for, 294–96

Rockefeller, John D., Jr., 186

Rocky Mountain Camp Company, 138, 186

Rocky Mountain National Park, 114, 169

Rodey, Bernard S., 70, 77, 80

Romero, David, 29, 34, 62, 93

Romero, Ernest and Ernestina (Montoya), 94

Romero, Victor and Luisa, 93

Roosevelt, Eleanor, 186

Roosevelt, Franklin D., 176, 178, 191, 204–5, 211–14

Roosevelt, Theodore, 70–71, 78–80, 158

Rost, Maynard T., 295, 303

Roybal, Diegito (Potsonutse), 49

Sagebrush Rebellion, 312

St. Peter's Dome, 271–73

Salfingere, Major Frank W., 228

Sánches, Antonio, 30, 94, 96

Sánchez, Antonio, 12, 34–36

Sánchez, Miguel, 63

Sánchez, Pedro, 12

Sánchez, Victoria, 34

Sánchez family, 33, 96

Sánchez Grant, 34

Sanchez v. Fletcher, 130

Sandia Peak, 1, 216

San Diego, 109–10

Sandoval County, 240–41, 276

Sangre de Cristo Girl Scout Council, 290

Sangre de Cristo Mountains, 1, 25, 90, 94, 104, 214, 216, 225, 271, 273

San Ildefonso, 8, 13–15, 93–94, 187, 199, 202–5, 289, 295–96

San Ildefonso Pueblo, 231, 236

San Pedro Parks Wilderness, 271

Santa Barbara Tie and Pole Company, 104

Santa Clara Indians, 104, 142, 145, 172, 202

Santa Clara Pueblo, 8, 13–14, 23–24, 41–42, 75, 79–80, 100–101, 142–43, 173, 236, 239

Santa Clara Reservation, 72, 81, 103, 108, 119, 143–44, 156, 165, 236

Santa Domingo, 264, 276

Santa Fe, 1, 14–15, 22–23, 31, 35–36, 40, 63, 86–87, 100, 104, 108–15, 117–18, 132, 134, 137–38, 148–49, 155–56, 162, 164, 172–73, 184, 186–87, 189, 192, 202–3, 210, 215, 222, 224, 228, 231, 246, 250, 274, 279, 290, 292–96, 299, 302

Santa Fe Art Museum, 151

Santa Fe Chamber of Commerce, 108–11, 113–18, 120, 122–23, 126–27, 130, 132–33, 135, 171

Santa Fe County, 35

Santa Fe Fiesta, 151

Santa Fe Indian Market, 151

Santa Fe Indian School, 72, 100, 142

Santa Fe National Forest, 145, 159, 162–63, 181, 183, 204–5, 218, 230, 249–50, 254, 271, 273, 279, 301–2

Santa Fe New Mexican, 64, 69–70, 111–12, 127, 192, 302

Santa Fe Ring, 22, 26, 34, 69, 221

Santa Fe Trail, 14, 22, 28

Save the Jemez, 300, 302

Sawyer, Daniel, 16–17, 24, 26

Schliemann, Heinrich, 89

School of American Archaeology, 86, 89, 100, 107, 109, 112, 115–116, 131, 151–52

School of American Research, 152, 154

Segre, Emilo, 225

Selig Movie Company, 293

Senate Public Lands Committee, 119, 161

Sequoia National Park, 60, 284

Sheldon, Charles, 158

Sheldon, Edward P., 25–26

Sheridan, J. J., 36

Sherman Anti–Trust Act, 52–53

Shu'finne, 133

Sierra Club, 259, 262, 273, 300

Smith, Winfield R., 25–27, 31–34

Smith, Zane, 271

Smithsonian Institution, 43, 69, 76, 86, 103

Snyder, Frederick C., 142

Soil Conservation Service (scs), 177–78, 199–205, 209

Soil Erosion Service, 199

Speers, L. C., 161

Stanfield, Sen. Robert N., 161

State of New Mexico ex. rel. S. E. Reynolds, State Engineer v. R. Lee Aamodt et al, defendant, 306–7

State of the Parks 1980, 288

Steen, Charlie, 252

Stevenson, James and Matilda Coxe, 41, 45

Stimson, Henry L., 213

Stone Lions, Shrine of, 120, 138

Stuart, Major Robert Y., 170, 173

Swanton, John, 44

Sweeney, Bo, 119–20

Szilard, Leo, 213

Tafoya, Cleto, 239

Tallman, Clay, 114, 119

Taos Pueblo, 199

Tarkio College, 49

Technical Cooperation–Bureau of Indian Affairs (tc–bia), 200

Teller, Edward, 213

Temple, Henry W., 158, 162, 164

Tewa Basin Study, 200–202

Tewa Indians, 1, 136, 216

Thomas, Chester A. (Art), 226–29, 248

Thornton (Santo Domingo), 14

Three–Mile Mesa, 29, 62

Tierra Amarilla, 32, 92, 275

Tijerina, Reies Lopez, 275

Tillotson, M. R., 169, 171, 228

Toll, Roger, 169–71

Tonner, A. C., 76

Tozzer, Alfred M., 112, 152

Tsankawi Mesa, 1, 253

Tsankawi Ruins, 75, 80, 142, 147, 155, 165, 294–95, 301

Tschirege, 12, 60, 64, 80, 104, 142, 146–47

Tugwell, Rexford, 204

Tyuonyi, 40, 63, 89, 95–96, 115, 188–91, 196–97, 246

Uhle, Max, 152

Union Geothermal Company of New Mexico, 296–97

Union Oil of California, 296, 298

United States v. Joseph, 75

United States v. Sandoval, 102

United States Bank and Trust Company (usb&t), 104, 116

U. S. Army, 208, 221, 226, 244

U. S. Army Corps of Engineers, 209, 227–28, 243, 263–64, 303–4

U. S. Department of Agriculture, 76, 80, 118, 120, 182, 199, 203

U. S. Department of Defense, 284

U. S. Department of Energy (doe), 288–89, 296–302, 307, 311

U. S. Department of the Interior, 16, 54, 57, 62, 66, 69, 72–73, 79–81, 85, 89, 97–99, 107, 116–18, 120, 122, 126, 137, 142–44, 147, 155, 158, 172, 182, 199, 204, 212, 291, 298

U. S. Forest Service (also usda Forest Service), 80, 92, 95, 113–14, 261; and Hewett, 85, 89–90, 103–5, 107; and confusion over land transfer, 97–98; and efforts to establish a national park, 118–20, 126–27, 129, 131, 133, 136, 143–46, 149–50, 153–54, 156–66, 168–70, 173–74; and establishment of Bandelier National Monument, 122–24; and New Deal

U. S. Forest Service *(cont.)*
   programs, 177, 181–85, 189–90, 192–
   93, 196, 201, 204–5; and Project Y,
   209, 216, 220, 227, 230–31; and post–
   war era; 234–36, 244, 247–50, 253–
   56; and RARE process, 269–75; and
   La Mesa fire, 279–81, 283–85; and
   gridlock, 289, 291–92, 294–96, 300,
   302–3
U. S. House Public Lands Committee,
   58, 61, 69, 75–76, 79, 120
University of California–Berkeley, 152,
   213–14
University of New Mexico Mountaineering Club, 267
Urey, Harold, 213

Valentine, Robert G., 101
Valle Grande, 130, 140, 155
Valles Caldera, 11, 165, 168, 204, 216
Van Stone, G. H., 114–15
Veeck, Bill, 218
Vidal, Gore, 218
Vigil, Alejandro Montes, 29, 35, 130
Vigil, Jose Ramón, 13, 24–25, 36
Vigil, Juan Montes, 28, 35

Walcott, W. D., 103
Wallace, Henry A., 204–5, 213
Walton, Rep. William, 141
Ward, E. J., 138, 140
Washington, D. C., 108, 127
Water Canyon, 12, 27, 32, 36, 138, 293
Wauer, Roland, 281–82

Welch, Major William A., 158
Westgate, 290–92
"Westgate Families," 291–92
Wetherill, Richard, 46, 48, 51–52, 54,
   56, 68, 71, 73, 75, 77, 79, 87–88, 136
White, George, 91–92
White, William Carpenter, 30, 37, 91
White Rock, 2, 243, 245, 275, 279, 288,
   294–95, 308
White Rock Canyon, 31, 137, 243, 272,
   280, 293
Wilderness Act of 1964, 259, 262–63,
   265, 267–69
Wilderness Society, 262, 273
Wilderness equipment, 260
Wild Horse and Burro Act of 1971,
   280–81
Wilson, Lucy, 134–37, 142
Winters v. *United States*, 305
Wirth, Conrad, 246, 251, 253, 262–63,
   266
Wissler, Dr. Clark, 170

Yard, Robert Sterling, 155–57
Yellowstone National Park, 57, 60, 154,
   160–61, 168, 272, 284
Yosemite National Park, 57, 60, 160,
   168, 247–48, 262, 267

Zahniser, Howard, 262
Zamora, Cristobal, 279
Zia Company, 238, 242–43
Zion National Park, 147, 156